THE ANTI-SOCIAL BEHAVIOU

SPECIAL BULLETIN

GW01392958

THE ANTI-SOCIAL BEHAVIOUR ACT 2003

SPECIAL BULLETIN

Helen Carr, Matthew Waddington, Ann Blair and Timothy Baldwin

JORDANS

2004

Published by
Jordan Publishing Limited
21 St Thomas Street
Bristol BS1 6JS

© Jordan Publishing Limited 2004

All rights reserved. No part of this publication may be reproduced, stored in a retrieval system, or transmitted in any way or by any means, including photocopying or recording, without the written permission of the copyright holder, application for which should be addressed to the publisher.

British Library Cataloguing-in-Publication Data

A catalogue record for this book is available from the British Library.

ISBN 0 85308 917 5

Typeset by Jordan Publishing Limited

Printed by APB Colour Print Ltd, Bristol

PREFACE

This special bulletin has been written by a team of authors. This has been a necessity because of the breadth of the Anti-Social Behaviour Act 2003 and, we hope, a virtue. The multiplicity of perspectives should add to the usefulness of the contents. For us it has also been a pleasure; each of us has welcomed the opinions and support of the others as we have been engaged in writing. Some of the team have been employed at the Law Commission during the production of the bulletin. We must make it clear that none of the views expressed within the bulletin are those of the Law Commission, but are solely those of the authors. Matthew Waddington left the Law Commission in November 2003 to work in Cyprus for three years. This disrupted his writing schedule more than anticipated and we were lucky that Tim Baldwin joined the team at that stage to ensure speedy completion of the script. Matthew, Ann and I are grateful for Tim's enthusiastic and efficient contribution to the finished product. Those of the authors who remain in the United Kingdom would also like to take this opportunity to wish Matthew and his family the best of luck for the future. He, however, like the rest of us, has joint responsibility for mistakes within the bulletin. Without doubt there will be some. We apologise in advance for any confusion they cause.

Helen Carr
London, 9 February 2004

CONTENTS

Chapter 5: Dispersal of Groups and Removal of Persons under 16 to their Place of Residence

Chapter 6: Firearms

Chapter 7: The Environment

TABLE OF ABBREVIATIONS

1968 Act	Firearms Act 1968
1971 Act	Misuse of Drugs Act 1971
1994 Act	Criminal Justice and Public Order Act
DDA 1995	Disability Discrimination Act 1995
HA 1985	Housing Act 1985
HA 1988	Housing Act 1988
HA 1996	Housing Act 1996
2001/02 British Crime Survey	Home Office, *Crime in England and Wales 2001/02* (2002)
ABC	acceptable behaviour contract
ASBO	anti-social behaviour order
BTP	British Transport Police
DEFRA	Department for Environment, Food and Rural Affairs
DETR	Department of the Environment, Transport and the Regions
DTLR	Department for Transport, Local Government and the Regions
ECHR	European Convention for the Protection of Human Rights and Fundamental Freedoms 1950
FCC	Firearms Consultative Committee
ISSP	Intensive Supervision and Surveillance Programme
LEA	local education authority
LGA	Local Government Association
NAS	UK National Noise Attitude Survey
NNO	Night Noise Offence
ODPM	Office of the Deputy Prime Minister
PAT	Policy Action Team
RSL	registered social landlord
TDPI	Transform Drug Policy Institute

CHAPTER 1

AN OVERVIEW OF THE ACT

Background

1.1   Anti-social behaviour has been high on the political agenda since the middle of the 1990s. The Labour Party, in particular, has been committed to action based on its rhetoric of rights and responsibilities and its belief that low-level crime and disorder exacerbates social exclusion. It established the Social Exclusion Unit shortly after its first election victory in 1997, and this was followed by the Crime and Disorder Act 1998 which has proved to be one of its most significant legislative measures. The Act established a framework for local, flexible, joined-up and victim-orientated responses to crime and disorder. Together, these initiatives represented action on the manifesto commitment, 'On crime, we believe in personal responsibility and in punishing crime, but also tackling its underlying causes – so, tough on crime, tough on the causes of crime'.[1]

1.2   The Social Exclusion Unit set up a number of Policy Action Team (PATs) at the end of 1998 to provide evidence for a national strategy for Neighbourhood Renewal. PAT 8 was concerned with anti-social behaviour.

1.3   The findings of the report,[2] published in March 2000, are summarised as follows. Anti-social behaviour is a widespread problem. It is a problem that is more prevalent in deprived neighbourhoods. Its effects are often most damaging in communities that are already fragile and where services are overstretched. Serious hard-core perpetrators are small in number, but their behaviour has a disproportionate impact on large numbers of ordinary people. There is no one accepted definition and anti-social behaviour can range from dropping litter to serious harassment. The lack of hard facts compounds the problem, but it is known that anti-social behaviour:

– is perceived to be twice as high in deprived areas than nationally;
– is considered to be a medium-to-large problem by three-quarters of social landlords, with some landlords recording figures of up to 285 complaints a year per 1,000 tenancies;
– appears to be increasing, with reports to the police of disorder offences increasing by 19% from 1995–96 to 1997–98 and complaints to environmental health officers about neighbours rising by 56% from 1993–97.

1.4   The recommendations focussed on tackling anti-social behaviour through prevention, enforcement, and effective resettlement of the perpetrators. One particular area of concern identified in the report was the need to improve the tools which were available to social landlords to respond to serious nuisance and harassment. In addition, PAT 8 highlights one of the major criticisms of anti-social behaviour, its lack of clear definition and its potentially wide scope.

---

[1]   Labour Party manifesto 1997.
[2]   National Strategy for Neighbourhood Renewal Report of Policy Action Team 8 Anti-social Behaviour (ODPM, March 2000).

1.5   Following the report, there has been continued legislative activity in the area of anti-social behaviour, particularly in improving the operation of anti-social behaviour orders[1], the extension of fixed penalty notices, and the provision of low-level policing powers for community support officers and accredited persons.[2]

1.6   The Queen's Speech of 13 November 2002 set out the government's intentions to legislate further on anti-social behaviour. The Prime Minister, in a press conference preceding the Queen's Speech stated that, 'Crime and anti-social behaviour is a Labour issue. For however much schools and hospitals improve, if people walk out of their doors and are confronted by abuse, vandalism and anti-social behaviour, they will never feel secure or able to take advantage of new opportunities'.[3]

1.7   In January 2003, shortly after the Queen's Speech, the Anti-social Behaviour Unit, a high-profile cross-departmental policy unit was established.[4] On 12 March 2003, the Home Office published *Respect and Responsibility – Taking a Stand against Anti-social Behaviour.*[5] It had been preceded by a number of other consultation papers from other government departments, for instance, *Tackling Anti-social Tenants*,[6] the *Review of the Noise Act 1996*[7] and *Living Places Powers, Rights Responsibilities.*[8] The Anti-social Behaviour Bill received its first reading on 27 March 2003.

1.8   Other Bills which received Royal Assent during the 2002–03 parliamentary session, such as the Fireworks Bill, the Licensing Bill, the Courts Bill and the Criminal Justice Bill, contain provisions relevant to reducing anti-social behaviour.

1.9   The Act therefore does not and cannot represent a complete statement of the current legislative provisions on anti-social behaviour. Its function is rather to reassure the public that the issue is still central to government policy. While the Act contains some innovation, it is more concerned with extending powers that were introduced in earlier legislation, improving some legislative provisions which have been less effective than anticipated, and providing a legislative vehicle for reforms which have been awaiting enactment. The broad range of anti-social behaviour has also allowed the Act to become a vehicle for legislation about things which concern backbench MPs such as raves, high hedges and graffiti removal.

1.10   This opened the Bill to criticism, as the Liberal Democrats pointed out at the first Standing Committee sitting, 'The Bill is a hotchpotch. Although we agree with some of the sentiments, we believe that they should be dealt with under other legislation'.[9] On the other hand, the breadth of the provisions within the Bill was described more positively by the Conservatives:[10]

> 'When scrutiny of the Anti-social Behaviour Bill started many months ago, few of us realised just what a Christmas tree it would become. In Standing Committee, I, my Hon Friends and the Liberal Democrats thought that we were pushing our luck in trying to introduce measures to deal with animal rights activists, travellers and raves, but all those things are now well and truly in the Bill, and I am delighted about that.'

---

[1]   Via amendments made to the Crime and Disorder Act 1998 by the Police Reform Act 2002.

[2]   Police Reform Act 2002.

[3]   Quoted in Alan Travis and Patrick Wintour 'Queen's speech New bill to target antisocial actions' (2002) *The Guardian*, Monday, November 11.

[4]   One of its most recent publications is the 'Together: Tackling Anti-Social Behaviour' Action Plan launched on 14 October 2003.

[5]   Cm 5778.

[6]   Department of Transport, Local Government and the Regions, April 2002.

[7]   Department of Environment, Transport and the Regions, 2000.

[8]   Department for Environment, Food and Rural Affairs, October 2002.

[9]   *Hansard*, HC Standing Committee G, 6 May 2003, col 005.

[10]   HC Deb, 17 November 2003, col 552.

Indeed, the Christmas tree effect was heightened by the addition at a late stage of provisions relating to 'high hedges'.

1.11 The Act will not end legislation on anti-social behaviour. The Housing Bill, for instance, published on 8 December 2003 includes measures increasing local authority powers to respond to anti-social behaviour in the private rented sector, and introduces further measures to respond to anti-social behaviour in the social housing sector.

The passage of the Bill

The House of Commons

1.12 Table 1.1 sets out the Commons stages of the Bill.

Table 1.1

Commons stages of the Anti-social Behaviour Bill, Parliamentary session 2002/03

Stage	Date	*Hansard* reference
First reading (HC Bill 83 Explanatory notes Bill 83-EN)	27 March	No debate
House of Commons Research Paper	*4 April*	*HC Research Paper 03/34*
Second reading	8 April	HC Deb, 8 April 2003, col 136
Standing Committee G 1st sitting	6 May am	Standing Committee Debates Anti-social Behaviour Bill, col 001
Standing Committee G 2nd sitting	6 May pm	HC Deb, 8 April 2003, col 043
Standing Committee G 3rd sitting	8 May am	HC Deb, 8 April 2003, col 085
Standing Committee G 4th sitting	8 May pm	HC Deb, 8 April 2003, col 121
Standing Committee G 5th sitting	13 May am	HC Deb, 8 April 2003, col 168
Standing Committee G 6th sitting	13 May pm	HC Deb, 8 April 2003, col 202
Standing Committee G 7th sitting	15 May am	HC Deb, 8 April 2003, col 258
Standing Committee G 8th sitting	15 May pm	HC Deb, 8 April 2003, col 293
Standing Committee G 9th sitting	20 May am	HC Deb, 8 April 2003, col 322
Standing Committee G 10th sitting	20 May pm	HC Deb, 8 April 2003, col 355

Table 1.1

Commons stages of the Anti-social Behaviour Bill, Parliamentary session 2002/03

Stage	Date	*Hansard* reference
Standing Committee G 11th sitting	22 May am	HC Deb, 8 April 2003, col 393
Standing Committee G 12th sitting	22 May pm	HC Deb, 8 April 2003, col 429
Joint Committee on Human Rights thirteenth report	*9 June*	
Remaining Commons stages (HC Bill 116)	24 June	HC Deb, 24 June 2003, col 896

1.13   The House of Lords stages of the Bill are set out in Table 1.2.

Table 1.2

Lords stages of the Anti-social Behaviour Bill, Parliamentary session 2002/03

Stage	Date	*Hansard* reference
First reading (HL Bill 84)	24 June	No debate
Second reading	18 July	HL Deb, 18 July 2003, col 1091
Joint Committee on Human Rights fifteenth report	*21 July*	
Committee sitting 1	11 September	HL Deb, 11 September 2003, col 431
Committee sitting 2	17 September	HL Deb, 17 September 2003, col 951
Committee sitting 3	7 October	HL Deb, 7 October 2003, col 223
Report stage 1st day	23 October	HL Deb, 23 October 2003, col 1760
Report stage 2nd day	3 November	HL Deb, 3 November 2003, col 538
Third reading	12 November	HL Deb, 12 November 2003, col 1438

1.14   The final stages in the House of Commons are set out in Table 1.3.

Table 1.3

Final Commons stages of the Anti-social Behaviour Bill, Parliamentary session 2002/03

Stage	Date	*Hansard* reference
Consideration of Lords amendments	17 November	HC Deb, 17 November 2003, col 517
Royal Assent	20 November	

The Act: key features

1.15   Noteworthy points of the Act are:

— the introduction of demoted tenancies for anti-social behaviour;
— extending the scope of the anti-social behaviour injunction;
— new powers to close crack houses;
— the extension of the fixed penalty notice regime;
— continued modifications and extensions to the anti-social behaviour order regime;
— new measures to respond to noise, graffiti, use of spray paints, and fly-tipping;
— new powers to disperse groups of children and remove unaccompanied under-16s to their place of residence at night;
— the introduction of 'parenting contracts' in cases of truancy, school exclusion and in respect of children and young persons who have been referred to Youth Offending Teams;
— the extension of powers to make 'parenting orders';
— the modification of public order legislation;
— further controls on firearms ownership;
— a dispute resolution scheme for 'high hedges'.

The scope of the Act and its implementation

1.16   Table 1.4 sets out the Parts of the Act indicating their subject matter, information on implementation and territorial coverage. Implementation details are provided in SI 2003/3300.

Table 1.4				
The Anti-social Behaviour Act 2003				
Part	**Title**	**Implementation details from the Anti-social Behaviour Act 2003 (Commencement No 1 and Transitional Provisions) Order 2003[1]**	**Implementation details (from Home Office Guide to Anti-social Behaviour Act 2003)**	**Territorial Coverage**
1	Premises where Drugs used Unlawfully	20 January 2004 ss 1–11 Draft non-statutory guidance published 7 November 2003		England and Wales
2	Housing		30 June 2004 (England only)	England and Wales

---

[1]   SI 2003/3300 (c 130).

Table 1.4

The Anti-social Behaviour Act 2003

Part	Title	Implementation details from the Anti-social Behaviour Act 2003 (Commencement No 1 and Transitional Provisions) Order 2003[1]	Implementation details (from Home Office Guide to Anti-social Behaviour Act 2003)	Territorial Coverage
			Guidance on s 12 to be published in June 2004	The National Assembly for Wales will commence the provisions separately.
3	Parental Responsibilities	27 February 2004 s 18 – final guidance to be available 26 February 2004 s 23 – draft guidance published 22 October 2003 ss 25–29 – final guidance to be available 26 February 2004 27 February 2004 (in **England only**) ss 19–22 – draft guidance published 22 October 2003 s 24 – draft guidance published 22 October 2003		England and Wales Parenting contracts and orders related to truancy and exclusion from school may be adopted by the National Assembly for Wales and if so will be commenced separately by the Assembly.
4	Dispersal of Groups etc	20 January 2004 ss 30–36 Draft guidance available on Home Office website		England and Wales
5	Firearms	20 January 2004 s 37; s 38; s 39(1),(2),(3) insofar as it relates to the purchase, acquisition, manufacture, sale or transfer of the prohibited weapon, (4), (5) and (6) – Home Office circular to police published 14 January 2004		England and Wales, and Scotland

Table 1.4

The Anti-social Behaviour Act 2003

Part	Title	Implementation details from the Anti-social Behaviour Act 2003 (Commencement No 1 and Transitional Provisions) Order 2003[1]	Implementation details (from Home Office Guide to Anti-social Behaviour Act 2003)	Territorial Coverage
		30 April 2004 s 39(3) to the extent it is not already in force and subject to the following – s 1(1)(a) of the Firearms Act 1968 shall not apply to a person who has in his possession any air rifle, air gun or air pistol which uses, or is designed or adapted for use with, a self-contained gas cartridge system where he has applied before 30 April 2004 for a firearm certificate under Part 2 of that Act and either the application is still being processed or any appeal in respect of it has not been determined.		
6	The Environment	20 January 2004 s 53	31 March 2004 s 40; s 41 – guidance will be included in DCMS guidance on the Licensing Act 2003 to be reissued in late 2004 s 42 – Noise Act circular will be reissued by DEFRA at end of January 2004 ss 43–47 – guidance will be produced by DEFRA in March 2004	England and Wales Closure of noisy premises; night noise; graffiti and fly-posting; waste and litter will be commenced separately by the National Assembly for Wales

Part	Title	Implementation details from the Anti-social Behaviour Act 2003 (Commencement No 1 and Transitional Provisions) Order 2003[1]	Implementation details (from Home Office Guide to Anti-social Behaviour Act 2003)	Territorial Coverage
			ss 48–52 (applies to 12 local authorities in England) – guidance will be published in March 2004 s 54 – guidance will be published in March	
7	Public Order and Trespass	20 January 2004 s 57; s 58; s 59 27 February 2004 ss 60–64 – guidance will be published in February 2004		England and Wales
8	High Hedges		1 October 2004 Draft guidance to be available for consultation in the summer	England and Wales
9	Miscellaneous Powers	20 January 2004 s 85(1),(2),(3), (4) insofar as it relates to s 1(10B) of the Crime and Disorder Act 1998, and (7) s 86(3) insofar as it relates to s 1C(9B) and (9C) of the Crime and Disorder Act 1998, (4), (5), and (6) s 87; s 89(1), (2), (3), (4), (6) and (7) 27 February 2004 s 85(8)		England and Wales

Table 1.4

The Anti-social Behaviour Act 2003

Table 1.4				
The Anti-social Behaviour Act 2003				
Part	**Title**	**Implementation details from the Anti-social Behaviour Act 2003 (Commencement No 1 and Transitional Provisions) Order 2003[1]**	**Implementation details (from Home Office Guide to Anti-social Behaviour Act 2003)**	**Territorial Coverage**
10	General	20 January 2004 s 92 insofar as it relates to the entries in Schedule 3 below		England and Wales, and Scotland
Schedule 1	Demoted tenancies			
Schedule 2	Curfew orders and supervision orders			
Schedule 3	Repeals	20 January 2004 The entries relating to: (a) the Firearms Act 1968 (b) the Prosecution of Offences Act 1985 (c) the Firearms (Amendment) Act 1988 (d) the Criminal Justice and Public Order Act 1994		

CHAPTER 2

PREMISES WHERE DRUGS ARE USED UNLAWFULLY

Introduction

2.1 Part 1 of the Act is designed to grant the police the power to close down flats and houses being used for the supply, use and production of Class A drugs where there is a nuisance or disorder associated with the premises. The service of a notice on the premises will close the premises to public access until a magistrates' court decides whether to make a final closure order on the premises. Under this Part of the Act, the court must consider the notice served on the premises within 48 hours of the service. If the court is satisfied that the relevant conditions are met for issuing a closure order, the court can make the order that closes the premises completely for a period of up to 3 months. The court has the power to extend this complete closure for up to a maximum of 6 months.

2.2 According to the 2001/02 British Crime Survey, 12% of 16–59-year-olds had taken an illegal drug in the previous year. Cannabis was the most commonly used drug. It is estimated that crack was used by about 1% of the population during the preceding year, with its prevalence of use being twice as high among 16–24-year-olds than 16–59-year-olds.[1]

2.3 In 2000, 584 people were found guilty or cautioned (418 guilty; 166 cautioned) under s 8 of the Misuse of Drugs Act 1971 for permitting premises to be used for unlawful purposes related to the use and supply of drugs. Of these, 41 people were sentenced to custody on average for 15 months with seven people being sentenced to 2 years or more but not exceeding 5 years.[2]

2.4 The use of the highly addictive form of cocaine known as crack cocaine appears to be of rising prominence. There appears to be evidence of a rise in crack consumption and availability from many quarters, with arrest referral workers encountering more people who use crack. Importation of crack through UK airports is reportedly rising. There appears to be increasing proliferation of crack houses in vulnerable and deprived communities in the UK. There are concerns about the damage crack causes in communities as a consequence of its greater availability, relative cheapness, its highly addictive qualities, and associated increase in crime, violence and intimidation. As crack is a relatively new drug in the UK, there is less experience in managing and treating it. Crack addiction appears very difficult to treat medically, as there are few treatments to overcome craving.[3]

2.5 A definition of crack house has been defined by Commander Alan Brown of the Metropolitan Police:

---

[1]   Home Office, *Crime in England and Wales 2001/02* (2002) ('the 2001/02 British Crime Survey'); *Home Office Findings 182* (2002); See Library Standard Note SN/SG/1862 *Drug Misuse Statistics* (available at http://hc11.hclibrary.parliament.uk/notes/sgss/snsg-01862.pdf).

[2]   Home Office, *Drug Seizure and Offender Statistics: United Kingdom 2000* (2002), supplementary table S2.13.

[3]   *Your Community Your Problem*, Crack Cocaine Conference, Conference Report, Birmingham 24–25 June 2002, Chapter 1 (http://www.drugs.gov.uk/ReportsandPublications/NationalStrategy/1038398896/Crack_report.PDF).

'But what is a "crack-house"? Well, usually a flat that has been taken over for the purpose of making and smoking crack. No great scientific knowledge or equipment is needed. In fact all you need is a microwave, a water supply and a bowl. Consequently the operations are highly mobile.

In many cases the people who run the "crack house" are unwanted guests of the flat's legitimate occupier. However they are able to remain by using intimidation and threats of extreme violence that underpins the crack trade.'[1]

2.6   Commander Brown went on to explain why crack houses are so problematic in a community:

'Once established, a "crack house" has a significant impact upon the local area. The level of crime in the vicinity escalates; much of it is violent acquisitive crime. The quality of life for members of the local community diminishes and the threat of violence pervades. Similarly, open "crack markets" exist in many of our cities.

They also attract their clientele and have a significant impact upon crime levels in the local areas. The commercial viability of the area dramatically reduces and members of local communities become fearful of using local facilities.'[2]

2.7   The comments of Commander Brown concerning the destructive impact of crack cocaine and crack houses on communities was re-iterated by the article of 'Sara Smith'[3] in *The Guardian*[4] that illustrates the inadequacy of the present police policy towards neighbourhood drug dealers and the nuisance and disruption they create, and the difficulties posed for communities in dealing with drug related crime:

'The oddest thing about living next to a crack den is how boring it becomes. After a while, the screaming rows, the urine-soaked steps and abuse from users becomes predictable and depressing rather than disturbing. I was scared when addicts tried to enter my home and wept with frustration when I had to scrape human faeces away from my front door. But I was largely inured to these problems until I turned the corner of my road one morning and saw the Crimestoppers posters. "Don't let London suffer the side effects of crack," the adverts thunder, urging us to shop dealers. At that point anger took over.

Well I have shopped and shopped and shopped and shopped, and so have my neighbours. We have shopped so enthusiastically we make Elton John look frugal. We have sung like a choir of canaries, offering times, dates and vehicle number plates.

Six months on, the crack house is thriving and pensioners are still scared to go out on their own. Hardly surprising since crack dealing is associated with aggression, violence and theft. Users spend almost twice as much on their habit as heroin addicts – £478 a month, on average – which might explain why they are so keen to get into our houses.'

2.8   For these reasons the author welcomed the then new guidelines for tackling such drug-related crime.

2.9   In its White Paper, *Respect and Responsibility – Taking a Stand Against Anti-Social Behaviour*[5] the Government proposed the following in relation to crack houses:

'For sometime local authorities, the police and local communities have been frustrated by their lack of powers to close down premises – rented, owner occupied or otherwise – where Class A drugs are being sold and used. We are determined to ensure that the ruin they can cause in communities is stopped.

We have to close down these properties from which drug dealers operate, or new dealers will simply move in. These dealers are sophisticated and devious in their methods. They prey on vulnerable people compelling them to give over their property whilst they deal and use drugs, and intimidate both the

---

[1]   *Your Community Your Problem*, op cit, Chapter 3.
[2]   Ibid.
[3]   'Sara Smith' is a pseudonym of a London-based journalist.
[4]   *The Guardian*, 11 March 2003, 'The crack den next door'.
[5]   Cm 5778.

residents and neighbours, sometimes making them too frightened to speak out for fear of retribution.

The new powers will give police the power, after consulting with the local authority, to issue notice of impending closure, ratified by the court, which will enable the property to be closed within 48 hours and sealed for a fixed period of up to six months. Drug dealers will be dealt with by the courts and the property will be recovered by the landlord.'[1]

2.10   The Government proposes to achieve these aims via this Part of the Act.

Table 2.1		
Summary of Part 1 of the Act		
Section Number	**Summary**	**Comment**
1	Closure notice	Provides the grounds for issuing, and the requirements of service and contents of a police closure notice.
2	Closure order	Provides for the procedure for granting a closure order and the legal test that has to be satisfied before granting such an order.
3	Closure order: enforcement	Provides for the procedure for the enforcement of closure orders.
4	Closure of premises: offences	Describes the offences created in relation to continued occupancy or obstruction of entry.
5	Extension and discharge of closure order	Procedures for extension and discharge of closure orders.
6	Appeals	Provides for procedures governing appeals in relation to closure orders.
7	Access to other premises	Describes procedure for applications to allow access to other premises affected by but not subject to closure orders.
8	Reimbursement of costs	Provides for reimbursement of costs for clearing, securing and repair of premises incurred by police or local authorities from owners.
9	Exemption from liability for certain damages	Gives police a limited exemption from liability in damages under this part of the Act.

---

[1]   Cm 5778, paras 3.12–3.14.

Table 2.1		
Summary of Part 1 of the Act		
Section Number	**Summary**	**Comment**
10	Compensation	Provides for the payment of compensation to those who suffer a financial loss as a consequence of the exercise of powers under this Part.
11	Interpretation	Provides for interpretation of terms used under this Part of the Act.

The social problem

2.11   There are several social problems that these provisions attempt to address. The overarching problem concerns the issue of addiction to illegal drugs in society. This is couched in terms of the general policy of harm reduction in relation drugs embodied in the manifesto statement by the Labour Party of 'Tough on crime, tough on the causes of crime'.

2.12   Here, the reforms are attempting to address the means of supply of the Class A drug, cocaine. Part of the Government's drug strategy is to attempt to limit its supply and distribution. Crack cocaine is highly addictive. Its manufacture and distribution have become commonly associated with manufacture and distribution from so-called crack houses. These establishments are often set up in vulnerable and deprived communities. The nature of the intensity of the addiction to crack cocaine and the existence of these premises has led to problems with anti-social behaviour and crime associated with these sources of manufacture and distribution. Also, the supply of crack cocaine from these premises is controlled by violent drug gangs. The existence of these gangs also leads to a growth in gun crime between rival gangs linked to enforcement of control of the drug supply. Often these gangs operate to take over the premises of vulnerable members of communities to use as a site for drug manufacture and supply. The existence of crack houses causes problems in vulnerable communities with the proliferation of crime and degeneration of particular neighbourhoods.

2.13   One of the Government's approaches to drug abuse is to increase the criminalisation of the supply and use of drugs. Although this is seen as one arm of attack on this problem it has led to concern that this policy alone may not promote the harm-reduction approach envisioned by the government. To this effect, the Home Affairs Select Committee recognised a problem in current drug policy in their third report of session 2001–02, *The Government's Drug Policy: is it working?*. Here, they provided two options that might alleviate the potential problems faced by those working in harm reduction initiatives:

> 'The first is draft an exclusion clause, which applied specifically to a defined group (eg drug agencies), or for a defined purpose (eg to provide safe injecting areas). The second, and perhaps the simpler, option is to draft an exemption which permitted a licensing [sic] system, whereby the Secretary of State would authorise specific harm reduction activities to take place on specified premises.'[1]

2.14   The problem faced by the Government is how to reduce the supply and exploitation of people addicted to Class A drugs via a scheme of enforcement by criminal sanctions combined with

---

[1]   Home Affairs Committee, *The Government's Drug Policy: is it working?*, 22 May 2002, HC 318-I 2001–2, Annex para 9.

a program of education and rehabilitation for addicts. The possible social danger of a scheme that is proposed is that mere closure of crack houses in a particular area will just mean that the problem moves elsewhere to other neighbourhoods or onto the streets. Also, such closures may lead to increased homelessness among certain groups of people who by virtue of their own addiction are increasingly vulnerable or prone to more serious acts of criminality. The question remains whether this reform in isolation will help alleviate the problem or perpetuate or worsen it.

The legal problem

2.15 The legal problem here, as illustrated below, is how to try and close a loophole in existing drugs laws without being excessively punitive or harming programs of rehabilitation or education. Clearly, the law at its most robust should attack those who exploit drug addicts rather than addicts themselves. However, in this context, the law should also attempt to protect the community from the unwelcome activities of drug addicts.

2.16 Curiously, the Government has chosen to tackle this from the standpoint of reducing anti-social behaviour and disorder associated with crack houses. The threshold for action by the police in relation to dealing with the closure of crack houses is the reasonable belief that they cause serious nuisance or disorder. The primary objective of this legislation appears to be to protect the surrounding community from drug addicts and drug dealers. Primarily, the powers are exercised by the police and supervised by the courts.

2.17 Addressing the legal problem by closure of and eviction from residential property, in the manner proposed by the Government, may promote problems of homelessness, increased drug use on the streets and increased crime. This approach may pose problems in the future in terms of risks of violation of the European Convention of Human Rights, for example Arts 2 and 3.

Public nuisance?

2.18 It is noteworthy that a local authority has used its powers under s 222 of the Local Government Act 1972 regarding prosecution of public nuisances to close crack houses in its area.[1] This is discussed in more detail in Chapter 10.[2]

Existing legislation

2.19 The Misuse of Drugs Act 1971 ('the 1971 Act') and the Misuse of Drugs Regulations 1985[3] do contain the potential for action to be taken against certain premises where drugs are produced or supplied. Section 8 of the 1971 Act provides for an offence where the occupier or person concerned in the control or management of a property knowingly permits or allows the following activities to take place in them:

(a) production or attempting to produce a controlled drug in contravention of s 4(1)[4] of the Act;

(b) supplying or attempting to supply a controlled drug to another in contravention of s 4(1) of this Act, or offering to supply a controlled drug to another in contravention of s 4(1);

---

[1] *Royal Borough of Kensington and Chelsea v Williams and others* [2003] EWHC 1933.
[2] See **10.8** et seq.
[3] SI 1985/2066, reg 13.
[4] 'Subject to any regulations under section 7 of this Act for the time being in force, it shall not be lawful for a person –
    (a) to produce a controlled drug; or
    (b) to supply or offer to supply a controlled drug to another.'

(c)   preparing opium for smoking;

(d)   smoking cannabis, cannabis resin or preparing opium;

[(d)   administering or using a controlled drug which is unlawfully in any person's possession at or immediately before the time when it is administered or used.][1]

2.20   However, as the House of Commons Research Paper[2] reports, this is not an absolute offence. According to the report of the Runciman Inquiry:

> 'Because it has to be committed "knowingly", the burden is on the prosecution to prove that the prohibited activities were taking place. An offence against section 8 is not a drug trafficking offence for the purpose of the Drug Trafficking Act 1994. Conviction therefore does not result in confiscation under that Act, although it may lead to forfeiture under section 27 of the [Misuse of Drugs Act 1971].'[3]

2.21   In fact the Runciman Inquiry recommended that s 8 should be repealed entirely:

> 'One possible solution would be, as has been recommended by ACPO and others, to extend paragraphs (c) and (d) to all controlled drugs. We prefer the alternative of repealing the paragraphs altogether. This would leave the more serious activities in relation to all controlled drugs to be caught by paragraphs (a) and (b). As far as offences of use are concerned, insofar as the law has an influence at present, it is likely to drive drug-taking out onto the street and other places where it is potentially far less safe. Our recommendation is intended to reverse that effect.'[4]

2.22   In response to this comment the 1971 Act, para (d) was extended as described above. Knowingly permitting the use of controlled drugs was an offence only in respect of smoking cannabis or opium.[5] According to the House Of Commons Research Paper,[6] the rationale behind this distinction was that the smoking of cannabis or opium ought to be readily detectable and thus owners and occupiers could be certain that such activities were illegal, whereas consumption of other drugs may be lawful. This amendments remains to come into force.

2.23   Thus, under the 1971 Act, the operators of crack houses are not liable for prosecution under the 1971 Act for allowing the use of crack cocaine on their premises. By contrast, however, they could be prosecuted for allowing the dealing or supply of the drug on their premises.

2.24   The Home Office has consulted with police and other government departments and other treatment and voluntary sector organisations prior to enactment of the modifications to s 8. This modification was not welcomed by many drug rehabilitation agencies as they believed that the change in the legislation would make those involved in helping to rehabilitate drug users and the homeless more liable to prosecution.[7]

---

1   Substituted by Criminal Justice and Police Act 2001, s 38, with the date in force to be appointed under s 138(2).

2   HC Research Paper 03/34, 4 April 2003, p 38

3   The Police Federation, *Drugs and the Law: Report of the Independent Inquiry into the Misuse of Drugs Act 1971* (2000), Chapter 5, para 35 (http://www.druglibrary.org/schaffer/Library/studies/runciman/default.htm).

4   Ibid, para 44.

5   The term 'opium' also refers to derivatives such as heroin.

6   HC Research Paper 03/34, 4 April 2003, p 38.

7   Transform Drug Policy Institute, *Response from the Transform Drug Policy Iinstitute to the Home Office Consultation on amendment to section 8 of the MDA 1971*, 8 November 2002 (http://www.tdpi.org.uk):

> 'Whilst Transform understands the impetus behind the updating of section 8 d, it believes that it has the potential to make the enforcement of the Act even more likely to increase the harm associated with the use and misuse of drugs.

> ... the amendment will do far more to impinge upon harm reduction initiatives than it will benefit police activities in increasing community safety and crime reduction.'

2.25 These concerns were ameliorated when the Home Office stated that they would wait on the impact of the implementation of the Anti-social Behaviour Act 2003 before deciding on whether to bring the s 8 modification into force.[1]

2.26 Roger Howard, the Chief Executive of DrugScope, welcomed the new measures outlined for the Anti-social Behaviour Bill:

> 'The government has produced a potent way of tackling the problems of houses used for crack dealing. DrugScope welcomes moves that will enable the police to quickly close those premises down. The new proposals will give communities the protection they deserve.'[2]

2.27 Transform issued a guarded response to the Anti-social Behaviour Bill. The Director stated that Part 1 of the Bill would provide useful measures for tackling problems in the community caused by crack houses but remained concerned that they would not solve the problems associated with crack cocaine.[3]

> 'However, any enforcement against crack house needs to be seen in a wider context. The illegal drug market is driven by demand and crack houses are a product of a high level of demand for crack combined with prohibitionist legislation. In this sense crack houses are actually the product of outdated prohibition-based drug laws. Assuming that we cannot eradicate crack use, users will always require somewhere to buy crack and smoke or inject it.

> This means that attempts to close places of use or sale of crack will only serve to displace these activities, not undermine the market itself. TDPI recognises that specific closure notices may reduce nuisance and increase community safety in one area. However, it is highly likely that this nuisance will only be moved elsewhere rather than stopped completely.'

Parliamentary session 2002–03

2.28 The issue of s 1 on closure notices was debated in the Standing Committee on 6 May 2003.[4]

Closure notices

2.29 Mr Hawkins (Conservative) tabled an amendment where local authority chief executives would have the same power as the police to issue closure notices. The Opposition stated that they believed that it was 'absolutely vital' that local authorities had to be involved in the enforcement and not just the police. Mr Hawkins noted that the problems of crack houses were not limited solely to poor neighbourhoods as there were problems with prosperous people dealing drugs in prosperous constituencies like his.[5]

2.30 Mrs Brooke (Liberal Democrat) stated that although she welcomed the support of crime and disorder partnerships between the police and local authorities[6] she felt strongly that the power to initiate such proceedings should remain with the police.[7]

---

[1] *The Guardian*, 19 March 2003, 'Harsh draft excluded: Drug workers cheer government's "crack house" law rethink'.

[2] DrugScope Press Release, *DrugScope gives mixed reaction to Anti-Social Behaviour White Paper*, 28 March 2003. (http://www.drugscope.org.uk)

[3] Transform Drug Policy Institute, *Response from Transform Drug Policy Institute (TDPI) to the Anti-social Behaviour Bill*, 28 March 2003, paras 3–4.

[4] *Hansard*, HC Standing Committee G, 6 May 2003, col 004ff.

[5] Ibid, cols 006–007.

[6] See Crime and Disorder Act 1998, ss 5–7; R Leng, R Taylor & M Wasik, *Blackstone's Guide to the Crime and Disorder Act 1998* (1998), pp 18–22.

[7] *Hansard*, HC Standing Committee G, 6 May 2003, col 007.

2.31   Mr Bob Ainsworth, the Minister for the Government, stated that the new powers being proposed are not designed as an additional resource to aid the police in combating dealing in Class A drugs. These powers are designed to protect people from the 'substantial nuisance' associated with the use and supply of Class A drugs. Mr Ainsworth went on to state that the powers were not designed to replace existing criminal law. 'Where there is evidence of the unlawful use and supply of drugs the police will continue to prosecute vigorously under the Misuse of Drugs Act 1971'.[1]

2.32   Mr Ainsworth continued that, for a number of reasons, it would not be appropriate for the extension of these powers to local authorities. For example, it would probably be very dangerous to enter premises to serve a notice where there had been serious nuisance or disorder associated with Class A drugs. Mr Ainsworth said that the powers should be maintained as police powers because police oversight and direction is vital to their use. Also, the powers are to be exercised in consultation with local authorities and thus local authorities should play an important role through these partnership arrangements.[2] The amendment was withdrawn.

2.33   Mr Hawkins (Conservative) tabled an amendment to extend the exercise of closure powers to encompass Class B and C drugs, for example cannabis, as well as those in Class A.[3] The argument was founded on the proposition that use and supply of such drugs also created disorder and nuisance in communities.

2.34   Mr Vernon Coaker welcomed the Government's proposals for Class A drugs. Although he accepted that there could be problems associated with houses dealing in Class B and C drugs, the anti-social behaviour associated with the dealing of Class A drugs was of a different magnitude to the other drugs. Mr Matthew Green supported this line of argument.[4] Mr Green welcomed the focus on crack houses and highlighted the distinction between the level of anti-social behaviour associated with Class A drugs versus Class B or C.

2.35   Ms Dari Taylor (Labour) noted that anti-social behaviour is associated with all classes of drugs. She noted that, if Classes B and C were included in the legislation, this would deflect attention from closure operations being targeted on crack cocaine. She specified that the focus of the police efforts should be on this drug.[5]

2.36   Ms Taylor expressed the hope that other legislation would deal with problems associated with Class B and C drugs. She noted that, if Class B and C drugs were included in closure operations, more than one third of the properties in her constituency would be targets for closure. She stated that 'The staggering scale of that, and the fact that children and young people are involved, mean that we should not enter into that debate until we understand the extent and involvement of the support services'. This she concluded should highlight concentration on Class A drugs first.[6]

2.37   Mrs Annette Brooke (Liberal Democrat) supported the statements of Ms Taylor stating '... it is right to concentrate resources on Class A drugs and to establish agencies that should be involved. ... I hope that the anti-social behaviour of a group of young people who regularly take cannabis would be picked up in other ways. ... I do not want young people to be criminalised by one act of

---

[1]   *Hansard*, HC Standing Committee G, 6 May 2003, col 008.
[2]   Ibid, col 008–009.
[3]   Ibid, col 017.
[4]   Ibid, col 019ff.
[5]   Ibid, col 021.
[6]   Ibid.

taking that drug. I want support measures to be included in the Bill, and I believe that there are other ways to deal with behaviour caused by cannabis use'. She concluded by reinforcing the distinction that should be made between crack houses and cannabis use.[1]

2.38   The Minister added that in this legislation:

'We are speaking of Draconian powers. We are talking about throwing people out of their homes. There must be a genuine need if that is to be done …Other amendments would decouple the issue of nuisance from Class A drug use, and Class A drug use from the issue of nuisance …

I believe that this part of the Bill should be confined to dealing with Class A drugs. The evidence shows that the overwhelming need is to deal with crack cocaine … The overwhelming need is to close crack dens … I believe that we now have adequate powers against the misuse of Class B and C drugs. We should at this stage, confine the powers to Class A drugs, to give the police powers that they require, where a real and proven nuisance exists.'[2]

2.39   Then there followed a debate on Liberal Democrat amendments that the clause should not apply to premises of certain charities that help drug addicts and the homeless. The Government stated that it believed that the power of the Secretary of State to exempt certain premises from the power in the clause is a necessary reserve power.[3]

2.40   The Minister clarified that, when a serious nuisance to the public is evident, the premises can be closed, even if no criminal charges against an individual involved in the supply of Class A drugs can be brought.[4] Clauses 1 and 2 (closure order) were ordered to stand as part of the Bill.

Closure enforcement

2.41   On the use of reasonable force, Mr Ainsworth stated, 'It is reasonable force against property. I know of circumstances where council employees have had to break windows to secure properties … Reasonable force has to be used to secure property for the tenants. This does not involve community support officers or accredited persons. We are not trying to get local authority workers to do the dangerous work needed, which is quite properly undertaken by properly trained police officers'. In answer to Mr Matthew Green, Mr Ainsworth stated, 'a constable may use reasonable force against individuals in the first place to effect the notice and assist those securing premises'.[5]

Extension and discharge

2.42   Mr Ainsworth stated, 'There will be no automatic denial of reoccupation [of the closed premises] by the individual but the period when the property is in effect sealed and they have been removed gives the local authority or registered social landlord the ability to take possession procedures to ensure that the individual does not return if that what they think is right and appropriate. In those circumstances the premises can be let to someone else. It is not a blanket ban. One can envisage circumstances in which it would be appropriate to allow someone to move back into the premises – perhaps a vulnerable person who has been abused, or whose property has been taken over'.[6]

---

[1]   *Hansard*, HC Standing Committee G, 6 May 2003, col 021–022.
[2]   Ibid, col 026.
[3]   Ibid, col 044–045.
[4]   Ibid, col 045.
[5]   Ibid, col 064–065.
[6]   Ibid, col 071.

Exemption from liability of certain damages

2.43 Mr Hawkins (Conservative) asked if this was an area of the law in which the Government might want to derogate from the European Convention on Human Rights. Mr Ainsworth answered by stating, 'The clause is designed to ensure that police officers and police forces are not liable for damages arising from the exercise of their powers under this part of the Bill. The clause is intended to prevent malicious attempts to seek redress for the actions of police from criminals who might have been involved with the supply of drugs. However, if the police officer fails to act within the boundaries of the Human Rights Act or acts in bad faith, it is entirely right that the matter should be addressed by the courts'.[1]

In the House of Lords

2.44 In the Committee stage, on 11 September 2003, on closure notices, there was a debate on the requirement to prove serious nuisance associated with drug use. The Government responded that it believed that if it were removed it would create the risk that individuals who posed no immediate problem, and who should be considered vulnerable or in treatment, could be evicted or denied housing. This would also create problems for voluntary sector organisations working in this area.[2]

2.45 On closure orders, Baroness Walmsley (Liberal Democrat) expressed concerns about children or elderly relatives or spouses who might be ignorant of what is going on, or powerless to stop it.[3] Lord Avebury (Liberal Democrat) sought assurances that, when an innocent person is made homeless as a result of the closure order, the local authority must have a duty to re-house them and that this must be incorporated under the strategies of the Homelessness Act 2002.[4] Baroness Maddock picked up on this point and noted that the Minister had not replied and expressed concerns about the existence of strategies to deal with this issue.[5]

2.46 On enforcement, Baroness Walmsley put forward an amendment that reasonable force in enforcing an closure should not be used in relation to children under 16. She expressed concerns about the application of criminal penalties expressed in the clause against children. The Minister responded by saying that the Government did not want to tie the hands of the sentencer and that this may be combined to meet the child's needs. Lord Wedderburn added that:

> '... if the government believe that we should presume that under-16s should not be sent to prison why not put that in the Bill? ... One begins to wonder about the attitude of our policy makers towards children ... if necessary we will lock them up for being on the premises. I do not think this is very intelligent penal policy.'[6]

2.47 The remaining clauses were not debated and were agreed to.

2.48 In the report stage in the House of Lords on 23 October 2003, Lord Dixon-Smith (Conservative) stated that there was wide concern that third parties who were not involved in anti-social behaviour or drug use would be adversely affected by closure orders. He was concerned about the impact this might have on those responsible for housing the homeless.[7] In response, the Minister said that any person made homeless had the right to seek re-housing from the local authority, but they would only be re-housed according to criteria laid down in law.

---

[1]   *Hansard*, HC Standing Committee G, 6 May 2003, col 076.
[2]   *Hansard*, House of Lords, 11 September 2003, col 435.
[3]   Ibid, col 440.
[4]   Ibid, col 441.
[5]   Ibid, col 445.
[6]   Ibid, col 449ff
[7]   *Hansard*, House of Lords, 23 October 2003, col 1760.

2.49 On closure orders, Baroness Walmsley attempted to introduce an amendment to ensure that those under 18 who commit offences under this Part of the Bill should only be subjected to community sentences. She was concerned that this had not been put on the face of the Bill.[1]

2.50 Baroness Scotland agreed that imprisonment should be the last resort for adults and juveniles but that it was impossible to legislate for such minutiae. The Minister said that the options available to the court were clear from the Powers of Criminal Courts (Sentencing) Act 2000, and judges are not obliged to hand out maximum sentences, yet imprisonment may be the most appropriate penalty for youth offenders.[2]

2.51 Lord Wedderburn (Labour) commented that the drafting of the clause did not make it clear that the penalties were not merely an option among many. The Minister replied that listing everything in the Sentencing Act would make things too complex in this Bill and that there would be guidance issued for juvenile offenders. Baroness Walmsley expressed the concern that sentencers may not look beyond the Bill because of its complexity.[3]

The provisions in detail

Closure notice

2.52 Section 1 of the Act sets out the conditions under which the police can issue a notice for closure of a premises where drug dealing occurs.

2.53 Subsection (1) of s 1 sets out the test that must be met before a police superintendent, or an officer of higher rank, can authorise that a closure notice on a premises is issued.

2.54 The authorising police officer must have reasonable grounds for believing that, at any relevant time, the premises have been used with the unlawful use, production or supply of controlled Class A drugs; and that the use of the premises is associated with the occurrence of disorder or a serious nuisance to members of the public.

2.55 Subsection (2) of s 1 requires the authorising police officer to be satisfied that the relevant local authority for the area in which the premises are situated have been consulted, and that reasonable steps have been taken to identify the persons living in the premises or those persons who have control or responsibility for or an interest in the premises before the authority for the issue of the notice is given.

2.56 Subsection (3) of s 1 provides that any authorisation given by the police under subs (2) may be given orally or in writing. However, if an authorisation is given orally the authorising officer must confirm it in writing as soon as is practicable.

2.57 Subsection (4) of s 1 sets out the contents that are required of the closure notice. These must include details that an application will be made to a court for a closure order, the time and the place of the court hearing in relation to the closure order and a statement that access to the property during the period of the notice is prohibited to someone other than someone who is usually resident in or the owner of the premises. The notice must also explain the effects of the notice and that a failure to comply with it amounts to a criminal offence. The notice must also contain information about local sources of legal and housing advice in relation to the notice and consequent order. Subsection (5) provides that the notice must be served by a police constable.

[1] *Hansard*, House of Lords, 23 October 2003, col 1766.
[2] Ibid, col 1767.
[3] Ibid, cols 1767–1768.

2.58   Subsections (6) and (7) of s 1 set out the requirements in relation to service of a copy of the notice, which must be attached to a prominent place on the premises, or its normal means of access, or to any outbuildings that appears to the constable to be used with or as part of the premises. A copy of the notice can be given to at least one person who appears to have control or responsibility to the premises, and giving a copy to person identified in pursuance of subs 2(b) and to any other person who appears to be the person matching a description of the person in that subsection. This is an attempt to avoid the fact that people may use alternative identities or avoid accepting service.

2.59   Subsection (7) of s 1 provides that service must also be effected on any person who occupies any other part of the building or structure in which the crack house is situated if the constable reasonably believes at the time of service that the person's access to other parts of the building will be impeded by the closure order.

2.60   Subsection (8) of s 1 provides that for the purpose of serving the notice or order that it does not matter whether or not any person has actually been convicted of a criminal offence in relation to use, control or supply of a controlled drug.

2.61   Subsection (9) of s 1 provides the Secretary of State for the Home Department with the power to make regulations to exempt premises or descriptions of premises from the application of this section, for example drug rehabilitation clinics or charities.

2.62   Subsection (10) of s 1 provides that the relevant time under subs (1) where an authorising officer may issue a closure notice is 3 months. This means that when the police officer authorises the issuing of a closure notice that this closure notice is only lawful if it relates to prescribed activities that are committed 3 months previously to the issue of the notice.

2.63   Subsection (11) provides the requirement that the information supplied on the closure notice must include names and a means of contacting persons and organisations providing legal and housing advice in the area.

Closure order

2.64   Subsection (1) of s 2 provides that once a closure notice has been issued under s 1 the police must apply to the magistrates' court to make a closure order.

2.65   Subsection (2) of s 2 provides that the magistrates' court must hear the application by the police within 48 hours of service of the notice on the premises.

2.66   Subsection (3) provides the test on which the court must be satisfied before making the closure order. The court must be satisfied, presumably to the civil standard of proof, of each of the following:

(1)   that the premises have been used in connection with the unlawful use, production or supply of a Class A controlled drug; and

(2)   that the premises is associated with causing serious nuisance or disorder to the public; and

(3)   that the making of the order is necessary to prevent disorder or serious nuisance for the period specified in it.

2.67   Subsection (4) of s 2 provides that a closure order is a court order closing access to all persons in respect of the premises for a period decided by the court that does not exceed 3 months.

2.68   Subsection (5) of s 2 provides the court with a discretion to include provisions in the order that it thinks appropriate for access to any part of the building or structure in which the premises are located, for example to stairways or shared parts. Also subs (8) provides that a closure order may be made in respect of only part of the premises affected by the closure notice.

2.69 Subsection (6) of s 2 provides the magistrates' court with the power to adjourn the hearing to allow the occupier or someone else with control, responsibility or an interest in the premises to show why a closure order should not be made. For example, because the problems have stopped or the occupiers have been evicted.

2.70 Under subs (7) of s 2, when a magistrates' court adjourns a hearing under subs (6), the court may order that the closure notice continues to have effect during this period of adjournment.

2.71 Subsection (9) of s 2 provides that it is immaterial in relation to making closure orders whether a person affected by the order has been convicted in relation to use, production or supply of a controlled drug.

Closure order: enforcement

2.72 When a closure order is made under s 2, s 3 provides that a constable or any other person authorised by the chief officer of police may enter and do anything reasonably necessary to secure the property against any other person. The person entering the premises as described may use reasonable force in relation to entry and making secure if it is necessary. This probably means not only the exercise of reasonable force against the property but also against persons in the premises in order to secure it.

2.73 Section 3(4) provides that the constable or authorised person must, if required to do so by the owner, occupier or other person in charge of the premises, provide evidence of identity and authority before entering the premises.

2.74 Section 3(5) provides that a constable or authorised person may enter the premises at any time during the order to carry out essential maintenance or repairs.

2.75 Section 3(6) provides that authorisation of the persons entering the property must be provided by the chief officer of police in the area of the premises.

Closure of premises: offences

2.76 Section 4 creates the criminal offences of remaining in or entering a property subject to a closure notice or order without reasonable excuse. Subsection (2) creates an offence if a person obstructs a constable or an authorised person acting in pursuance of the functions authorised by ss 1(6) or 3(2).

2.77 Subsection (3) provides that a person committing an offence under s 4 is liable on summary conviction to imprisonment for up to 6 months or a fine not exceeding level 5 on the standard scale, namely £5,000, or both.

2.78 Subsection (5) provides a constable in uniform with the power of arrest of a person they reasonably suspect of committing or having committed an offence under s 4.

Extension and discharge of closure order

2.79 Section 5 provides the police with the power to apply for an extension of the period for which the closure order has effect up to a maximum period of 6 months. This maximum of 6 months includes the period for which the original order had effect. Such an application for an extension can only be authorised by a superintendent or a police officer of higher rank.

2.80 The authorising officer must:

(1) have reasonable grounds for believing that the extension of the order is necessary for the purpose of preventing the occurrence of disorder or serious nuisance to other members of the public; and

(2)   be satisfied that the local authority has been consulted about the intention to make the application for the extension.

2.81   If an application is made to a magistrate then, under s 5(3), they may issue a summons directed to the persons on whom the closure notice relating to the closed premises was served (under subss (6)(d), (e), or (7) of s 1), or any other person who it appears has an interest in the closed premised but on whom the notice was not served.

2.82   Section 5(4) provides that if the court is satisfied that the order is necessary to prevent disorder and serious nuisance for a further period it may extend the period in which the notice has effect for a period not exceeding 3 months. However, subs (5) provides that a closure order must not have effect for more than 6 months in total.

2.83   Subsection (6) allows a constable, the local authority, persons on whom the closure notice was served under s 1 and any other person with an interest in the closed property, but on whom the closure notice was not served, to apply for the closure order to be discharged at any time.

2.84   Subsection (7) provides that, if an application is made under subs (6) by a person other than a constable, the magistrates may issue a summons directed to such constable as they think appropriate requiring the constable to appear at court to answer the application.

2.85   Subsection (8) specifies that a court must not make an order discharging a closure order unless it is satisfied that the closure order is no longer necessary to prevent disorder or serious nuisance.

2.86   Subsection (9) sets out the requirements relating to the service of notice on person summoned, under subss (3) or (7), to appear before the court under this section. To comply with this subsection a notice stating the date, time and place of the application must be served:

(1)   on the persons it is directed to if issued under subs (3);

(2)   by persons mentioned in subs (6)(c) and (d), apart from the applicant, if issued under subs (7);

(3)   by such a constable as the justice thinks appropriate, unless the constable is the applicant;

(4)   by the local authority, unless it is the applicant.

2.87   Under subs (10), an appropriate justice of the peace (magistrate) is a justice acting for petty sessions in the area of the premises relating to the closure order.

Appeal

2.88   Section 6 allows for appeals to the Crown Court against closure orders, under s 2 or s 5, and against a refusal to make one by all interested parties.

2.89   Under subs (2) of s 6, an appeal must be brought to the Crown Court before the end of a period of 21 days beginning with the day on which the decision relating to the order was made.

2.90   From subs (3) an appeal against an order made under s 2 or s 5(4) may be brought by a person on whom the closure notice was served, or a person with an interest in the premises but on whom no notice was served.

2.91   From subs (4), an appeal against a decision not to make an order can be brought by a constable or a local authority.

2.92   Subsection (5) provides that, concerning an appeal made under this section, a Crown Court may make such an order it thinks fit.

Access to other premises

2.93 Section 7 ensures that a court may make an order concerning access to any part of a building or structure in which the premises are situated, where the part itself is not subject to the closure order.

2.94 Under subs (2), a person to whom this section applies, who owns or occupies such a part of the building or structure, may make an application to the magistrates (s 2 or s 5 orders) or Crown Court (s 6 order) enabling them to retain the access to that part of the building or structure that he had before the closure order took effect.

2.95 Under subs (3), if an application is made under this section, notice of the date, time and place of the hearing of the application must be served on all persons mentioned in s 5(6).

2.96 Under subs (4), on hearing an application under this section a court may make any order as it thinks fit in relation to access to any part of the building or structure in which the closed premises are situated.

2.97 Subsection (5) provides that it is immaterial whether any provision has been made as mentioned in s 2(5).

Reimbursement of costs

2.98 Section 8 provides the court with the power to make an order against the owner of the premises relating to the closure order that they must reimburse any cost incurred by the police or local authority in clearing, securing or maintaining the premises.

2.99 Subsection (3) provides that an application made under this section is not to be entertained by the court unless it is made no later than the end of 3 months starting with the day that the closure order ceases to have effect.

2.100 Subsection (4) provides that an application made under this section must be served on the police authority for the area in which the premises are situated if made by the local authority, or the local authority if the application is made by the police, on the owner of the premises

Exception from liability in certain cases

2.101 Section 9 provides for an exemption from liability in damages claimed against the police in carrying out their functions under this part of the Act. It does not extend to acts of bad faith or acts that are in breach of the police's duty as a public authority to exercise their functions compatibly with the European Convention of Human Rights.

2.102 Subsection (4) provides that this section does not affect any other exemption from liability for damages, whether at common law or otherwise.

2.103 The relevant damages to which this section refers are damages awarded in proceedings for judicial review or for the tort of negligence or misfeasance in public duty.

Compensation

2.104 Section 10 provides for compensation payments to be made by the court, on application, out of central funds when it is satisfied that:

> 'A person has suffered a financial loss as a result of the closure notice being issued or the closure order having effect.'

2.105 Under subs (2) a person to whom this section relates may apply to a magistrates' court that considered the closure application, or the Crown Court if the order was made or extended by that court on appeal under s 6.

2.106 From subs (3), an application made under this section must not be entertained by the court if it is made later than the end of a period of 3 months, starting on either the day the court decides not to make the closure order, or the day the Crown Court dismisses an appeal against the decision not to make a closure order, or the day the closure order ceases to have effect, whichever is the later.

2.107 Subsection (4) provides that on application the court may order the payment of funds, in addition to proof of financial loss, if it satisfied that:

(1)   the person had no connection with the use of the premises subject to the notice or order for the supply or use of Class A drugs (such use having been associated with the occurrence of disorder or serious nuisance; or

(2)   if the person was the owner or occupier who took all reasonable steps to prevent that use; and

(3)   it is appropriate in all the circumstances to compensate the person for that loss.

Interpretation

2.108 Section 11 provides for interpretation of terms used in this Part of the Act.

2.109 Any reference to controlled drug and to production and supply must be construed in accordance with the Misuse of Drugs Act 1971. A Class A controlled drug is a controlled drug that is Class A within s 2 of the 1971 Act and includes crack cocaine.

2.110 Under subs (3) 'premises' are defined to include any land or other place whether enclosed or not; any outbuildings that are used as part of the premises. Thus, the definition of 'premises' is very broad; it is not necessarily restricted to flats and houses. It is such that it encompasses open spaces such as gardens or defined areas of open space where Class A drugs are used or supplied which could then become subject to a closure notice or order.

2.111 A closure notice is defined as a notice issued under s 1. A closure order is a court order made under s 2, extended under s 5, or an order made under s 6 which has like effect to an order made under ss 2 or 5.

2.112 Under subs (6), a local authority is defined to include a district council, a London borough council, a county council where there is no district council, the Common council of the City of London when acting as a local authority, the Council of the Isles of Scilly. In relation to Wales a local authority is defined as a county council or a county borough council.

2.113 References to a local authority are to the local authority for the area in which the premises to which the closure notice applies and the closure order has effect are situated.

2.114 Subsection (9) defines closed premises as premises in respect of which the closure order has effect.

2.115 Subsection (10) defines a person as the owner of a premises if either of the following applies to them:

(1)   they are a person (other than a mortgagee not in possession) who at the time being is entitle to dispose of the freehold, whether in possession or reversion;

(2)   they are a person who holds or is entitled to hold rents and profits of the premises under lease which (when granted) was for a term of less than 3 years.

Conclusions and problems

2.116 The legislation is designed to attempt to close a loophole in the law left by s 8 of the Misuse of Drugs Act 1971. The aim is to target dealing in Class A drugs, particularly from crack houses. This is founded on such premises provoking serious nuisance and disorder. It should be noted, however, that the statute does not provide a definition as to what constitutes a 'serious nuisance'. The remedy is to close the premises down and restore them to the rightful owner. The problem is that this approach may lead to harming vulnerable people by creating homelesness and subjecting vulnerable people to destitution. The success of this strategy will also be measured by the strategies that local authorities and Government create in response to drug treatment and homelessness issues.

CHAPTER 3

HOUSING

Introduction

3.1 Part 2 of the Anti-social Behavour Act 2003 presents a three-pronged approach to the problem of anti-social tenants. First, it provides a mechanism to ensure that social landlords focus upon their managerial/procedural responses to complaints of anti-social behaviour. Secondly, it provides further refinements of the existing legal tools available to local housing authorities and social landlords to respond to the problem of anti-social behaviour by enhancing and re-organising the injunction powers available to landlords and by ensuring that courts consider the impact of anti-social behaviour upon its victims when deciding whether to make a possession order. Thirdly, it provides for a new tool, the ability to demote a secure or assured tenant to a new less secure form of tenancy.

3.2 The provisions do not stand alone, but work by amending those sections of the Housing Act 1996 (HA 1996), the Housing Act 1988 (HA 1988) and the Housing Act 1985 (HA 1985), which enable landlords to take action against anti-social tenants. The complexity of the amendments and insertions is a reflection of the complexity of the legislation governing housing tenure.

3.3 Table 3.1 summarises the contents of Part 2.

Table 3.1

The contents of Part 2 of the Anti-social Behaviour Act 2003

Provision	Summary	Main amendment/insertion
s 12	Anti-social behaviour: landlords' policies and procedures	New HA 1996, s 218A which requires social landlords to publish policy and procedures relating to anti-social behaviour
s 13	Injunctions against anti-social behaviour on application of certain social landlords	Repeals HA 1996, ss 152, 153 New ss 153A–153E These re-organise and extend the injunction regime available to social landlords
ss 14 and 15	Demotion orders	Amends s 82 of the HA 1985 and inserts a new s 82A (in relation to secure tenancies) Inserts new s 6A into the HA 1988 (in relation to assured tenancies)

Table 3.1

The contents of Part 2 of the Anti-social Behaviour Act 2003

Provision	Summary	Main amendment/insertion
		Inserts new s 20B into the HA 1988 Creates a new form of tenancy which is less secure than the secure or the assured regime
s 16	Structured discretion in proceedings for possession on the basis of anti-social behaviour	Inserts new s 85A into the HA 1985 Requires court to take into consideration the broader effects of anti-social behaviour
s 17	Devolution: Wales	Makes appropriate amendments to Sch 1 to the National Assembly for Wales (Transfer of Functions) Order 1999 (SI 1999/672) to enable the provisions to be applied within Wales

The Housing Act 1996 and anti-social tenants

3.4   Legislative action specifically targeting the problem of anti-social tenants began with Part V of the HA 1996. The contractual and statutory powers which existed prior to the Act were considered to be ineffective or expensive and time consuming. One commentator explains the perceptions of social landlords, 'The courts are sometimes reluctant to grant possession, and it is often difficult to persuade residents to give evidence against difficult neighbours for fear of retaliation'.[1]

3.5   Several tools relating to the control of anti-social behaviour emanate from the HA 1996. There are essentially two strategic approaches underpinning these tools. The first concentrates on reducing the security of tenure of anti-social tenants by providing for introductory tenancies, by providing for new expanded grounds for possession for social tenants and by reducing the formalities required prior to the termination of a social tenancy as a result of anti-social behaviour. The second strengthens the powers of social landlords to intervene to prevent recurrence of anti-social behaviour by providing new injunctions with powers of arrest against anti-social tenants

Introductory tenancies

3.6   Introductory tenancies were introduced in s 124 of the HA 1996. Local housing authorities and housing action trusts can elect to operate an introductory tenancy scheme. Once the election is made, all new tenancies must be granted as introductory tenancies. The tenancy lasts for one year from the date of commencement unless proceedings are brought for possession of the property and the court makes an order for possession.

3.7   Proceedings for possession are governed by ss 127–128 of the HA 1996. The landlord must serve a notice of possession on the introductory tenant, which explains the procedure for possession, and the reasons why a possession order is being sought. The notice must also inform

---

[1]   James Driscoll, *A Guide to the Housing Act 1996* (Butterworths, 1996).

the tenant of his right to request a review of the landlord's decision to seek an order for possession and of the time within which such a request must be made.

3.8 The tenant has 14 days to seek a review. The procedure for review is governed by the Introductory Tenants (Review) Regulations 1997.[1] The decision in R *(on the application of McLellan) v Bracknell Forest BC, Reigate & Banstead BC v Benfield and Another*[2] decided that, whilst the authority's review of its own decision prima facie violates the tenant's right to a fair trial under Art 6, the procedure on internal review (combined with the availability of judicial review) contains sufficient safeguards to ensure compatibility.

3.9 The White Paper, *Our Future Homes*, suggested that landlords should be able to terminate the tenancies of introductory tenants 'who do not behave responsibly', which indicates that it is appropriate to use the summary procedure to evict not only unruly tenants but also non-payers of rent. The Department of the Environment advised that[3] 'it is envisaged that the majority of possession cases will relate to persistent anti-social behaviour or rent arrears'.

3.10 Registered social landlords (RSLs) are excluded from the introductory tenancy regime. Since the HA 1988, RSLs have been legally free to use assured shorthold tenancies.[4] Such use has been subject to more or less restrictive guidance from the Housing Corporation. Over recent years, the Corporation has approved their use as 'starter' tenancies, as a rough equivalent to introductory tenancies, and has encouraged experimentation.

3.11 Local authorities have been interested in RSLs' freedom to use assured shorthold tenancies outside of the first year of a new allocation. RSLs have, in turn, been interested in local authorities' ability to evict during the first 6 months of an introductory tenancy. Both have argued that some tenants deliberately refrain from causing a nuisance in their first year, and that others only develop nuisance behaviour later, typically when their children enter their teens or when a new partner moves in.

Extension of discretionary grounds for possession

3.12 Section 144 of the HA 1996 substituted a new, more extensive ground for possession on the basis of nuisance or annoyance to neighbours. The original ground, which was very close in formulation to the original legislation providing security of tenure for rented housing dating back to the beginning of the twentieth century,[5] was in two parts, the first relating to nuisance and annoyance to neighbours, the second concerned with convictions for illegal and immoral user.

3.13 The amendments to ground 2 in Sch 2 to the HA 1985 extend the ground so that the first part now includes the anti-social conduct of visitors. It no longer requires that actual nuisance is proved; the nuisance conduct includes behaviour which impacts upon visitors and those engaged in lawful activities in the locality as well as local residents, and the meaning of neighbour is extended to include all who live in the locality.

---

[1] SI 1997/72.

[2] [2001] EWCA Civ 1510, [2002] 1 All ER 899.

[3] DoE Circular 2/97, para 19.

[4] They are also legally free to terminate them for no reason, as is a private landlord, under HA 1988, s 21. The exception is if in the particular case the landlord counts as a 'public authority' for Human Rights Act 1998, ss 6–7. Then eviction would have to be justified as an interference with the tenant's home life. See *Poplar Housing and Regeneration Community Association v Donoghue* [2001] EWCA Civ 595, [2001] 3 WLR 183.

[5] Section 5(b) of the Increase of Rent and Mortgage Interest (Restrictions) Act 1920 provides that no order for the recovery of possession shall be made or given unless 'the tenant or any person residing with him has been guilty of conduct which is a nuisance or annoyance to adjoining occupiers, or has been convicted of using the premises or allowing the premises to be used for an immoral or illegal purpose, or the condition of the dwelling-house has, in the opinion of the court, deteriorated owing to acts of waste by or the neglect or default of the tenant or any such person'.

3.14 The second part of ground 2 is extended by the HA 1996 to include convictions for arrestable offences committed in or in the locality of the dwelling house, moving beyond its original focus upon the use of the house itself and it also includes the activities of visitors. The equivalent ground to ground 2, ground 14 in Sch 2 to the HA 1988 is extended in an identical way by s 148 of the HA 1996.

3.15 Ground 2 of Sch 2 to the 1985 Act and ground 14 of Sch 2 to the 1988 Act are both discretionary grounds, so evictions can only be ordered where it is reasonable to do so. The Court of Appeal has considered the meaning of reasonableness in the context of anti-social behaviour in a number of cases since 1996[1], for instance, in *Newcastle City Council v Morrison*,[2] to evict someone for the behaviour of their visitor or a member of their family even if they are not able to control that behaviour.

Expedited notice for possession

3.16 Section 147 of the HA 1996 amended the notice requirements set out in s 83 of the HA 1985 so that proceedings taken under ground 2 do not require a notice period prior to the issue of possession proceedings. The differentiation between this ground and the others is justified because of the necessity to expedite proceedings where the tenant is behaving in an anti-social manner. No order for possession can be made prior to the date which the landlord has given as the date when he is seeking possession (s 83(3)).

3.17 Section 151 of the HA 1996 amends s 8 of the HA 1988 to achieve the equivalent ability for RSLs to expedite possession proceedings as provided to local authorities under s 147 of HA 1996.

3.18 Section 147 of the HA 1996 also introduces a general discretion into the HA 1985 to dispense with the requirements of the notice of possession where it is just and equitable to do so. The discretion is on the lines of that which already exists in the HA 1988. So in extreme circumstances where housing managers consider that action needs to be taken swiftly it may be possible to dispense with a notice altogether.

Injunction powers

3.19 The landlord has a common law power to obtain an injunction against a tenant who breaches a term of the tenancy agreement. Other common law bases for injunction would include those arising from actions for trespass and nuisance. There is a range of statutory powers available to local authorities which would form the basis for applications for injunctions, in particular s 222 of the Local Government Act 1972.

3.20 Section 152 of the HA 1996 introduced a free-standing injunctive power in order to provide a local authority with a power specifically designed for the purpose of restraining anti-social behaviour in connection with local authority housing

3.21 Section 152 enables local authorities to obtain injunctions prohibiting a person from:

(a) engaging in or threatening to engage in conduct causing or likely to cause a nuisance or annoyance to a person residing in, visiting or otherwise engaging in a lawful activity in residential premises to which this section applies or in the locality of such premises;

(b) using or threatening to use residential premises to which this section applies for immoral or illegal purposes; or

(c) entering residential premises to which this section applies or being found in the locality of any such premises.

---

[1] See for a discussion of reasonableness in possession proceedings arising from anti-social behaviour Caroline Hunter and Kerry Bretherton, *Anti-Social Behaviour Law and Practice in the Management of Social Housing* (Lemos & Crane, 1998).

[2] [2000] 32 HLR 891.

3.22 The injunction is available in respect of secure and introductory tenancies and accommodation provided by the local authority under Part VII of the HA 1996 or Part III of the HA 1985. Tenancies are defined in s 158 of the HA 1996 to include licences.

3.23 Some difficulties have arisen with the use of the word 'locality'. In *Manchester City Council v Lawler*,[1] the Court of Appeal decided that it was a well-recognised phrase. It could be part of the whole of a housing estate, or parts of two housing estates, or include the local shops serving the housing estate but within its boundaries; whether or not the place in which the conduct occurred is within the locality is a question of fact for the judge. Judge LJ said:

> 'In this context "locality" is an ordinary, readily understood English word without specialised or refined meaning. The operation of the section is flexibly linked to a geographical place.'

3.24 However, for the purposes of s 152, there must be a link between the person whom the injunction is intended to protect and the residential premises or the locality of the residential premises referred to within the section. Residential premises for the purposes of s 152 are limited to local authority residential premises.[2] In *Enfield LBC v B (A Minor)*,[3] the application for an injunction was to restrain threats of violence against staff of the authority who worked in a social services office which was in the locality of local authority residential premises. Simply being in the locality was not sufficient; the Court of Appeal upheld the judge's refusal grant an injunction with a power of arrest under s 152, limiting the injunction to a common law injunction with a penal notice attached. As Buxton LJ stated:

> 'In my judgement therefore the judge was quite right in holding that there must be a link or connection between the activity that the persons protected by the injunction are engaging in and the local authority residential premises that give this sections its force and meaning.'

3.25 The Court of Appeal followed this decision in *Nottingham CC v Thames*.[4] Although it recognised the need of local authorities to protect staff and visitors to local authority offices from threats and acts of violence, it considered that s 152 did not provide the means of doing so.

3.26 Subsequently, a Court of Appeal case, *Manchester CC v Lewis Lee and Wigan MBC v G (A Child)*,[5] decided that premises occupied by owner occupiers on an estate where many properties were let by the local authority on secure or introductory tenancies fell outside of the definition of residential premises in s 152 of the Act. The court found that, despite the facts of both cases being sufficiently serious to provide for the threshold of conduct required by s 152, the nexus required by the court in *Enfield LBC v B* was not present where the victim was an owner-occupier.

3.27 The preconditions for the grant of the injunction mean that there is a relatively high threshold of anti-social conduct required before the injunction can be granted. The conditions are set out in s 152(3) as follows:

(a) the respondent has used or threatened to use violence against any person of a description mentioned in subs (1)(a); and

(b) there is a significant risk of harm to that person or a person of a similar description if the injunction is not granted.

3.28 'Harm' is defined in s 158 to mean ill-treatment or the impairment of health, and additionally in relation to a child includes the impairment of development. 'Health' includes physical or mental health and 'ill-treatment', in relation to a child, includes sexual abuse and forms of ill-treatment which are not physical.

---

[1] (1999) 31 HLR 119, CA.

[2] HA 1996, s 152(2).

[3] (1999) 32 HLR 799, CA.

[4] [2002] EWCA Civ 1098, [2002] All ER (D).

[5] [2003] EWCA Civ 1256 (7 August 2003).

3.29   The definition of 'harm' is clearly related to the Children Act 1989 definition, and suggests that the phrase 'significant risk of harm' is actually a drafting error and that what was intended was risk of significant harm, the threshold criteria for a care order under the Children Act 1989. There is considerable case law arising from the meaning of 'risk of significant harm'.

Power of arrest

3.30   A power of arrest is available to the court without any further threshold test of conduct.[1] The automatic availability of the power of arrest on the same level of conduct required to obtain the injunction has made the injunction very attractive to local authorities.

Power of arrest for breach of other injunctions against anti-social behaviour

3.31   The s 152 injunction is only available to local authorities. However s 153 of the HA 1996 provides social landlords – broadly defined – with the additional protection of a power of arrest when a tenant breaches an injunction restraining a breach of the tenancy in circumstances involving violence or threats of violence.

3.32   The court is given a discretion to attach a power of arrest to an injunction which it intends to grant in relation to a breach or anticipated breach of the terms of a tenancy where the applicant landlord is a local housing authority, a housing action trust, a RSL, or a charitable housing trust acting in its capacity as the landlord of the premises which are subject to the tenancy. The respondent – the person to be restrained by the injunction – is the tenant or a joint tenant under the tenancy agreement.

3.33   The breach, or anticipated breach, of the term of the tenancy must relate to the ground for possession for anti-social conduct. So the respondent must be engaging in or threatening to engage in conduct causing or likely to cause a nuisance or annoyance to a person residing, visiting or otherwise engaging in a lawful activity in the locality, using or threatening to use the premises of immoral or illegal purposes, or allowing any subtenant or lodger of his or any other person residing (whether temporarily or otherwise) on the premises or visiting him to act in an anti-social way.

3.34   The power of arrest can only be attached if the court considers that the anti-social conduct involves violence or threatened violence and there is a significant risk of harm to that person or a person of a similar description if the power of arrest is not attached to the injunction.[2]

Without notice applications

3.35   The same rules apply to applications for both s 152 and s 153 injunctions. Section 154 of the HA 1996 requires that the court considers all the circumstances surrounding an application for a power of arrest to be attached to an injunction when the person who is to be the subject of the injunction is not present at the hearing of the application. The section identifies two circumstances in particular that must be considered. These are:

(1)   whether it is likely that the applicant landlord will be deterred or prevented from seeking the exercise of the power if the power is not exercised immediately; and

(2)   whether there is reason to believe that the respondent is aware of the proceedings for the injunction but is deliberately evading service and that the applicant or the victim will be seriously prejudiced if the decision as to whether to exercise the power were delayed until substituted service is effected.

---

[1]   Section 152(6).
[2]   Section 153(6).

Other powers available to local authorities

3.36 Local authorities have other powers available to them which arise from their strategic responsibilities either for housing, or for crime and disorder and community safety, or more generally for the well being of the local authority area.

Selecting tenants

3.37 The Homelessness Act 2002 includes provisions designed to exclude or to reduce the priority of certain anti-social people within a local authority scheme of allocation of social housing. The Act amended the HA 1996 to give local authorities a discretionary power to exclude certain applicants on the grounds of behaviour.

3.38 A local housing authority can decide that an applicant is ineligible for allocation of accommodation if it is satisfied that:

(a) he, or a member of his household, has been guilty of unacceptable behaviour serious enough to make him unsuitable to be a tenant of the authority; and

(b) in the circumstances at the time his application is considered, he is unsuitable to be a tenant of the authority by reason of that behaviour.[1]

3.39 The 'only' behaviour which is unacceptable behaviour for the purposes of deciding ineligibility for housing is behaviour of a tenant or a member of his household which would entitle the authority to a possession order under the HA 1985 on any ground[2] (other than the ground which relates to failure to return to the original tenancy after completion of works).[3]

3.40 The Homelessness Act 2002 also amended the HA 1996 to provide that local authorities are entitled to take into account specific factors when determining the relative priority of applicants for the allocation of accommodation. These factors include any behaviour of a person or of a member of that person's household which affects his or her suitability to be a tenant.[4]

3.41 Local authorities have therefore been provided with the means to exclude potentially anti-social tenants from social housing. In the longer term, this may provide a very powerful weapon to control conduct in those areas where there is high demand for social housing.

Community safety

3.42 Local authorities have a role as community police over and above their role as social landlord. Local Government Act 1972, s 222 provides extensive powers to a local authority to prosecute or defend or appear in legal proceedings and initiate civil proceedings when it considers it expedient for the promotion or protection of the interests of the inhabitants of its area. The use of this power was recently considered by the Court of Appeal in the context of anti-social behaviour related to social housing provision in *Nottingham CC v Z*.[5] Nottingham City Council was seeking an injunction to restrain a drug dealer from entering a housing estate. The Court of Appeal held that the authority was entitled to institute proceedings under s 222 where activities interfered with the interests of local inhabitants, even where such activities were of a criminal nature. For further discussion of s 222 and the amendments to it contained in the Anti-social Behaviour Act 2003 enabling a power of arrest to be attached, see commentary on Part 9 of the Act.[6]

---

[1] HA 1996, s 160A(7).
[2] Ibid, s 160A(8).
[3] HA 1985, Sch 2, Ground 8.
[4] HA 1996, s 167(2A).
[5] [2001] EWCA Civ 1248, [2002] 1 WLR 607.
[6] At **10.96–10.109**.

3.43 The Crime and Disorder Act 1998 provided a further legislative emphasis to the community policing role of local authorities. In addition to anti-social behaviour orders (ASBOs) and other orders which target individual behaviour, local authorities have general statutory duties imposed upon them to reduce crime and disorder in their areas. Section 6 (the requirement to formulate and implement a crime reduction strategy) and s 17 of the Crime and Disorder Act 1998 (the duty to consider the crime and disorder implications of its decisions) combine to embed the prevention of crime and disorder into the strategic role of local authorities.

Anti-social behaviour orders

3.44 We consider ASBOs in Chapter 10.[1] They provide a tool to combat anti-social behaviour which complements and, to an extent, overlaps with the provisions of s 152 and s 153 of the HA 1996. The Anti-social Behaviour Act 2003 amends s 1 of the Crime and Disorder Act 1998 to add housing action trusts to the range of social landlords able to apply for ASBOs to provide protection from anti-social behaviour for people who reside in or who are in the vicinity of premises provided or managed by the social landlord.

Continued government attention

3.45 Anti-social behaviour within housing has continued to attract government attention since the implementation of the HA 1996. Following the election of the Labour Government in 1997, the Crime and Disorder Act 1998 was passed and the Social Exclusion Unit published Policy Action Team reports on anti-social behaviour and on unpopular housing,[2] both of which indicated that anti-social behaviour continued to be a serious problem with ramifications for social exclusion.

3.46 Constituency MPs and pressure groups such as the Social Landlords Crime and Nuisance Group continued to press for more powers to respond to anti-social behaviour. Problems emerged with the implementation of ASBOs which were partially tackled within the Police Reform Act 2000.

3.47 *Tackling Anti-social Tenants* was published by the Department for Transport, Local Government and the Regions (DTLR) in April 2002. It suggested that the problem of anti-social behaviour was threefold:

(a) a minority, through their offending behaviour, are creating a disproportionate and damaging impact on many neighbourhoods, particularly in deprived areas;

(b) whilst some landlords are using the current framework of legislation effectively to stop this behaviour, many are not; and

(c) some aspects of current legislation do not assist those landlords who are trying to stop this behaviour.

3.48 The consultation period for the proposals to improve the legal framework was from 2 April to 12 July 2002.

3.49 At the same time, the Law Commission published its proposals for the reform of tenure.[3] The report included suggestions for the reform of the legal tools necessary to enable social landlords to tackle anti-social behaviour, some of which were included in the DTLR consultation.

---

[1] At **10.04–10.37**.

[2] PAT 7 *Unpopular housing* and PAT 8 *Anti-social behaviour* (DETR, 2000).

[3] *Renting Homes 1: Status and Security* Consultation Paper 162 (The Law Commission, April 2002).

3.50 The Home Office published its White Paper, *Respect and Responsibility – Taking a Stand against Anti-Social Behaviour* on 12 March 2003, very shortly followed by the first reading of the Anti-social Behaviour Bill on 27 March 2003.

Targeting social tenants?

3.51 A major criticism of the HA 1996 provisions is that they concentrate on controlling the behaviour of social tenants, suggesting that anti-social behaviour is a problem of tenure. *Tackling Anti-social Tenants* makes it clear that:

'It is a problem which crosses all types of tenure. Households in the social and private rented sector and owner occupiers are all vulnerable to thoughtless offensive and sometimes criminal behaviour by other residents or visitors to their neighbourhood.'[1]

3.52 Nonetheless, the Local Government Association commented, in its response to the consultation paper:

'The Association is concerned that the emphasis of this paper is on social landlords and social tenants. There are two specific issues of concern here; The implication being that social tenants are a problem whilst private tenant, or owner occupiers are not; and that social landlords are the only ones who have to take action or do not take action. Social tenants already suffer an amount of stigmatising and the emphasis of this paper does nothing to get away from this. There are as many if not more problems in the private sector and to ignore this in this paper is a lost opportunity. Local authorities often have to use private sector landlords to house people and again there is no recognition of this in the paper.'[2]

3.53 The provisions of the Anti-Social Behaviour Act 2003 are susceptible to the same criticism. The Government's response has been that the scheme provided for in the Draft Housing Bill[3] for the selective licensing of private landlords in low demand areas is designed to target anti-social behaviour in the private rented sector.

3.54 The Housing Bill,[4] published on 8 December 2003, contains the selective licensing scheme. It also contains further responses to the anti-social behaviour of social tenants. It provides for introductory tenancies to be extended by 6 months in cases of anti-social behaviour and for the suspension of the right of mutual exchange and the landlord's obligation to complete a transaction under the Right to Buy where a relevant court order relating to anti-social behaviour has been applied for or obtained.

Provisions in detail

3.55 The Anti-social Behaviour Act 2003 further enhances the powers and responsibilities of social landlords in connection with anti-social behaviour. The focus moves beyond controlling the anti-social behaviour of social tenants and their visitors, to one which focuses on anti-social behaviour which impacts upon housing management. Many of the provisions of the Act are amendments to existing provisions.

3.56 The Act continues the strategic approaches of the HA 1996 of reducing security of tenure for anti-social tenants and streamlining procedures for obtaining injunctions. It also makes social landlords more accountable for their response to anti-social behaviour.

---

[1] Department for Transport, Local Government and the Regions, 2002.
[2] Local Government Association, *Response to Tackling Anti-social Tenants* (July 2002).
[3] *The Draft Housing Bill* (Office of the Deputy Prime Minister, March 2003), Cm 5793.
[4] The Housing Bill 11 53/3.

Policies and procedures

Section 12 – Anti-social behaviour: landlords' policies and procedures

3.57 This section imposes a new statutory duty upon social landlords to prepare, keep under review and publish anti-social behaviour policies. The statutory duty to publish anti-social behaviour procedures was proposed in *Tackling Anti-social Tenants*[1] as an alternative to imposing a specific statutory duty to tackle anti-social behaviour. The Government suggests that the particular problem with the more specific duty is enforcement and that 'the particular concern would be to avoid the kind of canvassing for legal work which has happened in disrepair claims'.[2]

3.58 However, it also suggests that the lack of a specific duty may be part of the reason for the wide variety of performance of landlords in tackling anti-social behaviour. The expectation is that publishing policies and procedures on anti-social behaviour 'would open the landlord to scrutiny with regard to the adequacy of the procedures and also as to whether they had followed their own procedure in any particular case. Whilst this would not have the specific force of a duty it would increase the landlord's accountability in this area of housing management'. [3]

3.59 The section operates by inserting a new s 218A into the HA 1996. The duty is imposed upon social landlords, defined as local housing authorities, housing action trusts and RSLs, which must prepare:

(a) a policy in relation to anti-social behaviour; and
(b) procedures for dealing with occurrences of anti-social behaviour.

3.60 Local authorities are familiar with statutory duties to publish policies and procedures. Section 168 of the HA 1996 imposes a duty on local housing authorities to publish summaries of their allocation schemes. Section 1 of the Homelessness Act 2002 imposes a duty on local housing authorities to carry out homelessness reviews for their district; and to formulate and publish homelessness strategies based on the results of that review.

3.61 The Housing Corporation is empowered to issue guidance with respect to the management of housing accommodation by RSLs under s 36 of the HA 1996. Section 12(2) of the Anti-social Behaviour Act 2003 amends s 36(2) of the HA 1996 to enable the Housing Corporation with the power to issue guidance under s 218A of the HA 1996.

3.62 The scope of anti-social behaviour policies is determined by the definition of anti-social conduct set out in s 153A and s 153B of the HA 1996. These sections are inserted into the HA 1996 by s 13 of this Act and are fully discussed below. Anti-social conduct is defined in s 153A as 'conduct which is capable of causing nuisance or annoyance to any person and which directly or indirectly relates to or affects the housing management functions of a relevant landlord' and in s 153B as conduct 'which consists of or involves using or threatening to use housing accommodation owned or managed by a relevant landlord for an unlawful purpose'. This indicates that anti-social behaviour policies have the potential to be extremely broad.

3.63 Bob Ainsworth, Parliamentary Under-Secretary at the Home Office, emphasised the role of the duty in increasing the accountability of social landlords in his evidence to the Home Affairs Committee on 25 March 2003:[4]

'It is about trying to make local authorities and social landlords accountable to the wider community. Publish what you are supposed to be doing, so that we can see what you are doing alongside what you are supposed to be doing. That is the motive behind obliging them to publish their policies.'

---

[1] Department for Transport, Local Government and the Regions, 2002.
[2] *Tackling Anti-social Tenants* (Department for Transport, Local Government and the Regions, 2002).
[3] Ibid.
[4] Department for Transport, Local Government and the Regions, 2002

3.64 Publication of policies and procedures is therefore going to feed into performance measurement by central government as well as increasing the capacity of victims to press their case for social landlords to take action. Publication also informs potential perpetrators of the action they may face and serves the additional purpose of enabling the sharing of good practice between social landlords.

3.65 The duty complements and overlaps with the duties on local authorities within s 6 and s 17 of the Crime and Disorder Act 1998. It reinforces RSLs' partnership role in reducing crime and disorder.

3.66 Social landlords will have 6 months from the commencement of s 12 of the Act to publish a statement of their policies and procedures. Social landlords must keep the policy and procedures under review and publish revised statements when they consider it appropriate to do so.

3.67 A model policy statement on anti-social behaviour for social landlords is annexed to *Tackling Anti-social Tenants*.[1] This model statement includes a general statement of commitment to tackling anti-social behaviour, procedures for initial responses to complaints, the provision of support and information to complainants and a commitment to take legal action when appropriate. It also makes reference to other policy statements such as procedures on racial harassment and the allocation of housing.

3.68 Guidance on the contents of the policies and procedures will be issued to local housing authorities and housing action trusts by the Secretary of State, to RSLs in England by the Housing Corporation and to RSLs in Wales by the National Assembly for Wales.

3.69 Lord Bassam of Brighton indicated that it was the Government's intention that the section would not be commenced until statutory guidance had been issued. Therefore social landlords will have 6 months from the issue of guidance to produce their policy and procedures.[2]

3.70 There was considerable discussion in Committee in the Lords about the contents of policies and procedures.[3] The Government indicated that matters such as the necessity for social landlords to record complaints and to monitor action taken would be dealt with in the guidance which would be produced following extensive consultation. Part of the function of the guidance would be to enable the development of best practice:

> 'We want to foster and to encourage more positive and proactive work because we see that as being a very important part, ..., of a holistic strategy.'[4]

3.71 The Government was also pressed to ensure that social landlords are made aware of their responsibilities in relation to the Disability Discrimination Act 1995 following concerns expressed by organisations such as Mind and the National Autistic Society.[5]

3.72 Baroness Scotland of Asthal responded on behalf of the Government:

---

[1] Ibid.

[2] *Hansard*, HL Deb, 11 September 2003, col 484.

[3] Ibid, cols 479–489.

[4] Ibid, col 485.

[5] Landlords need to be aware of the limitations that the Disability Discrimination Act 1995 imposes on possession proceedings when the tenant is disabled. In *North Devon Homes Ltd v Brazier* (2003) 6 CCLR 245 the landlord sought a possession order on the basis of her persistent anti-social behaviour including banging, shouting, using foul language and generally causing a nuisance and annoyance to her neighbours. It was accepted that the tenant was a disabled person within the meaning of the Disability Discrimination Act 1995, her disability arising from a mental impairment which had a substantial and long term effect on her ability to carry out normal day-to-day activity. On appeal, the court decided that the anti-social behaviour was caused by the tenant's disability. The court went on to consider whether eviction was necessary in order not to endanger the health or safety of any person which would include the disabled person herself or her neighbours. On the evidence presented to the court, there was no evidence that the eviction was necessary and in the circumstances the court decided that it was not reasonable to make a possession order under the HA 1988.

'The government are keen to ensure that the correct balance is maintained between ensuring that effective remedies against anti-social behaviour are available to protect all members of the community and that people with disabilities are not unfairly discriminated against.'

She indicated that the Government would address the issues in the guidance on policies and procedures. She expressed her hope:

'that that will make it crystal clear to social landlords that the provisions of section 22 – in particular, of section 22(3)(c), which as the noble Lord will know, expressly relates to evicting the disabled person or subjecting him to any other detriment – of the DDA 1995 which makes it unlawful for them to discriminate against a disabled person, will apply.'

3.73 The statement of the policy must be available for inspection at the social landlord's principal office and a copy provided on request for which a reasonable fee may be charged. Social landlords are also under a duty to prepare a summary of their current policy and procedures which must be provided free of charge to anyone who requests it. This is a parallel provision to s 3(9) of the Homelessness Act 2002. It is perhaps surprising that, given the importance attached to reducing the fear of crime amongst social tenants, that social landlords are not required to distribute summaries of the policy to their tenants.

Anti-social behaviour injunctions

Section 13 – Injunctions against anti-social behaviour on application of certain social landlords

3.74 Section 13 of the Anti-social Behaviour Act 2003 provides for three different types of injunction to respond to the problem of anti-social behaviour by tenants. The available injunctions are:

–   the anti-social behaviour injunction;[1]
–   the injunction against unlawful use of premises;[2]
–   the injunction against breach of tenancy agreement.[3]

3.75 The section repeals s 152 and s 153 of the HA 1996 and replaces them with ss 153A–153D. The combined effect of the new sections is that social landlords will be able to obtain injunctions against a very wide range of perpetrators of anti-social behaviour to protect a very wide range of victims.

The anti-social behaviour injunction

3.76 The anti-social behaviour injunction is based upon the injunction originally developed in s 152 of the HA 1996 but it is enhanced in a number of ways.

–   It extends the range of the conduct to which the powers apply. It utilises a two-tier test of conduct. A relatively low level of anti-social conduct referable to the housing management functions of a relevant landlord triggers the basic injunction. Additional protections of powers of arrest and exclusion orders are available where the conduct is violent or harmful.
–   It extends the range of landlords who may apply for the injunction. The original drafting of the HA 1996 limited the injunction against anti-social behaviour to local authorities. The Anti-social Behaviour Act 2003, defines relevant landlords for the purposes of the anti-social

---

[1]   Section 153A.
[2]   Section 153B.
[3]   Section 153D.

behaviour injunction as housing action trusts, local authorities and RSLs.[1] This provides an explicit recognition of the role of all social landlords in providing for community safety.

– It extends the range of victims who can be protected by the injunction.

– This provides a response to the unanticipated limitations on the scope of the protection provided by the original anti-social behaviour injunction.

3.77 The injunction no longer specifically provides for using or threatening to use the landlord's residential premises for immoral or illegal purposes or entering the landlord's residential premises or being found in the locality of such premises. These forms of anti-social conduct are now provided for in a new separate injunction set out in s 153B of the HA 1996, a new injunction against unlawful use of premises discussed below.

3.78 There are two preconditions which must be met before a court may grant an anti-social behaviour injunction. The first condition is that the person against whom the injunction is sought is engaging, has engaged or threatens to engage in anti-social conduct[2]

3.79 The threshold level of conduct set out in this condition is low. Conduct is anti-social if it is 'capable of causing nuisance or annoyance to any person'.[3] Therefore, there is no necessity for the behaviour to be intentional. The use of the word 'capable' is a significant departure from the phrase 'causing or likely to cause', used in the original injunction. It will require considerably less evidence to demonstrate and cover a wider range of behaviour. As the Minister explained in the Lords:

'New Section 153A deliberately widens the definition of anti-social conduct to include behaviour which is "capable" of causing nuisance and annoyance. That will enable social landlords to be more proactive in their management of anti-social behaviour and will avoid legal arguments about the exact severity or likelihood of anti-social behaviour causing nuisance and annoyance.'[4]

3.80 The low threshold is designed to enable early intervention by landlords to 'nip problems in the bud' and prevent escalation. The Minister explained in the Lords that the protection for the individual would be provided by the courts:

'it is for the court to determine whether the behaviour could cause nuisance or annoyance to a reasonable – not necessarily an ultra-sensitive – person and whether an injunction is both proportionate and necessary.'[5]

3.81 Either nuisance or annoyance is required, and not both. Nuisance or annoyance are given wide interpretation by the courts. As the Minister explained in the Lords:

'annoyance is assumed to mean something less than nuisance and to have a wider meaning than nuisance. Annoyance has been described as something that reasonably troubles the mind and pleasure, not of a fanciful person, but of the ordinary sensible person, although it may not appear to amount to a physical detriment to comfort.'[6]

3.82 Not all anti-social conduct enables a social landlord to obtain an anti-social behaviour injunction. There must be a connection between the conduct and the housing management functions of the social landlord. However, housing management functions are defined very broadly and the connection with the housing management functions may be direct or indirect.

3.83 Housing management functions[7] include, first, the functions conferred by or under any enactment and, secondly, the powers and duties of the landlord as the holder of an estate or interest

---

[1] Section 153E(7).
[2] Section 153A(3).
[3] Section 153A(1)(a).
[4] *Hansard*, HL Deb, 11 September 2003, col 497.
[5] Ibid.
[6] Ibid, col 498.
[7] Section 153E(11).

in housing accommodation. The definition, which is not exhaustive, embraces statutory roles and those arising from the contractual and property interests of a landlord.

3.84 The second condition is that the anti-social conduct is capable of causing nuisance or annoyance to:

(a) a person with a right to reside in or occupy housing accommodation owned or managed by the relevant landlord;

(b) a person with a right to reside in or occupy other housing accommodation in the locality of the housing accommodation owned or managed by the relevant landlord;

(c) a person engaged in lawful activity in or in the locality of the housing accommodation;

(d) a person employed by the relevant landlord wholly or partly in connection with his housing management functions.

3.85 This covers neighbours, whether tenants of the same landlord, tenants of another landlord, or owner-occupiers; it covers all other tenants of the same landlord; it covers those who visit, carry out businesses or other activities in the locality; and it covers the landlord's employees. The potential range of victims has been drafted to ensure that a number of victims of anti-social behaviour whom the courts considered to fall outside of the scope of the anti-social behaviour injunction provided for in the original wording of s 152 are now quite clearly included. So employees, owner-occupiers, and people who are temporarily absent from their homes may be protected by the injunction. As the Minister explained in the Lords:

> 'if someone has been forced out of their home by racial or sexual harassment an injunction under new section 153A should be available to protect them if they wish to return.'[1]

3.86 It is immaterial, for the purposes of the injunction, where the anti-social conduct takes place. The protection against, say, a landlord obtaining an anti-social behaviour injunction against someone who behaved anti-socially towards someone in the workplace, who also happened to live in a property rented from the same social landlord as them, is that their conduct must directly or indirectly relate to housing management functions. It means that the injunction will be available to restrain anti-social conduct in the landlord's offices even if these are some distance from the landlord's housing accommodation.

3.87 The first example of the anticipated operation of this provided by the Minister in the Lords concerned a housing officer who has refused a tenant a transfer, who could be protected if the aggrieved tenant later sees him in a supermarket some miles away and attacks him. The second concerned a tenant who, following a neighbour dispute, assaults another tenant outside her child's school. The Minister suggested that:

> 'the victim should not be refused the protection of an injunction with a power of arrest simply because the violent conduct took place away from her home. The dispute clearly related to the landlord's housing management function.'[2]

3.88 Locality retains some relevance. It restricts the range of victims with a more tenuous link with the landlord. So the protection is only available to people running businesses or people who do not live in accommodation provided by the landlord but are, for example, owner-occupiers and who must live in the locality of the landlord's housing accommodation. However, locality no longer restricts the protection available to tenants of the same landlord or employees. The meaning of locality is to be determined by judges on a case-by-case basis.

3.89 A court will be able to attach an exclusion order and/or a power of arrest to the anti-social behaviour injunction, where the anti-social conduct involves violence, threats of violence or a

---

1   *Hansard*, HL Deb, 11 September 2003, col 503.

2   Ibid, col 504.

significant risk of harm.[1] So, whilst the threshold level of conduct for the basic injunction has been seriously lowered by the amendment, the level of conduct which attracts a power of arrest remains the same.

3.90 The key similarities and differences between this injunctive power and HA 1996, s 152 are set out in Table 3.2:

Table 3.2		
The similarities and differences between s 152 and s 153A of the HA 1996		
Feature	*HA 1996, s 152*	*Anti-social Behaviour Act 2003, s 13 – a new s 153A*
Applicant	Local authority	A relevant landlord – a local authority, a housing action trust, a RSL
Subject of injunction	Anyone whose conduct is anti-social or is likely to be anti-social	Anyone whose conduct is anti-social or capable of being anti-social
Definition of anti-social conduct	Causing or likely to cause a nuisance or annoyance or Using or threatening to use premises for immoral or illegal purposes or Entering residential premises or being found in the locality of residential premises Plus violence or threat of violence and a significant risk of harm to relevant persons	Capable of causing nuisance or annoyance (nothing else necessary for injunction)
Connection with applicant	There must be a link or connection between the activity that the persons protected by the injunction are engaging in and the local authority residential premises	Conduct must directly or indirectly relate to housing management functions
Victims	Persons residing in, visiting or otherwise engaging in a lawful activity in or in the locality of the relevant housing	Persons with a right (of whatever description) to reside in or occupy housing accommodation owned or managed by the relevant landlord a person with a right (of whatever description) to reside in or occupy other housing accommodation in the locality of the housing accommodation mentioned in paragraph

---

[1] Section 153C(1).

Table 3.2

The similarities and differences between s 152 and s 153A of the HA 1996

Feature	HA 1996, s 152	Anti-social Behaviour Act 2003, s 13 – a new s 153A
		engaged in lawful activity in or in the locality of the relevant housing
		employed wholly or partly in connection with the relevant landlord's housing management functions
Locality	Relevant attribute of conduct	Immaterial where conduct occurs
		Material to restrict potential category of victims
Power of arrest	May be attached	Power of arrest if either
		(a) the conduct consists of or includes the use or threatened use of violence or
		(b) there is a significant risk of harm to a person described above
Exclusion order	Not specifically provided for	Exclusion from any premises or any area may be included within the injunction if
		(a) the conduct consists of or includes the use or threatened use of violence or
		(b) there is a significant risk of harm to a person described above
		Specific provision made to exclude a person from his normal place of residence.
Relevant housing	Secure, introductory tenancies or accommodation provided under local authority homelessness duties	Housing accommodation owned or managed by the relevant landlord
		Also protects housing accommodation in the neighbourhood of housing accommodation owned or managed by the relevant landlord

The injunction against the unlawful use of premises

3.91 The original anti-social behaviour injunction under HA 1996, s 152 included a power for a court to grant a local authority an injunction prohibiting someone from using or threatening to use residential premises for immoral or illegal purposes. The injunction could only be granted if the immoral or illegal use involved violence or threats of violence and a significant risk of harm to relevant persons.[1]

3.92 The Anti-social Behaviour Act 2003 separately provides for an injunction against unlawful use of premises.[2] The injunction is available to housing action trusts, local authorities and RSLs.[3]

---

[1]   HA 1996, s 152(1)(b) and (3).

[2]   Ibid, s 153B.

[3]   HA 1996, s 153E(7).

There is no requirement for the unlawful use to involve violence, threats of violence or significant risk of harm. There is no requirement for a victim.

3.93 The conduct which is being restrained is the unlawful use or threatened use of housing accommodation owned or managed by the landlord. This unlawful use of the social landlord's housing accommodation is implicitly defined as anti-social in itself.

3.94 The Bill, as originally drafted, additionally provided for the injunction to restrain immoral use of premises. However, it was amended by the Government to remove the 'immoral' basis for the injunction. It was explained:

> 'We do not think that it is appropriate that injunctions or demotion orders intended to prevent anti-social behaviour should be used to control the use of premises where no illegal activity is taking place and no nuisance is being caused.'[1]

3.95 This responds to concerns of the Joint Committee on Human Rights about the lack of objectivity and predictability in the interpretation of the phrase 'immoral behaviour'. The Committee acknowledged that, in the housing context, it has traditionally been interpreted restrictively to mean using premises for drug-dealing, prostitution and similar activities.[2]

3.96 The amendment has the effect of removing prostitution which is neither criminal nor causing nuisance nor annoyance from the ambit of the injunction. However, prostitution which is in breach of a tenancy agreement may be subject to an injunction (see below).

3.97 The ambit of 'unlawful' purpose is very wide. It embraces both civil and criminal offences. It includes trespass which was separately provided for within the original s 152.

3.98 The injunction does not require the perpetrator to have been convicted of any offence. This is in contrast to the equivalent ground of eviction set out in Sch 2 to the HA 1985 (for secure tenancies) and ground 2 and ground 14 of Sch 2 to the HA 1988 (for assured tenancies), which require conviction for using the dwelling house or allowing it to be used for immoral or illegal purposes or conviction for an arrestable offence committed in or in the locality of, the dwelling house.

3.99 Powers of arrest and exclusion orders are available where the unlawful use of the premises involves violence, threats of violence or a significant risk of harm to the range of victims provided for in the anti-social behaviour injunction.[3]

Injunction against breach of tenancy agreement

3.100 The third type of injunction available to social landlords to restrain anti-social conduct is one where the tenant or someone else that the tenant is 'allowing, inciting or encouraging' is behaving in such a way as to cause nuisance or annoyance to anyone in breach or anticipated breach of his tenancy agreement.[4] The injunction is therefore available prior to breach of the tenancy agreement in order to restrain a potential breach.

3.101 The definition of social landlords for the purpose of this injunction includes charitable housing trusts. 'Tenancy' agreement is defined to include any agreement for the occupation of residential accommodation owned or managed by a relevant landlord. Therefore licences, however informal, will be included.[5]

---

[1] *Hansard*, HC Deb, 24 June 2003, col 916.
[2] Joint Committee on Human Rights 13th Report, para 16.
[3] HA 1996, s 153C(1).
[4] Ibid, s 153D.
[5] Ibid, s 153D(5).

3.102 The conduct threshold level is the same as for the anti-social behaviour injunction (ie conduct that is capable of causing nuisance or annoyance). Therefore, an injunction can be obtained prior to breach on the basis of conduct which is capable of causing a breach.

3.103 The victim of the conduct could be any person. There is no need to restrain the scope of the injunction, since it is constrained by being dependent upon the behaviour of the tenant and by the contents of the tenancy agreement. However, the terms of the tenancy agreement must conform to the requirements of the Unfair Terms in Consumer Contracts Regulations 1999.[1]

3.104 Powers of arrest and exclusion orders are available where conduct which breaches or anticipates a breach of the tenancy agreement involves violence, threats of violence or a significant risk of harm to the range of victims provided for in the anti-social behaviour injunction.

Demotion of tenancies

Background

3.105 'Demotion' is a term coined for the idea of imposing a reduction in a tenant's security of tenure. As a response to anti-social behaviour, a local housing authority, housing action trust or RSL can now apply to court for a demotion order, which converts secure or assured tenants to one of two lesser forms of security for a year. This allows the landlord to take eviction proceedings without proof of reasons if they feel the need to do so during that period. If no possession action is taken during the demotion period, for example because the tenant's behaviour improves, then the tenancy is automatically promoted up to secure or assured status.

3.106 The idea is similar to introductory tenancies, created by the HA 1996. Under those, the landlord can insist that before someone becomes a secure tenant, they go through a probationary year of being subject to eviction for any reason without having to prove grounds in court.[2] However, they were only made available to local authorities and housing action trusts, rather than RSLs.

3.107 Demotion makes the principles behind introductory tenancies available at any point in the life of a tenancy rather than just in the first year. As well as making subsequent eviction easier, the demotion itself is meant to be a sanction for anti-social behaviour. It is less severe than eviction, offering a last chance to improve, but it includes removal of the right to buy and related rights. The prospect of promotion is also meant to offer an incentive for improvement in behaviour. The demotion period can be an opportunity for support services to be tried out, though there is no requirement that these should be available.

3.108 In April 2000, the Housing Green Paper *Quality and Choice: A Decent Home for All*[3] suggested considering new forms of tenure which could include 'introductory assured shorthold tenancies'. Meanwhile in Scotland, Housing (Scotland) Act 2001, s 35 created a power for landlords to demote by serving notice to convert a 'Scottish secure tenancy' into a 'short Scottish secure tenancy' where the tenant, or someone else living at the property, has been made subject to an anti-social behaviour order.

3.109 In 2002, the Law Commission developed this model[4] to suggest court orders for demotion

---

1   SI 1999/2083.

2   Following *McLellan v Bracknell Forest* [2001] EWCA Civ 1510, [2002] 1 All ER 899, it appears that introductory tenancies have survived the Human Rights Act 1998. However, they survived only on the basis that an introductory tenant can remove the element of speed and simplicity by insisting on adjourning the county court eviction procedure pending a judicial review application, as set out in *Manchester City Council v Cochrane* [1999] 1 WLR 809.

3   Office of the Deputy Prime Minister, April 2000.

4   *Renting Homes 1: Status and Security* (Consultation Paper 162, Law Commission, April 2002).

from their 'type I' to 'type II' agreements, based on breach of a housing-related anti-social behaviour order or of a housing injunction.

3.110 In 2003, the Law Commission's Report[1] retained the idea of demotion but suggested that it should be via a court order 'in the context of proceedings for breach of the [Law Commission's new] special anti-social behaviour term'. Demotion would only be available 'where the court is satisfied that otherwise it would have been reasonable to terminate the agreement', but the landlord is willing instead to produce a plan to provide appropriate support for the occupier to improve their behaviour during the year of demotion. The Law Commission's proposals are based on reducing the number of types of status to two, so they would produce only one mechanism to demote from the higher to the lower level, with only one status as the result of demotion. The 2003 Act borrows much from the Law Commission, but is built on the current plethora of types of status. It therefore adds a new status of 'demoted tenancy', and its mechanism for demotion depends on whether the tenancy is secure or assured, while the resulting status depends instead on whether the landlord is a local authority (or housing action trust) or a RSL.

3.111 Many of the complexities and problems described below may therefore be resolved in the not too distant future, if the Government takes up the Law Commission's final proposals for tenancy reform. On the other hand, the Government appears unwilling to take up the Law Commission's suggestion of tying demotion to provision of support.

Naming the two new types of demoted tenancy

3.112 Following demotion a new tenancy can be created, of which there are two types, as follows:

– a secure or assured tenancy from a RSL is replaced by a new sub-species of assured tenancy, the 'demoted assured shorthold tenancy';
– a secure tenancy from a local housing authority or housing action trust is replaced by a new species, referred to only as a 'demoted tenancy'.

3.113 This may lead to confusion because the Act uses 'demoted tenancy' as the collective name for the two types, but also singly for the type of demoted tenancy which is not assured, without providing a distinguishing name.[2] 'Demoted assured shorthold tenancies' need to be distinguished from those 'demoted tenancies' which are not assured. This book therefore offers the admittedly inelegant expression 'non-assured demoted tenancy' for the distinct new tenancy type resulting from demotion of a secure tenant of a local authority or housing action trust.[3] We reserve 'demoted tenancy' for use as the collective name covering both 'non-assured demoted tenancies' and 'demoted assured shortholds'.

---

[1] *Renting Homes* (Law Com 284, November 2003).

[2] See the collective use in s 14(2) of the 2003 Act inserting new HA 1985, s 82A(8) and the particular use for former secure tenancies with local authorities and housing action trusts in HA 1996, Part 5, Chapter 1A inserted by Sch 1 to the 2003 Act. Compare the practitioners' expression 'fully assured', to distinguish non-shortholds from shortholds when using the collective name of 'assured tenancies'.

[3] An accurate but memorable name will have to be found in practice. 'Formerly secure and now not assured demoted tenancy' is accurate and fully descriptive but does not trip off the tongue. During the Bill's passage through Parliament they were occasionally referred to as 'local authority demoted tenancies' (perhaps 'demoted council tenancies' would be shorter), and possibly this will catch on, given there are so few housing action trusts that their omission may not hurt. 'Demoted secure' would be potentially misleading, as secure tenancies with registered social landlords are replaced by demoted assured shortholds instead. Another temptation will no doubt be to call them 'Sch 1 tenancies' (from the 2003 Act numbering), but really they are 'Part 5, Chapter 1A tenancies' (from the 1996 Act amended numbering). Possibly practitioners will settle on 's 143A tenancies' from the defining section in the 1996 Act. The sooner a common parlance is established the less scope there will be for confusing the various permutations, but if the Law Commission's recommendations have been adopted by then that would remove the distinctions anyway.

3.114 Although there is a great deal of complexity in the differences between the various routes to and results of demotion, there is much in the Act which is repetitive as it is common between the different provisions. It is therefore easiest to consider first the points in common on each topic before going on to look at the differences.

Landlords

3.115 Demotion orders are available to local housing authorities, housing action trusts and RSLs. This list is the same as those who must publish anti-social behaviour policies and procedures under the new HA 1996, s 218A(1). A local housing authority or a housing action trust can apply to court for a demotion order against their secure tenants, while a RSL can apply for a demotion order against its secure or assured tenants.[1]

3.116 RSLs still have some secure tenants where the tenancy agreement for that property was entered into before HA 1988, Part I came into force on 15 January 1989. This covers around 195,000 properties, most of whose tenants still have the right to buy as well as other rights of secure tenants under the HA 1985.

3.117 Other landlords of secure tenants will not be able to use demotion.[2] Other residential landlords who do not have secure tenants are generally free, if they wish to achieve a similar result, to grant in the first place an assured shorthold tenancy or something of less security.

Notice

3.118 The landlord must serve notice before applying for the order.[3] The notice will be prescribed, but follows the existing model of notices seeking possession for secure and fully assured tenancies. However, the minimum length of notice is 2 weeks for an assured tenancy[4] and 4 weeks for a secure tenancy.[5] This contrasts with notice seeking possession on the nuisance grounds where notice can be given to take effect immediately.[6]

3.119 It is at this point that problems arise because the Act does not state whether demotion and possession can be sought as alternatives in one notice and set of proceedings. Nor, otherwise, does it set out at what stage a landlord must decide whether to go for demotion or possession (whether suspended or absolute).[7] The answer will initially depend on whether the Secretary of State prescribes forms which allow for a single notice to be used for both. Otherwise, it will be for the courts to decide whether both notices can be served without one cancelling out the other. Any attempt to combine the notices would have to take account of the different minimum lengths. If subsequent proceedings are issued it will be a question of whether the Civil Procedure Rules 1998 will allow for both applications to be made in one set of proceedings. The spirit of the Woolf reforms is generally against pleading alternative facts, but is more tolerant of claims for alternative

---

[1]   See s 14(2), inserting new HA 1985, s 82A(1), and s 14(4), inserting new HA 1988, s 6A(1).

[2]   See the 'landlord condition' in HA 1985, s 80, and the other types of landlords who still have secure tenants from before other amendments to that section. These landlords of secure tenants are also unable to use introductory tenancies, as HA 1996, s 124 similarly limits their use to local authorities and housing action trusts. Nor does a tenancy retain its demoted status if the landlord's interest is transferred to one of these landlords from a local housing authority or housing action trust – see new HA 1996, s 143C(2)(b) and (4) inserted by Sch 1, para 1 to the 2003 Act.

[3]   See s 14(3), inserting new HA 1985, s 83(4A), and s 14(4), inserting new HA 1988, s 6A(5)–(6).

[4]   Under HA 1988, s 6A(7), inserted by s 14(4) of the 2003 Act.

[5]   See HA 1985, s 83(4A), inserted by s 14(3)(c) of the 2003 Act, and HA 1985, s 83(5), amended by s 14(3)(d) of the 2003 Act.

[6]   See HA 1985, s 83(3)(a)(i) and HA 1988, s 8(4). However, under HA 1985, s 83(3)(a)(ii) and (5) the possession date sought by the landlord of a secure tenant must be at least 4 weeks later than the notice.

[7]   The landlord can issue notice and subsequent court proceedings for possession without having to decide whether to ask for a suspended possession order or an absolute one.

remedies based on the same set of facts. The factual basis for demotion can be the same as for possession, but does not have to be.[1]

3.120 Service of a notice also has the effect that the demoted status of the tenancy continues beyond the initial year of demotion, delaying its promotion to secure or fully assured status for up to a further 6 months if the landlord does not issue proceedings. This is a departure from the introductory model, where only issue of proceedings will prolong the introductory status, so the court can then control further progress.

3.121 It is not clear whether it would be acceptable for a landlord, who needs no particular reason to evict a demoted tenant, to serve notice expressly and solely for the purpose of extending the demotion period. A local authority or housing action trust could be judicially reviewed, but the court might accept that the landlord had legitimate reasons for wanting to extend the period without immediately pursuing proceedings. A RSL which is not a public body could only be challenged successfully if the court could be persuaded to extend its policy of rejecting 'shams' to cover the argument that the notice is a sham as it is not serious in stating that the court will be asked to make a possession order in the case of non-assured demoted tenancies,[2] or in stating that the landlord requires possession in the case of demoted assured shorthold tenancies.[3]

Grounds for demotion

3.122 The court can only grant the order if the tenant, or another resident of or visitor to the tenant's home, has used the premises for illegal purposes or has behaved in a way which is capable of causing nuisance or annoyance to any other person. The court must also be satisfied that it is reasonable to make the order.[4]

3.123 The required misconduct is that to which the new HA 1985, ss 153A or 153B apply. That is conduct defined in subs (1) of each of those sections, as part of the pre-conditions to granting injunctions against anti-social behaviour or unlawful use of premises. Those definitions are discussed above in relation to injunctions, but some contrasts can be made here.

3.124 To take the simpler provision on unlawful use first, this applies where the person is 'using or threatening to use housing accommodation owned or managed by a relevant landlord for an unlawful purpose'. The 'relevant landlord' definition for the injunctions is the same as the landlords who can apply for demotion of secure tenants, namely a local authority or housing action trust or RSL. What is not clear is whether the tenant of property A can be demoted because they have been visited by the tenant of property B who has made unlawful use of B rather than A. As with other aspects of demotion, it appears that a broad approach has been taken, relying on the requirement of reasonableness to avoid injustices. If the landlord is a public body then judicial review and human rights principles will also temper the court's view on reasonableness.

3.125 On other anti-social behaviour, the formula used in new HA 1985, s 82A(4)(a) appears to mean that only new s 153A(1) is relevant, as expanded by subs (5) (it is immaterial where the conduct occurs), rather than subss (2)–(4). The conduct must therefore be 'capable of causing nuisance or annoyance', but that can be to 'any person'. There is no need to consider whether the potential victim of the nuisance fits the categories in subs (4) of people with a link to the landlord's housing management functions or to the neighbourhood of the landlord's housing. The only limit

---

1   See below on the grounds for demotion and on differences between the test of reasonableness in demotion and possession. Contrast the Law Commission's view in LC 284 that demotion should be available 'where the court is satisfied that otherwise it would have been reasonable to terminate', which should mean the remedies can be advanced smoothly as alternatives.

2   Under HA 1996, s 143E(2)(A).

3   Under HA 1988, s 21(4)(a).

4   See s 14(2), inserting new HA 1985, s 82A(4), and s 14(4), inserting new HA 1988, s 6A(4).

is in subs (1)(b), that the conduct must directly or indirectly relate to or affect the housing management functions of a relevant landlord (which may or may not be interpreted here as meaning the same landlord as is applying for the demotion). It must also be reasonable to make the order based on that conduct.

Reasonableness

3.126 The requirement of reasonableness is familiar from secure and assured grounds for possession. It will mean that there should be no order in cases where the tenant is only technically on the wrong side of the rules. It will also mean that, as with possession, there should be no demotion orders by consent without the court considering reasonableness as a separate issue. Finally, it will mean that a hearing will be needed if the tenant defends and that each case will turn on its facts, so that the result is as unpredictable as a possession action on discretionary grounds.

3.127 Unfortunately, it will not be possible to draw continuing parallels on reasonableness with eviction cases. This is because in eviction cases the court's discretion is now 'structured' by the new HA 1985, s 85A, inserted by s 16 of this Act and described in more detail below. The court is required to consider the past and future effects of the behaviour.

3.128 However, that section does not apply to a demotion application, so the court's discretion will not be structured. It is not obvious whether this distinction was made for some purpose or merely for drafting convenience or by oversight. Defence lawyers may therefore try to argue that it should be taken to be a deliberate distinction, implying that in demotion applications the court should not put so much weight on the effects on others.

Perpetrators

3.129 Demotion is also available where the anti-social behaviour, as defined above, has been engaged in or threatened by someone other than the tenant. That other person must be residing in or visiting the home which is subject to the secure tenancy. Unlike the injunctions, which are against the perpetrator of the anti-social behaviour, the demotion order will affect the tenancy itself and so the status of the tenant, rather than directly affecting the perpetrator. The tenant may avoid the order if they can stop the perpetrator from living there or visiting in the first place. But the provisions are worded so that only one threat needs to have been made by someone who at the time was residing there or visiting.

3.130 The only limit on this is the requirement of reasonableness. Similar issues will arise, as have long arisen in eviction cases, where the court has to consider whether it is reasonable to evict an innocent tenant who has been unable, rather than unwilling, to curb someone else's behaviour, but the neighbours and the landlord cannot be expected to continue to suffer the consequences of the tenant's problems. In typical cases parents find it hard to evict their children, or women who have suffered domestic violence succeed in making the man leave but are unable to stop him from coming round to cause a nuisance.

Effects of demotion

3.131 A demotion order will end the secure or assured tenancy. If the tenant remains in occupation at the end of the tenancy, then a new demoted tenancy will begin on that date. Any rent that the tenant owes to the landlord at the date of the demotion order will still be owed under the demoted tenancy. Similarly, any overpayment or rent in advance will be credited to the tenant under the new tenancy.[1] The parties, period,[2] rental amounts and due dates will remain the same as under the

---

[1]   See s 14(2), inserting new HA 1985, s 82A(3), and s 14(4), inserting new HA 1988, s 6A(3).

[2]   But a fixed term will be replaced by a weekly periodic tenancy.

previous tenancy.[1] The landlord can then serve a statement on the tenant, picking which of the express terms of the former tenancy should be imposed on the new tenancy.[2]

3.132 This is a somewhat clumsy legal mechanism (contrast promotion which does not involve a new tenancy). It raises various questions as to the application of various statutory provisions which only apply to tenancies or contracts entered into after they came into force. So, it is possible that a tenant of, say, 20 years' standing would gain by finding that the new demoted tenancy attracts the provisions of the Unfair Terms in Consumer Contracts Regulations 1999,[3] the Landlord and Tenant (Covenants) Act 1995, and possibly even in some cases the Contracts (Rights Of Third Parties) Act 1999. It also raises questions as to whether the tenant could, after subsequent promotion, be evicted for unauthorised alterations to the property carried out during the original tenancy but discovered later. If the tenant later sues for disrepair they may have to sue under two contracts for periods under the old and new tenancies.

3.133 Following demotion, the new tenancy is categorised in one of two ways, as follows:

(1)   A secure or assured tenancy from a RSL is replaced by a new sub-species of assured tenancy, the 'demoted assured shorthold tenancy'. It is governed by the general law on assured shorthold tenancies, as varied by the new HA 1988, ss 20B and 21(5A).[4] The effect of s 20B is that the demoted assured shorthold is promoted to a higher level of security after a set period, as described below. The effect of s 21(5A) is that the landlord does not have to wait 6 months from the start of the new tenancy to be able to repossess using a s 21 notice and the accelerated possession procedure for shortholds.

(2)   A secure tenancy from a local housing authority or housing action trust is replaced by a new species, referred to only as a 'demoted tenancy'. It is governed by the new HA 1996, ss 143A–143P,[5] which are in most respects identical to or very similar to the provisions on introductory tenancies. This means that during the period of demotion tenants will not enjoy the right to buy, nor will time spent as a demoted tenant count toward the qualification period for the right to buy and the calculation of discount entitlement.

3.134 Both types of demoted tenancy rely on the tenant meeting the usual rules that they will lose their status, and be covered only by the Protection from Eviction Act 1977 at best, if the tenant ceases to be an individual occupying a separate dwelling as their only or principal home.[6]

Rights of non-assured demoted tenants compared to introductory tenants

3.135 The provisions on non-assured demoted tenancies and introductory tenancies (both now in the HA 1996 – all references under this heading are to that Act unless otherwise stated) are practically identical in respect of proceedings for possession, notice of proceedings for possession, review of decision to seek possession (although s 143F(5)(b) requires landlords to give reasons even for favourable decisions), restriction on assignment (although there is no right to assign to a potential successor), right to carry out repairs, provision of information, consultation, jurisdiction of county court, and meaning of dwelling house. The drafters of the demoted provisions chose to

---

[1]   See s 14(2), inserting new HA 1985, s 82A(5)–(6), and s 14(4), inserting new HA 1988, s 6A(8)–(9).

[2]   See s 14(2), inserting new HA 1985, s 82A(7), and s 14(4), inserting new HA 1988, s 6A(10). It is arguable that those terms, having been imposed in a fresh agreement, would then be subject to the Unfair Terms in Consumer Contracts Regulations 1999, even if they had previously been exempt because of being negotiated in the original agreement or because of pre-dating the Regulations.

[3]   SI 1999/2083.

[4]   Inserted by s 15(1) and (2) of the 2003 Act, respectively. New HA 1985, s 82A(8)(b), inserted by s 14(2) of the 2003 Act, and new HA 1988, s 6A(11), inserted by s 14(4) of the 2003 Act, apply new HA 1988, s 20B to formerly secure and formerly fully assured tenancies respectively.

[5]   Inserted by Sch 1, para 1 to the 2003 Act as Chapter 1A of Part 5 of the HA 1996.

[6]   See new HA 1996, s 143A(3), and the reference to an 'assured' tenancy in new HA 1988, s 20B(1).

improve on the wording of the introductory originals. While the resulting greater clarity is to be applauded, there is the inevitable uncertainty as to whether someone will be able to persuade a court to read a substantive difference into what was thought to be a merely technical rearrangement.

3.136 Table 3.3 sets out the equivalences between provisions on non-assured demoted tenancies and introductory tenancies:

Table 3.3		
Equivalent provisions between non-assured demoted tenancies and introductory tenancies		
Subject	**Non-assured demoted tenancies** – new HA 1996, Part 5, Chapter 1A – from ASB Act 2003, Sch 1, para 1	**Introductory tenancies** HA 1996, Part 5, Chapter 1
Definition	s 143A	s 124
Duration	s 143B	s 125
Change of landlord	s 143C	–
Licences	new HA 1985, s 82A(3)(b) – may attract HA 1985, s 79(3)–(4)	s 126
Proceedings for possession	s 143D	s 127
Notice of proceedings for possession	s 143E	s 128
Review of decision to seek possession	s 143F	s 129
Effect of proceedings for possession	s 143G	s 130
Succession	ss 143H–143J	ss 131–133
Restriction on assignment	s 143K	s 134
Right to carry out repairs	s 143L	s 135
Provision of information	s 143M	s 136
Consultation	new s 105(7) HA 1985, s 105(7) – from ASB Act 2003, Sch 1, para 2	s 137
Jurisdiction of county court	s 143N	s 138
Meaning of dwelling house	s 143O	s 139
Members of a person's family	s 143P	s 140

3.137 While new s 143G mirrors HA 1996, s 130 on the effect of beginning possession proceedings, this is to be seen in the light of new s 143B(3)–(4) which extends the demotion period where notice is issued, as explained above. For succession, the only significant difference from introductory tenancies is that same-sex couples are expressly included, and that even spouses must have been living with the tenant for 12 months before the death (but spouses are still preferred over other members of the family where there is more than one successor). Section 143P replaces 'live together as husband and wife' with 'live together as a couple in an enduring family relationship' in the definition of 'member of a person's family', and s 143P(2) states that it is 'immaterial' that the couple 'are of the same sex'. This wording should also be read as covering cases where one party is a transsexual following the European Court of Human Rights ruling in favour of recognition of such relationships in *Goodwin v UK*.[1] Otherwise, on succession there are minor and consequential drafting differences, such as where new s 143J contains elements from HA 1985, s 88, to allow for a demoted tenant to count as a successor if they were a successor in their previous secure tenancy. Although new s 143I is titled 'No successor tenant: termination', it is like s 143H(2) (and s 143B(2)(c) and (5), which awkwardly cover the same ground), in that it does not actually involve termination of the tenancy itself. Instead, it follows the model of secure and introductory tenancies in that if no statutory successor takes the tenancy (and it is not passed under certain family court orders), then the tenancy loses its demoted status. Under ss 143H(2)(b) and 143I(5), the tenancy does not gain secure status, so it continues as a common law tenancy protected only by the Protection from Eviction Act 1977.

3.138 New s 143C makes detailed provision for where a new landlord takes on the former landlord's interest in a non-assured demoted tenancy. Subsection (1) provides that, if it has been taken on by another local housing authority or housing action trust, the tenancy continues to be demoted and time spent under the previous landlord counts towards the demotion period. This matches introductory tenancies in the effect of the references in s 124 to such a landlord 'adopting' an introductory tenancy. Under s 125(5)(b), if some other type of landlord takes over a property subject to an introductory tenancy then the tenancy continues, but it ceases to be introductory. It will therefore become whatever is appropriate to the new landlord, but it cannot become secure. By contrast, new s 143C(4) provides that a non-assured demoted tenancy does become secure if the new landlord satisfies the 'landlord condition' in HA 1985, s 80, and is not a RSL.

3.139 The effect of new s 143C(3) is twofold:

(1) If the new landlord does not satisfy the landlord condition and is not a RSL, the tenancy converts to an ordinary assured shorthold. The landlord will not be able to use HA 1988, s 21 to obtain possession in the first 6 months after the conversion,[2] but the tenancy will not become fully assured at the end of the demotion period.

(2) If the new landlord is a RSL and does not satisfy the landlord condition, the tenancy converts to a demoted assured shorthold. This is because it meets the requirements of new HA 1988, s 20B(1), in that the continuing tenancy was created by a demotion order (albeit under HA 1985, s 82A) and the *current* landlord is a RSL. The time spent as a non-assured demoted tenant will still count towards the demotion period, because under HA 1988, s 20B(2) the demoted assured shorthold tenancy's demotion period is timed from the day the relevant demotion order took effect (even though its effect was initially to create a non-assured demoted tenancy). However, at the end of the demotion period, the tenant will be promoted to fully assured status, without attracting the 'preserved right to buy' which is kept by those who were not demoted at the time of transfer (see below on 'promotion').

3.140 Provision is made for the transfer of demoted tenancies in cases where the landlord's interest

---

[1]   (2002) 35 EHRR 18, ECHR.
[2]   As it will not be covered by either HA 1988, s 21(5A) or s 21(5)(b), as read with s 21(7)(a).

passes to another body (new s 143C). If the new landlord is a local authority or housing action trust, the tenancy will continue to be a demoted tenancy on transfer and will revert to a secure tenancy unless further action is taken. Where a local authority or housing action trust transfers its stock to an RSL, the demoted tenancy will become an assured shorthold tenancy (new s 143C(4)). If the tenant's behaviour gives no further cause for concern, these tenancies will revert to assured tenancies after the expiry of one year. It is normal for secure tenancies to become assured tenancies when local authority stock is transferred to a RSL, but tenants in occupation at the time of the transfer retain a 'preserved right to buy'. It appears that demoted tenants at the time of transfer to an RSL may not regain their preserved right to buy if and when they are 'promoted' to assured status.

3.141 Licences cannot be assured, but they can be secure (or introductory)[1] Since *Westminster City Council v Clarke*,[2] this only applies to licences with exclusive possession, which mainly means tied accommodation. It is not clear whether the demoted replacement for a secure licence would be a demoted licence. HA 1985, s 79(3)–(4) says the provisions of that Part, which includes the new s 82A(3)(b), apply to licences as they do to tenancies. But, in this case, it is a question of whether that means the new 'tenancy' is a licence, rather than whether an existing licence is secure. Presumably the courts would be likely to hold that demotion was not intended to give even the marginal benefits of being a tenant rather than a licensee (mainly to do with third parties, as a secure tenant and secure licensee have almost all the same statutory rights as against their landlord), and that the new arrangement was still a licence if its exclusive possession was referable to the contract of employment.

Promotion

3.142 Introductory tenancies are automatically promoted to 'secure' status at the end of a year, subject to limited exceptions. Similarly demoted tenancies are automatically promoted to a higher form of security after one year. As with introductory tenancies, there is no provision for tenants to apply for promotion early, but, if the landlord agrees to grant a fresh tenancy before the year is up, that tenancy would be secure or fully assured as appropriate.

3.143 However, if the landlord has served a notice of proceedings for possession during that year, the tenancy will remain demoted beyond the first year, until the notice is withdrawn or 6 months have passed without proceedings being issued. If proceedings are issued, the tenancy will remain demoted until the proceedings are determined in favour of the tenant.

3.144 On promotion, a demoted assured shorthold tenancy converts to a fully assured non-shorthold tenancy, and a non-assured demoted tenancy turns into a secure tenancy. The legal mechanism is that the same tenancy continues, but subject to a different statutory scheme. This contrasts with demotion where the tenancy terminates and the demoted tenancy is a new tenancy. This will mean the tenant does not regain the previous secure or assured tenancy as such. So, for example, some or all of the express terms of the original tenancy could be missing from the promoted tenancy, if the landlord had not chosen to incorporate them into the demoted tenancy by serving notice under new HA 1985, s 82A(7) or new HA 1988, s 6A(10). However, they regain all of the normal statutory rights of secure or assured tenants. Those who become secure become eligible again for the right the right to buy, but the time spent on demotion does not count towards qualification or discounts. Those assured tenants of RSLs who had the right to acquire under their original tenancy should regain it under the promoted tenancy.

3.145 The peculiar twist is that, on promotion, a demoted shorthold converts to fully assured, even if before demotion it was a secure tenancy with a RSL. This will mean secure tenants of RSLs lose

---

[1]   See HA 1985, s 79(3)–(4) and HA 1996, s 126, respectively.
[2]   [1992] 2 AC 288.

more by demotion and promotion than do assured tenants or other secure tenants. They will switch away from secure to assured rights, which will leave them without their previous right to buy, and in a weaker position on issues such as security, succession, consultation, lodgers, and so on. Most conversions from secure to assured status take place as part of stock transfer, where there is some consultation and negotiation and an attempt to offer more favourable terms than the basic assured package, but demotion will not have to involve any such approach. Tenants affected may seek to advance human rights arguments that there is no rational justification for treating them more harshly than other demoted tenants in respect of their rights to respect for their home life (ECHR, Art 8) and their rights to property (ECHR, Protocol 1, Art 1), so that the difference falls foul of the rules against discrimination (ECHR, Art 14).

3.146 The other group who lose out on the right to buy, despite promotion, are those with the 'preserved right to buy', generally former council tenants who became assured when their homes passed to RSLs on stock transfer. Under new HA 1985, s 171B(1A), inserted by para 2(3), Sch 1 to the 2003 Act, they lose the preserved right to buy if their new landlord demotes them. On promotion, they will then become ordinary fully assured tenants and there is no provision for them to regain the preserved right to buy.

3.147 The three resulting pathways for demotion and promotion are illustrated by Table 3.4:

Table 3.4 Emotion and promotion pathways			
Landlord	**Pre-demotion status**	**Demoted status**	**Promoted status**
Council or Housing Action Trust	Secure	Non-assured demoted tenancy	Secure
RSL	Secure	Demoted assured shorthold tenancy	Fully assured
RSL	Fully assured	Demoted assured shorthold tenancy	Fully assured

Procedure for termination of demoted tenancies

3.148 The procedures for terminating the two types of demoted tenancy are different from each other. The procedure for non-assured demoted tenancies is contained in new HA 1996, ss 143D–143F, which are a very close adaptation of the existing provisions on introductory tenancies. The procedure for demoted assured shorthold tenancies is under the same provisions of the HA 1988 as any other assured shorthold, but with some modifications.

3.149 The non-assured demoted tenant, like the introductory tenant, is therefore entitled to be given at least 4 weeks' notice, containing reasons and an explanation of the tenant's rights, and to seek an internal review before the landlord applies to the county court for a mandatory order. It is very likely, in view of the similarities, that the courts will hold that if the tenant applies for judicial review of the decision to evict, then the county court must adjourn the possession case pending the judicial review, in line with the decision on introductory tenancies in *Manchester City Council v Cochrane*.[1]

3.150 The demoted assured shorthold tenant can, in theory, be evicted under any of the normal HA 1988 assured grounds. In practice, the one of most interest will be the ability to serve

---

[1] [1999] 1 WLR 809.

2 months' notice without giving a reason and then use the accelerated possession procedure for shortholds. Demoted tenancies will always be periodic,[1] so notice can be served under HA 1988, s 21(4). The demoted tenancies will be fresh tenancies created after 1989, and so will fall under s 19A of that Act, but s 21(5) will be disapplied by new s 21(5A). The result is that the landlord will not have to wait the usual 6 months from the creation of the tenancy before using the shorthold repossession procedure.

Reasons for termination of demoted tenancies

3.151 The procedures for terminating the two types of demoted tenancy are different, but in both cases the demoted tenancy can be terminated for any reason. No reason at all is needed in the case of a RSL which does not count as a public authority for judicial review and human rights purposes (though a complaint could be made to the Independent Housing Ombudsman). So, although the demotion order is obtained only on proof of past anti-social behaviour, its effect is that the tenant can be evicted for later rent arrears or any other reason unconnected with anti-social behaviour. This point was raised by the Opposition in Parliament, who tried various ways to ensure the tenant was only evicted for further anti-social behaviour.

3.152 The Government successfully resisted on the basis that:

'A demoted tenancy is just that—a lesser form of tenancy where the tenant has forfeited certain rights. Once those rights are forfeited, it is our intention that tenants can regain them only by proving that they are responsible enough to be in receipt of those rights. That includes a general obligation to maintain their tenancy responsibly. ... Both local authority demoted tenancies and demoted assured shorthold tenancies can be ended without proof of anti-social behaviour. ... For the demoted tenancy to have a deterrent effect, tenants must be under no illusion that the effect of demotion orders is that they receive a very insecure form of tenancy. The onus is then on them to prove to their landlords' satisfaction that they are responsible tenants. If the landlord is not satisfied for any reason, including the accumulation of rent arrears, the tenancy may—and "may" is the important word—be ended swiftly.'[2]

3.153 This clear statement is likely to make it difficult to argue, in a judicial review or human rights proportionality challenge, that Parliament should be taken to have meant that any termination of the demoted tenancy should be for reasons in any way linked to the reasons which justified the original demotion order. Even in a case where a demoted tenant is evicted for reasons which are nothing to do with their activities, such as modernisation of an estate under HA 1985, grounds 10 or 10A, it seems from this statement that demoted tenants could be given less favourable treatment on alternative accommodation, or even offered none at all. In this they may be worse off than introductory tenants who do not have the stigma of having 'earned' their lower status.

3.154 A tenant will, at some point, inevitably challenge whether the eviction rules for demoted tenants are compliant with the Human Rights Act 1998. That will be a difficult job, following *R (on the application of McLellan) v Bracknell Forest BC*[3] and *Poplar Housing and Regeneration Community Association v Donoghue*,[4] in which introductory and assured shorthold eviction rules survived human rights scrutiny. However, the tenants' lawyers may try to use differences in demotion, such as the fact that a shortholder or introductory tenant never has had a right to have the merits of their case considered, whereas a demoted tenant would still have that right but for the demotion. This might be relevant in cases where the demoted tenant is now being evicted for something which is not their fault and has no proportionate relationship to the episode of anti-social behaviour which led to their demotion (for example that it is easier to evict them rather than their secure neighbour for a road-widening scheme).

---

[1]   Because of new HA 1988, s 6A(9).
[2]   Lord Bassam of Brighton – *Hansard*, HL 3rd Reading, 12 November 2003, col 1440.
[3]   [2001] EWCA Civ 1510, [2002] 1 All ER 899.
[4]   [2001] EWCA Civ 595, [2001] 3 WLR 183.

Comparisons with suspended possession orders

3.155 The success or otherwise of demotion will depend, first, on whether it is seen as a worthwhile tool in practice by landlords. It will have to be seen as more useful in some cases than its nearest equivalent, the suspended possession order. A landlord faced with anti-social behaviour may not feel an injunction would be adequate or appropriate to the particular situation, and may wish to look into possession, but may also feel unable or unwilling to obtain an absolute possession order. Previously they would have sought a suspended possession order. Now, they will need to consider whether to apply for a demotion order instead. This decision will involve considering how a demotion order compares to a suspended possession order.

3.156 A landlord may prefer to apply for a demotion order, rather than a suspended possession order, for the following reasons:

(a) It suspends the right to buy or right to acquire immediately, rather than only when a suspended possession order is breached.

(b) The demoted tenancy can be terminated for any reason. No reason at all is needed in the case of a demoted shorthold with a RSL which does not count as a public authority for judicial review and human rights purposes (although a complaint could be made to the Independent Housing Ombudsman). By contrast, the suspended possession order can only be activated by a breach of the original order. So, if the possession is suspended on terms that there is no further anti-social behaviour, the tenant cannot be evicted for later rent arrears.

(c) If the tenant wants to challenge the termination of the demoted tenancy they will only be able to do so on technical grounds rather than on the merits. Even if the landlord is subject to judicial review and human rights, there will not be a challenge on the full merits. With a suspended possession order, the tenant, when applying to stay or suspend execution of the warrant, can raise arguments on the merits given the court's general discretion in secure and assured tenancies.[1]

3.157 A landlord may prefer to apply for a suspended possession order, rather than a demotion order, for the following reasons:

(a) The landlord can apply for a possession order on the nuisance grounds by giving notice which takes effect immediately.[2] To obtain a demotion order, the landlord must give at least 2 weeks' notice for an assured tenancy[3] and 4 weeks' for a secure tenancy.[4]

(b) The landlord can issue notice and subsequent court proceedings for possession, but only decide later whether to go for a suspended possession order or an absolute one. An application for demotion on its own could not be converted part-way through into an application for possession. If the landlord is willing to give an extra chance but wishes to retain the ability to apply for immediate eviction, it will be safer therefore to go for possession. Even if it is possible to apply for demotion and possession as alternatives in the same notice and proceedings, this will be a more complex and risky task.

(c) A demoted tenancy requires a further notice and court application before the landlord can obtain possession. In the case of a non-assured demoted tenancy, the tenant can also use the review procedure. In the case of a demoted assured shorthold, the landlord must give 2 months' notice (though there need be no hearing under the accelerated possession procedure for shortholds). By contrast, once the landlord believes a suspended possession order has been

---

[1]   See HA 1985, s 85(2) and HA 1988, s 9(2), respectively.

[2]   See HA 1985, s 83(3)(a)(i) and HA 1988, s 8(4). However, under HA 1985, s 83(3)(a)(ii) and (5), the landlord must seek a possession date at least 4 weeks later than the notice.

[3]   Under HA 1988, s 6A(7), inserted by s 14(4) of the 2003 Act.

[4]   See HA 1985, s 83(4A), inserted by s 14(3)(c) of the 2003 Act, and HA 1985, s 83(5), amended by s 14(3)(d) of the 2003 Act.

breached, the landlord can simply make an administrative application for a bailiff's warrant. It is up to the tenant to apply for a hearing if they wish to challenge the landlord's action.

(d)   Where the landlord is subject to judicial review and human rights, the tenant will be able to use the *Cochrane* procedure[1] to adjourn the county court application for termination of the demoted tenancy pending judicial review. Whatever the result, this is likely to cause more delay than would be caused by the county court having to list a tenant's application to stay or suspend a warrant under a suspended possession order. However, the availability of *Cochrane* adjournments does not seem to have brought use of introductory tenancies to a halt.

Structured discretion

3.158 The final section of this Part of the Act provides a procedural refinement to the court's decision on the reasonableness of granting a possession order.

Section 16 – proceedings for possession: anti-social behaviour

3.159 This section is designed to ensure that courts hearing applications for possession on the basis of the conduct of tenants, of others who live in the property or visitors to the property, take into account the impact of the nuisance and annoyance caused to other people when deciding whether it is reasonable to make an order for possession.

3.160 It responds to social landlords' concerns that there was insufficient predictability in the outcome of possession proceedings for anti-social behaviour. *Tackling Anti-social Tenants*[2] reported that:

> 'some landlords have said that they would find it easier to sustain witnesses if they themselves had more confidence in the outcome. They have pointed to individual cases where failure to secure an order from the court has damaged not only the confidence of individual witnesses, but also the confidence "in the system" of residents in whole neighbourhoods. Moreover, the failure of the court to grant an order can greatly embolden the perpetrator to create a worse, rather than better, situation for residents and for staff managing the tenancy. The individual case can have a disproportionate effect.'

The advantages of structuring discretion are identified in *Tackling Anti-Social Tenants* as increasing the likelihood of securing the possession order and assisting judges who are unfamiliar with housing law.

3.161 Section 16 inserts a new s 85A into the HA 1985 and a new s 9A into the HA 1988. The new sections require that the court consider the past impact of the anti-social conduct on other people, the likely continuing effect of the nuisance and the likely future effect of any repetition of the conduct, when considering whether it is reasonable to make an order for possession. The structured discretion only applies to the anti-social behaviour grounds for possession set out in ground 2 in Part 1 of Sch 2 to the HA 1985 and in ground 14 in Part 2 of Sch 2 to the HA 1988. This contrasts with the Law Commission recommendations[3] that judges' discretion is structured in all actions for possession based upon discretionary grounds.

3.162 Several questions arise in connection with s 16. The court is required to consider the effect of conduct and its continuing effect and the effect if the conduct is repeated. This requires the court to speculate about the impact of conduct which has not happened.

3.163 Effects, no doubt, will go beyond physical harm, to include stress and psychological harm arising from anti-social behaviour. How much further should the meaning of effect be stretched?

---

[1]   See *Manchester City Council v Cochrane* [1999] 1 WLR 809.

[2]   Department for Transport, Local Government and the Regions, 2002.

[3]   *Renting Homes*, Law Com No 284, November 2003.

Does it include social and economic harm? For instance, can the landlord provide evidence of the deterioration of the quality of the neighbourhood due to nuisance? Could a local authority provide evidence of the financial impact of the anti-social behaviour when it is considering the financial package associated with the transfer of an estate to an alternative landlord? It will be interesting to see the extent of the effects that the courts take into consideration.

3.164 The Law Commission recommendations provide greater certainty but, at the same time, attempt to retain breadth. The Report[1] recommends that the court should be required to consider all the relevant circumstances, including, but not necessarily limited to, those set out in a statutory list. The statutory list is to be constructed to include consideration of the interests of the occupiers of the property, the landlord, the landlord's other occupiers, people on a waiting list, other neighbours who are not renting from the landlord and the local community.

Conclusion

3.165 Part 2 of the Act contains a broad range of provisions which considerably enhance the tools available to social landlords. Table 3.5 provides a summary of the housing-related anti-social behaviour tools and indicates how the Act continues developments started in the HA 1996.

Table 3.5			
Focus	Mechanism	Development	Anti-social Behaviour Act 2003
The social landlord's role in controlling anti-social behaviour	Tenancy agreements	Explicit anti-social behaviour clauses added	
	Policies and procedures		s 12 – duty to prepare and publish policies and procedures in relation to anti-social behaviour
New forms of tenure	Grounds for possession	Reasonableness requirement re-interpreted by the Court of Appeal New extended grounds available for anti-social behaviour following HA 1996	s 16 – structures the discretion of the court in cases of anti-social behaviour
	Injunctive powers	New statutory powers introduced by HA 1996	Re-organised and enhanced by s 13 of the Act

---

[1] *Renting Homes*, Law Com No 284, November 2003.

Table 3.5			
Focus	**Mechanism**	**Development**	**Anti-social Behaviour Act 2003**
		Introductory tenancies – 12-month discretionary probationer tenancies introduced by HA 1996 for local authorities Starter tenancies available to RSLs	Demoted tenancies – 12-month reduction in security of tenure for the tenants of local authorities, housing action trusts and RSLs
Social landlords community safety role	Anti-social behaviour orders	Local authorities originally followed by RSLs able to apply for ASBOs	s 85 – housing action trusts able to apply for ASBOs
Local authority as housing provider	Allocation schemes	Homelessness Act 2002 increases the power to exclude potential anti-social tenants from accessing social housing	
Local government	Local Government Act 1972, s 222	Courts confirm its applicability in anti-social behaviour cases	s 91 – Power of arrest available
	Strategic and planning duties	Crime and Disorder Act 1998, ss 6 and 17	These duties are elaborated on in the context of housing by the new duty to publish policies and procedures

3.166 The table demonstrates that powers are both broad based and extend to all social housing providers. Social landlords will now be required to respond to problems of anti-social behaviour. The questions will be to what extent will they do so, and what will be their preferred mechanism?

CHAPTER 4

PARENTAL RESPONSIBILITY

Introduction

4.1   The notion of parents bearing responsibility for the criminal or anti-social conduct of their children strikes many chords. Poor parenting is commonly seen as a, if not *the*, cause of young people's bad behaviour. The responsibilities of parenthood can be seen to include a duty to respond to a child's bad behaviour in order to prevent repetition; or it might be a responsibility to provide some form of recompense or to pay a financial penalty. The Act touches all of these aspects of parental responsibility, and the place it does so most directly is in Part 3. This contains three basic sets of provisions:

(1)   the introduction of a 'parenting contract', either in cases of truancy or exclusion from school or in cases where the child has engaged, or is likely to engage, in criminal or anti-social behaviour;

(2)   the introduction of new situations where a 'parenting order' can be imposed; and

(3)   the introduction of fixed penalties for unauthorised absence from school.

4.2   Part 3 falls into two parts, the first relating to truancy and exclusions and the second to criminal conduct and anti-social behaviour. However, apart from the new fixed penalties for truancy, the provisions that apply to education are broadly replicated in the youth justice provisions. For the sake of clarity and to avoid unnecessary repetition, the treatment of Part 3 is organised by reference to the new orders and penalties it introduces rather than by following the precise sequence of the Act. During the course of the debates on the Bill, many concerns were raised about the appropriateness of these provisions, these are considered as they arise in discussion of the various sections of the Act.

4.3   Table 4.1 summarises the contents of Part 3:

Table 4.1 – The contents of Part 3 of the Anti-social Behaviour Act 2003		
Provision	**Summary**	**Main amendment/insertion**
s 18	Parenting orders	Amends Crime and Disorder Act 1998, s 8
s 19	Parenting contracts, in cases of exclusion from school or truancy	
s 20	Parenting orders, in cases of exclusion from school	
s 21	Provisions supplemental to s 20	

Table 4.1 –

The contents of Part 3 of the Anti-social Behaviour Act 2003

Provision	Summary	Main amendment/insertion
s 22	Appeals against parenting orders under s 20	
s 23	Penalty notices for parents, in cases of truancy	Inserts new ss 444A and 444B into the Education Act 1996
s 24	Interpretation of ss 19–21	
s 25	Parenting contracts in respect of criminal conduct and anti-social behaviour	
s 26	New power for Youth Offending Teams to apply for free-standing parenting order in respect of criminal conduct and anti-social behaviour	Adds to existing powers in Crime and Disorder Act 1998, s 8
s 27	Provisions supplemental to s 26	
s 28	Appeals against parenting orders under s 26	
s 29	Defines the scope of ss 25–27 and makes a consequential amendment	Minor amendment to Crime and Disorder Act 1998, s 38(4)

Parenting contracts

Introduction

4.4 Parenting contracts are introduced by ss 19 and 25 of the Act and during the Parliamentary debates on the Bill assumptions were made that the parenting contracts will have much in common with home–school agreements and acceptable behaviour contracts (ABCs). Home–school agreements are found in ss 110 and 111 of the School Standards and Framework Act 1998; ABCs are non-statutory, but used increasingly in the youth justice system, and have been recognised in Home Office Guidance.[1] In reality, the parenting contract has far more in common with the non-statutory ABC than it does with the home–school agreement and the question of effectiveness of ABCs has, it seems, been assumed rather than proven through detailed research. Nevertheless, comments made on the Bill raised little by way of serious concern on parenting contracts,[2] and in Parliament the consensus seems to have been that ABCs work, home–school agreements are unproblematic and that, therefore, these contracts raise no significant concerns.[3]

---

[1] It does not seem that parallels have been drawn with the form of 'contracts' found attached to referral orders introduced by the Youth Justice and Criminal Evidence Act 1999 and now made under the Powers of Criminal Courts (Sentencing) Act 2000. These are discussed at **4.16**.

[2] Liberty, *Second Reading Briefing on the Anti-Social Behaviour Bill in the House of Commons* (2003). Joint Committee on Human Rights, *Thirteenth report – Anti-social Behaviour Bill* (2003), HL Paper 120, HC Paper 766.

[3] See comments in *Hansard*, HC Standing Committee G, 8 May 2003, col 092, where an Opposition amendment to make the contracts enforceable on parents but not on LEAs or governing bodies failed.

4.5 Parenting contracts are made available in cases of exclusion from school and truancy by s 19. They are made available in cases of criminal conduct and anti-social behaviour among young people who have been referred to the Youth Offending Team by s 25. These have much in common and are considered in turn.

Parenting contracts in cases of exclusion from school or truancy

Definition

4.6 According to s 19(4), a parenting contract is:

'a document which contains—

(a) a statement by the parent that he agrees to comply with such requirements as may be specified in the document for such period as may be so specified, and

(b) a statement by the local education authority or governing body that it agrees to provide support to the parent for the purpose of complying with those requirements.'

Parties

4.7 The contract is entered into between either the Local Education Authority (LEA) or the governing body of the relevant school[1] and the parent of the pupil (s 19(3)) and must be signed by the parent and signed on behalf of the LEA or the governing body (s 19 (7)).

Scope

4.8 According to s 19(1) and (2), parenting contracts are available in two education situations:

(1) where a pupil has been excluded from school (either permanently or for a fixed term); and

(2) where a child of compulsory school age has failed to attend regularly at a school where he or she is registered as a pupil.

Content

4.9 The only matter specified in the Act is that the contract may include a requirement to attend a counselling or guidance programme (s 19(5)). Although the Act gives no other indication of what the contracts might potentially contain, in carrying out their functions in relation to parenting contracts, LEAs and governing bodies must have regard to statutory guidance. This is to be issued by (in England) the Secretary of State for Education or (in Wales) the National Assembly for Wales (ss 19(9) and 24(1)). It would seem probable that examples of the kinds of requirements that might (or might not) be suitable for inclusion in the contract will be provided in the guidance.

4.10 At the time of writing, draft guidance produced by the Department for Education and Skills was out to consultation.[2] A final version of this guidance will be available as the provisions of s 19 are brought into force on 27 February 2004. This part of the guidance is stated to be non-statutory guidance. Disappointingly, the draft guidance is extremely vague about what should and what should not be included in parental side of the contracts, specifying only that general and specific requirements should be balanced. Further, the draft guidance states that the governing body/LEA side of the contract is 'a statement that it agrees to provide the parents with support for the

---

[1] A relevant school is a maintained school (be it a community, foundation or voluntary school, or a community or foundation special school, or a maintained nursery school), a city technology college, a city college for the technology of the arts, or an Academy or a pupil referral unit.

[2] Department for Education and Skills, *Consultation on the Education Related Provisions Included in the Anti-social Behaviour Bill* (2003) (DfES/0710/2003). Guidance on the youth justice provisions is issued separately by the Home Office and discussed at **4.13** and **4.18**.

purpose of complying with the requirements' with no indication of what this support might consist of.[1] This seems a somewhat one-sided bargain, although the consultation does ask for comment on what the contract should include and the type of support that might be helpful to a parent.

4.11   According to ordinary principles of public law, the content of the contract should also be constrained by the legislative purposes of s 19. These purposes are spelled out in s 19(6). This states that the purposes of the requirements imposed on parents by s 19(4)(a) are:

(a)   in a case of exclusion, to improve the behaviour of the pupil, and

(b)   in a case of truancy, to ensure that the child attends regularly at the relevant school at which he is a registered pupil.

4.12   Any requirements that could not be fairly stated to relate to these purposes would be ultra vires and could potentially make the contract void. However, this doctrine is difficult and expensive to use. Further, it is hardly going to be at the forefront of the minds of most parents and schools at such times. Indeed, it is unlikely to be the first thought of most LEAs when dealing with these sorts of issues. As such, it seems quite possible that, unless the guidance is made much more explicit, the contracts will in some cases be used wrongly for purposes other than the statutory purposes.

Legal status

4.13   These contracts are not contracts in the ordinary sense of the word and s 19(8) specifically provides that breach (on either side) does not create liability in either the law of contract or the law of tort. The intended impact is on practical parenting skills rather than the creation of legal consequences. However, parenting contracts can have an indirect legal effect through s 21. This provides that, in deciding whether to make a parenting order (discussed below) the court must take various matters into consideration. These considerations include any refusal by the parent to enter into a parenting contract or, if the parent has entered a parenting contract, a failure to comply with the requirements specified in the contract (s 21(1)). Liability arises only on breach of the parenting order, but these provisions ensure that LEAs and governing bodies do have leverage and this significantly affects the nature of what would otherwise be purely voluntary arrangements. Guidance given on the use of non-statutory acceptable behaviour contracts in the sphere of criminal justice already emphasises the importance of using such leverage and encourages the explicit invoking of possible consequences to encourage compliance.[2] This is reiterated in Home Office draft guidance on the use of parenting contracts and parenting orders.[3] Provisions emerging in the Department for Education and Skills draft guidance on the school-based parenting contracts is not as strong as this but notes that 'staff responsible for overseeing the contract may wish to warn that further action may be taken'.[4] These contracts are clearly aimed at modifying the behaviour of both parents and pupils before serious sanctions become necessary and, despite their bilateral appearance, the coercive nature of the parenting contract is fairly close to the surface.

---

[1]   Department for Education and Skills, *Consultation on the Education Related Provisions Included in the Anti-social Behaviour Bill* (2003) (DfES/0710/2003)., paras 224 and 225.

[2]   Home Office *A Guide to Anti-social Behaviour Orders and Acceptable Behaviour Contracts* (Home Office Communications Directorate, 2002), at pp 52 and 59.

[3]   Home Office *Consultation on Guidance for Parenting Orders and Contracts* (2003) at paras 2.12–2.13, 3.18–3.21 and 5.10.

[4]   Department for Education and Skills *Consultation on the Education Related Provisions Included in the Anti-social Behaviour Bill* (2003) (DfES/0710/2003) at para 240.

Parenting contracts in respect of criminal conduct and anti-social behaviour

Location in the youth justice system

4.14 In the broadest terms, s 25 gives Youth Offending Teams similar powers to those given to schools and LEAs to enter into parenting contracts. Youth Offending Teams were established by s 39 of the Crime and Disorder Act 1998. Their statutory purpose is to co-ordinate the provision of youth justice services for all those in need of them in a particular area (NB a local authority may establish more than one Youth Offending Team and may act with other local authorities to establish Youth Offending Teams in their area).

4.15 The principal aim of the youth justice system, as established by the Crime and Disorder Act 1998, is to 'prevent offending by children and young persons' and all persons carrying out youth justice functions have a statutory duty to have regard to this aim (Crime and Disorder Act 1998, s 37). The local authority also has a duty, in co-operation with other agencies, to secure that appropriate youth justice services are available in their area. In support of this the chief of police, police authority, probation committee and health authority have a statutory duty co-operate with the local authority in the discharge of this duty (Crime and Disorder Act 1998, s 38). Youth Offending Teams operate within this framework and within the purview of the Youth Justice Board for England and Wales, which was established by Crime and Disorder Act 1998, s 41. To a large degree, the finer detail of the responsibilities and composition of Youth Offending Teams is determined by the local Youth Justice Plan which local authorities are obliged to draw up by virtue of Crime and Disorder Act 1998, s 40. These plans are submitted to the Youth Justice Board.

Parenting contracts in the youth justice system

4.16 The parenting contract in s 25 adds a new tool to those already established within the youth justice system for preventing offending by children and young people. The power to enter into these contracts only arises in respect of a child or young person who has been referred to a Youth Offending Team. This is not a referral to a Youth Offender Panel established by the relevant Youth Offending Team, as is the case with a 'referral order'.[1] It is much wider than this. However, this produces another interesting point of comparison because one of the main outcomes of a referral order is the use of a 'youth offender contract'. This is somewhat akin to the parenting contract in that it has a clear statutory basis for its existence, but this apart, the contracts made under the referral order are more like the ABCs, because the contract is with the young offender, not with the offender's parent. A referral order can only be used where there has been criminal behaviour. A parenting contract is rather more pre-emptive in intent. It may be sought where a member of the Youth Offending Team 'has reason to believe that the child or young person has engaged, or is likely to engage in criminal conduct or anti-social behaviour'. This means that the parenting contract can be used where the behaviour is anti-social behaviour that does not amount to criminal conduct. Equally, it can be used where the child has not engaged in either form of conduct but is thought to be likely to do so.

Definition

4.17 The definition of a parenting contract in s 25 is almost identical to that in s 19 except that in the second part of the definition the statement that support is agreed to be provided is made by the Youth Offending Team rather than a LEA or a school's governing body. As with the educational orders, the requirements that the parent can be asked to agree to include '(in particular) a

---

[1] As introduced by the Youth Justice and Criminal Evidence Act 1999 and consolidated within the Powers of Criminal Courts (Sentencing) Act 2000.

requirement to attend a counselling or guidance programme' (s 25(4)). The parenting contract must be signed by the parent and on behalf of the Youth Offending Team (s 25(6)).

Purpose

4.18   The statutory purpose of the requirements the parents are asked to agree to is 'to prevent the child or young person from engaging in criminal conduct or anti-social behaviour or further criminal conduct or anti-social behaviour' (s 25(5)). As is the case for LEAs and governing bodies under s 20, Youth Offending Teams in carrying out their functions must have regard to guidance issued by the Secretary of State. However this is separate guidance issued by the Home Secretary, not that issued by the Secretary of State for Education under s 21.[1] The discussion relevant to the draft Department for Education and Skills guidance above is relevant here, but the existence of separate guidance raises the possibility that the two versions of the parenting contract might develop in quite different ways. As with s 19, the parenting contract does not create obligations under the law of contract or tort (s 25(7)).

Content

4.19   The comments made above in respect of contracts under s 19 also apply here. At the time of writing, the Home Office guidance had appeared in draft form. This includes a wider range of examples of what might be included on the parent's side than the draft Department for Education and Skills guidance. It suggests that parents could be required to ensure that the child complies with some or all of the following requirements:

–   to stay away from places where they have misbehaved unless under supervision;
–   to be supervised at certain times;
–   to avoid contact with certain disruptive individuals;
–   to avoid contact with someone that they have been harassing;
–   to attend school; and
–   that the parents themselves should attend all school meetings.

4.20   The detail of what should be included on the Youth Offending Team side is less detailed but the guidance specifies that it should include details of specific support that will be provided to the parents.

Costs

4.21   One of the issues that might govern the extent and nature of the use of parenting contracts is the question of who bears the costs. Draft Department for Education and Skills guidance suggests that governing bodies may delegate the power to enter the contracts to the head teacher, but emphasises that in this case the head teacher will be able to commit the school's funds to meet the costs. In view of this, it seems doubtful that a large proportion of schools will wish to include expensive elements such as a requirement to attend guidance and counselling in the contracts. In the case of a s 24 parenting contract, the costs are borne by the Youth Offending Team.

---

[1]   This is due to be published as s 24 is brought into force on 27 February 2004.

Parenting orders

Introduction

4.22 Parenting orders have a more established character than ABCs yet, perversely, they have proved much more controversial than parenting contracts. Parenting orders were introduced by Crime and Disorder Act 1998, ss 8 and 9. Under these provisions, parenting orders could be made in any court proceedings in four basic circumstances:

(a) where the court has made a child safety order in respect of the child; or

(b) where the court has made an anti-social behaviour order or a sex offender order in respect of the child; or

(c) where the child has been convicted of an offence; or

(d) where a person[1] has been convicted of an offence in relation to the child's truancy under Education Act 1996, s 443 or s 444.

4.23 A new situation is added to the basic list by s 324 of Schedule 34 to the Criminal Justice Act 2003, where a referral order is made in respect of the young person or where in such cases the case has been referred back to court because the parent has failed to co-operate with the Youth Offender Panel or attend meetings of the panel.

4.24 The order should only be granted *if* the order would be desirable in the interests of preventing the conduct which gave rise to the order or the conviction (Crime and Disorder Act 1998, s 8(6)).

4.25 The core terms of the order require the parent to attend guidance or counselling sessions over a 3-month period. However, the order may specify other requirements that the parent must comply with. Failure to comply with any requirement included in the order is a criminal offence punishable by a fine.

4.26 A principal objection to parenting orders seems to have been the perceived contradiction in ordering a parent to attend a programme designed to improve parenting skills where the success of such programmes depends on participants engaging with the process whole-heartedly. The orders have been available for a considerable period, but courts and professionals (and parents) showed little enthusiasm for them in the initial stage.[2] These concerns were reflected in the debates but the Government refused to give ground on the basis that it has been shown that even parents who were initially reluctant to participate had benefited from compulsory participation.[3]

Parenting orders under the 1998 Act

4.27 These provisions build on those first established by the Crime and Disorder Act 1998. Section 18 of the Anti-social Behaviour Act 2003 amends Crime and Disorder Act 1998, s 8 in subtle but important ways to ensure that the new and existing orders carry the same effect. It does this by substituting new sub 8(4) and 8(5) for the existing provisions and by adding a new s 8(7A). The effect of the new s 8(4) is to eliminate a proviso that an order could not compel a parent to attend counselling or guidance sessions more than once in any week (and hence the need to define what was meant by a 'week'). The new s 8(5) was required as a drafting amendment to acknowledge that parenting orders are now to be found in both the Crime and Disorder Act 1998 and the Anti-social Behaviour Act 2003 and a further drafting amendment to Crime and Disorder Act 1998, s 8(5) is found in Anti-social Behaviour Act 2003, s 25(2).

---

[1] The parent rather than the child.

[2] D Ghate and M Ramello, *Positive Parenting: The National Evaluation of the Youth Justice Board's Parenting Programme* (Policy Research Bureau for the Youth Justice Board, 2002).

[3] See *Hansard*, HL Deb, 18 July 2003, col 1130; *cf* col 1153.

4.28   As already noted, the initial order requires the parent to attend a counselling or guidance programme (s 8(4)(b)). The overall impact of s 8(5) is to enable (but not to compel) the courts when issuing a subsequent order to require further attendance at a programme of counselling or guidance. The manner in which the content of the order is defined seems to anticipate that both elements will be present in the initial order and that other requirements will be present in any subsequent order although further counselling and guidance need not. However, the statute itself gives no guidance as to what the other requirements might consist of and may mean that an order (initial or subsequent) need contain only the requirement to attend counselling or guidance. A strict interpretation seems to preclude this, as the term 'such requirements' is integral to the definition of a parenting order. If a restrictive interpretation were accepted to be correct, it would be possible for court to order minimal other requirements if the main purpose in seeking the order in a particular case is to ensure that the parent is required to attend counselling or guidance.[1]

4.29   The other effect of s 18 is to add a new Crime and Disorder Act 1998, s 8(7A). This provides that the programme of counselling or guidance may include a residential element. This can only be ordered if the court is satisfied that two conditions are made out:

(1)   this is likely to be more effective than attendance at a non-residential course in preventing the behaviour at which the order is targeted;

(2)   any interference with family life that is likely to result from the parent attending a residential course is proportionate in all the circumstances.

The provisions in s 18 are reflected in the new parenting orders introduced by ss 20 and 26 and were introduced to the Bill at the Commons committee stage.[2]

4.30   The references to effectiveness, to family life and to the need for any interference in family life to be proportionate are obvious attempts to prevent the provisions, and decisions made under them, being assailable on the grounds that they infringe Art 8 (the right to privacy and family life) of the European Convention on Human Rights. This is necessary to prevent possible breach of the Human Rights Act 1998. It remains possible that if used inappropriately there could still be a breach of the Human Rights Act 1998 on these grounds. Draft guidance on the use of these powers draws explicit attention to this possibility.[3]

Parenting orders in cases of exclusion from school

4.31   Section 20 adds to these powers by introducing a new 'free-standing' parenting order in cases of exclusion from school. First, it might be useful to note that, while these provisions are contained wholly within the Anti-social Behaviour Act 2003, the provisions that relate to truancy remain within the scope of the newly amended s 8 of the Crime and Disorder Act 1998. In addition, whereas the provisions relating to truancy only apply where a parent is being prosecuted under the relevant provisions of the Education Act 1996, no underlying court action is required before an order can be applied for or granted under s 20; only the fact of exclusion from school is necessary.

4.32   The LEA may apply to the magistrates' court[4] for a parenting order where 'a pupil has been excluded on disciplinary grounds … for a fixed period or permanently' and 'such conditions as may be prescribed in regulations made by the appropriate person are satisfied' (s 20(1)).

---

[1]   Note that the Department for Education and Skills draft guidance presumes that it is possible to have an order with only a counselling and guidance component.

[2]   *Hansard*, HC Standing Committee G, 8 May 2003, cols 103–104.

[3]   Department for Education and Skills, *Consultation on the Education Related Provisions Included in the Anti-social Behaviour Bill* (2003) (DfES/0710/2003) at para 4, and Home Office, *Consultation on Guidance for Parenting Orders and Contracts* (2003).

[4]   Section 20(2).

4.33 If such an application is made the court may make a parenting order in respect of the parent of the pupils 'if it is satisfied that making the order would be desirable in the interests of improving the behaviour of the pupil' (s 20(3)). The regulations limit the use of such orders in the case of fixed-term exclusions to situations where a child has been excluded from school for a fixed term on more than one occasion.[1]

4.34 A parenting order is defined in s 20(4) and in s 26(4) in terms identical with those in Crime and Disorder Act 1998, s 8.

'A parenting order is an order which requires the parent—

(a) to comply, for a period not exceeding twelve months, with such requirements as are specified in the order, and[2]

(b) subject to subsection (5), to attend, for a concurrent period not exceeding three months, such counselling or guidance programme as may be specified in directions given by the responsible officer.'

4.35 Provisions in ss 20(5) and 26(5) replicate the amended provisions of Crime and Disorder Act 1998, s 8(5) to allow residential guidance and counselling courses as discussed above in relation to s 18. The effect produced by the new Crime and Disorder Act 1998, s 8(7A) is reproduced by ss 20(6)–(8) and 26(6)–(8) of the Anti-social Behaviour Act 2003. The only differences relate to what the effectiveness of a residential programme has to be assessed by reference to.

Requirements

4.36 The draft guidance from the Department for Education and Skills is sketchy about what requirements should be included in the order. This may reflect the relative lack of experience that there is with the educational use of parenting orders as compared with their use in the youth justice system; the Home Office draft guidance is much more detailed and is discussed below.

4.37 Section 9(4) of the Crime and Disorder Act 1998, which is applied by s 21(3), states that the requirements and directions in the order must, as far as practicable, avoid any conflict with the parent's religious beliefs and any interference with the times that the parent normally works or attends an educational establishment.

Free-standing parenting orders in respect of criminal conduct and anti-social behaviour

4.38 As we have already noted, the courts have had the power to issue parenting orders since the provisions of the Crime and Disorder Act 1998 were brought into force. The innovative impact of s 26 is that this order can be applied for to the magistrates' court without being parasitic upon a criminal prosecution for the behaviour that is complained of on some other court order. This new measure is intended to allow the courts to address early patterns of offending behaviour and, as such, sits alongside the new power introduced by the Criminal Justice Act 2003 to introduce parenting orders in situations where a referral order has been made.

4.39 The content and effect of these orders is worded almost identically to s 20. Section 26(3) provides that:

'If such an application is made, the court may make a parenting order in respect of a parent of the child or young person if it is satisfied—

(a) that the child or young person has engaged in criminal conduct or anti-social behaviour, and

---

[1] Education (Parenting Orders) (England) Regulations 2004, SI 2004/182.

[2] The Department for Education and Skills draft guidance suggests that even where the only requirement in the order is to attend guidance and counselling, the order could be made for 12 months to allow for the possibility of breach and for variation.

(b)   that making the order would be desirable in the interests of preventing the child or young person from engaging in further criminal conduct or further anti-social behaviour.'

4.40   Differences arise in relation to who can apply for them and their statutory purpose.

4.41   By contrast with parenting contracts, it is significant that they may only be applied for where the child has engaged in criminal conduct or anti-social behaviour.

Requirements

4.42   As noted above, the Home Office draft guidance includes several quite detailed suggestions for requirements that could be included in the s 26 parenting order. These include ensuring that the child or young person:

- attends school or other relevant educational activities;
- avoids certain areas unsupervised;
- remains at home or is supervised during certain hours of the night; and
- that the parent attend, for example, an anger management programme or a drug/alcohol misuse programme

4.43   As with the s 20 orders, Crime and Disorder Act 1998, s 9(4), which is applied to s 26 by s 27(3), states that the requirements and directions in the order must, as far as practicable, avoid any conflict with the parent's religious beliefs and any interference with the times that the parent normally works or attends an educational establishment.

Overlap between s 20 and s 26 of the Anti-social Behaviour Act 2003 and s 8 of the Crime and Disorder Act 1998

4.44   The potential for the use of parenting contracts in the education system to develop in a different way from those in the youth justice system was noted earlier. That discussion is as relevant to parenting orders as it is to parenting contracts. In most cases, this seems unlikely to be problematic in practice. However, it leaves open the possibility that behaviour that has led to exclusion and a parenting order with the LEA might produce a significantly different outcome if the behaviour had instead resulted in the child being referred to the Youth Offending Team. Although it should be noted that the structure of Youth Offending Teams should mean agencies working together, there does not seem to be anything in the legislation that would preclude parents being subject to two different contracts or orders at the same time. If this were to happen, they might possibly be drawn up in quite different terms and seek compliance with different requirements. This seems a curious possibility in itself, but is more curious given the possibility that they might be made in respect of the same or very similar behaviour. The only saving provision seems to be that, following the initial parenting order, it is not necessary for the order to include the guidance and counselling component in ss 20(4)(b) and 26(4)(b) of the Act and in s 8(4)(b) of the Crime and Disorder Act 1998. It is to be hoped that working practices would be developed to avoid other unnecessary or unhelpful overlap or conflicts.

Parenting orders: supplemental provisions

Costs

4.45   Section 21(4) allows for regulations to be made to determine how the costs of parenting orders, including the costs of the counselling and guidance provision are to be met. In relation to the education provisions, the regulations provide that the LEA will meet the cost except where the LEA has been requested to apply for a parenting order by the school. In this case, the costs will usually be met by the school, although it may negotiate for the LEA to meet the costs.[1] As observed earlier, this seems unlikely to encourage schools to make best use of the powers that the Act introduces. Youth Offending Teams will meet the costs of the s 26 orders.

Considerations in deciding whether to make an order

4.46   Sections 21(1) and 27(1) outline factors that must be taken into consideration in deciding whether to make a parenting order. These contain the provisions discussed at **4.13** that link the making of the order to the refusal by a parent to enter a parenting contract or the failure to comply with the requirements of parenting contract.

Information that must be before the court

4.47   Sections 21(2) and 27(2) outline information that must be before the court before an order is made. Section 21(2) states that, in the case of a pupil under the age of 16, a court must obtain information about the pupil's family circumstances and the likely effect of the order on those circumstances. Section 27(2) states the same in respect of a 'child or young person'. This is clearly designed to meet the concern that in some situations a parenting order might do more harm than good.

4.48   Similar information will also clearly be necessary before directing the parent(s) to attend a counselling or guidance programme with a residential component. Without such information, it is hard to see how the court could ensure that the residential programme is more likely to be effective than a non-residential programme. Possibly more importantly, it would be necessary to be certain that any interference with family life likely to result from the attendance is proportionate in all the circumstances. Draft guidance emphasises the need for LEAs and Youth Offending Teams to be alert to the human rights implications of this requirement.

Other considerations

4.49   Sections 21(5) and 27(4) state that LEAs, head teachers, Youth Offending Teams and responsible officers must, in carrying out their functions, have regard to any guidance issued by the Secretary of State for Education, the National Assembly for Wales, or the Secretary of State for the Home Department as appropriate.

4.50   Sections 21(3) and 27(3) apply certain of the supplemental provisions that apply to parenting orders under the Crime and Disorder Act 1998 to parenting orders made under ss 20 and 26. This is achieved by applying s 9(3)–(7) of the Crime and Disorder Act 1998 to ss 20 and 26. These provisions are important.

Explaining the effect of the order

4.51   Crime and Disorder Act 1998, s 9(3) specifies that, before making a parenting order, a court must explain to the parent the effect of the order and of the requirements proposed to be included in it. The court must also explain the consequences of failure to comply with any of those requirements and explain that the court has power to review the order on the application of the parent or the responsible officer. These must all be explained 'in ordinary language'. Guidance emphasises the fact that these orders are designed to help parents and that they should not be represented as being punitive.

---

[1]   See also the draft guidance.

4.52 It is expected that parents will be at court and there are methods of compelling attendance. Where the parent is not in court, the Home Office draft guidance suggests that the court could write to the parents to make the necessary explanation, but would need proof that the letter had been served before the order could be made.

Variation and discharge of the order

4.53 On the application of the responsible officer or the parent, the order may be varied in one of three ways: by discharging the order; by cancelling any provision included in the order; or by inserting into it any additional or replacement provision that could have been included in the order at the time that the original order was made. The only grounds for variation under Crime and Disorder Act 1998, s 9(5) are that this appears appropriate to the court that made the original order. If an application for discharge under s 9(5) is dismissed, no further application for its discharge can be made by any person, except with the consent of the court that made the order (Crime and Disorder Act 1998, s 9(6)).

Penalties for breach of a parenting order

4.54 Finally, and importantly, these provisions import into the Anti-social Behaviour Act 2003 the penalties for breach of the parenting order that are found in Crime and Disorder Act 1998, s 9(7). This provides that:

> 'If while a parenting order is in force the parent without reasonable excuse fails to comply with any requirement included in the order, or specified in directions given by the responsible officer, he shall be liable on summary conviction to a fine not exceeding level 3 on the standard scale.'

Parenting orders: appeals

4.55 Appeals against the making of a s 20 or s 26 parenting order are to the Crown Court (ss 22(1) and 28(1)). Appeal provisions in Crime and Disorder Act 1998, s 10(2)–(3)[1] provide that on appeal the Crown Court:

(a) may make such orders as may be necessary to give effect to its determination of the appeal; and

(b) may also make such incidental or consequential orders as appear to it to be just.

4.56 This means that on appeal the Crown Court can direct the magistrates' court to rehear the application. If any other order is made, Crime and Disorder Act 1998, s 10(3) provides that, for the purposes of Crime and Disorder Act 1998, s 9(5)–(7), this order is to be treated as if it were an order of the court from which the appeal was brought and not an order of the Crown Court. This allows variation or enforcement to be carried out by the magistrates' court not the Crown Court.

4.57 In the interests of completeness, it is worth noting that where a child or young person is convicted of an offence, the appeal against a parenting order issued as part of those proceedings is to the same court that would hear the appeal against the offence. This will arise in cases brought under the original Crime and Disorder Act 1998 provisions, but not in cases brought under the provisions in the Anti-social Behaviour Act 2003.

4.58 One area of concern that has not been raised so far arises out of the preventive nature of many interventions by the Youth Offending Team. A child can become involved merely on the basis of a potential for criminal or anti-social behaviour. Once referred, the child and its parent can then be asked to sign a 'voluntary' parenting contract and if, having committed an offence, they refuse or breach its terms, be subjected to a parenting order and subject to a fine if they breach it.

---

[1] Applied by Anti-social Behaviour Act 2003, ss 22(2) and 28(2).

In the majority of cases, one would anticipate that genuine concerns would justify this sort of intervention. However, it is well within the bounds of possibility that parents whose approach to their children's upbringing is merely unconventional might potentially be subject to fines in respect of a child whose offending is very minor. This possibility makes the existence of the right of appeal crucial.

Interpretation

Interpretation of ss 19–21

4.59 Many of the definitions used in the school-based provisions of Part 3 are already referred to in the discussion above. Most of the remainder is fairly self-explanatory with definitions being adopted from the Education Act 1996. However, one or two points are worth noting.

Definitions

4.60 In this Part of the Act, a parent is someone who falls within a modified version of the definition of s 576 of the Education Act 1996. This can include both natural parents, a person with parental responsibility as defined by the Children Act 1989 and any person who has care of the child (ie some that the child lives with and who looks after the child). A 'corporate parent', the local authority in the case of a child in care, is removed from the s 576 definition for these purposes by s 24. This definition of parent is used throughout the school-based provisions of Part 3.

4.61 The definitions of 'child of compulsory school age' and 'local education authority' are the same as in the Education Act 1996.

4.62 'Pupil' is defined by Education Act 1996, s 3(1) and (1A). This means a person for whom education is being provided at a school. This is subject to three exceptions:

(1) it does not include persons aged 19 or over who are receiving further education; or
(2) any person being provided with part-time education suitable to the requirements of persons of any age over compulsory school age; or
(3) any person receiving education provided under the governing body of a maintained school's power to provide community facilities.

4.63 This definition includes those who will be pupils following admission to a school and pupils who were receiving education at school before they were excluded from school. 'Registered pupils' has the same meaning as in Education Act 1996, s 434(5), 'a person registered as a pupil at the school in the register kept under [s 434]'.

4.64 'Responsible officer' in relation to s 20 parenting orders means an officer of the LEA or a head teacher or someone nominated by a head teacher. However, the head teacher, or person appointed by the head teacher. must consent to taking on the role. The draft guidance suggests that it will normally be most appropriate for this to be an officer of the LEA but that a head teacher can carry out the role if the governing body approves. The need for approval recognises that behaviour policy remains the overall responsibility of the governing body. 'Head teacher' includes acting head teacher, teacher in charge and acting teacher in charge.

Interpretation of ss 25–27 and consequential amendment

4.65 Section 29(1) defines terms used in the youth justice parts of Part 3.

4.66 The definition of 'anti-social behaviour' that applies in this Part of the Act is 'behaviour by a person which causes or is likely to cause harassment, alarm or distress to one or more other persons not of the same household as the person'. 'Criminal conduct' is defined as;

'conduct which—

(a) constitutes a criminal offence, or

(b) in the case of conduct by a person under the age of 10, would constitute a criminal offence if that person were not under that age.'

4.67 In this Part of the Act, the 'responsible officer' means a member of a Youth Offending Team who is specified in the order.

4.68 In these provisions, 'parent' includes guardian, and 'guardian' is defined as having the same meaning as in the Children and Young Persons Act 1933. This is a person who 'has for the time being the care of the child or young person'.

4.69 'Child' means a person under the age of 14 and 'young person' means a person who is over the age of 14 and not yet 18, as in the Crime and Disorder Act 1998.

4.70 Section 29(2) amends the Crime and Disorder Act 1998 to include the performance of functions under the youth justice parts of Part 3 in the definition of youth justice services under that Act.

Fixed penalties for truancy

Introduction

4.71 One of the most controversial aspects of this Part of the Act is the introduction of penalty notices for parents who have failed to ensure that their child attends school on a regular basis. This allows an 'authorised officer' who has reason to believe that an offence has been committed under Education Act 1996, s 444(1) (failure to secure regular attendance at school) to issue a penalty notice.

4.72 The introduction of these provisions in the face of significant concerns reflects the Government's concern with the importance of education. The risks associated with poor school attendance include an increased risk of criminal behaviour, increased risks of poverty and social exclusion, greater risks of teenage pregnancy and even an increased risk of running away from home. Many of these issues are discussed in the 2003 Green Paper *Every Child Matters*[1] which notes the role that schools can play in problems so diverse as to include child abuse. Fixed penalties are seen as a response to the difficulties of expense and time involved in a decision to prosecute parents for their child's non-attendance at school under the Education Act 1996.

4.73 In consultations on the proposals, teacher unions, the Local Government Association, the National Children's Bureau and the Association of Education Welfare Management all expressed concerns about the impact of these new powers, especially the potential impact on relationships between schools and parents.[2] The argument that was used to deflect these criticisms was that these new provisions create a power that some schools might welcome and that schools that do not wish to use them would be under no obligation to do so. Whilst there is no doubt that this is the effect of these provisions, it seems quite likely, given the concerted opposition to this element of Part 3, that very few schools will choose to use these powers. In view of this, it seems more than likely that in some future debate an opposition may well be repeating arguments that were heard often in Parliament during the course of this Bill, that the proposed powers are unnecessary because existing powers are not being used.

---

[1] Cm 5860.

[2] HC Research Paper 03/34. See also *Hansard*, HC Standing Committee G, 8 May 2003, cols 107–118. This was taken up at various points in the debates on the Bill. See for example, *Hansard*, HC Deb, 8 April 2003, col 152 and *Hansard*, HL Deb, 18 July 2003, col 1129.

Penalty notices for parents in cases of truancy

Relationship with truancy offences

4.74 The overall structure of s 23 is very detailed but the strategy is to add new powers to deal with truancy to those that already exist in the Education Act 1996. Of course, it should be remembered that one of the powers to deal with truancy is the new parenting contract and another is the parenting order in Crime and Disorder Act 1998, s 8. This order is not 'free-standing' like the order in s 20, but is parasitic on a parent having been convicted under either s 443 or s 444 of the Education Act 1996.[1] In the interests of completeness, it is worth outlining these offences before explaining how s 23 adds to them.

4.75 Section 443 creates an offence where a parent has failed to comply with a 'school attendance order'. A school attendance order may be issued in the circumstances outlined in s 437. This applies where it appears to a LEA that a child of compulsory school age in their area is not receiving a suitable education, either by regular attendance at school or otherwise. The issuing of the order is subject to certain procedural requirements. Once made, the order will remain in force so long as the child is of compulsory school age unless revoked by the authority or unless a direction is made in respect of the order in subsequent court proceedings under s 443 or s 447. The order requires the parent to cause the child to become a registered pupil at the school named in the order (s 437). If the order names a maintained school the governing body must admit the child (s 437(6)), but this does not affect the power to exclude a pupil from a school that he or she is registered at (s 437(7)).

4.76 The offence in s 443 is to fail to comply with the requirements of the order. There is a defence if the parent proves that that he is causing the child to receive suitable education otherwise than at school. In effect this means that the child is being educated adequately at home. Liability is set as a fine not exceeding level 3 on the standard scale.

4.77 The other basic offence is in s 444. Section 444(1) provides that the parent of a child is guilty of an offence if a child of compulsory school age who is a registered pupil at a school fails to attend regularly at the school. Section 444(1A) creates a further and more serious offence where a parent knows that the child is failing to attend regularly and fails without reasonable justification to cause the child to do so.[2] A person guilty of the offence under s 444(1) is liable to a fine not exceeding level 3 on the standard scale. A person guilty of the offence under s 444(1A) is liable to a fine not exceeding level 4 or to imprisonment for a term not exceeding 3 months or both (s 444(8) and (8A)). There are various defences to both offences outlined in s 444(3)–(6), and in addition to the fines and possible imprisonment the court may issue a parenting order.

Summary

4.78 A parent can be issued with an order to cause their child to attend school. If they fail to do so, they may be convicted of an offence under s 443 and whether or not there is such an order, a parent who does not ensure regular attendance at school may be convicted of one of the offences under s 444. The basic offence is one of strict liability (subject to defences)[3] but the offence under s 444(1A) increases the penalties where the parent knows of the non-attendance but fails to cause the child to attend school regularly.

---

[1] For the rest of this part of the discussion, section numbers between s 437 and s 444B all refer to the Education Act 1996.

[2] This subsection was added by the Criminal Justice and Court Services Act 2000.

[3] In *Barnfather v Islington London Borough Council* [2003] ELR 263, the legitimacy of the offence under s 444(1) was challenged on Human Rights Act 1998 grounds that strict liability was in conflict with the presumption of innocence in Art 6(2) of the European Convention on Human Rights. This argument was rejected.

New Education Act 1996, s 444A

4.79 Section 23 adds new ss 444A and 444B to the Education Act 1996. Section 444A allows an 'authorised officer' who has reason to believe that an offence has been committed under s 444(1) and that the school the child has failed to attend is a 'relevant school'[1] to give a penalty notice in respect of the offence. According to s 444A(2):

> 'A penalty notice is a notice offering a person the opportunity of discharging any liability to conviction for the offence under s 444(1) to which the notice relates by payment of a penalty in accordance with the notice.'

4.80 Note that the penalty notice does not apply to the more serious offence in s 444(1A). However, it is suggested that as in practice the lesser offence will always be made out where the more serious offence is committed, it will always be possible to allege the lesser offence and to seek a fixed penalty where it is thought that this would have a preferable outcome.

Effect

4.81 The effect of the notice is to give parents a specified period of time[2] during which liability to conviction under s 444(1) can be discharged by payment of a penalty in accordance with the notice.

4.82 The impact of this is that if the penalty is paid the parent cannot be convicted of this offence (s 444A(4)). No proceedings should be issued for the offence to which the notice relates or for an offence under s 444(1A) arising out of the same circumstances until the end of a prescribed period (s 444A(3)). Of course it may be that the notice does not cover all of the instances of truancy which leaves it open that the parent could be convicted for instances not specified in the notice, and in the case of a serial non-attender it will always be possible to prosecute for a future offence.

'Authorised officer'

4.83 The definition of 'authorised officer' includes:

(a) a constable;
(b) an officer of the LEA who is authorised to give penalty notices; or
(c) (most controversially) an authorised staff member.

4.84 'Authorised staff member' means a head teacher of a relevant school or a member of the staff of a relevant school who is authorised by the head teacher to give penalty notices. The regulations clarify that the authorised member of staff must be either a deputy head teacher or an assistant head teacher; answering concerns raised at various stages throughout the debates that an authorised staff member should be a senior member of staff (see s 444B(4)).[3] An amendment to the Police Reform Act 2002 extends the power granted to constables under s 444A to community support officers (s 23(3)).

4.85 The proceeds of the fixed penalties are paid to the LEA (s 444A(5)) and the use of the funds may be specified in regulations (s 444A(6)). The regulations allow them to be used to defray the costs of administering the penalty system.

---

[1]   'Relevant school' means (a) a maintained school, (b) a pupil referral unit, (c) an Academy, (d) a city technology college or (e) a city college for the technology of the arts (s 444B(4)).

[2]   Under the Education (Penalty Notices) (England) Regulations 2004, SI 2004/181, this period is set at 42 days.

[3]   See *Hansard*, HC Standing Committee G, 8 May 2003, cols 107–118 and the Education (Penalty Notices) (England) Regulations 2004, SI 2004/181.

New Education Act 1996, s 444B

4.86 There are additional provisions in the new s 444B.

Power to make regulations

4.87 Section 444B(1) outlines the scope of powers to make regulations governing the operation of the fixed penalty system. In addition to those already mentioned these include:

– provisions as to the form and content of the notices and as to the amount of and the time at which the penalty is to be paid;
– provision for determining which LEA the penalty should be paid to, how the penalties should be paid and what records should be kept;
– provision limiting the circumstances in which authorised officers may give penalty notices;
– provisions relating to repayment of any sums paid under a notice which is withdrawn and prohibiting proceedings that relate to a withdrawn notice;
– provision of a certificate stating that payment was, or was not received by a date specified in the certificate that can be used as evidence of these matters;
– provisions relating to the action to be taken if the penalty is not paid;
– provision in connection with the preparation of codes of conduct in relation to the giving of penalty notices (s 444B(1)(a)–(k)); and
– 'such other provision in relation to penalties and penalty notices as the Secretary of State thinks necessary or expedient' (s 444B(1)(l)).

4.88 As already noted, some of these regulations were emerging in draft form before the Bill had completed its passage through Parliament.

Amounts

4.89 The Education (Penalty Notices) (England) Regulations 2004 specify different amounts depending on the circumstances as expressly envisaged and permitted by s 444B(2):

– a penalty of £50, where the sum is paid within 28 days of receipt of the notice;
– a penalty of £100 where the sum is paid within 42 days of receipt of the notice

Duty to have regard to guidance

4.90 Section 444B includes a statutory duty to have regard to guidance issued by the Secretary of State (s 444B(3)).

Consequential amendments

4.91 In addition to the introduction of these two new sections to the Education Act 1996, s 23 of the Anti-social Behaviour Act 2003 also includes minor drafting amendments to other legislation. This includes changes relating to the service of notices in the Education Act 1996 (s 23(2)) and changes to Schs 4 and 5 to the Police Reform Act 2002 in respect of the role of community support officers (s 23(3)–(8)).

Territorial scope

4.92 Note that these provisions apply only to England at the present time. However the Welsh Assembly may adopt the provisions of ss 444A and 444B by amending the section to remove the words 'in England' (s 23(9)). If these provisions are applied to Wales, the functions exercised by the Secretary of State in England will be exercisable by the National Assembly for Wales (s 23(10)).

Date in force

4.93 The powers in Part 3 are brought into force from 27 February 2004. Sections 18 and 25–29 apply to the whole of England and Wales. At present the powers in ss 19–24 apply only to England.

CHAPTER 5

DISPERSAL OF GROUPS AND REMOVAL OF PERSONS UNDER 16 TO THEIR PLACE OF RESIDENCE

Introduction

5.1 Part 4 of the Act is concerned with the fear and alarm caused to the public by groups of people, predominantly young people, gathering in public places. Part 4 also deals with the presence of young people under the age of 16 in public places after 9 pm who may, in prescribed circumstances, be returned to their home.

5.2 Prior to the enactment of the Anti-social Behaviour Act 2003, the police already had considerable powers under the Public Order Act 1986, the Criminal Justice and Public Order Act 1994 and the Criminal Justice and Police Act 2001, as well as the common law power where there is a threat to breach of the peace, to arrest and to move groups of people on, where their behaviour amounts to a criminal offence or serious disorder is threatened. The call for additional powers has been largely to make it easier for the police to disperse groups that pose the risk of relatively minor disturbance,[1] but it seems also to have stemmed from apparent unwillingness to use powers created by the Crime and Disorder Act 1998 to designate areas for the use of child curfew schemes. These powers bear a striking resemblance to some of the new powers in Part 4.

Impact on civil liberties and human rights

5.3 The Anti-social Behaviour Bill followed close on the heels of the publication of the White Paper *Respect and Responsibility: Taking a Stand Against Anti-social Behaviour*, and the Government was criticised for not engaging in significant consultation prior to the publication of the Bill.[2] Even so, it is striking that the White Paper contains little by way of justification of the power to disperse groups and the power to return under 16s to their homes. The White Paper noted only that:

> '4.12 It is important that communities are not afraid to use parks, playgrounds, streets and shopping centres. Young people gathering together in groups can be very intimidating to the public and trouble does sometimes occur when gangs gather together in the street. In the year 2000 32% of respondents to the [British Crime Survey] cited teenagers hanging around in the street as a big problem in their area.

> 4.13 The police, in consultation with local authorities, will therefore be given the ability to designate areas with significant levels of anti-social behaviour. Within these specified areas the police will be able to disperse groups of people and will have access to automatic, fast-track child curfew powers.'

5.4 The White Paper also contained no reference to the local child curfew schemes that one of these new powers resembles so closely and criticism during the course of the Bill's Parliamentary progress noted this in strong terms:

---

[1] *Hansard*, HC Deb, 24 June 2003, col 935.
[2] Ibid, col 174.

'... the Minister must explain some points. The proposition has come up at a pretty late stage in the government's thought processes on anti-social behaviour. It follows what the government must accept as the abject failure of child curfew orders which have not worked as intended. The government should think carefully about the detail of what is proposed.'[1]

5.5   Criticism was also received from many agencies and associations concerned with civil liberties and youth justice. The Local Government Association[2] raised concerns that the legislation will simply reinforce negative perceptions of young people as troublemakers and jeopardise their future life chances. Similar concerns were raised by the National Children's Bureau in their comments on the White Paper.[3] More worryingly, the House of Lords and House of Commons Joint Committee on Human Rights Report on the Bill[4] considered that the potential intrusion on private life contained in the use of the powers in s 30, especially in proportion to the proposed benefits of such action, might, in practice, result in breaches of the Human Rights Act 1998 due to the lack of guidance on the circumstances in which it might be appropriate to exercise them. They noted:

> 'It suggests that the proposed powers are not intended to be a response to threats of serious disorder, but rather to allow the police to manage people in public spaces in such a way as to prevent any more remote risk of minor disorder. It is true to say that this power does not currently exist in the law. There is a reason for that: it has heretofore been regarded as an unnecessary intrusion on the liberty of the individual to allow a constable to give orders to someone where there is no threat of crime or danger to safety.'[5]

5.6   Less liberal concerns, that the area designation requirement would mean that the powers would not be available generally, or would simply mean shifting a problem to the boundaries of a defined area, were rejected during the course of the legislative process.[6]

The structure of Part 4

5.7   The strategy of Part 4 of the Act is to enable senior police officers to designate areas where the presence of groups and young people in public places is seen as particularly problematic, and to allow the new powers to be exercised only in these designated areas.

5.8   Part 4 consists of seven sections, but these all relate to the two basic powers found in s 30. These consist of the power to disperse groups and the power to remove children and young persons to their place of residence. These are considered in turn.

5.9   The powers have two distinct stages: First, the area designation and, secondly, the exercise of the power within the designated area.

Area designation

5.10   Section 30(1), (2) allows officers of a certain rank to authorise powers conferred on a constable by s 30 to be exercised as specified in the authorisation. Authorisations apply only to a 'relevant locality' and only for a specified and limited period.

---

[1]   *Hansard*, HC Standing Committee G, 8 May 2003, col 139, Mr Paice.

[2]   Local Government Association, *Anti-social Behaviour Bill: Second Reading Briefing*, 8 April 2003 (Local Government Association, 2003); Local Government Association, *Lords Second Reading Briefing*, 18 July 2003 (Local Government Association, 2003).

[3]   National Children's Bureau letter to the Home Affairs Committee dated 17 March 2003.

[4]   HL Paper 120, HC Paper 766 (17 June 2003).

[5]   Ibid, para 35.

[6]   *Hansard*, HC Standing Committee G, 8 May 2003, col 139.

Trigger criteria

5.11   An area may only be designated under s 30 if certain criteria are satisfied. Section 30(1) provides:

'This section applies where a relevant officer has reasonable grounds for believing—

(a)   that any members of the public have been intimidated, harassed, alarmed or distressed as a result of the presence or behaviour of groups of two or more persons in public places in any locality in his police area (the 'relevant locality'), and

(b)   that anti-social behaviour is a significant and persistent problem in the relevant locality.'

'Presence or behaviour'

5.12   Some of the most sustained criticism of these provisions has arisen from the fact that the powers can be triggered by the presence or behaviour of groups of people.[1] The particular issue here is that it is not necessarily the *behaviour* of a group that causes alarm, etc, but the simple *presence* of a group. Clearly, if a group, or members of it, are rowdy or behaving in an offensive, abusive or threatening manner, concerns may be legitimate. Where the members of the groups are simply gathered together, it is harder to see why another person's reaction to this should interfere with their apparently legitimate use of public space. This concern is made more acute by the fact that the group might be as small as two persons. Further, it takes no flight of fancy to imagine that some members of the public might be alarmed by the mere presence of a small number of black people or young people where they would be unaffected by the presence of a group of white people or older people. If it is the behaviour of the group that is at issue, the danger of the power being used in a prejudiced or biased way is minimised; if it is simply the group's presence that is at issue, a real possibility arises that the powers could be used on the basis of stereotypes rather than any real assessment of culpability. A code of practice (discussed at **5.58**), which had not been produced at the time of writing, should clarify the proper scope of the use of these powers, but if they had been directed solely at behaviour the risk of improper use would have been reduced significantly.[2]

'Intimidated, alarmed, harassed or distressed'

5.13   It is clear that these terms are alternatives and, as such, it is only necessary that members of the public have been affected in one of these ways by a group of at least two persons in the relevant locality. The stronger pre-conditions of 'intimidation' or 'harassment' are not necessary conditions for the exercise of these powers. Suggested amendments to the wording of this part of the Act during the Parliamentary progress of the Bill which would have removed the terms 'distress' and 'alarm', because these were felt to be too minor to justify the potential risk to the right to freedom of association were rejected. Other amendments to ensure that the distress or alarm was a reasonable response to the behaviour or presence were not accepted either, although the debate presumed that designation would not take place except where the relevant officer saw this as a serious and persistent problem.

5.14   It would be helpful to be able to give an indication of how the terms used in the Act have been interpreted in legislation using the same or similar terminology in the past. However, there has been remarkably little litigation on what measure of conduct exactly amounts to 'intimidation' 'alarm', 'harassment' and 'distress'. A recent case, *Norwood v Director of Public Prosecutions*[3] concerned the question of whether the display of a poster in a window was likely to cause religiously

---

[1]   *Hansard*, HC Deb, 8 April 2003, col 184 and 24 June 2003, col 931; *Hansard*, HC Standing Committee G, 8 May 2003, cols 146–147; *Hansard*, HL Deb, 18 July 2003, cols 1100 and 1112.

[2]   *Hansard*, HC Standing Committee G, 8 May 2003, cols 142–143.

[3]   *The Times*, 30 July 2003.

aggravated 'harassment, alarm or distress' under s 5(1)(b) of the Public Order Act 1986 (as amended). The poster showed one of the World Trade Centre's twin towers in flames with the words 'Islam out of Britain' and 'Protect the British People'. The Divisional Court found that the interpretation of these words was a mixed question of value and fact and that the district judge had been entitled to come to the view that the posters were likely to cause 'harassment, alarm or distress' to passers-by as a matter of common sense. The effect could be judged by reference to the impact on any right-thinking member of society who was concerned about the issues it raised. It did not matter that followers of Islam were unlikely to see it in a street in a small market town in Shropshire. An argument that this was an unjustified infringement on the right to freedom of expression under the Human Rights Act 1998 was rejected.

5.15   *Percy v Director of Public Prosecutions*[1] raised the issue of the compatibility of s 5 of the Public Order Act 1986 with the Human Rights Act 1998 because of its impact on the right to freedom of expression in Art 10 of the European Convention on Human Rights. In this case, the district judge at first instance had decided that the desecration of the American flag in the presence of American citizens was an offence because of the distress it had caused. In the course of the appeal, having decided that there was a pressing social need to protect citizens and visiting foreign nationals from intentionally and gratuitously insulting behaviour that would cause them alarm and distress, it was held that:

> 'It is therefore, in my view a legitimate aim, provided of course that any restrictions on the rights of peaceful protestors are proportionate to the mischief at which they are aimed. Some people will be more robust than others. What one person finds insulting and distressing may be water off a duck's back to another. A civilised society must find an appropriate balance between the competing rights of those who may be insulted by a particular course of conduct and those who wish to register their protest on an important matter of public interest. The problem comes in striking that balance, giving due weight to the presumption in the accused's favour of the right to freedom of expression.'

5.16   The court went on to hold that, in this case, the balance had not been struck appropriately because the judge had placed too much emphasis that on the fact that the protest did not require behaviour of this kind and that the distress could have been avoided. This failed to address adequately the question of proportionality. The conviction was quashed.

5.17   Obviously the right that will be affected most often by s 30 will be the right to freedom of association which has a slightly less well protected status than the right to freedom of expression under s 12(4) of the Human Rights Act 1998. However, taken together, these cases give an indication that establishing distress might not require a high threshold, but that this needs to be balanced against the impact on rights under the Human Rights Act 1998. The code of practice, when it is produced, will need to address this if legal challenges are to be minimised.

'Anti-social behaviour is a significant and persistent problem'

5.18   The area cannot be designated under s 30 unless the officer has reasonable grounds for believing that anti-social behaviour is both a significant and a persistent problem in the relevant locality.

'Anti-social behaviour'

5.19   This is defined in s 36 as 'behaviour by a person which causes or is likely to cause harassment, alarm or distress to one or more other persons not of the same household as the person'.

---

[1]   [2002] Crim LR 835.

'Significant and persistent problem'

5.20 In the Commons committee stages of the Bill, it was accepted that this definition should not be restricted or refined any further so as not to be over-prescriptive.[1] The understanding was that it would, rather, be developed through statutory guidance. This had not been published at the time of writing, but, as it stands, the wording means that sporadic or occasional instances of people gathering should not be caught, leaving serious but infrequent or 'one-off' disturbances to be dealt with through pre-existing legislation. In the light of this, one would think that gatherings that have no significant anti-social effect should remain outside the scope of this legislation and should not justify area designation. However, the way in which the power is defined leaves it open that the relevant anti-social behaviour might have nothing to do with groups of people gathered together, but might be the result of individual acts with no connection to groups gathering in the locality.

5.21 The way in which these provisions are interpreted by the police and by the courts will have a significant impact on the extent of the use of these powers. If the purpose of the powers is to address the potential for harm caused by disorderly groups of people, then one would hope that the power would be confined to areas where such groups do cause real problems in a community. The alternative is that a limited or technical reading of these provisions would allow groups of people, particularly groups of young people, to be prevented from gathering simply because some members of the community behave in a persistently anti-social manner and some members of the community find the presence of even small groups of people makes them fearful.[2] It is to be hoped that the code of practice, when it is published, will satisfactorily clarify the proper extent of the use of these powers.

Role of area designation in the removal power

5.22 As noted at the outset, the area designation process has to be in place before groups can be dispersed or the power to return under-16-year-olds to their place of residence can be used. It is interesting to note, therefore, that the criteria that are used to determine whether an area designation is appropriate contain no reference to the presence of unaccompanied under-16-year-olds being a problem to the relevant locality. The criteria relate only to anti-social behaviour being a significant and persistent problem and to groups of persons having caused intimidation, alarm, harassment or distress. This lack of a requirement to identify a particular problem in a locality before the power to make a scheme is invoked is consistent with the provisions relating to local child curfew schemes under Crime and Disorder Act 1998, s 14. However, it seems curious that the exercise of the powers should be conditional upon having established the existence of another unconnected problem of anti-social behaviour. Guidance produced in relation to the designation of local child curfew schemes presumes that these powers will only be used where the presence of young children in public places is a particular problem (see **5.24**). In view of this, it seems reasonable to assume that similar provisions will be included in a code of practice on the operation of s 30 (see **5.58**).

Relevant officer

5.23 The relevant officer who is empowered to designate the area is a police officer above the rank of superintendent (s 36).

---

[1]   *Hansard*, HC Standing Committee G, 13 May 2003, col 171.

[2]   But see the discussion at **5.15** and **5.16** above.

Relevant locality

5.24   The relevant locality is 'any locality in his police area' and the Parliamentary debates clarified that this could be as wide as the whole of a police command area.[1] The area will have to be defined in the authorisation, but the Act contains no guidance on how widely or narrowly the area should be drawn. Obviously, if the designated area is set very narrowly it is likely to result in merely displacing a problem to another area close by.[2] If the area is set too wide, this might unjustifiably infringe the liberty of those living and working in the area. Similar considerations are dealt with in Home Office Guidance on the designation of areas for the use of local child curfew schemes:

> 'The local child curfew notice will focus on a specific area which has an identified problem of unsupervised children who are engaged in anti-social or potentially criminal behaviour. This will need to be a clearly defined geographical area which may include, for example, part of a housing estate or a town or a city centre (s 14(2) of the 1998 Act). Care needs to be taken in gauging the extent of the curfew to ensure that unintended consequences are minimised. For example, avoiding the application of numerous notices covering small geographical areas or displacing problems to adjoining areas.'[3]

5.25   Arguments raised during the course of the debates on the Bill that the powers should be available in all parts of England and Wales were rejected. The rejection recognised that these powers do impact on the exercise the right of freedom of association and should therefore only be available where local conditions justify it.[4]

Length of designation

5.26   According to s 30(2), the authorisation for the use of powers in the designated areas may be for a period of not more than 6 months. Arguments in the committee stages of the Bill that this was too short were rejected on broadly the same grounds as those discussed in the previous paragraph.

The area designation process

5.27   Section 31 sets out various procedural conditions that must be satisfied before an area designation can take effect. First, the designation must be in writing and signed by the relevant officer. In addition, it must specify:

(a)   the relevant locality;
(b)   the grounds on which the authorisation is given; and
(c)   its duration.

Role of the local authority

5.28   In view of the concerns expressed above regarding fears that the designation might be granted too easily, it is significant that a late amendment to the Bill ensured that each local authority whose area includes the whole or part of the relevant locality must consent to the authorisation. This is found in s 31(2), which replaced the initial provisions in the Bill that would have required consultation with such local authorities but not their agreement.

---

[1]   *Hansard*, HC Standing Committee G, 13 May 2003, col 292.
[2]   A concern noted at *Hansard*, HC Standing Committee G, 13 May 2003, col 174 and at *Hansard*, HL Deb, 18 July 2003, col 1098.
[3]   Home Office, *Guidance on Local Child Curfews* (1998) Circular 46/98 at para 4.22.
[4]   *Hansard*, HC Standing Committee G, 8 May 2003, col 161, and *Hansard*, HC Deb, 24 June 2003, col 946.

5.29 In England, 'local authority' means a district council or a county council in counties that have no district councils, a London borough council, The Common Council of the City of London or the Council of the Isles of Scilly. In Wales, 'local authority' means a county council or a county borough council (s 36).

Publicising the designation

5.30 The designation must be publicised by means of an 'authorisation notice'. This must either be placed in a newspaper circulating in the relevant locality, or posted in some conspicuous place or places in the relevant locality or both (s 31(3)). An authorisation notice is a notice that states that the authorisation has been given, specifies the relevant locality and specifies the duration of the authorisation (s 31(4)). The notice must have been published or posted before the commencement of the period specified in the authorisation.

Withdrawal of authorisations

5.31 An authorisation may be withdrawn either by the officer who made it or by another officer of the same rank or a higher rank (s 31(6)). Consultation must take place with any local authority whose area includes the whole or part of the relevant locality before an authorisation is withdrawn (s 31(7)).

5.32 The withdrawal does not affect the exercise of any powers that occurred before the withdrawal took place (s 31(8)) and it does not prevent the giving of further authorisations in the whole or any part of the relevant locality at a future date (s 31(9)).

Challenges to area designation

5.33 There is, it should be noted, no formal method by which members of an affected group or community can challenge the legality of, or the need for, area designation. It might be that concerns could be raised with the local authority who might reflect on reasonable concerns and refuse to consent to the order. However, if this was not possible or the designation had been made before local people realised its potential impact, only the police can withdraw the designation. There is no formal mechanism by which an individual or group, or indeed the local authority, can even request its withdrawal.

5.34 In view of this, the only method that individuals in the affected community would have for challenging the legality of the designation would be through judicial review. Given the limitations of judicial review, a successful claim would be difficult. However, in the case of significant procedural irregularity, failure to comply with the statutory requirements or where the decision to designate the area was '*Wednesbury* unreasonable', this would be a possibility. In practical terms, the greatest safeguard against abuse of process is the fact that the designation is time-limited and concerns could be raised with a local authority if a re-designation was proposed.

5.35 A further possibility for challenge might arise in the case of a person who has been prosecuted under s 32(2) for failing to obey a direction to leave the area (see **5.47**). Here, it should be possible to use significant illegality in the designation process as a defence. For an example of this, see *Boddington v British Transport Police*.[1] However, it should be remembered that the courts will give public authorities a wide margin for the exercise of their discretion.

---

[1]   [1998] 2 All ER 203.

Authorisations by the British Transport Police

5.36   The power to designate an area may also be applied to property covered by the Railways and Transport Safety Act 2003. In this case, the designation is carried out by an officer of the British Transport Police (BTP). Section 35(1) and (2) of the Anti-social Behaviour Act 2003 achieves this by substituting alternative wordings in ss 30(1) and 31(6)(b).

Dispersal of groups

Power to disperse groups in a designated area

5.37   Once an area has been designated using the procedures outlined above, a constable in uniform may give various directions to persons in groups within the relevant locality, again provided that certain conditions are satisfied.

5.38   The preconditions for the exercise of the powers are that 'a constable in uniform has reasonable grounds for believing that the presence or behaviour of a group of two or more persons in any public place in the relevant locality has resulted, or is likely to result, in any members of the public being intimidated, harassed, alarmed or distressed' (s 30(3)).

'A group of two or more persons'

5.39   According to s 30(7), 'any reference to the presence or behaviour of a group of persons is to be read as including a reference to the presence or behaviour of any one or more of the persons in the group'. This raises the issue of the relationship between the conduct of individuals and the perceived conduct of the group as a whole. The balance that s 30 has drawn between the right of members of a group to associate with each other and the need of a community to be able to exist free of disturbance is tilted firmly away from freedom of association by this section. The concern raised here is that the presence of a single rowdy individual[1] within a group could be used to prevent a significant number of other people whose conduct is exemplary from gathering in a public place. Clarification of the situations where the use of this proviso is appropriate through a code of practice will be most welcome and may be necessary if possible infringement of the Human Rights Act 1998 is to be avoided.

A public place

5.40   According to s 36 'a public place' means any highway and 'any place to which at the material time the public or any section of the public has access, on payment or otherwise, as of right or by virtue of express or implied permission'.

Intimidated, harassed, alarmed or distressed

5.41   This will be recognised as identical wording to the condition that applies to the designation of the area in the first place. Many of the comments that were made in discussing this earlier are relevant here. A proposed amendment that the relevant officer should believe that this reaction is reasonable was withdrawn. However, it was accepted that this should be specified in associated guidance.[2]

---

[1]   Or, as mere presence will trigger this, it could be the presence of a single heavily tattooed individual, or a single individual in leathers and chains, within the group.

[2]   *Hansard*, HC Standing Committee G, 8 May 2003, col 175.

Possible directions that can be given

5.42   There are three possible directions that the constable can give. These are laid out in s 30(4) which provides that the constable may give one or more of the following directions:

(a)   a direction requiring the persons in the group to disperse (either immediately or by such time as he may specify and in such a way as he may specify);

(b)   a direction requiring any of the persons whose place of residence is not within the relevant locality to leave the relevant locality or any part of the relevant locality (either immediately or by such time as he may specify and in such a way as he may specify); and

(c)   a direction prohibiting any of those persons whose place of residence is not in the locality from returning to the relevant locality or any part of the relevant locality for such period (not exceeding 24 hours) from the giving of the directions as he may specify.

5.43   Concerns were raised during the debates that, under para (c), a person who did not live in the relevant locality, but who worked or attended school there might place themselves in breach of a direction by simply going to school or work. This was not felt to be a sufficiently grave risk as to require amendment of the Bill.[1] Other concerns about the likely effect of the power to specify how the group should disperse were confirmed to be essentially about the routes that should be taken.[2]

The form of the direction

5.44   According to s 32(1), a direction to disperse may be given orally. It may be given to an individual or to two or more persons together.

Withdrawal of the direction

5.45   The direction may be withdrawn or varied by the person giving it (s 32(1)(c)).

Groups to whom these powers do not apply

5.46   In view of the importance of the right to freedom of association, it would be expected that limits would be imposed on the power to disperse groups. Two sorts of gatherings are exempted from the scope of s 30, by s 30(5). These are groups picketing in furtherance of a trade dispute and public processions. The scope of the right to picket peacefully that remains unaffected by s 30 is set out in s 220 of the Trade Union and Labour Relations (Consolidation) Act 1992. In cases of doubt, one should refer to a specialised employment law text. The scope of the right to take part in processions is as outlined by Public Order Act 1986, s 11 and applies to processions to: demonstrate support for or opposition to any views or action; to publicise a cause or campaign; or to commemorate an event. In this case, s 30 does not apply as long as either a written notice has been given in accordance with Public Order Act 1986, s 11 or no such notice is required. This applies where it is not reasonably practicable to give such written notice, or where the procession is one that is commonly or customarily held in the area, or where it is a funeral procession.

Effect of a direction under s 30

5.47   Once a direction has been given, it is an offence if a person that the direction has been given to knowingly contravenes the direction (s 32(2)).

5.48   Where a power is exercised, any local authority whose area includes the whole or part of the relevant locality must be notified (s 32(4)).

---

[1]   *Hansard*, HC Standing Committee G, 8 May 2003, col 163.
[2]   *Hansard*, HC Standing Committee G, 13 May 2003, col 180.

Penalties

5.49 A constable in uniform may arrest a person he reasonably suspects has committed an offence under s 32(2) without a warrant (s 32(3)).

5.50 According to s 32(2), a person who commits an offence under s 30(4) is liable on summary conviction to a fine not exceeding level 4 on the standard scale, or imprisonment for a term not exceeding 3 months.

5.51 The need for a power to imprison for failing to observe a direction was challenged during the course of the debates. The response was that the power would be necessary in the 'worst kinds of cases'; what exactly these would amount to was not specified.[1] The amendment that would have removed this was withdrawn, but this withdrawal was accompanied by a request that this should be clarified in guidance.

Removal of persons under 16 to their place of residence

5.52 The second power in s 30 relates solely to young people. This power applies to remove a person that a constable believes to be under the age of 16 to their place of residence. This power applies only where the area has been designated under s 30(1) and (2). It applies only to children and young persons in public places between the hours of 9 pm and 6 am. It applies only where the person under the age of 16 is not under the effective control of a parent or adult (s 30(6)).

5.53 Significantly, it is also restricted where the constable 'has reasonable grounds for believing that the person would, if removed to that place, be likely to suffer significant harm' (s 30(6)). This was subject to some discussion during the debates. It was noted that a constable might not be aware of circumstances at home which made the removal ill-advised until he had arrived at the residence with the child or young person.[2] No amendment was made, but further clarification through the guidance was requested.[3]

Relationship to child curfew schemes

5.54 It was noted in the introduction to this chapter that this power bears a striking resemblance to the power to create a local child curfew scheme. These powers were introduced by Crime and Disorder Act 1998, ss 13 and 15 to allow local authorities to designate areas where children under the age of 10 could be removed to their place of residence between the hours of 9 pm and 6 am. This power was never used and, in the Criminal Justice and Police Act 2001, the powers were extended so that they could be applied in the case of children and young persons under the age of 16. Significantly, the powers were also extended so that a scheme could be applied for by the chief officer of police of the relevant police area as well as by the local authority. This amendment came into force in August 2001, but again the power has never been invoked.[4] It might be that having designated an area under s 30 primarily to deal with problem groups, the police will be willing to use the power of removal. If so, this power may not fall into disuse in the way that the child curfew powers have, but unless a consensus is built around the benefits of these powers, as compared with perceived disadvantages, the rate of use may again prove very low.[5]

---

[1] *Hansard*, HC Standing Committee G, 13 May 2003, cols 195 and 197.
[2] Ibid, col 185.
[3] Ibid, at col 102.
[4] Although a similar power under Scottish legislation has been used in one area. An evaluation of the scheme can be found in McGallagly et al, *Evaluation of the Hamilton Child Safety Initiative* (Scottish Office Crime and Criminal Justice Research Findings No 24) (1998) (http://www.scotland.gov.uk/cru/documents/crf24-00.htm).
[5] For an expression of doubt as to the likely usefulness of these powers see *Hansard*, HC Deb, 24 June 2003, col 950.

'Responsible person'

5.55   The powers only apply if the child or young person is not accompanied by a parent or a 'responsible person' aged 18 or over (s 30(6)(b)). This term raised some concerns during debates because it is not defined in the Act. It was confirmed during the Commons committee stages that the term 'responsibility' does not refer to any form of legal responsibility but only to practical control of the child or young person.[1]

General provisions

Constable in uniform – the role of community support officers

5.56   The powers that are conferred by s 30 on a constable in uniform to disperse groups and to remove under-16s to their place of residence may also, by virtue of s 33, be exercised by a community support officer where the chief officer of police of any police force has designated community support officers to perform this role under s 38 of the Police Reform Act 2002. Section 33 achieves this by adding the powers under s 30 to the list in Police Reform Act 2002, Sch 4 through a new para 4A. The Anti-social Behaviour Act 2003 also extends the power of the community support officer to detain persons for short periods[2] to cases where the officer has reason to believe that an offence has been committed under s 30. A person who refuses to give their name or address, or who makes off while under this detention, is liable to a fine not exceeding level 3 on the standard scale.

5.57   Further powers are extended to community support officers by the addition of a new para 4B to Sch 4 to the Police Reform Act 2002. This concerns the power of a constable under s 15 of the Crime and Disorder Act 1998 to remove a child to its place of residence under a child curfew notice. This is not strictly relevant to the powers in Part 4, and it is presumed that it has been included here simply as a matter of convenience.

Code of practice on s 30 powers

5.58   Many of the concerns that have been raised about the potential for heavy-handed use of the powers in s 30, which might at the extreme infringe the Human Rights Act 1998, could be allayed by clear guidance on how the powers are to be used.

5.59   This guidance is most likely to take the form of a statutory code of practice as provided for by s 34(1). This provides that:

'the Secretary of State may issue a code of practice about—

(a)   the giving or withdrawal of authorisations under s 30, and

(b)   the exercise of the powers conferred by s 30(3)–(6).

(2)   The Secretary of State may from time to time revise the whole or any part of a code of practice issued under this section.

(3)   The Secretary of State must lay any code of practice issued by him under this section, and any revisions of such a code, before Parliament.

(4)   In giving or withdrawing an authorisation under s 30, a relevant officer must have regard to any code of practice for the time being in force under this section.

(5)   In exercising the powers conferred by s 30(3)–(6), a constable in uniform or community support officer must have regard to any code of practice for the time being in force under this section.

(6)   A code of practice under this section may make different provision for different cases.'

---

[1]   *Hansard*, HC Standing Committee G, 13 May 2003, col 191.

[2]   This applies where they fail to give their name or address, or where the Community Support Officer has reasonable grounds to suspect that the name or address is false or inaccurate.

5.60 Given the risk to important rights under the Human Rights Act 1998 and the assurances that were given at many times during the course of the legislative process on the role of guidance, it could have been assumed that the power to issue a statutory code of practice would be invoked before Part 4 was brought into force. However, these powers came into force on 20 January 2004, at which time no code of practice had been made. It is anticipated that this will be produced in 2004 but not until after a draft code has been put out to consultation. Given the need for care in the use of these powers to avoid, in particular, any possible conflict with the Human Rights Act 1998, one might anticipate that the powers will be used sparingly until the code is available. A brief account of the powers is available in Home Office Circular 004/2004.[1]

---

[1] Available at http://www.homeoffice.gov.uk/docs2/hoc0404.html.

CHAPTER 6

FIREARMS

Introduction

6.1   Part 5 of the Act is designed to introduce a number of changes into the Firearms Act 1968 with a view to tackling the misuse of air weapons and imitation firearms. Also, this Part of the Act introduces stricter controls over especially dangerous air weapons.

6.2   In the Government's White Paper, *Respect and Responsibility – Taking a Stand Against Anti-social Behaviour*,[1] the Government notes that in 2001/02, there were 12,340 recorded offences where air weapons were used. Of these offences, 166 resulted in serious injury to a person and in two cases the injuries proved fatal.[2] Incidents involving injuries by airguns are still commonly reported.[3]

6.3   The Government also noted that airguns are used to cause property damage, injury to pets and, often, to shoot at people.[4]

6.4   In addition to misuse of air weapons, the Government noted that the misuse of replica weapons can cause serious alarm and fear. The Government stated that, in inner cities, the police estimate that 50% of the call-outs of armed response units result from a sighting of an imitation firearm in public. The Government expressed concern that there is a real risk that a person carrying an imitation firearm in public would be shot by the police if they appear to use it to threaten either the police or members of the public. The Government also suggested that there was evidence that replica firearms were used to threaten victims; also that young people in certain areas have taken to carrying imitation firearms as a fashion accessory and in order to intimidate other people.[5]

6.5   The Government noted a problem that certain air weapons, powered by a self-contained gas cartridge, can be converted to take ammunition from more conventional firearms. These weapons have a very realistic appearance and have become popular with criminals and have been used in a number of serious crimes. As a result, the Government is looking to ban the importation, sale and manufacture of these weapons. The Government proposed that, if people already owned these unconverted weapons, they required a licence for ownership.[6]

6.6   This is part of the Government's overall strategy to tackle gun crime in the UK.

6.7   Prior to the Government's White Paper, the Firearms Consultative Committee (FCC) addressed several of these issues in its 11th Annual Report published on the 19 March 2002.[7] The FCC is an independent body established by an Act of Parliament to keep under review the workings of the Firearms Acts.

---

[1]   Cm 5778 (March 2003).
[2]   Ibid, para 3.15.
[3]   *The Times*, 10 November 2003, p 14, 'Airgun incident. A girl of 12 was seriously injured after being shot by a rogue airgun pellet'.
[4]   Cm 5778, para 3.16.
[5]   Ibid, para 3.17.
[6]   Ibid, para 3.19.
[7]   HC Paper 501.

6.8   On air weapons, the FCC noted that the Government had rejected the idea of a licensing ownership of air weapons.[1] The FCC did not make any specific recommendation about increasing the age for ownership of such weapons, but expressed concern about the lack of education of the young concerning misuse of air weapons.[2] As part of these recommendations, they suggested that there should be greater public education and practical demonstrations of the safe use of airguns.[3] They did note that there were problems with the enforcement of the existing law. They considered that there should be changes in the existing law but that this should be clearly backed up by providing the resources for enforcement.[4] The FCC expressed the view that prosecution policy should not favour mere cautions and that the courts should be clearly involved in issues of airgun misuse;[5] moreover, in circumstances of misuse, that the weapon should be confiscated. The FCC went as far to recommend that air weapons should be forfeited in cases of misuse independently of whether criminal proceedings are instituted.[6]

6.9   On replica weapons and imitation firearms, the FCC noted similar problems as expressed by the Government concerning the misuse, and the proliferation of the misuse, of imitation and replica firearms.[7] The FCC noted that the existing law was to prevent the sale of blank-firing imitation weapons that could be converted to fire live ammunition.[8] They went on to note that there may be legitimate uses for imitation firearms, for example for historical re-enactments, as toys and for collectors, and that any interference with ownership of such weapons had to be proportional to any legitimate aim under the Human Rights Act 1998.[9] They recommended that they would support a measure for the carrying of imitation firearms in public that was consistent with that for knives and other offensive weapons (ie the defence of lawful authority or reasonable excuse).[10]

6.10   The Government proposed to increase the age for the lawful ownership of an air weapon to 17 and to tighten the law concerning adult supervision. There would also be a new offence of having an air weapon in a public place without lawful authority or reasonable excuse; also, to create a new offence of having an imitation firearm in a public place without lawful authority or reasonable excuse. Air weapons and imitation firearms could also be confiscated.

Table 6.1
Summary of Part 5 of the Act

Section Number	Summary	Comment
37	Prohibition of possession of air weapons or imitations fire arms in a public place.	This creates an arrestable offence for carrying an air weapon or imitation firearm in a public place without lawful authority or a reasonable excuse.

[1] HC Paper 501, paras 9.1 and 9.2.
[2] Ibid, paras 9.5–9.12.
[3] Ibid.
[4] Ibid, para 9.19.
[5] Ibid, paras 9.20–9.21.
[6] Ibid, para 9.22.
[7] Ibid, paras 3.6–3.8.
[8] Ibid, para 3.10.
[9] Ibid, paras 3.16–3.17.
[10] Ibid, paras 3.33–3.35.

Table 6.1 Summary of Part 5 of the Act		
Section Number	**Summary**	**Comment**
38	Imposition of new age limits on acquisition and possession of air weapons.	This raises the age from 14–17 for ownership of air weapons and ammunition but allows for supervised use by adults of person under 17.
39	Prohibition of certain types of especially dangerous air weapons.	This prohibits air weapons that use gas cartridges as propellant mechanisms because of their easy conversion to use of conventional ammunition.

The social problem

6.11   The key social problem concerning the use and ownership of firearms relates to an increasing fear of gun violence and the manifestation of firearms on the streets in the UK. There is the increasing use of firearms in crime and the link of the use of firearms in the trade in illegal drugs and by youth gangs.[1] Also, as a result of misuse of air weapons and replica weapons, there is a growing concern that Britain is developing a 'fashionable' gun culture that mimics that seen in the USA. This may be a consequence of social and cultural changes promoting violence. The use, and the threat of use, of weapons generally instils fear and disruption in communities.

6.12   Part of this problem seems to be the increasing misuse, and the unsupervised and careless use, of air weapons by youths. This creates a nuisance and damage to property, with the attendant risk of serious harm or injury to people.

The legal problem

6.13   The legal problem is to develop an approach whereby the law can achieve the aims outlined by the Government above while accommodating the lawful use of such weapons in controlled circumstances. The law should not merely act as a blunt instrument, but instead accommodate an educational aspect to firearms use, to create a notion of a responsible citizen, rather than merely to alienate groups who may resort to the use of other weapons. Moreover, although the law may be fairly easy to develop and a great deal of consensus exists about its development, there has to be clear and robust enforcement of such law in order for it to be effective.

---

[1]   See *The Independent*, 11 October 2003, p 1, 'A very British way of life and death'; *The Independent on Sunday*, 26 October 2003, p 12, 'MPs press for ban on the sale of replica guns'; *The Times*, 5 January 2003, p 12, 'Silenced by the rule of the gun'.

Existing legislation

6.14 The ownership, licensing and use of firearms in the UK is regulated by the Firearms Act 1968. This Act deals with the ownership and use of air weapons and of replica or imitation firearms.

Parliamentary session 2002–03

6.15 In the Standing Committee on 20 May 2003, James Paice MP (Conservative) tabled an amendment based on the suggestion that that air gun misuse is being exaggerated. He referred to statistics suggesting that 'air weapon crime increased by 21%, but non-air weapon crime increased by 35%' and that '84% of all air weapons offences resulted in no injury to anybody'. He added that s 19 of the Firearms Act 1968 already made it a criminal offence to carry a loaded air weapon in a public place. In response, Dari Taylor MP (Labour) referred to an accident with an air gun that led to the death of a 14-year-old boy. Subsequently, the amendment was withdrawn.

6.16 It was agreed that the age limits and the prohibition on certain types of air weapons, as amended, should stand as part of the Bill.

6.17 In the Committee stage of the second reading in the House of Lords on 7 September 2003, Earl Attlee (Conservative) introduced an amendment to ensure that the age at which a person can use an air weapon without supervision remains at 14 rather that 17. Lord Moynihan (Conservative) argued that increasing the age limit would prevent young people from taking part in shooting sports, by making it illegal for them to carry guns in public without supervision. Lord Moynihan argued that the clause restricts the Labour Party manifesto promise of not acting to restrict the sport of shooting. In reply, Baroness Scotland stated that there had been an increase by 21% in the misuse of air weapons in 2001–02, and that the ability of the police to arrest those carrying such weapons in public would help to tackle this. Baroness Scotland argued that the amendments to exempt air weapons if they were carried in a cover and being carried directly to or from a legitimate shooting event were not practical and that the approach of requiring adult supervision was correct. The clause was agreed to.

6.18 In the report stage on 31 November 2003, Lord Dixon-Smith (Conservative) moved an amendment to set the age limit for ownership and transport of airguns to 16. Lord Dixon-Smith said that 16-year-olds could do many things and if they are treated responsibly they will behave responsibly. In reply, the Minister noted the concern of shooting organisations but stated that the Government had allowed for the use of air weapons by young people on private property to alleviate this. Baroness Scotland said that 17 had been chosen as the new age limit in order to catch the group that was most likely to be involved in misuse of air weapons, adding that 17 is consistent with other age limits imposed by firearms laws.

6.19 Lord Monyihan followed by introducing an amendment to allow persons under 17 to carry air weapons from home to a place of legal use without adult supervision so long as it was in a locked case and the ammunition was separate. Lord Moynihan was concerned that the new Act could seriously jeopardise the participation of the young in shooting sports. He reminded the House that there had not been a single offence concerning a sports shooter of 14–17 concerning misuse of their right to carry their weapon. The Minister replied that someone under 17 could carry an air weapon if they had a reasonable excuse to do so and were supervised by an adult. The Minister argued that the concern of the Government was not for those sports shooters who act improperly but about those who might take the air weapon from them. The Minister suggested that the raft of amendments and conditions would make it very difficult for the police to enforce the law effectively. The amendments were defeated.

The provisions in detail

Possession of air weapon or imitation firearm in a public place

6.20   Section 37 of the Act amends s 19 of the Firearms Act 1968 ('the 1968 Act'), which created an offence of carrying a firearm in a public place. Section 37 extends the prohibition in s 19 of the 1968 Act to include air weapons and imitation firearms. The amendment means that it will be an offence to carry an air weapon, whether loaded or not, or any other firearm, whether loaded or not, together with ammunition suitable for use in that firearm, or an imitation firearm in a public place without lawful authority or without a reasonable excuse. An imitation firearm is defined by s 57(4) of the 1968 Act. This definition covers anything that has the appearance of being a firearm, whether or not it is capable of discharging a bullet or shot.

6.21   This amendment is inserted in s 37(2).

6.22   Subsection (3) provides that carrying a firearm or imitation firearm, as defined above, makes this an arrestable offence by adding the new offence to para 5 (now 5A) of Sch 1A to the Police and Criminal Evidence Act 1984. This will be subject to the maximum penalty of 6 months' imprisonment.

Air weapons: age-limits

6.23   Section 38 amends ss 22, 23 and 24 of the 1968 Act in order to raise the age of a person who may own an air weapon and add further restrictions on when such a weapon may be used when unsupervised by an adult.

6.24   Subsection (2) raises the present age-limit for acquisition and possession of firearms by minors from 14 years of age, under s 22 of the 1968 Act, to 17 years of age.

6.25   This means that no person under 17 will be able to own or have an air gun in their possession at any time unless supervised by someone who is at least 21 or as part of an approved shooting club or shooting gallery.

6.26   Subsection (3) provides that 14–16-year-olds, inclusive, will be permitted to have air weapons unsupervised when on private land, provided that they have the consent of the occupier. However, it will be an offence for the minors to shoot beyond the boundaries of the land. Under subs (5), on summary conviction, improper use of an air weapon on private land could lead to a fine up to level 3 on the standard scale; this is £1,000 at present.

6.27   However, subs (4) modifies s 24(4) of the 1968 Act and makes it an offence to give an air weapon or ammunition to a person under 17.

Prohibition of certain types of weapon

6.28   Section 39 of the Act provides for a ban on air weapons that use a self-contained gas cartridge system that acts as the propellant. These weapons are vulnerable to conversion to fire conventional gunpowder-based ammunition. Subsection (3) of s 39 adds these types of weapons to s 5(1) (weapons subject to general prohibition) of the 1968 Act, thereby making them prohibited weapons which cannot be possessed, purchased, acquired, manufactured, sold or transferred without the authority of the Secretary of State of the Home Office.

6.29   Subsection (4) does allow for existing owners of such weapons to retain them, provided that they obtain a firearms certificate from the police. However, subs (5) prevents the application of subs (4) to possession in the circumstances described in s 8 of the 1968 Act, which involves authorised dealings.

6.30 Subsection (6) of s 39 creates an order making power for the Secretary of State for the Home Office to prohibit or provide controls in respect of any air weapon that appears to the Secretary of State to be especially dangerous.

Conclusions

6.31 In general, these reforms have been welcomed and seem a sensible solution to part of the problem with gun crime. Their success will depend on a combination of effective enforcement and compliance combined with cultural, social, political and educational changes concerning the use of violence and firearms in society. The ban on the self-contained gas cartridge weapons is being introduced in two stages. From 20 January 2004 making, selling, purchasing, transferring or acquiring these weapons becomes an offence. Then from 1 May 2004 it will be an offence to possess one of these weapons without a firearms certificate and owners have until that date to either obtain a certificate or surrender the weapon to the police.

CHAPTER 7

THE ENVIRONMENT

Introduction

7.1 Part 6 of the Anti-social Behaviour Act 2003 (ss 40–56) consists of a series of provisions which enable the appropriate authorities to respond to a range of behaviours: excessive noise, graffiti, fly-posting and the illegal dumping of household and industrial waste, all of which can be characterised as having undesirable environmental impacts.

7.2 This Part of the Act therefore concentrates on one particular aspect of the range of behaviour which is commonly described as anti-social and responds to the Government's belief that anti-social activities which damage the local environment have a disproportionate effect on the character of an area with damaging social and economic consequences.

7.3 The Office of the Deputy Prime Minister, for instance, explains that:

'Dirty and dangerous places encourage graffiti, vandalism and anti-social behaviour, which in turn undermine public confidence in them and lead people to avoid them. An unattractive and threatening local environment encourages people to use their cars for short journeys and to move to a better area if they can. It can discourage investment and lead to abandonment and dereliction. A high quality local environment is a big influence in making people visit a place, spend money and invest in it. Conversely a low quality environment can lead to places becoming stigmatised and drive people, businesses and investment away.'[1]

7.4 ENCAMS, an environmental campaigning charity, comments, in its first annual survey of environmental quality:[2]

'In recent years, there has been an increasing recognition of the links between neglect, wilful environmental damage, and crime. In particular, these forms of poor local environmental quality send out signals to law-abiding people and businesses that can cause them to become fearful of crime. Research also indicates that these environmental problems may also signal to criminals that policing (in its various forms) in the affected areas is less vigilant, and that offences are easier to commit.'

7.5 The provisions of this Part of the Act respond to these concerns. They utilise a similar range of preventative and punitive techniques as used elsewhere in the Act, such as closure orders and fixed penalty notices and extend the powers of local authorities and community support officers enabling rapid response to environmental nuisances. The focus is on providing local authorities with the necessary legal tools to tackle environmental problems and not on developing the strategic role of local authorities, managing their performance or on publicising to the public the existence and extent of the powers available to local authorities

7.6 The Government has also used the opportunity provided by the Act to remedy some difficulties in the effective implementation of current environmental protection legislation. The

---

[1] ODPM, *Living Places, Cleaner, Safer, Greener* (October 2002).
[2] ENCAMS, *The Environmental Quality Survey for England, 2001–2002* (September 2002).

Department for Environment, Food and Rural Affairs (DEFRA) reviewed the current legislative framework and concluded:

'... that the current extensive set of powers, duties and guidance is not working as effectively as it should be. Some of the reasons for this failure include confusion and misunderstanding within and between service providers, an unawareness of the responsibilities associated with the right to have a clean and safe local environment and inadequate and unmanageable powers for tackling irresponsible and anti-social behaviour.'[1]

7.7   DEFRA was concerned to create the legal basis for local authorities to assume strategic responsibility for the environment. It suggested that there were three principal powers that must be in place for a local authority to play a strategic role. These are:

–   the power to enforce all other relevant bodies to meet their respective duties;
–   the power to intervene and take remedial action when the other bodies fail to meet their duties; and
–   the power to recover any costs incurred during intervention.[2]

7.8   Moreover, it highlighted the current weaknesses in the legislative framework:

'At present these powers are limited because they are: made up of disparate provisions within various statutes; only applicable for dealing with narrowly defined aspects of public space and the local environment; or untested and so wide-ranging that local authorities are not yet sure of the power's suitability for dealing with specific problems.'

7.9   Whilst the provisions of this Part of the Act address some of the specific legislative weaknesses identified by DEFRA, they do not provide for all of the suggestions for legal reform.

7.10   Part of the Government justification for the powers within the Act is the increased public awareness of environmental crime. *Crime in England and Wales*[3] uses the British Crime Survey and the number of crimes recorded by the police to provide a comprehensive account of the latest patterns and trends in high volume crimes. The statistics demonstrate that, over the last 7 years, there has been an increasing awareness of environmental anti-social behaviour. Since 1996 the proportion of people who say that vandalism, graffiti and other acts of property damage are a very or fairly big problem in their area has increased from 23% to 35% in 2002/03 and those reporting rubbish and litter as a problem rose from 26% to 33% in 2002/03.

7.11   Research indicates that there is a considerable variation in the spatial distribution of environmental problems. So ENCAMS, for instance, points out that their survey indicated that most areas are 'completely or substantially unaffected by these environmental crimes. However, on a small proportion of the sites where they are present, the problems are intense'. Noise nuisance is disproportionately suffered by those living in medium/high-rise flats and exposure to noise is higher in wards which suffer from greater levels of deprivation, including the 10% most deprived wards in England.[4]

7.12   *Crime in England and Wales* also suggests differential experience of environmental anti-social behaviour, indicating that, in 2002/03, 52% of people living in the inner city saw rubbish or litter as a very or fairly big problem compared with 19% of those who lived in rural areas. 54% of those living in the inner city saw vandalism, graffiti and other deliberate damage to property as a very or fairly big problem compared with 20% of those who lived in rural areas.[5]

---

[1]   DEFRA Consultation Paper, *Living Places – Powers, Rights and Responsibilities* (October 2002).
[2]   Ibid.
[3]   *Crime in England and Wales 2002/03* (Home Office Statistical Bulletin, July 2003).
[4]   *Neighbour Noise Public Opinion Research to Assess its Nature, Extent and Significance*, Research Study conducted for DEFRA by MORI Social Research Institute in October 2003.
[5]   *Crime in England and Wales 2002/03* (Home Office Statistical Bulletin, July 2003), Table 8.13.

7.13 There seems to have been a general welcome for the new powers provided in this Part of the Act. The Local Government Association, in its briefing prepared for the Lords Report Stage, commented:

'The appearance of the local environment is a priority for local people and a poor environment encourages anti-social behaviour and fuels the fear of crime. The LGA supports the additional powers provided in the Bill, which provide local authorities with more 'tools' to maintain and care for the environment.'[1]

7.14 However, the Local Government Association makes it clear that:

'further mechanisms are needed to take forward the remaining proposals set out in DEFRA's review. In particular we would like to see local authorities being given a more strategic responsibility for managing the local environment.'[2]

7.15 Responses in Parliament have also been generally supportive. Dissent seems to have focused upon proposals to prevent the sale of aerosol paint to under 18s, a measure that the Government rowed back on. Other concerns which have been expressed relate to the adequacy of resources and the need, not just for legislative powers, but a commitment to enforcement.

7.16 Table 7.1 summarises the provisions of this Part of the Act:

Table 7.1

The provisions of Part 6 of the Anti-social Behaviour Act 2003

Section	Summary	Comment
40–41	Closure of noisy premises	New power for local authorities to close licensed premises and events for 24 hours
42	Dealing with noise at night	Amendments to the Noise Act 1996 which allow all local authorities to respond to night time noise
43–47	Penalty notices for graffiti and fly-posting	New power for local authorities and community support officers to issue fixed penalty notices of £50 for graffiti and fly-posting
48–52	Graffiti removal notices	New power for local authorities to serve notices requiring that graffiti is removed or works carried out in default
53	Display of advertisements in breach of regulations	Increase in fine levels from level 3 to level 4
54	Sale of aerosol paint to children	New preventive measure which creates an offence of selling aerosol point to children under sixteen
55–56	Unlawfully deposited litter	Amends Control of Pollution (Amendment) Act 1989 and Environmental Protection Act 1990 to extend the powers of local authorities as waste collection authorities

[1] *Anti-social Behaviour Bill Lords Report Stage Briefing* (Local Government Association, 23 October 2003).
[2] *Anti-social Behaviour Bill Briefing for Commons remaining stage* (Local Government Association, 17 November 2003).

The problem of noise

7.17 Noise pollution is an increasingly significant environmental problem. Findings of a survey of more than 5,000 people carried out by DEFRA in 2000 indicated that 21% of respondents reported that noise spoilt their home life to some extent, with 8% saying that their home life was spoilt either 'quite a lot' or 'totally'.[1]

7.18 The research found that only a small proportion of respondents who were bothered by noise from neighbours complained to the environmental health department of the local authority, which DEFRA suggests may mean that noise complaint statistics may greatly underestimate the extent of community dissatisfaction.

7.19 Statistics from the Chartered Institute of Environmental Health for England and Wales covering noise complaints per million of the population show that domestic complaints rose from 2,264 in 1990/91 to 5,001 in 2000/01 with construction/demolition accounting for 325 in 2000/01 and industrial/commercial recorded at 1,381 in the same year.

7.20 In October 2003, DEFRA has published public opinion research on the nature, extent and significance of neighbour noise.[2] The findings indicate that nearly two thirds of the population hear noise from their neighbours to some extent. Fewer are actually annoyed by it, although annoyance occurs among just fewer than half of those who hear noise, or close to one in three among the population as a whole. One in seven of the 6,116 respondents identified neighbour noise as a problem that affects their quality of life, fewer than are annoyed by litter, vandalism and graffiti but comparable to abandoned vehicles, street drinking and drug abuse. Amongst particular groups, such as residents in high-density flats, it is one of the most significant quality of life issues.

7.21 Whilst neighbour noise is not as widespread as some noises, such as traffic, neighbour noise causes a great deal of annoyance. Neighbour noise is irregular, has no apparent utility and is seen as demonstrating a lack of consideration. Loud music, shouting and banging are the most annoying sounds, with 'one-off' noises, such are parties, being seen as less of a problem.

7.22 The research emphasises the social context of noise:

'Noise disputes often involve a package of problems with a neighbour (including litter, dog fouling and rubbish) with noise the focal point for these wider grievances. These need to be addressed concurrently.'[3]

7.23 The research indicated a link between tenure and noise:

'Noise sufferers tend to be in social rented accommodation while noise makers tend to be in either social rented or private rented accommodation. Many noise sufferers feel that private-renting tenants do not care about their neighbours or the area given the short term nature of their stay. There is also resentment in areas of mixed tenure where there are different "rules" depending on people's tenure status. There also appears to be a particular problem with private landlords who are perceived to not be interested in problems relating to their tenant.'[4]

7.24 Respondents to the survey identified speedy response to the initial complaint and expeditious dispute resolution as their priorities. There was also widespread support for new powers of intervention, including fines and evictions. However, stakeholders such as social landlords and environmental health officers stressed 'the need for an impact assessment of any new legislation to ensure that is practicable, resourced and enforceable on the ground'.[5]

---

[1]   The UK National Noise Attitude Survey (NAS) 1999/2000.

[2]   *Neighbour Noise Public Opinion Research to Assess its Nature, Extent and Significance* Research Study conducted for DEFRA by MORI Social Research Institute in October 2003.

[3]   Ibid.

[4]   Ibid.

[5]   Ibid.

Noise policy

7.25 Noise policy in the UK is being driven by European developments, in particular the recent European Union Directive 2002/49/EC, which imposes a requirement to assess environmental noise exposure levels, to map noise levels in local areas and to produce appropriate action plans. In response, the Government has developed a strategic approach to problem of noise which has four elements: research, design, information and enhanced legal remedies.

7.26 First, it intends to continue to research both the extent of the problem and the particular characteristics of noise makers and noise sufferers so that policy can be appropriately targeted. Secondly, it intends to reduce the level of domestic noise pollution through improving sound insulation standards via building regulations, the 'Decent Homes' initiative and the reform of housing grants. Thirdly, it intends to increase the information about noise available to consumers when buying domestic equipment by building upon European labelling initiatives, including the expansion of the energy labels on domestic goods scheme, to include air conditioners, the transposition of a Directive covering noise labelling, and limits for outdoor equipment and increased investment in the European Flower 'Ecolabel', which indicates products with high environmental and performance standards.

7.27 Finally, the Government has decided to improve the anti-noise legislative framework to allow for more speedy and effective interventions to stop excessive and inappropriate noise and uses this Act as the legislative vehicle to achieve this.

The legal framework

Statutory nuisance

7.28 A statutory nuisance is a matter which is listed within s 79 of the Environmental Protection Act 1990 which causes nuisance or is prejudicial to health. Section 79 also requires that local authorities investigate complaints of statutory nuisances. The Act enables local authorities to issue abatement notices and courts can impose penalties upon people who fail to abate the nuisance. If a local authority fails to act an individual may apply to the magistrates' court for an abatement order.

7.29 Under ss 80 and 81 of the Environmental Protection Act 1990 (as amended by the Noise and Statutory Nuisance Act 1993), local authorities have a duty to deal with any noise which they consider to be a statutory nuisance. The Act includes powers which enable local authorities to seize people's music equipment. Statutory nuisance has provided the traditional legal control on noisy environments. However, complaints about noise require particularly speedy responses and concerns have been raised as to the amount of time it can take for complaints to be dealt with under the statutory nuisance regime.

Public nuisance

7.30 Public nuisance provides another potential avenue for the control of noise. Like statutory nuisance, public nuisance is a criminal offence. However, it is not defined by statute but is a common law offence. It is committed when a person 'does an act not warranted by law, or omits to discharge a legal duty, if the effect of the act or omission is to endanger life, health, property, morals, or comfort of the public, or to obstruct the public in the exercise or employment of rights common to all Her Majesty's subjects'.[1]

7.31 This has been described as 'an amorphous and unsatisfactory area of the law covering an ill-assorted collection of wrongs, some of which have little or no association with tort and only appear

---

[1] *Archbold's Criminal Pleading, Evidence and Practice* (Sweet & Maxwell, 1999).

to fill a gap in the criminal law'.[1] The particular difficulty which may arise when considering whether noise can be controlled as a public nuisance concerns the number of people who need to be affected before the noise could be described as a public nuisance.

7.32 Local authorities can enforce the law of public nuisance, in particular by obtaining injunctions utilising s 222 of the Local Government Act 1972. However, the problem of noise requires legal control which is flexible and speedy. Public nuisance does not provide an opportunity for enforcement officers to shut down noise at the time of its occurrence. The Noise Act 1996 was designed to achieve this.

The Noise Act 1996

7.33 The Noise Act 1996 created a new Night Noise Offence (NNO), for neighbour noise occurring between the hours of 11pm and 7am, clarified procedures for the seizure and forfeiture of noise-making equipment and introduced a fixed penalty scheme for breach of warning notices made under the Act. The NNO was additional, and complementary, to the existing statutory nuisance procedures within the Environmental Protection Act 1990.

7.34 Any local authority in England, Wales and Northern Ireland may choose to adopt the NNO. However, certain resource-intensive criteria must be fulfilled if it does so: it must do so for the whole of its geographical area; the local authority must appoint an officer who must take reasonable steps to investigate complaints between 11pm and 7am hours. These requirements proved to be significant deterrents to the adoption of the offence.

7.35 The Government honoured a commitment to review the effectiveness of the Noise Act 1996 2 years after its implementation. The review[2] found that there had been a very low adoption rate of the powers provided by the Act with only 14 local authorities taking up the powers on offer. The main explanations offered for the low adoption rate were:

– that there was no local demand (38%);
– that the local authority had insufficient resources to fund the full requirements of the 1996 Act (55%); and
– that their current service was adequate (41%).

7.36 The Chartered Institute of Environmental Health provided additional explanations for the failure of the NNO in their response to the Government review:

'... it offers only one real advantage – that of short-circuiting an often protracted judicial process with the option of a fixed penalty notice – over the powers co-existing under Pt III of the 1990 Environmental Protection Act. Otherwise, the scope of the NNO is actually more limited, ie in the hours during which it is applicable, in the origin of the noise to which it relates and in the use of a fixed sound pressure level as an intervention threshold, this latter feature imposing a resource requirement which few authorities have been able to justify by reference to their pattern of noise complaints. ... By contrast, the long-standing health-based standard of statutory nuisance is applicable at any time of the day or night, in relation to all classes of premises, and to a wider variety of noises, including vibration. While the investigation of statutory nuisances is, like that of complaints under the 1996 Act, mandatory, with no need under the 1990 Act actually to measure a sound pressure level that investigation can be delayed if officers are not available. Evidence can be, and often is, collected later. That may not put a stop to a nuisance immediately, of course, but nor necessarily does an intervention under the 1996 Act while an abatement notice at least normally prohibits recurrence and for all these reasons, Pt III continues to provide the powers-of-choice in nearly all cases, including (unexpectedly and unexplained by the research) those occurring in districts which have adopted the 1996 Act.'

---

[1]   Deacon et al, *Markesinis and Deakin's Tort Law*, 5th edn (OUP, 2003).
[2]   Review of Implementation of the Noise Act 1996 (DEFRA, 2000):
       http://www.DEFRA.gov.uk/environment/consult/reviewofnoise.

7.37 Legal control of domestic noise levels should also be considered in the context of housing-related anti-social behaviour powers.[1] All landlords, whether social or private, have powers to take action against tenants who are breaching their tenancy agreement. This may include injunctions to prevent noise, which can be highly effective preventive measures which reduce the nuisance caused whilst allowing people to keep their homes. Social landlords (local authorities, housing action trusts and housing associations) can ask the courts to attach a power of arrest to such injunctions if there is violence, or a threat of violence. Eviction is available to be used by landlords as a last resort against those who continue to make their neighbours' lives a misery despite warnings.

The new provisions in detail

7.38 Within this Part of the Act there are three different measures designed to reduce noise pollution and address public concern about the control of noise. The first provides for the temporary closure of noisy premises, the second improves the night-time noise offence and the third allows local authorities to use monies raised by fixed penalty notices to fund local noise services.

Temporary closure of noisy premises

7.39 Section 40 of the Act allows the chief executive officer of a local authority to make a closure order, for a period which cannot exceed 24 hours,[2] in relation to licensed premises, or premises in respect of which a temporary event notice is in effect, if he or she reasonably believes that a public nuisance is being caused by noise coming from the premises, and that the closure of the premises is necessary to prevent that nuisance.

7.40 The Government considered that:

'... the decision whether a public nuisance is occurring should be left to the investigating environmental health officer's judgment, based on his skills, experience and training ... Such a discretion would allow the investigating officer to take into account not only the volume and duration of the noise, but also the characteristics of the neighbourhood; the type and frequency of the noise; the time of day or – more likely – night when it occurs; and what alternative measures could be taken. He could also assess whether the licensee is taking reasonable steps to control the noise.'[3]

7.41 The section requires the noise to come from within the premises in question. In response to the observation that, to a great extent, noise nuisance is generated outside of the licensed premises or entertainment venue as patrons leave, the Government explained:

'As regards areas outside premises, clearly, the local authority enforcement officers will want to work closely with the police. They are, after all, responsible for dealing with noise in the streets. They have a range of powers already to deal with the order and supporting guidance, including, controversially, fixed-penalty notices. There is a working relationship and we expect that to develop. Furthermore, it falls to them to deal with the public order aspects of noise nuisance on the streets and in the community.'[4]

7.42 The power to make closure orders may be, and is likely to be, delegated to environmental health officers who are experts in the policing of noise.[5] As the Government pointed out in debate in standing committee in the Lords, environmental health officers have the training, skill and expertise for dealing with noise, public nuisance and abatement orders. The delegation power is

---

[1]   See the discussion of Part 2 of this Act in Chapter 3.

[2]   Section 40(3)(a).

[3]   *Hansard*, HC Deb, 12 November 2003, col 1454.

[4]   Ibid.

[5]   Section 41(2).

limited to environmental health officers. The Government did not want to see people without such experience exercising what they described as a 'stringent, Draconian statutory power'. [1]

7.43   A closure order is defined as an order which requires that the premises must be kept closed during a specified period which cannot exceed 24 hours and which begins when the manager of the premises receives written notice of the order.[2] The order may be cancelled by written notice to the manager of the premises, and must be cancelled as soon as reasonably practical if it is no longer necessary.[3]

7.44   The limited duration of the power reflects the fact that its purpose is to stop the noise. As the Government pointed out:

> 'It is not of itself a penalty or a warning; it seeks to ensure that the disturbance caused by the noise stops. … the 24-hour period seeks to ensure that the particular nuisance that is being caused is ended instantly.'

If the disturbance ceases there is no reason why the premises cannot re-open with the permission of the enviornmental health officer prior to the expiry of the 24 hours. As the Government Minister pointed out in the Lords:

> 'within 20 minutes of the order having been issued, everything might have calmed down with everyone having gone home for the night. Therefore, there is no reason why the pub should not open for the normal, quiet, decent regulars the next morning.'[4]

7.45   It is an offence to open premises in contravention of a closure order[5] and if found guilty a person is liable to imprisonment for a term not exceeding 3 months or a fine not exceeding £20,000, or both.[6] However, there is probably more deterrent value in the requirement that notice of the closure order must be given to the licensing authority, which will undoubtedly take the making of closure orders into account when making future decisions on licences.

7.46   The section provides environmental health officers with very similar powers to those given to the police as a result of amendments to the Licensing Act 1964 made by the Criminal Justice and Police Act 2001.[7] To make a closure order under that Act, a senior police officer must reasonably believe that there is likely to be disorder in, or in the vicinity of and related to, the premises in question, and that closure is necessary in the interests of public safety, including customers; or that there is disorder already taking place in, or in the vicinity of and related to, the premises, and closure is necessary in the interests of public safety; or that he reasonably believes that a disturbance is being caused by excessive noise emitted from the premises, and that closure is necessary to prevent the disturbance. So a closure order can be made for example where there is noise disturbance to local residents living in the neighbourhood of the premises concerned.

7.47   The Joint Committee on Human Rights considered that s 40 of the Anti-social Behaviour Act 2003 raised issues relating to the right to a fair hearing under ECHR, Art 6(1) and the right to peaceful enjoyment of possessions under Art 1 of Protocol 1 of the ECHR, since it did not require the intervention of the court and there were insufficient safeguards built into the section to ensure that a fair balance was struck between the interests of the community and the rights of the owner or occupier of the premises.[8]

---

[1]   *Hansard*, HL Deb, 7 October 2003, col 232.

[2]   Section 40(3).

[3]   Section 41(1).

[4]   *Hansard*, HL Deb, 7 October 2003, col 231.

[5]   Section 40(4).

[6]   Section 40(5).

[7]   Section 17 of the Criminal Justice and Police Act 2001 inserted new ss 179A, 179B, 179C, 179D, 179E, 179F, 179G, 179H, 179I, 179J and 179K into the Licensing Act 1964.

[8]   Joint Committee on Human Rights Thirteenth Report.

7.48 It considered that the power given by the Act to the local authority went beyond the similar power given to senior police officers to make closure orders. The committee had, when considering the Criminal Justice and Police Act 2001, decided that its provision was justifiable as a proportionate response to the need to protect public safety and prevent disorder. The provision allowed the order to be made only if the officer reasonably believed that closure was 'necessary in the interests of public safety' and the order lasted only for a day at a time unless a magistrates' court made a further order after a proper hearing.

7.49 The Government responded to the Committee's criticism by explaining that, in its opinion, the use of the power in the Anti-social Behaviour Act 2003 is a control of the use of possessions under Art 1 of Protocol 1 rather than a deprivation of property, and that, 'the temporary interference with the rights of the licensee would strike a fair balance between the public interest in controlling noise nuisance and the protection of individual rights'.[1]

7.50 In view of the very limited duration of the closure order and the requirement that it must be necessary to stop a nuisance caused by noise, the Committee accepted the provisions struck an appropriate balance between the public interest and individual rights, as required by Art 1 of Protocol 1 of the ECHR.

7.51 The Committee also accepted that the lack of court scrutiny of the power would not be incompatible with Art 6 because the limited interference with civil rights resulting from the exercise of the power would not amount to a 'determination' of those civil rights. Any steps taken subsequently by the licensing authority (for example, to deny a licence to the licensee in the future) would be subject to court proceedings which would guarantee compliance with Art 6.

Dealing with noise at night

7.52 Section 48 of the Anti-social Behaviour Act 2003 removes the need for local authorities to provide a 24-hour on-call service for the whole of its area in order to be able to access the powers of the Noise Act 1996 and thus dismantles the significant and often disproportionate resource barrier to local authorities taking action against night-time noise.

7.53 It does this by amending the Noise Act 1996 by substituting a power to investigate complaints of noise at night for the original duty[2] to investigate complaints.

7.54 As a result, the Government is able to make the NNO available nationally. This is achieved by introducing a new s 1 into the Noise Act 1996 which provides that ss 2–9 of the Act apply to the area of every local authority in England and Wales. Prior to the implementation of this section of the Act, ss 2–9 of the Noise Act 1996 only applied to a local authority if the authority had passed a resolution that it did or the Secretary of State had provided that it did by order.

7.55 It is intended that the Noise Act 1996, as amended, will provide a national, flexible and speedy system to respond to individual's complaints of noise from dwellings between 11 pm and 7 am. If environmental health officers are satisfied, following investigation of a complaint, that there is noise which exceeds permitted levels,[3] they may serve a warning notice on the person responsible for the noise.[4] Anyone responsible for noise from the dwelling which exceeds the permitted level of noise, following the service of the warning notice, will be guilty of an offence.

7.56 Offenders can be served with fixed penalty notices which offer the opportunity of discharging any liability to conviction for that offence by payment of a fixed penalty within 14 days of service of the fixed penalty notice.

---

[1]   Letter from the Home Secretary appended to the JCHR Thirteenth Report.
[2]   Contained in s 2 of the Noise Act 1996.
[3]   The permitted level of noise is set by regulation.
[4]   Noise Act 1996, s 3.

7.57   The Government Minister explained:

> 'We want to make the powers as easy to use as we can because the fact that they have been adoptive has
> militated against local authorities taking such action. Increasingly, when these powers are taken together
> with some of those to deal with noisy licensed premises under the licensing legislation, we will begin to
> have a coherent set of powers that really can help to attack the tremendous nuisance caused by excessive
> noise. Some people have to live with noise day in, day out – or rather night in, night out – which has a
> detrimental effect on their well-being.'

Fixed penalty receipts

7.58   A final amendment to the provisions of the Noise Act 1996 was introduced by the
Government in the Report Stage in the Lords. The amendment[1] substitutes a new s 9(4)–(4F) for
the original provision which provided that sums received by a local authority under the fixed
penalty scheme must be paid to the Secretary of State. From the implementation of this section of
the Anti-social Behaviour Act 2003, local authorities will be able to use sums they receive as penalty
receipts for the purpose of carrying out functions under the Noise Act 1996 and for functions
which are to be specified in regulations made by the Secretary of State.

7.59   The amendment makes it clear that the regulatory power is broad enough to allow the
Secretary of State to permit receipts to be used for any local authority function. This was explained
as enabling the Government to consider giving additional flexibility in future in the use of such
receipts by local authorities.[2] The Secretary of State will also be able to request, from local
authorities for monitoring purposes, information on the level and use of such income.[3]

7.60   The change is expected to have two benefits:

> 'First it will encourage local authorities to make more use of the night noise offence by way of fixed
> penalty notices, and secondly it will provide consistency with the proposed handling of receipts from
> fixed penalty notices issued for graffiti and fly-posting.'[4]

Graffiti and fly-posting

The problem

7.61   ENCAMS, the environmental campaigning charity responsible for the 'Keep Britain Tidy'
campaign, defines graffiti as 'any informal or illegal marks, drawings or paintings that have been
deliberately made by a person or persons on any physical element comprising the outdoor
environment, with a view to communicating some message or symbol etc to others'.[5]

7.62   Their environmental quality survey published in September 2002[6] suggested that graffiti
levels for the whole country were, overall, satisfactory, that graffiti is a problem in particular areas
and is a greater problem in London than in any other region. Even in London, the overall standard
was satisfactory, with graffiti being either absent or light on just over 80% of transects, although
there was a significant minority of sites on which members of the public would have found graffiti
to be either noticeable or obtrusive.

7.63   Fly-posting is the display of advertising material on buildings and street furniture without
the consent of the owner, and contrary to the law. The ENCAMS environmental survey found that

---

[1]   Section 42(5).

[2]   *Hansard*, HL Deb, 3 November 2003, col 577.

[3]   Section 42(5).

[4]   *Hansard*, HL Deb, 3 November 2003, col 577.

[5]   On www.ENCAMS.org.uk.

[6]   ENCAMS, *The Environmental Quality Survey for England, 2001–2002* (September 2002).

the most widespread form of fly-posting was small stickers (placed on lamp posts and highways posts), followed by entertainments posters (mainly on vacant shop fronts and public utility boxes, and sometimes on walls and railings). Other forms of fly-posting were infrequent, and included old planning and highway notices that had not been removed, political posters, and personal material (such as lost cat posters).

7.64 Significant quantities of fly-posting were most common in retail and commercial areas and in areas such as seaside promenades. In other land uses, the great majority of fly-posting was light.

7.65 Fly-posting and graffiti are commonly perceived to be activities of young people. However, businesses, in particular the music industry, are a major source of illegal advertising. *The Guardian* reported that:

'Big business and local government are spending millions of pounds each year on fly-posting. The difference is, companies are pocketing a massive profit from illegal advertising while councils are left to pick up the bill for keeping the streets clean. There is no city or large town that has not seen streets blighted by the sight of peeling wall posters overlaid with the latest news of a record release or a band on tour. For people in the music business, and other companies wanting to hit the young and hip, fly posting reaches a specific market and gives the brand the instant image of street credibility. But if using the streets to get the message across rings the corporate cash tills, there is also the cost to the local authority and its council tax payers.' [1]

7.66 The article goes on to explain the financial benefits to companies:

'One of the problems is that fly posting is a relatively cheap form of advertising. The Department of the Environment, Transport and the Regions (DETR) estimates that a company is charged £1.50 for each poster used in its campaign. For a large record company, seeing 50,000 of these posters on the streets promoting a band's album is money well spent. With 250,000 posters going up in a good week, it is also a big earner for the handful of fly posting companies that control the distribution business throughout Britain. No one is going to go without a fight.'

Government responses

7.67 Graffiti and fly-posting are identified by the Government as contributing to poor environmental quality and acting as a barrier to regeneration. It has a disproportionate impact on particular areas and is financially burdensome. Reducing the extent of graffiti and fly-posting is seen as critical to the overall policy aim of improving the quality of public spaces and reducing fear of crime and anti-social behaviour.

7.68 For instance, the Minister for Policing, Crime Reduction and Community Safety commented in an adjournment debate on graffiti in July 2002:[2]

'Just to confirm the impact of graffiti, a Home Office study published in 2000 estimated the cost of criminal damage, which includes graffiti, to be £4.1 billion in the year 1999–2000. Of course, that is not all down to graffiti, but it is a significant issue. …it has a social cost and can have a negative impact in terms of making an area feel run down and contributing to the fear of crime. It can also be a factor in deterring small or large businesses from investing in an area that looks neglected.'

7.69 More evidence of the cost of graffiti is provided in a report published by the Greater London Assembly:[3]

'We have identified expenditure by London Boroughs and transport companies of approximately £13 million per annum. This figure rises to £23 million if all the etched glass on the underground is replaced, but does not include costs to businesses, utilities, rail companies and homeowners. Costs go beyond just removal costs and include damage to economic development and loss of capital values to people's homes.

---

[1] *The Guardian*, 14 February 2001, 'Taking a Pasting'.
[2] Ibid.
[3] *Graffiti in London*, Report for the London Assembly Graffiti Investigative Committee London Assembly, May 2002.

We were unable to identify accurately these additional costs, but we estimate that when they are taken into account the cost of graffiti to the London economy each year exceeds £100m.'

7.70   Graffiti and fly-posting are also a major concern of constituency MPs. For instance Siobhain McDonagh MP stated in the Commons that:

'People, particularly the elderly, are scared to go out if their neighbourhood is targeted by graffiti vandals. If we are serious about doing more to tackle crime and the fear of crime, we must do more to tackle graffiti. My constituents are deeply aggravated by graffiti vandalism. They want effective action on it, as do most Hon Members, I am sure.'[1]

7.71   Back-bench pressure was highly influential in extending the ambit of this Part of the Act. Graffiti removal notices, the recovery of expenditure for removing graffiti in default, and the increased level of fines for illegal advertising were all amendments proposed by back-benchers.

Current legal provisions

7.72   The perpetrators of graffiti can be prosecuted under the Criminal Damage Act 1971. Magistrates can impose fines of up to £5,000 (level 5) and impose sentences of up to a year for criminal damage. Damage over £5,000 is prosecuted in the Crown Court. Persistent fly-posters or graffiti artists can be made subject to anti-social behaviour orders under the Crime and Disorder Act 1998.

7.73   Fly-posting is an offence under the Town and Country Planning Act 1990, and there are also provisions in the Highways Act of 1980.

7.74   However, there are concerns that courts and enforcement agencies do not regard graffiti and fly-posting as serious offences.

The provisions in the Act

7.75   Sections 43–47 and s 53 of the Act target the problem of the disproportionate costs of prosecution for environmental crime by introducing, first, a power for local authorities and community support officers to impose fixed penalty notices for certain graffiti and fly-posting and, secondly, by raising the level of fine payable for illegal advertising. Sections 48–52 target those businesses which do not remove graffiti from their businesses by providing for graffiti removal notices, and s 54 targets retailers by making it an offence to sell aerosol points to anyone under the age of 16.

Penalty notices for graffiti and fly-posting

7.76   Fixed penalty notices have been available for litter offences under the Environmental Protection Act 1990. The provisions of this Part of the Act extend the regime by enabling local authorities' officers[2] and community support officers[3] to issue fixed penalty notices for a range of offences arising from graffiti and fly-posting.

7.77   The offences to which the fixed penalty notice applies are:[4]

(1)   affixing posters;
(2)   defacement of streets with slogans;
(3)   damaging property, which involves the painting or writing on, or the soiling, marking or other defacing of, any property by whatever means;

---

[1]   *Hansard*, 11 July 2002, col 1138.
[2]   Section 43(1).
[3]   Section 46.
[4]   Section 44.

(4)   obliteration of a traffic sign;

(5)   painting or fixing things on structures on the highway;

(6)   displaying advertisements in contravention of regulations.

7.78   Once a person is issued with a penalty notice, no proceedings may be commenced for that offence within the next 14 days. If the financial penalty (currently set at £50[1]) is paid within the 14 days, the person may not be convicted of the offence.[2]

7.79   Penalties will be applicable only to the person committing the offence.[3] So, for instance, in relation to the displaying of an advertisement in contravention of regulations, the penalty notice can only be issued to the person who personally affixed or placed the advertisement.[4]

7.80   Section 87 of the Anti-social Behaviour Act 2003 extends the fixed penalty notice scheme to 16- and 17-year-olds.[5] The section also provides the Secretary of State with the power to extend fixed penalty notices to children aged 10 and over. So, young people can be issued with penalty notices for graffiti and fly-posting.

7.81   A fixed penalty may not be issued if the officer considers the offence to be racially aggravated criminal damage (under s 30 of the Crime and Disorder Act 1998) or motivated by religious or racial hostility.[6] As the Government Minister explained in the Lords:[7]

> 'the intention is to use fixed penalties for minor instances of offences that would not otherwise have been worth the expense of prosecution, although prosecution will still remain an option. We do not think that fixed penalty notices are at all appropriate for offences that are racially or religiously targeted or motivated. The clause therefore specifically excludes those and they would therefore be subject to prosecution.'

7.82   The penalties are payable to local authorities which may use the money for grafitti and fly-posting activities and other functions as specified in regulations.[8]

7.83   Section 46 of the Act amends the Police Reform Act 2002 to provide community support officers and accredited persons with the same power as local authority officers to issue penalty notices in respect of graffiti or fly-posting.[9]

Graffiti removal notices

7.84   At the third reading in the Commons, provisions relating to graffiti removal notices were introduced into the Bill.

7.85   Graffiti removal notices are notices served by local authorities which require a person who is responsible for a surface such as the wall of a business, or street furniture, which has been defaced to remove or clear or otherwise remedy the defacement.[10]

7.86   If the defacement is not removed within the period specified in the notice, which must not be less than 28 days from the service of the notice, the local authority may remove the defacement and recover their costs.[11] The provisions provide authority for entry onto land for the purposes of

---

[1]   Section 43(10).

[2]   Section 43(4).

[3]   Section 44(1).

[4]   Section 43(3)

[5]   Section 87(2), amending s 2(1) of the Criminal Justice and Police Act 2001.

[6]   Section 43(2).

[7]   Ibid.

[8]   Section 45.

[9]   For a discussion of the roles of community support officers and accredited persons see **10.77** et seq.

[10]   Section 48.

[11]   Section 48(4).

doing this.[1] Costs may only be recovered if the local authority serves a notice setting out the amount of and the details of the expenditure which it proposes to recover.[2]

7.87 Graffiti removal notices can only be served when the local authority considers that the defacement is detrimental to the amenity of an area or is offensive, and the defacement is on public land or visible from public land, or the defacement is visible to members of the public using the services or facilities of a statutory undertaker or an educational institution.[3]

7.88 If the local authority is unable to identify the person responsible for the surface, the authority may fix the graffiti removal notice to the defaced surface and may enter land in order to do so. Such action will be the equivalent of personal service.[4]

7.89 People are defined as responsible for a relevant surface if they own, lease, occupy, control operate or maintain it.[5]

7.90 A person on whom a graffiti removal notice is served has a right of appeal within 21 days to the magistrates' court against the notice. The grounds for appeal are that the defacement is neither detrimental to the amenity of the area nor offensive, that there is a material defect or error in the notice, or that the notice should be served on another person.[6]

7.91 A person is also given a right of appeal to the magistrates' court where a local authority has removed the defacement and served a notice detailing the amount of the expenditure it intends recovering on the grounds that the amount is excessive. Again the appeal period is 21 days.[7]

7.92 The Local Government Association responded as follows:

'While this new measure is also very much welcome, we need to be able to recover the costs for removing graffiti in these instances in the same spirit as new measures allowing local authorities to keep receipts from issuing fixed penalty notices in this area.'[8]

7.93 The Government emphasised the importance of piloting the provision and developing detailed guidance:

'We shall pilot this whole provision in 12 local authority areas. It is important that we secure full co-operation and engagement with industry, and I believe that we will do so. ... but we seek to produce guidance to cover all the issues, such as dealing with delicate property, damage to property in general, health, safety and so forth. I think that that is the way to proceed rather than seeking to provide exemptions, which would allow less scrupulous companies to escape their obligations by signing up to a single local graffiti initiative. A single, comprehensive and coherent guide to good practice in this area, which is the intention behind providing statutory guidance. The clauses will come into effect on the due commencement date—which we will debate later—but the statutory guidance will not be finalised until the pilots have been completed. We intend to start the pilots in April 2004 and to select the areas between now and then. The pilots will run for a number of months before we can finalise the statutory guidance. I hope that clarifies the issue; we will have draft guidance; we will have the 12 pilot schemes testing out that draft guidance; and the powers will commence in those areas only for that period. Once we have completed the pilots and developed the final guidance, the powers will roll-out more generally.'[9]

---

[1] Section 48(5).

[2] Section 49(2).

[3] Sections 48(9) and (10).

[4] Section 48(8).

[5] Section 8(11).

[6] Section 51.

[7] Section 51(6).

[8] Anti-social Behaviour Bill Briefing for Commons remaining stage (Local Government Association, 17 November 2003).

[9] *Hansard*, HL Deb, 7 October 2003, col 242.

Advertisements

7.94 The Government has taken the opportunity to raise the level of fine for the display of advertisements in contravention of regulations, which is an offence under s 224(3) of the Town and County Planning Act 1990. Fines which were levied at level 3, a fine of up to £1,000, are from the implementation of this section of the Act to be levied at level 4, a fine of up to £2,500.[1]

7.95 The Government Minister pointed out that the 'increase recognises the growing incidence of fly-posting, and the need for a more punitive deterrent for those responsible for that environmental crime'.[2]

7.96 The amendment was first proposed by Baronness Hamwee who explained that:

'Illegal fly-posting tends to happen at night and is done very quickly. The chances are that not many successful fixed-penalty notices will be issued. The amendments would approach the issue from another direction by amending the current legislation. Under the Town and Country Planning Act 1990, local authorities can give notice in writing to a person who displays, or causes to be displayed, a poster or placard on an illegal site. The notice served states that the offender has 48 hours to remove or 'obliterate' the poster. If they do not do so, local authorities can recover reasonable expenses. I understand that the standard recharge fee per poster is around £100. If the same promoter puts up a poster in the same locality within 28 days, the local authority can take action resulting in prosecution. The average fine is around £500. That figure does not reflect the amount of work that goes into tackling the problem. Local authorities must identify the marketing company. The people who undertake fly-posting, being fairly fly themselves, tend to use unmarked vehicles so that they are difficult to identify. The costs of identifying those behind what is being advertised is also a difficulty.'[3]

7.97 The unequal relationship between the cost of removing fly-posters and the penalties applied to offenders is highlighted in a *Guardian* article:

'For years, cash-strapped local authorities have been weighed down by the cost of cleaning up fly posting. Camden council, in north London, estimates it spends £100,000 a year. It has street cleaning teams out removing posters; covers lamp posts with textured paint which cannot be glued to; builds timber strips on hoardings to make them unusable for fly posting; and spends time advising owners of derelict and empty properties how to keep their sites clean … When the authority successfully prosecuted Creation Records over fly posting for the Oasis album Stand By Me, the company received a fine of £1,800 and was ordered to pay costs of £2,000.'[4]

7.98 The effect of this provision should be to redress to a very slight extent the imbalance between the vast profits to be made from fly-posting and the level of the fines payable.

Sale of aerosol paint to children

7.99 Young people appear to be disproportionately responsible for the problem of graffiti, although evidence also suggests that older people carry out graffiti as a lifestyle choice.[5]

7.100 In an attempt to reduce the amount of graffiti created by young people, the Act creates a new offence which is committed when a person sells paint in an aerosol paint container to people under 16. A person found guilty of an offence under the section will be liable on summary conviction to a fine not exceeding level 4.[6]

7.101 Originally, the Government proposed it would be an offence to sell aerosol paint to young people under the age of 18. However:

[1] Section 53.
[2] *Hansard*, HC Deb, 17 November 2003, col 530.
[3] *Hansard*, HL Deb, 7 October 2003, col 237.
[4] *The Guardian*, 14 February 2001, 'Taking a Pasting'.
[5] *Graffiti in London* (Report of the London Assembly Graffiti Investigative Committee, May 2002).
[6] Section 54.

'The Government have been open to argument on that point throughout the passage of the Bill. We remain convinced of the need to take the tools of the criminal damage trade out of the hands of the taggers, but the precise age at which it is proportionate to restrict sale of those items is a matter for debate. Having listened carefully to arguments both in this House and in another place, we agree that an age limit of 16 is more appropriate than one of 18.'[1]

7.102 The Opposition spokesman reminded the House of the Government's original position:

'They will remember how totally and utterly the Government rejected the logic of the arguments put by my Hon Friends and me for reducing the age at which someone should be prevented from buying an aerosol. I remember drawing attention to the fact – I think it was on Second Reading – that someone can, at 16, use a shotgun, go into a pub and have a drink, or even get married. At that age, they can have a driving licence and buy a car, but if they bend the car, they cannot go and buy the paint to mend it until they are 18. That seems utterly ludicrous.'[2]

7.103 The new offence is accompanied by an amendment made by the Criminal Justice Act 2003 to the Police and Criminal Evidence Act 1984 which provides increased powers for the police to stop and search those they believe are carrying spray paints or other items used for graffiti.[3]

7.104 Two defences are provided to the seller of aerosol paint:

(1) that the seller took all reasonable steps to determine the purchaser's age and that he or she reasonably believed that the purchaser was not under the age of 16;

(2) if someone (the defendant) is charged under the section when the sale was made by another person, it is a defence to prove that the defendant took all reasonable steps to avoid the commission of an offence under the section.[4]

7.105 This section has proved to be one of the more contentious provisions of this part of the Act. It was characterised by the opposition as illiberal and inappropriately penalising the shopkeeper rather than the offender.

Waste and litter

Fly-tipping

The problem

7.106 Stockport Council's website explains the problem of fly-tipping clearly:

'Fly-tipping is the illegal depositing of waste onto land that is not licensed to accept rubbish. Waste can be every sort of material; garden refuse, large items such as fridges, mattresses, building rubble, chemicals, asbestos, tyres, in short virtually anything.

As well as the expense of clearing a site that has been tipped, money that could have been spent elsewhere, there are other environmental costs. Wild animals and pets are injured sometimes fatally by rubbish that has been tipped. Illegally dumped chemicals pollute land and watercourses. Fires are started in heaps of waste items such a car tyres. Dumped rubbish will attract and harbour vermin. An area that has been targeted by fly-tippers will attract other anti-social elements such as vandals, graffiti "artists" and further fly-tipping. Piles of rubbish are detrimental to the appearance of an area, which discourages investment and can lead to a general decline.'[5]

---

[1]　*Hansard*, HC Deb, 17 November 2003, col 530.

[2]　Ibid.

[3]　Section 1 of the Criminal Justice Act 2003, amending s 1(8) of the Police and Criminal Evidence Act 1984.

[4]　Sections 54(4) and (5).

[5]　http://www.stockport.gov.uk/council/eed/eh/fly_tipping.htm.

7.107 The Government believes that fly-tipping is on the increase, although there is a lack of reliable evidence.[1] In 2002, the Environment Agency responded to 4,997 incidents of fly-tipping.[2] There appears to be a number of reasons that people resort to fly-tipping, including poor collection services, lack of proper disposal facilities, limited opening hours at civic amenity sites, charges for bulky refuse collection, charges for trade waste collection, ignorance and the desire to avoid paying landfill tax.

7.108 Fly-tipping is a crime and both the Environment Agency and local authorities can prosecute fly-tippers under the Environmental Protection Act 1990. In 2002/03, the Agency won 197 successful prosecutions against fly-tippers. Fines can be up to £20,000 or 6 months' imprisonment (or both) if convicted in a magistrates' court. If prosecuted in the Crown Court, the fine is unlimited with the possibility of between two and five years' imprisonment if hazardous waste is involved.

The legal framework

7.109 Legal controls on waste in the United Kingdom have developed very slowly from the first recorded law of 1297 which made householders keep the front of their house clear from refuse. This law was largely ignored, establishing something of a tradition in the control of waste. It was not until Victorian times that waste regulation began with the Public Health Act 1848. The Public Health Act 1875 imposed the first responsibilities on local authorities which had to arrange the removal and disposal of waste to replace the previously widespread practice of scavenging. It was this Act which required that householders keep their waste in a 'movable receptacle' (a dustbin), which the local authorities had to empty every week. The Public Health Act 1936 established the crime of statutory nuisance, and local authorities were given the power to prosecute where there was an accumulation of waste which is prejudicial to health, or a nuisance. So, uncontrolled dumping, cesspools and scavenging could be prosecuted. The Act also prohibited building upon contaminated land and provided for the regulation for the management of landfill sites.

7.110 During the 1980s, increased European interest in waste regulation led to the Environmental Protection Act 1990, which separated waste regulation from operational work in local authorities and provided for more regulations and controls. It established a new licensing system covering all controlled wastes (certain household, commercial and industrial wastes) and required local authorities to consider recycling in their waste strategies. Regulations made under the Environmental Protection Act 1990 established a duty of care whereby anyone who 'imports, produces, carries, keeps, treats or disposes of controlled waste' must take responsibility for it.

7.111 The Environment Act 1995 established the Environment Agency with the principal aim of protecting or enhancing the environment so as to achieve sustainable development.[3] Its Chairman, Sir John Harman, explains its purpose:

> 'We are the leading public body for protecting and improving the environment in England and Wales. It's our job to make sure that air, land and water are looked after by everyone in today's society, so that tomorrow's generations inherit a cleaner, healthier world.'[4]

7.112 The Environment Agency has a number of functions, one of which is as waste regulator. The Agency regulates waste management through a system of licences. It also registers and monitors people who transport waste and must be informed before anyone moves potentially dangerous waste (special waste).

---

[1] See HC Research Paper 03/34.

[2] http://www.environment-agency.gov.uk/yourenv/eff/pollution.

[3] See Environment Act 1995, s 4(1).

[4] http://www.environment-agency.gov.uk/aboutus.

7.113 The establishment of the Environment Agency resulted in a change in the responsibilities of local authorities for waste. Their waste regulation role was transferred to the Agency. Local authorities however retained their waste collection role.

Legal problems

7.114 A number of legal problems have resulted from the split of responsibilities between the Environment Agency and local authorities which have made the control of fly-tipping more difficult.

7.115 The first problem has been solved by the amendment of regulations. Section 34(1) of the Environmental Protection Act 1990 imposes a duty of care on any person who imports, produces, carries, keeps, treats or disposes of controlled waste or, as a broker, has control of such waste. The duty requires such persons to ensure that there is no unauthorised or harmful deposit, treatment or disposal of the waste, to prevent the escape of the waste from their control or that of any other person, and on the transfer of the waste to ensure that the transfer is only to an authorised person or to a person for authorised transport purposes and that a written description of the waste is also transferred.

7.116 This means that companies which produce waste remain responsible for the waste, even when someone has removed it from their site. If it is fly-tipped, the company who manufactured the waste can be prosecuted, as well as the firm fly-tipping it. Clearly it is very important to police these requirements.

7.117 The Environmental Protection (Duty of Care) Regulations 1991[1] impose requirements upon the transferor and transferee of non-domestic waste to document the transfer. The waste transfer note must identify the waste in question and state its quantity, how it is stored, the time and place of transfer, the name and address of the transferor and the transferee, whether the transferor is the producer or importer of the waste, which (if any) authorised transport purpose applies, in which category of person the transferor and the transferee are and certain additional information. Breach of the duty of care or of the regulations is a criminal offence.

7.118 The regulations impose a duty on those required to document transfers to provide copies of the documents to a waste regulation authority if required to do so by the authority. When local authorities ceased to be waste regulation authorities, they lost the power to require businesses to produce waste transfer notes. However the Environmental Protection (Duty of Care) (England) (Amendment) Regulations 2003[2] which came into force on 20 February 2003 amended the 1991 Regulations to give waste collection authorities the same powers as waste regulation authorities.

7.119 The second problem is addressed by the provisions of this Part of the Anti-social Behaviour Act 2003. The Control of Pollution Amendment Act 1989 gave waste regulation authorities, which at that time were local authorities, powers to carry out spot checks on vehicles carrying waste and fine them if they were not registered carriers, and to seize vehicles that had been used to commit the offence. This power was transferred from the authorities to the Environment Agency, following its creation in 1996.

7.120 Joan Ruddock introduced the Waste Bill as a 10-minute rule Bill in April 2002 to address the problem and extend the powers of the Control of Pollution Amendment Act 1989 to local authorities. She explained:

'the Environment Agency estimates that removing fly-tipped waste costs it £500,000 per annum. By contrast, a recent Local Government Association survey of fly-tipping provided evidence that the estimated cost of clean-ups to English and Welsh local authorities was £25 million per annum. It found

---

[1] SI 1991/2839.

[2] SI 2003/63.

that 94% of the 128 responding authorities' had recorded incidents of fly-tipping, with 20% recording more than 1,000 incidents. Furthermore, 84% believed that local authorities did not have sufficient powers to deal with fly-tipping, and 97% supported a change in regulations.'[1]

The Bill failed.

7.121 Thirdly, problems have arisen in the effective use of s 59 of the Environmental Protection Act 1990. This section allows waste regulation and waste collection authorities to require removal of unlawfully deposited waste. However, DEFRA points out that it is almost never used by local authorities and rarely by the Environment Agency:

'The power to recover costs only applies when the occupier/owner of the land caused or permitted the deposit of waste. This can be very difficult to prove and limits the power's usage to the Environment Agency, which has stronger powers of evidence gathering, surveillance than local authorities.'[2]

7.122 The investigation powers of the Environment Agency are set out in the Environment Act 1995, s 108. DEFRA explains that 'several local authorities have suggested that they could be more effective at dealing with and preventing fly-tipping if they had these powers'.[3] Again the provisions of this Part of the Anti-social Behaviour Act 2003 specifically address this problem.

The provisions in detail

7.123 Section 55 of the Anti-social Behaviour Act 2003 provides additional powers to local authorities in their waste management roles to help them deal with the problem of fly-tipping and provides for greater government direction in the removal of unauthorised waste.

7.124 It amends the Control of Pollution (Amendment) Act 1989 by substituting the words 'waste regulation authority' for the words 'relevant authority' in s 7(1) of the Act.[4] This is described in the explanatory notes as 'correcting an error'.[5] It then redefines 'regulation authority' to include waste collection authority as defined in s 30 of the Environmental Protection Act 1990.[6]

7.125 In this way, local authorities are given the same powers as the Environment Agency to carry out spot checks on vehicles carrying waste, to impose fines if they are in breach of the requirements and to seize used to commit the offence.

7.126 The Act also gives the Secretary of State additional powers to issue directions to local authorities and the Environment Agency under s 59 of the Environmental Protection Act 1990.[7] This was explained by the Government as clarifying the current voluntary arrangement between the Environment Agency and local government:

'These directions will allow the government to set priorities for different categories of waste for local authorities and the Environment Agency when those authorities are requiring the removal of unlawfully deposited waste. The section specifically provides for priorities to be different in different authorities ... Broadly speaking, the Environment Agency is supposed to deal with the fly-tipping of hazardous waste and serious environmental crime, and local authorities are supposed to deal with incidents involving non-hazardous waste.'[8]

7.127 The Secretary of State is also given the power to require the Environment Agency and local authorities to supply information about the exercise of powers under s 59 of the Environmental

---

[1] *Hansard*, HC Deb, 20 April 2002, col 813, quoted in HC Research Paper 03/34.
[2] DEFRA Consultation Paper, *Living Places – Powers, Rights and Responsibilities* (October 2002).
[3] Ibid.
[4] Section 55(1).
[5] Bill 83 – EN.
[6] Section 55(2).
[7] Section 55(4).
[8] *Hansard*, HL Deb, 7 October 2003, col 259.

Protection Act 1990 and any other action relating to the deposit or disposal of controlled waste.[1] These powers are designed to address the lack of reliable evidence about the extent of the problems and ensure that authorities report on any action taken in relation to fly-tipping. The Government explained:

> 'There are currently no national data on levels of fly-tipping. The Environment Agency and most local authorities already collect some data, but not in any standardised way. It is important that we develop our information base on the extent of fly-tipping, to help inform future policy development both nationally and regionally. Local authorities will also benefit from the measure, as they will be able to access reports from the database.'[2]

7.128 Section 108 of the Environment Act 1995 is amended to provide the investigation and surveillance powers of the Environment Agency to local authorities. This is done by amending s 108(15) by the insertion of the words 'waste collection' authority, by inserting that pollution control functions in relation to a waste collection authority mean the functions conferred by s 59 of the Environmental Protection Act 1990 and by defining waste collection authority in accordance with s 30 of the Environmental Protection Act 1990.[3]

7.129 DEFRA points out that the benefit of this should be increased enforcement of fly-tipping offences by local authorities 'who may be in a better position than the Environment Agency to be aware of local issues'.[4]

7.130 The Government acknowledges that there will be relatively substantial costs resulting from the measures in the short term. These, however, will be offset by an increase in fine receipts and a reduction in expenditure by the Environment Agency:

> 'Costs are expected to fall in future years, as more funds are spent on prevention, better detection and more effective enforcement of fly-tipping legislation and less is spent on clearing up the illegally deposited waste. In time, the measures are expected to be cost-neutral. In addition, there are expected to be unquantified benefits associated with an improved environment, cleaner streets and fewer pollution incidents.'[5]

Litter

7.131 Litter is of major public concern as 'Crime in England and Wales' indicates.[6] It is taken seriously by the Government in developing its 'liveability' agenda. Additional evidence is provided by the one-day count of anti-social behaviour carried out by the Government on 10 September 2003 to provide a snapshot of the extent of anti-social behaviour in England and Wales.[7] The results suggested that litter was the most prevalent anti-social behaviour problem. 10,686 reports of litter and rubbish were made at an estimated cost to agencies per day of £1,866,000.

7.132 ENCAMS explains that:

> 'Legally speaking, the word litter is given a wide interpretation. Litter can be as small as a sweet wrapper, as large as a bag of rubbish, or it can mean lots of items scattered about. ENCAMS describes litter as waste in the wrong place caused by human agency. In other words, it is only people that make litter.'

7.133 In a Local Environmental Quality Survey carried out by ENCAMS in 2002, cigarette-related litter was found in 77% of all locations surveyed and confectionery-related litter such as sweet wrappers was found in 53% of locations. Drinks-related litter such as cans and bottles was found in

---

[1]   Section 55(5).
[2]   *Hansard*, HC, 17 November 2003, col 530.
[3]   Section 55(6).
[4]   DEFRA Consultation Paper, *Living Places – Powers, Rights and Responsibilities* (October 2002).
[5]   Bill 83 – EN.
[6]   *Crime in England and Wales 2002/03* (Home Office Statistical Bulletin, July 2003).
[7]   *The one day count of anti-social behaviour: September 10th 2003* (Home Office, 2003).

31% of all locations. ENCAMS estimates that £342 million a year is spent by local authorities in England on street cleaning and litter clearance.

7.134 Part IV of the Environmental Protection Act 1990 provides a range of powers to local authorities to tackle litter. The Act provides that it is an offence for a person to drop, throw, deposit or leave anything so as to cause defacement in a public place. However, the number of prosecutions for littering is in decline. In 1990, there were 2,543 litter prosecutions, whilst in 1999 there were only 501 prosecutions.

7.135 The Environmental Protection Act 1990 also provides a fixed penalty system for littering offences. Local authority officers and/or litter wardens can give an on-the-spot £50 fixed penalty notice for littering. Section 119 of the Local Government Act 2003 which commenced on 18 November 2003 allows local authorities to keep the revenue raised from the issue of fixed penalty notices.

7.136 Local authorities also have the power to serve litter abatement notices, which require that litter and refuse is cleared up within a specified time and prohibits further defacement. The power only applies to certain types of land: relevant Crown land, the land of designated statutory undertakers and educational institutions and land within a Litter Control Area. If a person served with a litter abatement notice fails to comply with it, the litter authority has the power to enter onto the land, clear the litter and recover its costs. However, not all of the land covered by the litter abatement notice procedure is covered by this power. Crown land and the land of statutory undertakers is excluded.

The legal problems

7.137 The DEFRA Consultation Paper[1] indicates a number of problems with the law on litter. For instance, there are currently no clear requirements on clubs, institutes and sports arenas to require the clean-up of the street within a prescribed area of the premises after special events; legislative controls on litter do not include aquatic environments, such as beaches, rivers and canals; and chewing gum does not clearly fall within the definition of litter.

7.138 DEFRA also identifies the limitations on the power of local authorities to clear Crown land and land of statutory undertakers which has been served with a litter abatement notice.

The provision

7.139 It is this concern which is addressed by the final provision of this part of the Act. It amends s 92(10) of the Environmental Protection Act 1990 so that the power of local authorities, in their role as litter authorities, is extended to include entering Crown land and land owned by statutory undertakes to deal with litter, if a litter abatement notice is not complied with.[2] The authority is then able to recover any reasonable expenditure.

7.140 'Statutory undertaker' is defined in the Environmental Protection Act 1990 as:

(a)   any person authorised by any enactment to carry on any railway, light railway, tramway or road transport undertaking;

(b)   any person authorised by any enactment to carry on any canal, inland navigation, dock, harbour or pier undertaking; or

(c)   any relevant airport operator (within the meaning of Part V of the Airports Act 1986).

7.141 However, Crown land which is occupied for military purposes is still excluded, as is any land belonging to a statutory undertaker that the Secretary of State designates as excluded.

---

[1]   *Living Places – Powers, Rights and Responsibilities* (October 2002).
[2]   Section 55.

Conclusion

7.142 This Part of the Act contains the largest number of sections, and the most diverse range of provisions. It attempts to respond to a range of difficulties in the control of environmental anti-social behaviour. The individual measures may well prove very valuable to some local authorities and have been widely welcomed.

7.143 However, questions remain about the resources available to local authorities in connection with their new powers, about improving the enforcement of provisions and about the remaining recommendations made by DEFRA. Questions have also been raised about the extent to which local authorities are given a clear strategic responsibility for the environment. There is no doubt that the strategic role of the local authority is enhanced by powers to carry out certain environmental works in default and claim costs for doing so. However, there is no clear statement of the leadership role of local authorities and no consolidation of environmental legislation. These matters would require a further piece of legislation, and competition for Parliamentary time would suggest that there will be a long wait before there are further improvements to the law.

CHAPTER 8

PUBLIC ORDER AND TRESPASS

Introduction

8.1   Part 7 of the Anti-social Behaviour Act 2003 is designed to enhance police powers under the various public order Acts to deal with assemblies of groups of people, raves, aggravated trespass and encampments of gypsies and travellers on land without the permission of the landowner. Unlike the other provisions of the Act, there has been comparatively little introduction or discussion by the Government concerning why these provisions were introduced into the Act.

8.2   In the Government's White Paper, *Respect and Responsibility – Taking a Stand Against Anti-Social Behaviour*[1] there is no mention of modification of the existing public order legislation as a mechanism to control anti-social behaviour. It may have been introduced as a mechanism to deal with some of the underlying policy issues raised by the Government. The points raised in the White Paper that may touch on issues of public order in public places relate to harassment, intimidating or offensive behaviour, drugs, and supporting crime and disorder partnerships. However, it is unclear where these proposals for modification of the Acts governing issues of public order originated. Moreover, the Government's press release issued prior to the second reading of the Bill in the House of Lords does not mention the introduction of these provisions in the Act.

8.3   On 9 June 2003, in the Thirteenth Report of Session 2002–03,[2] the Joint Committee on Human Rights commented on Part 4 of the Bill, which concerns groups of children. They considered that the Bill would introduce extensive police powers for the dispersal of groups of two or more persons in areas where it is reasonably believed that anti-social behaviour is a significant and persistent problem with intimidation and harassment by such groups.[3] It was noted by the Committee that the Government accepted that such provisions might give rise to issues relating to Arts 5, 8, 10 and 11 under the European Convention of Human Rights (ECHR).[4]

8.4   The Government proposed that there was a legitimate aim and pressing social need to prevent crime and disorder and protect communities that would provide a justification under the ECHR for the introduction of this legislation.

8.5   The Committee accepted that there were important problems in certain areas. However, they questioned how such measures would, in practice, make it easier to deal with the problems than at present. The Committee noted that the police already had extensive powers under the Public Order Act 1986, the Criminal Justice and Public Order Act 1994 and the Criminal Justice and Police Act 2001.[5] They also noted that common law powers for dealing with an apprehended breach of the peace may be applied. The Government responded that these powers would be entirely directed to

---

1   Cm 5778 (March 2003).
2   HL Paper 120, HC Paper 766, 9 June 2003.
3   Ibid, para 29.
4   Ibid, paras 30–32.
5   Ibid, para 33.

allow for potentially threatening situations to be defused before any harm or disorder becomes imminent.[1]

8.6   The Committee remained concerned about the introduction of these new powers. They suggested that this was not a response to threats of serious disorder, but rather to allow police to manage people in public spaces in such a way as to prevent any more remote risk of minor disorder. They agreed that this power did not exist in law, but felt that the reason for this was that it represented an unnecessary intrusion on the liberty of the individual, to allow a constable to give orders to someone where there is no threat of crime or danger to safety. The Committee drew this issue to the attention of both Houses of Parliament.[2]

8.7   In a second briefing paper[3] on a second reading of the Bill in the House of Lords, Liberty noted that Part 7 (then Part 8) was only introduced into the Bill after it had finished in the House of Commons and noted the modifications to s 14 of the Public Order Act 1986 as described below. Liberty expressed the concern that any situation where the police can self-authorise restrictions on the right to assemble and possibly protest should be treated with great caution. Liberty acknowledged that the police should have appropriate powers to deal with violent protests but raised concerns about the manner in which these powers give rise to criminal sanctions for behaviour that would not itself be criminal apart from imposition of these conditions. Liberty felt that it was 'incredible' that the Government considered that two people could form an assembly and was unclear of the justification.[4]

8.8   Liberty went on to note that, while ss 68 and 69 of the Criminal Justice and Public Order Act 1994 had been amended to apply to buildings, it remained concerned about the wide-ranging powers contained in the Act. While Liberty was pleased that, on removal of vehicles and caravans in the amendment to s 62 of the Criminal Justice and Public Order Act 1994, a police officer was required to consider a alternative site, it still expressed reservations. It was concerned that too much relied on the exercise of an opinion by the officer and that this exercise of discretion should extend to local authorities to find alternative sites.[5]

8.9   On modification of s 62 of the Criminal Justice and Public Order Act 1994, Liberty was concerned that the creation of new criminal offences was entirely disproportionate in relation to any forms of trespass. The Bill greatly extended the range of potential criminal liability for groups such as travellers for acts that would normally be civil torts.

8.10   The Joint Committee on Human Rights returned to scrutiny of the Bill in its 15th Report of Session 2002–03.[6] Their main conclusion was that Part 8 of the Bill (now Part 7 of the Act) could give rise to a risk of incompatibility with human rights guaranteed under the ECHR in relation to public assemblies for dealing with trespassers.[7] They noted that Part 8 of the Bill was introduced by way of Government amendment at the Report Stage in the House of Commons.[8]

8.11   On the issue of redefining a public assembly, the Committee considered that the conditions would have to meet the requirements of Arts 10 and 11 of the ECHR if they were to be lawful. They considered it distinctly odd to consider that two people could constitute a public assembly in order to prevent resulting disorder. They considered that the reduction to two people might

---

[1]   HL Paper 120, HC Paper 766, 9 June 2003, para 34; Annex A to the report, the Home Secretary's letter page 27, paras 4–7, where it specifically identified a problem of perception in many communities that groups of teenagers caused intimidation, harassment, alarm and distress to others based on evidence from the British Crime Survey.

[2]   Ibid, para 35.

[3]   July 2003.

[4]   *Liberty's second reading briefing on the Anti-social Behaviour Bill in the House of Lords* (July 2003).

[5]   Ibid, paras 28–29.

[6]   HL Paper 149, HC Paper 1002, 14 July 2003.

[7]   Ibid, para 1.9.

[8]   Ibid, para 1.1.

undermine the claim of a legitimate aim for such an imposition under Arts 10 and 11 of the ECHR. Also, they felt that it would give rise to consideration that these powers would be used in a disproportionate way.[1] In a letter to the Committee, which is annexed to the report, the Home Secretary stated that he was content that the proposals in the Bill were necessary and consistent with the requirements of the ECHR.

8.12 The Committee noted that, although safeguards remained in place for the exercise of these powers, they felt that the imposition of the restriction could provide for a 'chilling effect' on freedom of expression and association on small groups of individuals who are inherently less likely than larger groups to cause public disorder.[2] The Joint Committee went on to recommend that the Government should clarify the mischief at which this extension of powers was aimed and should explain why existing powers are insufficient to deal with this mischief. The Committee suggested that this would allow Parliament to assess the legitimacy of these provisions, and the general necessity for allowing the police to exercise the powers over very small groups of people and its proportionality.[3]

Table 8.1

Summary of Part 8 of the Anti-social Behaviour Act 2003

Section Number	Summary	Comment
57	Public assemblies	Lowered the threshold to two people from 20 to constitute assembly for police to exercise their powers under s 14 of the Public Order Act 1986.
58	Raves	Redefined a rave in the Criminal Justice and Public Order Act 1994 to comprise 20 or more people, makes unlicensed indoor as well as out door raves illegal.
59	Aggravated trespass	Penalties for aggravated trespass in the Criminal Justice and Public Order Act 1994 now apply to buildings as well as land in the open air.
60, 61 and 62	Power to remove trespassers: alternative site Failure to comply with direction: offences Failure to comply with direction: seizure	These provisions are aimed at dispersing encampments of gypsies and travellers who are on land without the permission of the landowner Creates a new power in the Criminal Justice and Public Order Act 1994 for police to give directions to leave land combined with a consideration of the availability of new sites for travellers Creates a new offence in the Criminal Justice and Public Order Act 1994 for failing to comply with a direction made under s 60 above

---

[1] HL Paper 149, HC Paper 1005, 14 July 2003, para 1.4.
[2] Ibid, para 1.5.
[3] Ibid, para 1.6.

Table 8.1

Summary of Part 8 of the Anti-social Behaviour Act 2003

Section Number	Summary	Comment
		Creates a power of seizure of vehicles and property in the Criminal Justice and Public Order Act 1994 for failing to comply with a direction under s 60 above
63	Common land: modifications.	Makes necessary modifications of the Criminal Justice and Public Order Act 1994 in its application to common land
64	Interpretation.	Gives interpretation of terms used in this Part of the Act

The social problem

8.13 The central social problem that this Part of the Act attempts to address is the idea that certain groups of individuals have been involved in disruptive behaviour in communities. The activities appear to extend to apparent harassment and intimidation of members of the community. In particular, this has been associated with gangs of youths in the inner cities.[1] The question is whether this is a transient cultural change that will die out without the intervention of the law or whether it requires such intervention. The alternative is that perhaps targeting resources to education and social development and regeneration would be a better response than extending police powers.

8.14 In addition to street gangs, other groups or gatherings of people are considered exceptionally problematic. The tactics of certain groups of activists, for example certain animal rights activists, are perceived as problematic. Organisations such as the Animal Liberation Front and Stop Huntington Animal Cruelty have made it clear that they are not interested in peaceful protest and debate. Rather, such organisations prefer intimidation, coercion and threats, combined with direct invasions of property.[2] Nevertheless, it may be the case that these tactics are justifiable when there is obvious wrongdoing by the object of the protest, or when regulators fail to intervene to rectify the situation.[3]

8.15 Gypsies and travellers are other groups that tend to attract the attention of public order legislation. It is clear that encampments of gypsies and travellers can cause a great deal of disruption to a community.[4] This problem is exacerbated by the lack of 'official' campsites for gypsies and travellers that provide necessary and appropriate facilities.[5] This long-running problem has lead to serious tension between gypsies and travellers and local communities.[6] The key social problem here

---

[1]   See *The Times*, 6 November 2003, p 11, '"Psycho" leader of teenage gang admits 37 charges'; *The Times*, 3 October 2003, p 1, 'Scots ban to drive teenage gangs from "hot spots"'; *The Independent*, 21 August 2003, p 1, 'Teenage gang attacks 2 Portuguese men'; *The Guardian*, 16 July 2003, society page 2, 'A leap of faith: some are classed as gangs, others peer groups'; *The Guardian*, 1 July 2003, home page 6, 'Street gangs ruled by machismo'.

[2]   See *The Guardian*, 17 August 2003, leader, p 27, 'Animal behaviour: a tough court order-but justifiably so'.

[3]   Ibid.

[4]   See *The Times*, 8 November 2003, p 15, 'Farmers want law to cut £100m cost of travellers'.

[5]   *The Times*, 4 November 2003, 'Providing sites for gypsies'.

[6]   *The Times*, 3 November 2003, p 9, 'Race inquiry after gypsy caravan burnt'.

is: how does a society deal fairly with a nomadic group of people who exhibit a different lifestyle and express different values that are often at odds with mainstream society without criminalising them and devaluing their traditions?

8.16 Finally, groups of people gathering to engage in parties where loud music is played throughout the night are generally considered especially disruptive to communities. Previous legislation has attempted to deal with outdoor 'raves' in the countryside. However, it did not necessarily deal with such events that occur indoors, in cities and built-up areas where, arguably, the disruption could be greater. Also, such unlicensed gatherings often attract crime, drugs and major considerations of control of the health and safety of the participants. The question is: how are such gatherings dealt with fairly when, for example, other gatherings (eg private garden parties or private wedding receptions with music) remain immune? Moreover, how far does the law go to deal with these activities fairly without being perceived as unfairly targeting and criminalising the young or other groups?

The legal problem

8.17 The key legal problem is: how should the law respond to this behaviour in order to assuage fear and disruption in communities without being overly heavy handed, unnecessarily infringing individuals' civil rights and liberties, or selecting particular groups or vulnerable communities for exceptional treatment? There may be additional risks associated with over-criminalising certain activities. Moreover, there is a risk of placing too much power in the hands of police forces and individual policemen without sufficient judicial scrutiny. Furthermore, the exercise of such powers by the police could be damaging to community relations and promote distrust and an expansion of criminality as a result. In the most unfortunate circumstances, this could lead to a militaristic style of policing at odds with traditional police practice which can lead to rioting such as seen in Brixton[1] and elsewhere.

Legal background

Public Order Act 1986 (the '1986 Act')

8.18 The background to this Act can be found in several wide-ranging documents and is the subject of a number of books.[2] The Green Paper Review of the Public Order Act 1986 and Related Legislation[3] initiated the move towards change. The Fifth Report of the House of Commons Home Affairs Committee, *The Law Relating to Public Order*[4] was an influential report dealing with many aspects of public order law and practice. It concentrated on statutory provisions relating to processions and assemblies. The Law Commission focused largely on common law offences in its report *Offences Relating to Public Order*[5] and it working paper.[6]

8.19 The Government's White Paper, *The Review of Public Order Law*,[7] drew the various documents together and produced proposals that have been largely incorporated into the Act. It is noteworthy

---

[1] See *The Brixton Disorders 10–12 April 1981*, Report of an inquiry by the Rt Hon The Lord Scarman OBE, Cmnd 8427, paras 4.1–4.97.

[2] J Marston, *Public Order: A Guide to the 1986 Public Order Act* (Fourmat Publishing, 1987); ATH Smith, *Offences Against Public Order: Including the Public Order Act 1986* (Sweet and Maxwell, 1987); R Card, *Public Order Law* (Jordans, 2000).

[3] (1980) Cmnd 7891.

[4] (1979–1980) HC 756.

[5] Report No 123.

[6] No 82.

[7] Cm 9510.

that, in *R v Shivpuri*,[1] Lord Hailsham regretted the departure of the Act form the draft Bill produced by the Law Commission.

8.20   The Government's White Paper refers to a 'right of peaceful protest' and 'right to march'. Prior to the enactment of the 1986 Act, there were no general statutory provisions for the control of public assemblies. Part II of the 1986 Act deals with both public processions and assemblies. Common law and statutory powers related to the control of certain assemblies remain.

8.21   In s 16 of the 1986 Act, 'public assembly' means an 'assembly of 20 or more persons in a public place which is wholly or partly open to the air.' The word 'assembly' is not explained any further, however for the purposes of the 1986 Act an assembly is distinguished from a procession.

8.22   Examples of assemblies within the Act are pickets,[2] lobbies, vigils, pop festivals, queues for buses and tickets and a group of people drinking in a pub garden. It would also include football matches and notably trespassory assemblies introduced by the Criminal Justice and Public Order Act 1994. The meaning appears not to be limited to static assemblies. Thus, a group of circulating protestors, which does not amount to a procession, might fall to be an assembly within the meaning of the 1986 Act. From the Act, it is unclear if an assembly is defined by reference to the location, the organisers, the participants, the objective or a combination of these factors or other considerations. For example, a group of people in the entrance to a shop might move from place to place and the participants of the group might change from time to time.

8.23   'Public place' is defined in s 16 of the 1986 Act. It is only in relation to public assemblies that the meaning of 'public place' is likely to be an important factual issue, for example whether the entrance to a shop is a public place.

8.24   The reference is to 'open to the air'. 'Partly open to the air' must mean more than a *de minimis*.

8.25   Section 14 in the 1986 Act allows conditions to be imposed on public assemblies. The 1986 Act does not affect the powers of the police under their general preventative duty or other powers. Also, the 1986 Act does not affect the civil liabilities, rights or obligations of any other persons, for example the ability to obtain an injunction.

8.26   Under s 14, conditions may be imposed either before or during an assembly by a senior police officer. A senior police officer may be, in relation to an assembly intended to be held, the chief officer of police under s 14(2)(b), subject to delegation under s 15, and the direction must be given in writing under s 14(3). In relation to an assembly being held, the senior police officer is the most senior rank of police officer at the scene under s 14(2)(a) and the directions need not be in writing.

8.27   The conditions may be imposed on either the organisers or those taking part in the assembly. In light of the requirement of knowledge in the offences, it appears appropriate for the organisers of the assembly to be served with a copy of the written directions, or for them to be told of the direction personally. Appropriate steps should be taken to inform the participants as early as possible in order to avoid a breach

Criminal Justice and Public Order Act 1994 ('the 1994 Act')

8.28   The provisions of the 1994 Act can be traced to a number of sources. Central to the provisions of the Act were those in Part V related to public order. In an article in *The Times* on 8 March 1994, Peter Thornton, the then chairman of the Civil Liberties Trust, argued that the public order provisions of the 1994 Act extended the law 'to a point not far short of a straight law

---

[1]   [1987] AC 1, [1986] 2 All ER 334.
[2]   However, see s 220 of the Trades Union and Labour Relations (Consolidation) Act 1992.

of criminal trespass'. In the debate on the second reading of the Bill, Mr Butler MP[1] expressed the hope that they would lead to a full law of criminal trespass. On the other hand, Mr Gunnell MP[2] was sure that '... the clauses on trespass will create a new class of lawbreakers. The time and resources that the police will devote to them will therefore detract from the current use of police resources'.

8.29 One of the most controversial areas concerned the repeal, by s 80 of the 1994 Act, of the provisions in the Caravans Act 1968, which had imposed a duty on local authorities to provide sites for gypsy encampments. The *duty* is replaced by a *power*, but this led to the concern that this change meant that the police will be employed merely to confront and move on gypsies who have no designated site available to them where they can go.

Raves[3]

8.30 Section 63 of the 1994 Act introduced sets of police powers for dealing with persons attending or preparing for an unlicensed[4] rave. Raves were a cultural phenomenon of the early to mid-1990s characterised as large gatherings of people in the open air, with very loud music at night. The music at raves was commonly of a low frequency that could penetrate buildings and could be heard over a long distance. The large number of people at or making their way to a rave posed potential public order problems and severe congestion on highways for several miles around the rave. Although the 1994 Act did not specifically address the issue of drug abuse, it was a perception at the time that this was a major problem at raves.

8.31 Neither the police nor local authorities had statutory powers to intervene or deal with an unlicensed rave that had the permission of the landowner where it was held. The only available powers to the police were the common law powers to deal with an actual or apprehended imminent breach of the peace. These common law powers could be used to forbid the rave or to turn people away. The local authorities did have powers to serve abatement notices under the Environmental Protection Act 1990[5] to deal with noise nuisance, but in general they were not well equipped to deal with such an event rapidly and effectively.[6] Section 63 powers also bear on ss 64–67 of the 1994 Act. These sections provide police with the following powers:

–   to enter and seize sound equipment if necessary (s 64); and
–   to redirect people on their way to a rave (s 65);

and provides the court with powers concerning:

–   the forfeit of sound equipment (s 66); and
–   the retention and charges for seized property (s 67).

8.32 In replying, on behalf of the Government, at the end of the second reading of the Bill, David Maclean MP, Minister of State at the Home Office, explained that the purpose of the provisions in

[1] *Hansard*, HC Deb, 11 January 1994, col 87.
[2] Ibid, col 131.
[3] M Wasik and R Taylor, *Blackstone's Guide to the Criminal Justice and Public Order Act 1994* (1995), para 4.2.
[4] Section 63 of the 1994 Act does not apply to a gathering authorised by a local authority entertainment licence (s 63(9)); there are two types, private and public licence.
[5] See ss 80–82 of the Environmental Protection Act 1990, empowering a local authority to issue an abatement notice if it is satisfied that a statutory nuisance exists. A failure to comply with such a notice is an offence. Section 82 of the 1990 Act provides that a person aggrieved by an actual statutory nuisance may bring proceedings in a magistrates' court, where an abatement notice and a fine can be issued against the defendant. The 1994 Act confines itself to raves on land in the open air or partly open to the air, and it does not deal with noisy commercial parties in empty buildings. These parties can be dealt with by way of prosecution for not having an entertainment licence (1990 Act, s 79) or under s 82 of the 1990 Act.
[6] R Card and R Ward, *The Criminal Justice and Public Order Act 1994* (Jordan Publishing Limited, 1994), para 3.94.

ss 63–67 of the 1994 Act was to prevent the mischief of '… the appalling distress caused by unlicensed night-time raves on open land. Their incessant noise can keep residents for miles around awake all night'.[1]

8.33 Section 63 of the 1994 Act applies in relation to gatherings on land in the open air, or partly open to the air, of 100 or more persons, whether or not they are trespassers, at which amplified music is played during the night, which, by reason of its loudness and duration is likely to cause serious distress to inhabitants of the locality. Music for the purposes of this section 'includes sounds wholly or predominantly characterised by the emission of a succession of repetitive beats' (s 63(1)(b)).

8.34 It is unclear why the threshold for attending a rave is set at 100 for the engagement of dispersal under this section. Gatherings of less than 100 that play loud music can cause distress to the local community. The question that arises is that, if the playing of loud music is the essential mischief behind s 63 as a public order provision of the 1994 Act, why should there be a minimum number in attendance?[2] Card and Ward suggest that the danger with fixing any number is that the devious can always get around it, for example issuing 90 tickets with nine organisers present. A figure as high as 100 is likely to exclude private parties in people's gardens at which loud music is played. It may be that some individuals consider that the latter should also be subject to s 63 if the music persists into the night. It may be the case that the distinction between raves and garden parties is that the former is most likely to be attended by the young and the latter by older people, and not necessarily based on the volume of noise. Moreover, this may link to the general concept that attendant public disorder may be more prevalent amongst young people than older people at gatherings of large numbers.

8.35 It is clear that raves are not limited to trespassory conduct or gatherings. Also, unlike the provisions concerning aggravated trespass and trespassory assemblies, the provisions are not limited to activities in the open air as s 63(10) of the 1994 Act defines a rave and 'includ[ing] a place partly open to the air'. Would this necessarily mean that 'indoor' raves, where a window was open in a large room? David Maclean MP[3] stated at the Committee stage in the House of Commons that a Dutch barn and an aircraft hanger were partly open to the air for the purposes of s 63. Also, the Minister went on to state that a marquee would be regarded as partly open to the air.[4]

8.36 Spontaneous gatherings of 100 or more trespassers can constitute a rave if the other conditions are satisfied. There is no requirement that the rave is an organised event. The amplified music must be played 'during the night'. If it is only played at some other time, the gathering is not a rave, even if the gathering continues during the night. 'Night' is not defined in the 1994 Act. At the Committee stage in the House of Commons, David Maclean MP stated that he was content that the provision should be left vague.[5]

8.37 By reason of its duration, loudness and time, the amplified music must be such as is likely to cause serious distress to the local inhabitants. 'Serious distress' is not defined in the 1994 Act. It appears to be more than annoyance or a nuisance.

8.38 A direction to leave the site is given under s 63(2) of the 1994 Act. If a police officer, of at least the rank of superintendent, reasonably believes that, as respects land in the open air:

(a)   two or more persons are making preparations to hold a rave;

(b)   10 or more people are waiting for a rave to begin; or

(c)   10 or more people are attending a rave which is in progress,

---

[1]   *Hansard*, HC Deb, 11 January 1994, cols 116–117.

[2]   R Card and R Ward, *The Criminal Justice and Public Order Act 1994* (Jordan Publishing Limited, 1994), para 3.98.

[3]   HC Committee, col 592.

[4]   Ibid, col 593.

[5]   Ibid, col 595.

he may issue a direction. However, in order to give such a direction the superintendent must reasonably believe that 100 or more would attend the gathering in order for it to be a rave. The requirement that 100 or more will attend is a precondition for the exercise of the power.

8.39 The direction under s 63 is to the persons mentioned in the paragraph above and to any others who come to prepare or wait for or attend the rave. The direction is to leave the land and to remove any vehicles or other property that they have with them. A direction to leave does not apply to the occupier of the land in question, any members of their family, any employee or agent, or any person whose home is on the land.

8.40 A person who knows that a direction that applies to them has been given and who:

(a) fails to leave the land as soon as reasonably practicable,[1] or
(b) leaves but returns within 7 days,

commits a summary offence punishable by a fine not exceeding level 4 or up to 3 months in prison or both (s 63(6)). Also, s 63(8) creates a power of arrest without warrant for this offence. However, s 63(7) provides a defence to a charge under s 63 for the accused to demonstrate they had a reasonable excuse for failing to leave as directed, or returning to the land within 3 months.

8.41 Once the s 63 thresholds are met and a direction lawfully given, s 64 of the 1994 Act provides powers for entry and seizure. Once a superintendent reasonably believes that the circumstances exist for giving a direction under s 63, they may authorise any constable to enter the land without a warrant to determine if such circumstances exist. If the circumstances do exist following a s 63 direction, and the constable reasonably suspects that any person subject to the direction has:

(a) failed to leave; or
(b) has failed to remove any vehicle or property; or
(c) has been arrested for an offence,

the constable may seize and remove a vehicle or sound equipment connected with the gathering.

8.42 Section 65 of the 1994 Act provides a police officer with a power to stop persons and direct them not to proceed to a gathering where a s 63 direction is in force. This power may be exercised at a place within 5 miles of the boundary of the site of the gathering.

8.43 Section 66 of the 1994 Act provides that, where a person is convicted of an offence under s 63, sound equipment seized may be forefeited.

8.44 Section 67 of the 1994 Act specifies the arrangements that apply in respect of retention and charges for property, namely vehicles and sound equipment, seized under s 64 powers.

Aggravated trespass

8.45 Section 68(1) of the 1994 Act created a new offence of aggravated trespass. Section 69 of the 1994 Act provides police with a power corresponding to that under s 61 to direct people to leave the land. The offence of aggravated trespass is committed when a person trespasses on land in the open air and, in relation to any lawful activity, that persons are engaging in, or are about to engage in, on that land or adjoining land in the open air, does anything that is intended by the trespasser to have the effect of:

---

[1] For 'reasonably practicable', see *Krumpa v DPP* [1989] Crim LR 295. The Divisional Court held that trespassers should leave as soon as they reasonably could in the circumstances. The test is an objective one applied in light of all the circumstances (ie unroadworthiness of vehicles), and it cannot be determined entirely by the police officer's view of how soon the trespassers might be expected to leave.

(1)   intimidating those persons or any of them so as to deter any of them from engaging in their lawful activity; or

(2)   obstructing that activity; or

(3)   disrupting that activity.

8.46   'Land in the open air' does not include a metalled highway or road (s 68(5)), but does extend to footpaths, bridleways or byways that are used as public paths (see s 61(9) of the 1994 Act). This definition of land in s 61(9) specifically excludes most buildings.

8.47   The activity on the land in question appears to be lawful for the purposes of s 68(1) of the 1994 Act if the persons engaged in that activity are committing no criminal offence or trespass (s 68(2) of the 1994 Act). However, the language used is such that an activity is lawful if the persons 'may engage in the activity on the land on that occasion' without committing an offence or trespassing on the land. This appears to cater for a landowner giving a limited permission for persons to use the land on a specific occasion for a specific purpose. The activity is lawful if the limited permission has been given.

8.48   These provisions were specifically aimed at anti-hunting protesters who go beyond peaceful protest, people who disrupt horse races, people who disrupt anglers[1] and people who demonstrate on land to prevent the building of new roads.

8.49   These provisions were especially controversial both inside and outside Parliament. The concerns that were aired were that the provisions were drafted too widely and may catch peaceful protests and freedom of access.

8.50   A constable may arrest without warrant for an offence under s 68. A person found guilty under s 68 will be liable on summary conviction for up to 3 months' imprisonment, a fine up to level 4 or both.

8.51   Section 69 of the 1994 Act creates powers for the removal of persons committing or participating in an aggravated trespass. If a senior police officer who is present at the scene holds the reasonable belief that:

(1)   a person is committing, has committed or intends to commit the offence of aggravated trespass; or

(2)   that two or more persons are trespassing on land in the open air with the common purpose of intimidating people so as to deter them from engaging in a lawful activity, or to obstruct or disrupt this activity,

the police officer may direct the trespassers to leave. Under s 69(3) of the 1994 Act, a person who knows that a direction has been given that applies to them, and who fails to leave the land as soon as practicable, or, having left, returns as a trespasser within 3 months of the direction, is committing an offence and is subject to arrest and punishment as above.

8.52   Under s 69 of the 1994 Act, it is a defence for the accused person to show that they were not trespassing on the land, or that they had a reasonable excuse for failing to leave the land, or return as a trespasser.

Trespassory assemblies

8.53   Although trespassory assemblies are not directly addressed in the Anti-social Behaviour Act 2003, they are indirectly affected through modification of s 14 of the Public Order Act 1986 by the new Act.

---

[1]   The Home Secretary, *Hansard*, HC Deb, 11 January 1994, col 29.

8.54 Sections 70 and 71 of the 1994 Act amended the Public Order Act 1986 by inserting ss 14A, 14B and 14C. As noted above, the original s 14 provided police powers for imposing conditions on public assemblies. Sections 14A, 14B and 14C respectively provide a general statutory power for prohibiting an assembly in open air, if it is trespassory, various offences in relation to the contravention of the prohibition, and provide a power to stop people progressing to a banned assembly.

8.55 In the Public Order Act 1986, the Government decided against a ban on static demonstrations on the grounds that it would be a substantial limitation on freedom of expression and freedom of assembly that would be disproportionate. However, it could be argued that it is not easy to understand, if a power to ban processions is necessary, why there should not also be a power to ban assemblies in similar circumstances.[1]

8.56 Sections 70 and 71 of the 1994 Act introduced compromise provisions based on the perceived need to protect communities from serious disruption caused by trespassory assemblies and to protect ancient monuments, for example Stonehenge, from damage. Previously, only the common law power of the prevention of an apprehended breach of the peace applied. This power extended to the prevention of a meeting,[2] but not to the anticipated situations within s 14A of the 1986 Act.

8.57 Section 14A of the 1986 Act created a new power for the relevant chief police officer to apply to the local council for an order prohibiting, for a specified period, the holding of all trespassory assemblies in specified areas. The granting of such an order by the council requires the consent of the Secretary of State. The chief officer may make an application for such an order if he reasonably believes that an assembly of 20 or more persons is intended to be held on land in the open air to which the public has no right of access or a limited right of access; and that the assembly:

(1) is likely to be held without the permission of the occupier, or to exceed that permission or to exceed the public's right of access; and

(2) may result in serious disruption to the life of the community, or significant damage to land, or to a building or monument on that land, where the land, building or monument is of historical, architectural, archaeological or scientific importance.

8.58 If the order is made, it must not prohibit the holding of such assemblies for a period exceeding 4 days, or prohibit an assembly being held outside an area within 5 miles from a specified centre (s 14A(6)). There is no route of appeal from this decision to ban apart from judicial review.

8.59 Section 14B of the 1986 Act creates three new offences for persons organising trespassory assemblies, those who take part in them, or those who incite people to take part in them. All three offences are summary and arrestable without warrant. Organising a trespassory assembly is punishable with imprisonment for a term up to 3 months, or a fine up to level 4, or both (s 14B(5)). Taking part in a trespassory assembly is not an imprisonable offence, but is punishable by a fine not exceeding level 3 on the scale (s 14B(6)). Inciting a trespassory assembly is punishable in the same manner as for organising it.

8.60 Section 14C of the 1986 Act was created by s 71 of the 1994 Act. The power created parallels with that for raves in s 65 of the 1994 Act. This provides a uniformed police officer who reasonably believes that a person is on the way to a trespassory assembly subject to a s 14A order with the power to stop that person and redirect them away from the assembly. This may be exercised within a 5-mile radius of the assembly.[3]

---

[1] R Card and R Ward, *The Criminal Justice and Public Order Act 1994* (Jordan Publishing Limited, 1994), para 3.64.

[2] *Duncan v Jones* [1936] 1 KB 218.

[3] In defending this position, Earl Ferrers said that they were considering assemblies that may attract tens of thousands of people: *Hansard*, HL Deb, 7 July 1994, col 1489.

Section 62: seizure of vehicles and property

8.61 Section 62 of the 1994 Act creates supplementary powers of seizure as a result of directions given under s 61 of the 1994 Act. Where a s 61 direction has been given and any person to whom that direction applies has failed to leave, failed to remove vehicles or property or has been arrested for an offence, the police, after a reasonable period, may seize and remove any vehicle from the land that was under the control of the person who was subject to the direction under s 61.

8.62 The s 61 power in the 1994 Act provided police with new powers to remove trespassers from land. The Government had in mind groups such as new age travellers.[1] David Maclean MP stated that 'new age travellers are the main offenders' against whom these provision were directed, but that 'there may be other groups'.[2]

8.63 It is noteworthy that s 39 of the 1986 Act, which contained similar provisions, was repealed by the 1994 Act, with s 39 being replaced by s 61. ATH Smith commented that the impetus for enactment of s 36 in the 1986 Act was concerned about incidents of mass trespass.[3] ATH Smith doubted whether such an offence was necessary given the availability of civil proceedings to evict trespassers and the likelihood of commission of criminal offences in the course of trespass, for example criminal damage. Also, it may be the case that local authorities could use their statutory powers related to public nuisance in these circumstances.

8.64 Section 61 of the 1994 Act provides that where a senior police officer at the scene reasonably believes that two or more people are trespassing on land, and are present there with the common purpose of residing there for any period, and reasonable steps have been taken by the occupier to ask them to leave and that either:

(1) damage has been caused to the land or property on the land, or threatening, abusive or insulting words or behaviour have been used by any of those people to the occupier; or

(2) those persons have between them six or more vehicles on the land,

then the senior police officer, or an officer acting on their behalf, may direct the persons to leave the land and remove their vehicles and property.

8.65 The definition of 'land' in the 1994 Act includes common land as defined in s 22 of the Commons Registration Act 1965 and is extended to cover certain forms of tracks.

Parliamentary session 2002–03

Commons

8.66 The clauses were introduced at the Report Stage on 24 June 2003 prior to the third reading of the Bill. The Bill was read for the third time and passed.

Lords

Public assembly

8.67 On the second reading of the Bill in the House of Lords, Baroness Linklater, Liberal Democrat, noted the criticisms of the Joint Committee on Human Rights in its Thirteenth Report of the Session 2002/03. Also, she noted that, on the dispersal of groups, the Association of Chief Police Officers has stated that 'the initial reaction of the forces suggest that it would not be

---

[1]   M Wasik and R Taylor, *Blackstone's Guide to the Criminal Justice and Public Order Act 1994* (1995), p 82.

[2]   *Hansard*, HC Deb, 13 April 1994, col 296.

[3]   ATH Smith, *Offences Against Public Order* (Sweet & Maxwell, 1987), paras 14–18.

enthusiastically used in an operational environment'.[1] Although this criticism was aimed primarily at the provisions in Part 4, it may be equally applicable to the modifications of the Public Order Act 1986.

8.68 In the Report Stage, on 3 November 2003, Lord Lester, Liberal Democrat, thought that it was odd to speak of two people as a public assembly, in light of the fact that the Public Order Act 1986 was designed to combat serious threats to public disorder. Lord Lester noted the potential 'chilling effect' of such a provision on basic freedoms and the fact that the clause was introduced into the Bill without debate. Lord Lester, with the support of Lord Monson and Lord Avebury, asked the Minister for an explanation of the mischief that this clause was aimed at. Lord Lester further noted that the Protection from Harassment Act 1997 could be used to deal with threats from animal rights extremists or others.[2] In response, Baroness Scotland stressed the problems faced by police, faced with protestors who know the law and meet in groups of 19 or less. She stated that, while there were powers to deal with intimidating individuals, there were none to deal with the collective behaviour of an intimidating group.[3]

8.69 In the Committee Stage of the House of Lords, on 7 October 2003, the clauses that constitute Part 7 of the Act were agreed to.

8.70 Lord Dixon-Smith, for the Conservatives, introduced an amendment to increase the clause's definition of a public assembly from 2 to 10 people.[4] Lord Avebury, with the agreement of Lord Hylton, went on to ask the Minister what circumstances the Government had in mind for this reform and why not just reduce it to one person.

8.71 In reply, Baroness Scotland, Minister for the Government, said that the proposals were intended to give powers to the police to deal with those assembling for intimidatory purposes and not against those assembling peacefully. Also, this power would give the police the power to disperse the group to remedy the solution quickly.[5] Lord Dixon-Smith withdrew his amendment.

8.72 From this followed a debate on the possible use of the powers in the Protection from Harassment Act 1997, or ss 4A or 14 of the Public Order Act 1986 instead. Baroness Scotland argued that the Public Order Act 1986 would not allow the police to act against groups of less than 20, and that protesters frequently used this fact to avoid police action. The example given was that of animal rights activists protesting at Huntington Life Sciences.[6]

Raves

8.73 Lord Bassam, Minister for the Government, introduced an amendment to insert a new clause to define powers relating to raves. The clause was introduced to rectify the fact that tactics and circumstances have changed in relation to organising and holding raves. The Government's proposals were to increase powers to act against raves by making indoor trespassory events illegal, and by lowering the number of persons required to be present to qualify as a rave when outdoors from 100 to 20.[7] Lord Bassam states that the aim of this legislation was to make unlicensed raves commercially unattractive by redefining the numbers constituting a rave. Also, the intention of this legislation was to cover both indoor and outdoor raves. This amendment was agreed to.[8]

---

[1] *Hansard*, HL Deb, 18 July 2003, cols 1097ff.
[2] *Hansard*, HL Deb, 3 November 2003, cols 581ff.
[3] Ibid, col 587.
[4] *Hansard*, HL Deb, 7 October 2003, col 260.
[5] Ibid, cols 261–262.
[6] Ibid, cols 262–263.
[7] Ibid, cols 263–265.
[8] Ibid, col 268.

Power to remove trespassers: alternative sites

8.74 On the second reading of the Bill in the House of Lords on 18 July 2003, Baroness Walmsley, Labour, stated of Part 8 of the Bill (now Part 7 of the Act):

'The very fact that something specific on gypsy and traveller families has been tacked onto the Bill about anti-social behaviour encourages the public to have racist attitudes about them. It suggests that the nomadic way of life, linked with the shortfall in sites is itself criminal behaviour.'[1]

8.75 Lord Wedderburn, Labour, stated that he believed that the Bill failed to address issues of civil liberties. With the issue of trespass, he said that the Bill did not afford the opportunity to question the belief of a police officer that an alternative site was available for travellers.[2]

8.76 In the Report Stage of 23 October 2003, Baroness Turner, Labour, introduced a series of amendments after being approached by the Children's Society. She expressed the view of the Gypsy's Council that there were inadequate numbers of suitable sites for travellers and noted that the proposals would not produce any more, and thus would criminalise travelling communities. Baroness Turner sought assurances that the powers would not be used to split up families; and that the powers would only be used when an actual alternative site was made available to those in need of it, rather than the mere possibility of an available site. Baroness Turner asked that police officers exercising these powers should receive training on the application of the Human Rights Act 1998, the Race Relations Act 1976 and the Children Act 1989, bearing in mind that there may be children travelling alone and that there should be protection for all those under 18. Baroness Turner expressed the view of the traveller community that the Government might use these powers to separate them from their children.[3]

8.77 Lord Avebury, Liberal Democrat, was concerned that the Government was not providing local authorities with incentives to provide extra sites for travellers. He also noted that many authorities did not mention travellers in their homelessness strategies, and that few referred to them in race equality statements or references to the Race Relations Act 1976. Moreover, no local authorities could offer trespassing travellers a place on an official site because none were available.[4]

8.78 Baroness Scotland, for the Government, denied that the Government was attempting to portray travellers as a criminal element, or that the provisions would separate travellers from their children. Baroness Scotland recognised that there was a shortage of sites but that the new powers were an important tool for police to compel travellers to move to local authority sites. Baroness Scotland stressed that there were genuine problems faced by other members of the community when travellers settle illegally. Baroness Scotland stated that travellers would not always be split up and that it would be unnecessarily bureaucratic that all directions should be communicated in writing as this would undermine a swift response to a problem.[5]

8.79 This clause and subsequent clauses were agreed to.[6]

8.80 In the Report Stage of 3 November 2003, Lord Dixon-Smith, Conservative, attempted to introduce an amendment on the issue of aggravated trespass in relation to destruction of genetically modified crops that was defeated.[7]

8.81 Lord Avebury, Liberal Democrat, introduced a new amendment to introduce a clause 'powers relating to trespassers and unauthorised campers: alternative site available'. Lord Avebury

[1] *Hansard*, HL Deb, 18 July 2003, col 1113.
[2] Ibid, cols 1126–1128.
[3] *Hansard*, HL Deb, 23 October 2003, col 153.
[4] Ibid, col 1169.
[5] Ibid, col 1170.
[6] Ibid, col 1172.
[7] *Hansard*, HL Deb, 3 November 2003, col 591.

argued that before the police can exercise these powers to move travellers to another site they must ensure that there is another site for them to go to. The main concern was the potential threat of imprisonment for a failure to comply with a direction.[1]

8.82 The Minister responded by stating that the new powers would be used alongside existing powers under s 61 of the 1994 Act. The Minister added that, where further local authority sites are available, under the new powers trespassers on unauthorised sites will be moved on. However, if this were not the case, then police can use their powers under s 61 of the 1994 Act, but only after reasonable steps have been taken to ask the occupiers to leave and they have caused damage to the land or property on the land. The Minister stated that it is not desirable for the police to be unable to take action where damage has occurred because there is no alternative site available. However, the Minister stressed the efforts of the Government to upgrade existing sites and the creation of others. The Minister responded that there was a range of sentences available but that imprisonment may be the appropriate sanction in certain circumstances.[2]

8.83 Baroness Turner, Labour, stated that there were still concerns about the impact of the Bill on gypsy and traveller children and their families. Her concern was that it was wrong that there was a disparity between the treatment of those evicted from houses and those evicted from traveller sites. Also, a forced eviction is frightening and would not be in the best interests of the child. Moreover, the fact was that issues of good race relations had been raised in the Committee Stage but the issue remained to be addressed. Baroness Turner looked to the Deputy Prime Minister to issue guidance in consultation with the CRE on this part of the Bill. Baroness Turner stated that she would like to see an extension of the defence of children to all those under 18 on the site and not just those travelling with parents or guardians specifically given the powers under the Children Act 1989 concerning child welfare.[3]

8.84 Lord Wedderburn, Labour, demanded to know why a local authority should not have to certify that there is another site available to house families and children. Lord Wedderburn stated that the rights of the child were paramount and questioned why steps are not there to protect children under 18 regardless of whether they are travelling with their parents or guardian. Lord Wedderburn suggested that these policies gave the impression that travellers' children do not count and that the Government had adopted an illiberal attitude.[4]

8.85 In response, the Minister, Lord Bassam, denied that the Government was being illiberal or hardline. On the issue of a police officer giving the direction and consulting with local authorities about alternative sites, the Minister stated that this was better left to guidance rather than by a rigid statutory scheme in the Bill. The Minister stated that it would not always be possible to ensure that large extended families would be housed on the same site when moved. The Minister gave assurances that the police would receive the appropriate training. The Minister stated that the removal of the requirement that the child must be living with a parent or guardian would lessen police powers to act swiftly, but the Minister said that the powers were unlikely to be used against those under 18.[5]

8.86 Lord Avebury responded to the Minister on the issue of guidance by stating that this tactic had left children of travellers as the most deprived section within schools.[6]

8.87 The Government amendments were agreed to.

---

[1] *Hansard*, HL Deb, 3 November 2003, cols 596–598.
[2] Ibid, col 600.
[3] Ibid, col 599.
[4] Ibid, cols 606–607.
[5] Ibid, col 607.
[6] Ibid, cols 610–611.

The provisions in detail

Public assemblies

8.88   As discussed above, s 14 of the Public Order Act 1986 gives a senior police officer the power to impose conditions on public assemblies. In order to exercise this power lawfully, the senior police officer must reasonably believe that serious public disorder, serious damage to property or serious disruption to the life of the community might result from the assembly, or that its purpose is the intimidation of others with the view to compelling the other people to act in a particular way. The conditions that a senior police officer can impose on such an assembly include determining its location, its maximum duration or the maximum numbers of people who may assemble. At present, these conditions can only be imposed on assemblies of 20 or more people.

8.89   Section 57 of the Anti-social Behaviour Act 2003 amends the definition of an assembly in s 14 of the Public Order Act 1986 from '20 or more persons' to 'two or more persons'. Thus, the threshold for the exercise of powers imposing conditions on public assemblies under the 1986 Act is lowered and applies to groups of two or more people.

8.90   This section will not affect peaceful picketing by members of a trade union at their place of work (Trades Union and Labour Relations (Consolidation) Act 1992, s 220).

8.91   This amendment will also alter the threshold by which an order can be sought by the police for banning trespassory assemblies under ss 14A, 14B and 14C of the 1986 Act. A ban may now be sought for an assembly of two people and thus the powers and punishments provided for under ss 14B and 14C of the 1986 Act exercised. This amendment has been made despite Earl Ferrers' statement that the justification for such powers was the apprehension that tens of thousands of people would turn up to such assemblies.[1]

Questions and problems

8.92   The obvious problem with this change is the small number of people now required to be a gathering for the purposes of attracting the police powers to deal with unlawful assemblies and trespassory assemblies. The obvious potential civil liberty problems have been highlighted by the discussions above. These changes might have been 'piggy-backed' onto the changes presented is Part 4 of the Act to deal with groups of children. It may have been the case that the Government saw problems with identifying groups as containing only children under 16 for the exercise of these powers. However, the powers provided by Part 4 have been subject to criticism by Baroness Linklater in the Lords' debates as being in potential breach of basic civil liberties and rights of the child.

8.93   At this point, it may be of interest to revisit the proposals forwarded by the Law Commission,[2] which received judicial support from Lord Hailsham. On the existing law at the time in Part V of the report[3] on the unlawful assembly and Part VI on riot[4] it was noted that there was a common purpose for unlawful assembly and riot that the number of people required was three or more.[5] The Law Commission, in its draft Bill, recommended that a minimum of 12 person should be the lower limit for a gathering for a common purpose of a threat of unlawful violence.[6]

---

[1]   Earl Ferrers, *Hansard*, HL Deb, 7 July 1994, col 1489.
[2]   *Offences Related to Public Disorder*, 24 October 1983, Law Com No 123.
[3]   Ibid, paras 5.1ff.
[4]   Ibid, paras 6.1ff.
[5]   Ibid, para 6.11–6.16.
[6]   Clause 1 of Criminal Disorder Draft Bill 1983.

8.94 In addition to the obvious civil liberties problems, this legislation may create policing problems. Baroness Linklater in the Lords' debates noted that there was not an enthusiastic reaction to this reform from police forces, since it may provide problems for the police in terms of increased litigation via judicial review of their actions in dispersing groups. It may also increase civil claims against police if their actions under this provision are held to be unlawful. Thus, the police response may be not to become involved in circumstances where their intervention in necessary. The counterpoint to this argument may be that there is inadequate judicial supervision of the exercise of this power via judicial review. This can lead to major problems where community trust of police is further eroded, especially among ethnic minorities. At the extreme end, it could result in a 'militaristic' style of policing which can precipitate rioting. Also, the policy behind the anti-social behaviour legislation is to reduce crime and disorder in deprived and vulnerable communities. If, in the exercise of these provisions, community relations with the police are damaged, people who are viewed to benefit from this legislation may, in fact, be harmed further if they remain victims of crime and disorder rather than be helped by legislation.

Raves

8.95 Section 58(2) of the Anti-social Behaviour Act 2003 amends s 63 of the 1994 Act to reduce the threshold of a definition of the numbers of persons constituting a rave from 100 to 20 or more. Thus, a rave can constitute a gathering of 20 people or more. Therefore, a gathering of 20 people can engage the exercise of the powers under ss 63–67 of the 1994 Act.

8.96 Subsection (3) inserts an additional section after s 63(1) of the 1994 Act, such that s 63(1) also applies to a gathering of 20 or more persons who are trespassing on land, and that it would be a gathering of the kind (ie a rave) if it took place in the open air.

8.97 Subsection (4) removes the requirement that the direction relates to land 'in the open air' under s 63(2) of the 1994 Act.

8.98 Subsection (5) modifies s 63(7) of the 1994 Act to replace the words 'this section' for 'subs (6) above'. Thus, the defence under s 63(7) only applies to the offences committed under s 63(6) of the 1994 Act.

8.99 Subsection (6) provides for the addition of an extra offence under s 63 of the 1994 Act. Subsection (6) inserts a new Part after s 63(7) of the 1994 Act. A person commits an offence if he knows a direction has been given under s 63(2) of the 1994 Act that applies to him, and he makes preparations for or attends a rave within 24 hours of the direction being given. If a person is found guilty of this offence, he is liable for up to 3 months' imprisonment, or a fine up to level 4 on the scale or both.

8.100 The purpose of this reform is to attempt to reduce the nuisance and disruption associated with unlicensed raves by making them commercially unattractive. Also, the aim is to target indoor raves. The potential problems which may arise relate to effective exercise of the police powers in the 1996 Act to control movement and travel of people to a rave.

Aggravated trespass

8.101 Section 59 of the Anti-social Behaviour Act 2003 amends ss 68 and 69 of the Criminal Justice and Public Order Act 1994 ('the 1994 Act') to extend the provisions relating to the offence of aggravated trespass to cover trespass into buildings as well as in the open air. Thus, the offence of aggravated trespass will be constituted where a person trespassing, either in a building or in the open air, does anything that is intended to intimidate or deter persons from engaging in a lawful activity, or to obstruct or disrupt that activity.

8.102 From the explanatory notes to the initial draft of the Bill, the Government speculates that these provisions might be used in respect of activists, for example animal rights activists who invade a building of a company with the intention of conducting an intimidating or disruptive protest.

8.103 Subsection (2) of s 59 amends subs (1) of s 68 of the 1994 Act by removing the words 'in the open air' so that the offence under s 68 of the 1994 Act becomes aggravated trespass on land.

8.104 Subsection (3) of s 59 amends subs (1) of s 69 of the 1994 Act by removing the words 'in the open air'. Thus, where a senior police officer reasonably believes that a person is committing or participating in an aggravated trespass, the police officer has the power to direct them to leave the land. 'Land' is defined in the Interpretation Act 1978 so as to include buildings.

Questions and problems

8.105 This extends the offence of aggravated trespass to buildings. The aim was to address the activities of certain activists and other groups. The question that remains as to whether this will unjustifiably limit peaceful and legitimate protests and gatherings.

Powers to remove trespassers: alternative site available

8.106 Section 60 inserts a new s 62A into the 1994 Act to create a new power for a senior police officer to direct a person to leave the land and remove any vehicle or other property with him on that land. This power relates to a senior police officer who is present at the scene who holds a reasonable belief that the conditions set out in s 60(2) are satisfied in relation to the person on the land.

8.107 Subsection (2) provides the following conditions that a senior police officer ought to reasonably believe to be satisfied that:

(1)   at least two persons must be trespassing on the land including the person to whom the direction is given;
(2)   the trespassers must have between them at least one vehicle on the land;
(3)   the trespassers must be present on the land with a common purpose between them of residing on the land;
(4)   if it appears to the police officer that the person to whom the direction is given has one or more caravans in their possession or under their control on the land, there are relevant caravan sites available for the trespassers to move to;
(5)   the occupier of the land or a person acting on behalf of the occupier must have asked the police to remove the trespassers.

8.108 Subsection (3) permits a direction given by a senior police officer under subs (1) to be communicated to the person who is the subject of the direction by a police constable at the scene.

8.109 Subsection (4) provides that subs (5) applies if the senior police officer proposes to give a direction under subs (1) and it appears to the police officer that the person who is the subject of the direction has one or more caravans in their possession or under their control on the land in question.

8.110 Following satisfaction of the conditions in subs (4), subs (5) provides that the police officer issuing a direction under subs (1) must consult with every local authority in the area of the land, with the caravan(s) on it, to determine whether there is an alternative suitable pitch for the caravan(s) on a relevant caravan site that is situated in the local authority's area.

8.111 Subsection (6) provides a series of definitions of terms used specifically in this section:

(1) The terms 'caravan' and 'caravan site' are to have the same meaning as in Part 1 of the Caravan Sites and Control of Development Act 1960.[1]

(2) A 'relevant caravan site' means a caravan site, as defined above, that is situated in the area under the control of a local authority within whose area the land subject to the direction is situated, and is managed by a relevant site manager.

(3) A 'relevant site manager' means either a local authority within whose area the land is situated; or a registered social landlord.

(4) A 'registered social landlord' means a body registered as a social landlord under Chapter 1 of Part 1 of the Housing Act 1996.[2]

8.112 Subsections (7) and (8) enable the Secretary of State to make an order by statutory instrument, which is subject to annulment by resolution of Parliament, to change the definition of the term 'relevant site manager' either by adding persons or changing the description of persons who can be a relevant site manager for the purposes of this Act.

Failure to comply with direction: offences

8.113 Section 61 inserts a new section, s 62B, into the 1994 Act. The effect of this new section is that a person commits an offence if they fail to comply with a direction given to them under s 62A of the 1994 Act and leave the land as soon as is reasonably practicable, or if within 3 months of the direction being given they return to any land in the area of the relevant local authority as a trespasser with the intention of living on the land. A person found guilty of an offence under s 62B is liable to imprisonment for up to 6 months or a fine not exceeding level 4 on the standard scale, or both.

8.114 Subsection (4) of s 62B provides a constable in uniform with the power of arrest without a warrant of a person that they reasonably suspect is committing an offence under this section.

8.115 Subsection (5) of s 62B provides a defence to the offence specified in subs (4) if the accused was not a trespasser, or had a reasonable excuse for failing to leave or returning to the land, or was under 18 and living with their parents or guardian when the direction under s 62A was given.

Failure to comply with direction: seizure

8.116 Section 62 inserts s 62C into the 1994 Act. This provides a power for any constable, whether in uniform or not, to seize and remove vehicles, if they reasonably suspect that the person who owns or controls the vehicle has committed an offence under s 63B, and the offence relates to this vehicle.

8.117 It also provides for modification of s 67(1) where after 's 62(1)' '62C(3)' is inserted into s 67(1).

Common land: modifications

8.118 Section 63 introduces s 62D into the 1994 Act and makes necessary modifications to ss 62A–62C of the 1994 Act in their application to common land. These modifications provide for

---

[1] Section 29 provides for the interpretation of Part I. Subsection (1) provides that in this Part of this Act, unless the context otherwise requires:

'section 1(4) defines caravan site as follows:

In this Part of this Act the expression "caravan site" means land on which a caravan is stationed for the purposes of human habitation and land which is used in conjunction with land on which a caravan is so stationed.'

[2] See, in particular, s 2 of the Housing Act 1996 for eligibility of bodies to be registered as a social landlord.

identification of the nature of trespass on common land, and identities of occupiers and commoners and the exercise of their rights combined with exceptions to those who might be trespassers.

8.119 Subsection (2) provides that references to trespassing and trespassers are to have effect as if they were references to acts, and persons doing acts that constitute a trespass against the occupier, or infringement of commoners' rights.

8.120 Subsection (3) provides that references to the occupier in the case of land where the public has access are to include the local authority and any commoner, and in any other case are to include the commoners or any of them.

8.121 Subsection (4) provides that subs (1) of s 62D does not require action by more than one occupier, or to make persons trespassers against any commoner or local authority if they are permitted to be there by the other occupier.

Travellers' rights: questions and problems

8.122 The main questions raised by these provisions concern whether gypsies and travellers are being criminalised for their way of life by the creation of new offences. Although the new legislation introduces the consideration of use of dispersal of travellers and gypsies to alternative sites by the police the problems remain of availability of such local authority sites. The Government has promised more investment in such sites.

Interpretation

8.123 Section 64 provides for insertion of s 62E into the 1994 Act. This section provides for interpretation of terms used in ss 62A–62D.

8.124 The definition of 'land' does not include buildings other than agricultural buildings within the meaning of paras 3–8 of Sch 5 to the Local Government Finance Act 1988, or scheduled monuments within the meaning of the Ancient Monuments and Archaeological Areas Act 1979.

8.125 The term 'local authority' means in London, a London Borough or the Common Council of the City of London; in England outside London, a county council, a district council or the Council of the Isles of Scilly; in Wales, a county council or county borough council.

8.126 The terms 'occupier', 'trespass (and 'trepassing'/'trespasser') have the meanings given by s 61 of the 1994 Act.

8.127 The term 'relevant land' means land to which a direction under s 62A(1) is given.

8.128 The term 'relevant local authority' means that if the relevant land is situated in the area of more than one local authority (except for the Isles of Scilly), the district or county borough council within whose areas the relevant land is situated.

8.129 The term 'vehicle' has the same meaning as under s 61. This includes any vehicle whether it is in a fit state or not for use on roads, a chassis or body with or without wheels, or any load carried by or attached to such a vehicle. This also includes a caravan as defined under s 29(1) of the Caravan Sites and Control of Development Act 1960.

8.130 A person may be regarded as having the purpose of residing in a place or on land if they have a home elsewhere.

CHAPTER 9

HIGH HEDGES

Introduction

9.1   Part 8 of the Anti-social Behaviour Act 2003 provides local authorities with enforcement powers to deal with high hedge disputes. It was inserted into the Anti-social Behaviour Bill at the Report Stage in the Lords by the Government following the failure of Stephen Pound MP's High Hedges (No 2) Bill in June 2003.

9.2   There are about 17,000 problem hedges in England and Wales[1] and the victims of these problem hedges regularly contact their local authorities, central government and their constituency MPs for help. The lack of an effective dispute resolution procedure for hedge disputes means that many MPs are sympathetic to the need for legislation to provide a simple and proportionate dispute resolution procedure.

9.3   Neighbour disputes caused by inappropriately high hedges, most notoriously leylandii hedges, can be distinguished from other types of anti-social behaviour targeted by the provisions of the Act in that the consequences of an overgrown hedge impacts upon individuals rather than the community. The problems which arise are overwhelmingly suburban rather than urban.

9.4   However, the Government did not accept these distinctions:

'In truth, to those who suffer the most extreme forms of the problem, it can be just as antisocial as graffiti or noisy neighbours. We should not accept the stereotype that antisocial behaviour is only about teenagers on low-income estates.'[2]

9.5   The insertion of a Private Member's Bill into a Government Bill is highly unusual, since Private Member's Bills rarely receive the necessary level of parliamentary scrutiny. Nonetheless, the Government, having promised legislative action in 2000, and surprised by the failure of the High Hedges (No 2) Bill, considered that the Anti-social Behaviour Bill provided the best vehicle for prompt enactment of the measures.

9.6   In fact, the series of unsuccessful attempts to legislate on this matter have ensured that there has been extensive parliamentary scrutiny. There have been seven Private Member's Bills[3] on the issue since 1997 and Stephen Pound MP's Bill received 22 hours and 20 minutes of parliamentary debate.[4] Moreover, all-party support in both Commons and Lords no doubt provided the Government with sufficient justification for the unusual procedure.

---

[1]   DETR, *High Hedges: Possible Solutions*, A consultation paper covering England and Wales (November, 1999).

[2]   *Hansard*, HC Deb, 17 November 2003, col 551.

[3]   Including the Hedges (Control) Bill, Bill 29 of 1998–99; the Control of Residential Hedgerows Bill, Bill 61 of 1998/99; the Statutory Nuisances (Hedgerows in Residential Areas) Bill, HL Bill 10 of 1999/2000; and the High Hedges Bill, Bill 13 of 2000–01.

[4]   *Hansard*, HC Deb, 17 November 2003, col 561.

The social problem

9.7   The problems caused by high hedges have received extensive publicity and are outlined in a House of Commons research paper published in 1999:

> 'There is a widespread problem of people losing light in their gardens and houses, because of the planting of a high hedge in the neighbouring garden. This is often associated with leylandii (*cupressocyparis leylandii*), that can grow by four feet in a year and reach a height of 100 feet or more. Gardens and even houses, can be thrown into the shade.'[1]

9.8   High hedges also block views and cause damage to drains and other structures. Neighbours can feel oppressed and that their enjoyment of their homes and gardens has been reduced. The resulting tension between neighbours can impact upon people's mental and physical health.

9.9   The press coverage following the Government announcement of the amendment indicates the extent and seriousness of and public interest in the problem of high hedges. For instance *The Independent* commented:

> 'The end is finally in sight for "skyscraper" leylandii hedges which block light, cause subsidence and dramatically reduce property values. For years MPs have been inundated with protests about neighbours' hedges, which can rocket to 40ft in 10 years. This year, one dispute over a hedge led to a 66-year-old man shooting his neighbour dead in Lincolnshire and later hanging himself in a jail cell.'[2]

9.10   The Government had advocated non-legal solutions to the problem. In 1998, it established the leylandii working group which agreed a voluntary code of practice on information to be provided at the point of sale.[3] It also recommended mediation. However, neither of these remedies resolves problems of existing problem hedges where neighbours are unwilling to compromise.

The legal problem

9.11   The existing common law and statutory provisions have proved inadequate to deal with the problem of high hedges.

9.12   The Government had advised that the use of the statutory nuisance procedure under the Environmental Protection Act 1990 may provide an appropriate legal remedy.[4] A statutory nuisance is a matter which is listed within s 79(1) of the Act which causes nuisance or is prejudicial to health. Section 79(1) of the Act also requires that local authorities investigate complaints of statutory nuisances. The Act enables local authorities to issue abatement notices and courts can impose penalties upon people who fail to abate the nuisance. If a local authority fails to act, an individual may apply to the magistrates' court for an abatement order.

9.13   However, high hedges are not one of the categories of nuisance listed in s 79(1) of the Act and there has been no court decision that a particular high hedge does constitute a statutory nuisance. Proceedings under the Environmental Protection Act 1990 are criminal proceedings and the burden of proof is therefore 'beyond reasonable doubt'. Local authorities are unwilling to risk potentially expensive litigation when the outcome is so uncertain. There is no legal aid available for individuals to pursue criminal cases so the individual's avenue for dispute resolution when the local authority does not intervene is not a viable one.

---

[1]   HC Research Paper 99/35, 25 March 1999, *The Control of High Hedges*.

[2]   *The Independent*, 18 October 2003.

[3]   *The right hedge for you* (DETR).

[4]   DETR, *Possible remedies to problems with high hedges in gardens*, advice sent to individuals quoted in HC Research Paper 99/35, 25 March 1999, *The Control of High Hedges*.

9.14 It may also be that, as a result of the public health origins of the Environmental Protection Act 1990, statutory nuisances require there to be a risk of disease or illness. Moreover, as a House of Commons research paper published in 1999 points out:

> '... high hedges are very different from other nuisances. One particular problem with any type of remedy is that the owner of the hedge has to take positive action, at considerable expense, to prevent the hedge growing. Repeated action will be required perhaps with repeated abatement notices or repeated court appearances for a recalcitrant owner.'[1]

9.15 English common law upholds the rights of the owners of land to use their land as they will. Therefore growing hedges which interfere with a neighbouring owner's light cannot be prevented unless a right to light has been acquired as an easement. This could be demonstrated for instance by showing that the light has been enjoyed uninterrupted for 20 years. The 1999 House of Commons Research Paper suggests that, whilst theoretically legislation such as the Prescription Act 1832 may provide a legal solution to a dispute, in practice the law is not useful to those suffering from the problems caused by high hedges.[2]

9.16 The law of private nuisance is concerned with substantial interference with a neighbour's land. It applies when branches overhang a neighbour's property or when roots encroach upon the property. The neighbour is able to cut down the branches as long as he or she does not enter the land where the tree is growing, and, in appropriate cases, may claim remedial expenditure.[3] However, hedge disputes are not concerned with encroachment on the land, but on the less physical impacts of high hedges.

9.17 The case of *Stanton v Jones*[4] indicates the difficulties involved in litigating about leylandii hedges. Michael Jones, who subsequently founded the pressure group Hedgeline[5] which provides advice and campaigns for appropriate legal remedies for those suffering from the problems of high hedges, was ultimately successful in litigation against his neighbour. However, the costs of the case were reported to be as much as £50,000, the litigation took a number of years and the facts of the case are narrow since the hedge provided the boundary of the properties and, as a party hedge, both occupiers were responsible for its maintenance. If the hedge had been within his neighbour's property 'it is questionable whether anything'[6] could have been done about the hedge.

9.18 There is no need to apply for planning permission to plant a hedge, in contrast with erecting a fence over 2 metres in height, and therefore planning law does not apply.

Consultation

9.19 The Department of the Environment, Transport and the Regions published a consultation paper, *High Hedges*, in November 1999.[7] This suggested four options for resolution of the problem: the promotion of existing procedures; a non-legislative approach; the extension of easements of light; and a system based on complaints.

9.20 The consultation paper considered that a complaints-based system would address hedge problems effectively, would provide for minimal interference with people's property, since it would only affect people's right to grow their own hedge if it interfered with their neighbour's right to enjoy their own property, and would provide a relatively transparent basis for action.

---

[1] HC Research Paper 99/35, 25 March 1999, *The Control of High Hedges*.
[2] Ibid.
[3] *Delaware Mansions Ltd and another v Westminster City Council* [2001] UKHL 55.
[4] *Charles Bernard Stanton v Clarence Michael Jones*, Birmingham County Court, 30 November 1995.
[5] www.hedgeline.org.uk.
[6] HC Research Paper 99/35, 25 March 1999, *The Control of High Hedges*.
[7] DETR, *High Hedges: Possible Solutions*, a consultation paper covering England and Wales (November 1999).

9.21 The DETR received 3,062 responses to the consultation paper, demonstrating a huge level of interest. The responses overwhelmingly preferred the establishment of a statutory complaints system run by local authorities. The Government press release committed the Government to legislative action:

> 'The government is to work up new laws to be introduced in England as soon as there is space in the Parliamentary timetable. Specially designed to tackle nuisance garden hedges, such as Leylandii, the legislation would mean that people could ask their local council to settle their hedge disputes, if they could not resolve matters amicably.'[1]

9.22 The Government has not introduced its own Bill, but John Taylor MP presented a Private Member's Bill in the parliamentary session 2000–01. His High Hedges Bill,[2] which was based upon the complaints-based system proposed in the consultation, had Government support.[3] The Bill failed due to lack of time caused by the calling of the 2001 General Election.

Parliamentary session 2002–03

9.23 Stephen Pound MP, for Ealing North, drew fourteenth in the annual ballot for Private Member's Bills. He chose to introduce a Bill to enact the complaints-based system. The Government supported his Bill[4] and was prepared to provide sufficient time to enable the Bill to become law.

9.24 At the same time, Baroness Gardner introduced a similar Bill in the House of Lords.[5] She indicated that she would work with Stephen Pound MP to increase the chances of his Bill becoming law.

9.25 The amendments made to Lady Gardner's Bill, which had no prospect of success, formed the basis of the Bill presented by Stephen Pound at second reading and no further amendments were required at the Committee Stage. However, Stephen Pound's Bill was talked out at the Report Stage in the Commons by Christopher Chope MP for Christchurch on 20 June 2003.

9.26 Lady Gardner proposed an amendment to the Anti-social Behaviour Bill to include the whole of the Government-drafted High Hedges (No 2) Bill. This was not initially successful, but in what was described as a 'surprising, albeit worthwhile, piece of initiative on their part'[6] the Government decided to do what it had previously rejected and enact the High Hedges (No 2) Bill by incorporating it into the Anti-social Behaviour Bill.

The provisions in detail

9.27 Part 8 of the Anti-social Behaviour Act 2003 provides for a statutory complaints-based system which will enable local authorities to resolve and enforce solutions to disputes caused by high hedges impacting upon domestic property. It requires that complainants have exhausted other means of dispute resolution, including mediation, prior to having recourse to the complaints mechanism. Local authorities are given the power, in the last resort, to carry out the work to reduce the height of the hedge themselves and bill the owner for the work.

---

[1] DETR Press Release 540/00, 'Nuisance hedges to get the chop', 10 August 2000, quoted in HC Research Paper 01/20, 7 March 2001, *High Hedges Bill.*
[2] Bill 13 of 2000–2001.
[3] *Hansard*, HC Deb, 14 February 2001, col 150.
[4] High Hedges (No 2) Bill.
[5] High Hedges Bill [HL].
[6] Mr Paice MP, *Hansard*, HC Deb, 17 November 2003, col 553.

9.28   The table below (Table 9.1) summarises the main provisions of this Part of the Act.

Table 9.1 Summary of the main provisions of Part 8 of the Anti-social Behaviour Act 2003		
Section	**Summary**	**Comment**
65–67	Definitions of complaints, high hedges and domestic property	The definition of high hedges is critical to the scope of the statutory remedy. It can be amended by regulation.
68	Complaints procedure	Considerable discretion is given to local authorities in deciding if and how to proceed. Fees may be charged by local authorities to determine complaints.
69–70	Remedial notices	Remedial notices can provide for both immediate action and longer term maintenance
71–73	Appeals	An independent appeals procedure is available to both complainants and those responsible for problem hedges
74	Powers of entry	These are provided to enable entry for the purposes of determining the complaint, the appeal and to carry out work in default.
75–78	Enforcement powers	Failure to comply with a remedial notice will be a criminal offence. Additionally local authorities are given default powers to do the necessary works and recoup the costs
79–84	Supplementary provisions	The most significant provision is the power to amend the scope of complaints and amend the definition of high hedge

9.29   Local authorities are already anticipating the measures:

‘Councils up and down the country are welcoming the chance, not because they wish to act like some local government *gauleiter* and dictate how things should or should not be done, but because they have an immense problem and have not been willed the tools to address it.’[1]

The scope of the complaints system

9.30   Complaints can be made by the owner or the occupier of domestic property who considers that his or her reasonable enjoyment of the whole or part of the domestic property is impaired by the height of a high hedge planted on another person's land.[2] Complaints are restricted to the effect of the height of the hedge.

9.31   The Act does not apply to complaints about the effects of roots.[3] The Government considers that other remedies are available to deal with root-related property damage and pointed

---

[1]   *Hansard*, HC Deb, 17 November 2003, col 557.
[2]   Section 65(1).
[3]   Section 65(4).

out that in such cases 'the issues tend to be about who is liable for the damage and the level of compensation rather than about remedial works to the hedge'.[1]

9.32   The section provides for a broad basis for complaints and is not restricted to the reduction of light caused by the high hedge. This provides flexibility, so that a range of difficulties caused by high hedges can be addressed. For instance, a complaint could be based on damage to plants caused by the high hedge, or where a small garden was dominated by the neighbouring hedge reducing the amenity value of the garden.

9.33   An owner does not have to occupy the domestic property in order to make a complaint.[2] Where the complainant is not in occupation, the basis of the complaint is the effect that the height of the hedge would have on the reasonable enjoyment of the property by a prospective occupier.[3]

9.34   Complaints can be transferred to new owners and occupiers when the original complainant ceases to own or occupy the property.[4]

9.35   'Domestic property' is defined as a dwelling or a garden or yard which is used in connection with the dwelling.[5] The limit to domestic property reflects the aim of this Part of the Act, which is to enable people to enjoy their homes. Where premises have mixed domestic and commercial uses, the Act applies to protect the living quarters from the effects of a neighbouring hedge:

> 'Where the boundaries between the business and living quarters are more blurred, the local authority would need to use its good sense and consider the facts of each case to determine whether the legislation should apply.'[6]

The definition of a high hedge

9.36   A high hedge is one which forms a barrier to light or access, is made up of a line of two or more evergreens, is wholly or predominantly evergreen, and is more than 2 metres high.[7] A deciduous hedge is therefore not a high hedge for the purposes of the Act. However, an evergreen hedge which also contains a few deciduous trees would constitute a high hedge for the purpose of the Act.

9.37   This definition provides an interesting contrast with that provided by the judge in *Stanton v Jones*:

> 'a number of woody plants, whether capable of growing into trees or not, which are so planted as to be intended to be in line and which, when mature, to be so integrated together as to form both a screen and a barrier.'[8]

9.38   Limiting the definition to coniferous species was justified within the DETR consultation paper on the basis of a lack of evidence of problems with other types of tree:

> 'It would seem sensible, therefore, in the interests of proportionality, to restrict any new law regulating high hedges to the species which are causing problems.'[9]

---

[1]   *Hansard*, HL Deb, 28 February 2003, col 498.
[2]   Section 65(2).
[3]   Section 65(2)(b).
[4]   Section 65(5).
[5]   Section 67.
[6]   *Hansard*, HL Deb, 9 January 2003, col 1150.
[7]   Section 66.
[8]   *Stanton v Jones*, Birmingham County Court, 30 November 1995, quoted in DETR, *High Hedges: Study of the Problem and Feasibility of Possible Solutions* (1999).
[9]   DETR, *High Hedges: Possible Solutions*, a consultation paper (November 1999).

The Act, however, only requires the hedge to be predominantly evergreen. This prevents avoidance of the procedure by the person responsible for the hedge planting an alder or another deciduous tree within the hedge.

9.39 The Act avoids listing prohibited species. Listing dangerous breeds has proved problematic in other legislation.[1] It defines evergreen broadly to include semi-evergreen trees or shrubs.[2] A semi-evergreen plant is one which retains most of its foliage throughout the year, and therefore would include privet.

9.40 The height of 2 metres appears to have been chosen to reflect practice in other countries as well as UK planning restrictions on fences and walls. In both France and Germany, a victim can take civil action where a hedge exceeds 2 metres.[3]

9.41 A line of evergreens, as a result of the gaps between the evergreens at a height of more than 2 metres, does not form an effective barrier to light or access.[4] This means that gaps between trees or shrubs below 2 metres will not prevent the hedge from being defined as a high hedge unless there are also gaps above the critical 2 metre mark.

9.42 The section does not require that the hedge is a boundary hedge and therefore the provisions apply wherever the hedge is located on the neighbouring land. It does require that the hedge forms a barrier to light or access. The word barrier has two effects. It will 'focus attention on the dense screens that evergreens tend to create, which the cause of complaint. Secondly it would help to filter out complaints that have little chance of success before they reach the local authority'.[5] The Government intends to provide guidance on what is a barrier:

> 'It will obviously have to reflect to some degree its location and mass. The decision in general will necessarily involve consideration of the extent to which the hedge in question acts as a barrier and its effect; its obstacle to light, access, visibility and so on.'[6]

9.43 The Secretary of State (for England) and the National Assembly for Wales have the power to change the definition through regulations. The Government Minister in the Lords pointed out that 'Getting the precise definition of a hedge right is far from easy, and only time will test the present definition'.[7] By providing a regulatory power to change the definition, the Government is given the flexibility to respond quickly to changing circumstances and to new and other problems which may emerge. The regulations would be subject to the affirmative resolution procedure which would require them to be debated and approved by both Houses of Parliament.[8]

The complaints procedure

9.44 The complaints procedure is set out in s 68 of the Act. The complaint must be made to the local authority and, if a fee is required, then it must be paid at the time of the complaint.

9.45 Prior to the complaint being made, the expectation is that the complainant should inform the hedge owner that they intend making the complaint. However, this expectation is to be made explicit within leaflets published for the public which explain the complaints procedure, rather than including the requirement on the face of the Act.

---

[1] See the Dangerous Dogs Act 1991.
[2] Section 66(3).
[3] DETR, *High Hedges: Possible Solutions*, a consultation paper (November 1999).
[4] Section 66(2).
[5] *Hansard*, HL Deb, 9 January 2003, col 1134.
[6] Ibid, col 1137.
[7] *Hansard*, HL Deb, 28 February 2003, col 503.
[8] Regulatory Impact Assessment, *High Hedges (No 2) Bill*.

9.46 Extensive discretion is given to local authorities to decide whether to proceed with complaints where the complainant has not taken all the steps that should have been taken prior to complaining to the local authority or where the local authority considers the complaint to be frivolous and vexatious.[1] There was some discussion in Parliament as to whether local authorities should be empowered to exclude malicious complaints. However, the Government considered that it was not appropriate to ask local authorities to make judgements about the motivation of complainants:

> 'It is intended that the Bill should take the heat out of hedge disputes by local authorities acting as independent third parties in examining issues as objectively and dispassionately as they can . Our view is that local authorities should be left to weigh the facts of each case in a fair and impartial manner, unencumbered by questions of the different and varying motivations of the parties involved.'[2]

9.47 The provision of discretion will, as a result of normal public law principles, require local authorities to develop a complaints system which is responsive to individual circumstances, allows parties the opportunity to be heard and enables the local authority to develop solutions that are reasonable and proportionate to the problems caused.

9.48 If the authority decides to proceed with the complaint, it must decide whether or not to uphold the complaint and, if the complaint is upheld, whether or not to issue a remedial notice. Decisions not to take action, together with reasons, must be notified to the complainant and to the owner and occupier of neighbouring land as soon as reasonably practicable.[3] Decisions on whether or not to take action can be appealed.

Remedial notices

9.49 Remedial notices are issued by the local authority following a complaint which it has decided to act upon. The notice must inform the owner or occupier of the neighbouring land:

- of the authority's decision to uphold the complaint;
- of the initial action that must be taken before the end of the compliance period;
- of the preventative action which will be required in the future; and
- of the consequences of failure to comply with the remedial notice.[4]

9.50 Remedial notices cannot require that the hedge is reduced below 2 metres in height, or removed.[5] The Government Minister in the Lords explained that:

> 'implicitly the Bill is saying to people that hedges can be grown to 2 metres without them having any adverse effect on neighbours. Reducing the height of the hedge below this limit or removing it entirely would, therefore, go beyond what was necessary to remedy the adverse effects of the hedge. ... the government believe that requiring removal of a high hedge would represent a disproportionate response to the problem.'[6]

9.51 The remedial notice can provide for both the immediate solution to the problem, and for a longer-term remedy. It is therefore potentially binding on future owners of the hedge, which may cause difficulties in practical enforcement. Remedial notices are local land charges.[7] Reduction in the height of the hedge is not the only course of action that can be specified in a remedial notice.

---

[1] Section 68(2).
[2] *Hansard*, HL Deb, 9 January 2003, col 1153.
[3] Section 68(5).
[4] Section 69(2).
[5] Section 69(3).
[6] *Hansard*, HL Deb, 28 February 2003, col 510.
[7] Section 69(8).

Local authorities are given flexibility in designing solutions so that, for example, the person responsible for the hedge could be required to reduce the width of the hedge.

9.52 The operative date of the notice must be at least 28 days after the issue of the notice and the compliance period, which starts to run from the operative date of the notice, must give the person responsible for the hedge a reasonable period to take the required action.[1]

9.53 Local authorities can decide to withdraw a remedial notice or waive or relax a requirement within the notice. If they do either of these, they must inform the complainant(s) and the owners and occupiers of the neighbouring land.[2] Such decisions can be appealed.

Appeals

9.54 An independent appeals system is necessary to fulfil the requirements of natural justice and Art 6 of the ECHR. Complainants and owners and occupiers are given rights to appeal against local authority decisions to issue or withdraw a remedial notice or to relax or waive its requirements.[3] Complainants are additionally given rights of appeal over local authority decisions not to uphold the complaint or to take no action in relation to the complaint. This goes further than the consultation paper suggested, presumably because such decisions would be open to judicial review, and therefore might as well be included in a less elaborate and cheaper form of appeal.

9.55 Appeals, on the face of the Act, will be to the Secretary of State (in England) or the National Assembly for Wales (in Wales).[4] Details of the appeals procedure are to be dealt with by way of regulation, which may include the delegation of the appeal function. The regulatory impact assessment suggests that the Planning Inspectorate is the most likely forum, utilising the relatively cheap and speedy written representations procedure.

9.56 The regulatory impact assessment estimates that the appeal rate may be as high as 20% during the first few years of the complaints system whilst the backlog of complaints is dealt with. However, after the initial period, the number of cases and, therefore, the number of appeals is likely to fall dramatically.[5]

Enforcement

9.57 If the person responsible for the hedge fails to comply with a remedial notice within the compliance period, or, for works which are required by the notice to be carried out in the future, in the time set out in the notice, he will commit an offence which, following conviction in the magistrates' court, will be liable to level 3 fine (ie up to £1,000).[6]

9.58 The person responsible for the hedge, and therefore liable for prosecution, is likely to be the owner of the land. However, where the property is leasehold or tenanted, the local authority would normally prosecute the person who has legal responsibility within the lease for looking after the hedge.

9.59 Two defences will be available:

(1) that the person responsible did everything that could be reasonably expected to secure compliance;

---

[1] Section 69(5).
[2] Section 70.
[3] Section 71.
[4] Section 71(7).
[5] Regulatory Impact Assessment, *High Hedges (No 2) Bill*.
[6] Section 75(1).

(2)   that he or she was not sent a copy of the notice as required by the Act.[1]

However, if the person is the owner of the land and the notice is registered as a local land charge, he or she will be presumed to have knowledge of the remedial notice.

9.60   The magistrates' court will have option of ordering compliance with the remedial notice within a set period of time, either in addition to or instead of imposing a punishment. Failure to comply with such an order will be an offence.[2]

9.61   Continued failure to comply with the court order will also constitute an offence for which a fine can be imposed, not exceeding one-twentieth of the level 3 fine per day of non-compliance.[3]

9.62   The regulatory impact assessment comments on court proceedings, suggesting that:

> 'only the most intractable cases are likely to require such intervention. And if the courts use the full range of penalties at their disposal – including daily fines for a continuing failure to comply with a remedial notice – this should act as a powerful deterrent to others.'[4]

9.63   A local authority is able to carry out the necessary work itself and charge the person responsible where the work required by the remedial notice has not been carried out during the compliance period.[5] These powers can be used, whether or not a criminal prosecution is pursued. Unpaid expenses as a result of carrying out works are a local land charge.[6]

9.64   Local authority charges are likely to be considerably higher than if the owner employed contractors directly. The threat, therefore, of the local authority carrying out works will probably provide sufficient incentive for compliance. If the local authority does carry out the works, hedge owners would, in effect, be penalised for non-compliance, but without having to be labelled as criminals and fined, which in certain circumstances may be considered excessive.

Powers of entry

9.65   In order for the complaints procedure to work effectively, local authority officers and appeals inspectors must be able to access the land where the hedge is located. In most cases, the landowner is likely to give permission but, in circumstances where permission is not forthcoming, the Act provides extensive powers of entry for the purposes of complaints and appeals. A local authority officer may enter the neighbouring land to obtain information which will enable them to make necessary decisions about complaints and remedial notices, including information that remedial notices have been breached. Appeals inspectors are given similar powers to enter the land to obtain the information necessary for an appeal.[7]

9.66   Anyone exercising a power of entry under this section must give at least 24 hours' notice to every occupier, produce evidence of his authority if required, and ensure that the land, if unoccupied, is as secured against unauthorised entry as it was when he entered it.[8]

9.67   The power of entry allows the officer to take with him other necessary people, which may include the police, and/or equipment and materials, and to remove samples of the trees or shrubs which make up the hedge to enable species identification.[9]

---

[1]   Section 75(3) and (4).
[2]   Section 75(9).
[3]   Section 75(10).
[4]   Regulatory Impact Assessment, *High Hedges (No 2) Bill.*
[5]   Section 77.
[6]   Section 77(3).
[7]   Section 74.
[8]   Section 74(3).
[9]   Section 74(5).

9.68 Local authority officers are also empowered to enter land to carry out remedial work in default of the person responsible for the hedge. In these circumstances, 7 days' notice must be given, providing a final opportunity for the work to be carried out by the hedge owner. [1]

9.69 It is an offence to obstruct someone exercising a power of entry.[2]

9.70 The Government explained its approach to powers of entry:

'… entry to land is always a sensitive issue, especially when it involves access to someone's home or, as in this case, garden. We would therefore expect the powers to be used sparingly, and for local authorities and appeals inspectors to proceed by agreement wherever possible. Where the voluntary approach does not work, we believe that the powers provide a vital fallback, helping to ensure that the legislation works fairly and effectively.'[3]

Consultation on regulations

9.71 Details of the fees payable, appeals procedures and other matters are to be provided for in regulations. The Government stated:

'We aim to have regulations published and out for consultation as rapidly as possible. We will consult over the course of next year with the aim, if possible, of having the measures fully implemented toward the end of 2004.'[4]

The Government intends that the consultation will be wide and include not only local government but also a range of interested organisations.

Interaction with existing laws on trees and hedges

9.72 The consultation paper suggested that tree preservation orders and the controls on conservation areas may take precedence over remedial notices. However, the Government pointed out that s 198(6)(b) of the Town and County Planning Act 1990 states that a tree preservation order does not apply 'to the cutting down, uprooting, topping or lopping of trees in compliance with any obligations imposed by or under an Act of Parliament. So remedial notices issued under the Act would automatically override the requirements of a tree preservation order'.[5] Moreover the Government indicated that it would consider revising the regulations on tree management in conservation areas to provide an exemption from requirements to obtain permission for the topping or lopping of evergreen hedges as part of normal management.

Expiry date

9.73 The consultation paper suggested that the legislation should be time-limited. Not only would the number of new cases decline but also:

'People are more likely to maintain their hedges so as not to cause problems, or respond informally to complaints from neighbours once new laws are in place.'[6]

It suggested that at the end of a set period of, for example, 10 years the law should lapse:

'This would be preceded by a review to establish whether there was a continuing need for such a system. If that showed complaints were still running at a high level, Parliamentary approval would be needed to renew the legislation.'[7]

---

[1] Section 77(2) and (5).
[2] Sections 74(7) and 77(9).
[3] *Hansard*, HL Deb, 28 February 2003, col 513.
[4] *Hansard*, HC Deb, 17 November 2003, col 550.
[5] *Hansard*, HL Deb, 9 January 2003, col 1159.
[6] DETR, *High Hedges: Possible Solutions*, A consultation paper covering England and Wales (November 1999).
[7] Ibid.

This suggestion has not been followed in the Act.

Funding

9.74 The provisions apply to existing hedges so that the complaints mechanism will apply to outstanding cases. This gave rise to considerable concern about the funding of local authorities to deal with the estimated 10,000 outstanding cases. Although fees can be levied, the Government Minister promised that if there was a shortfall 'we will follow the established procedure for recompensing local authorities for new burdens'.[1] It is expected that after the backlog of cases has been dealt with there will be far fewer complaints. In the long term, costs are likely to fall.

9.75 The Government intends to take a number of steps to limit recourse to the statutory complaints system, and therefore reduce the burden on local authorities. The regulatory impact assessment states:

> '... we will develop an advice and information pack that local authorities can send out when anyone asks them for help with hedge problems. This will include advice on the steps they might take to settle things amicably (an updated version of our existing leaflet *Over the Garden hedge*) and information on any local mediation services; there will be guidance on the legislation, including on how local authorities might assess and weigh the various factors and issues raised by complaints. Although aimed primarily at local authorities, the guidance will be widely available. Householders would, therefore, also be able to use the information to help them present their case persuasively in negotiations with the hedge owner; even after a formal complaint has been submitted, local authorities will be encouraged – where it is appropriate – to point people towards mediation. As an incentive to participate, the proposed fee would normally be refunded if the mediation succeeds.'[2]

Conclusion

9.76 After a long gestation period, Parliament has now provided a mechanism to resolve disputes about high hedges. It appears to have been generally welcomed, for instance, by the Local Government Association, whose only reservation is about the costs of administering the legislation. The procedure provides a number of opportunities for the disputants to resolve their differences and avoid criminal sanctions, yet has sufficient teeth to work.

9.77 Hedgeline described the legislation as 'the best possible news for tens of thousands of hedge victims'. They continued:

> 'We urge the anti-social hedge bullies – those people who have repeatedly ignored their neighbours' reasonable requests over many years – to cut their hedges down to size now or face the consequences of a public enforcement procedure that includes heavy fines and criminal prosecution.'[3]

---

[1] *Hansard*, HC Deb, 17 November 2003, col 561.

[2] Regulatory impact assessment *High Hedges (No 2) Bill*.

[3] Statement on www.hedgeline.org.uk.

CHAPTER 10

MISCELLANEOUS POWERS

Introduction

10.1 Part 9 of the Anti-social Behaviour Act 2003 contains a range 'miscellaneous powers' designed to provide further tools for the police, the courts and local authorities to respond to a range of anti-social behaviour. The provisions were originally contained in Part 5 of the Bill and headed 'sanctions', indicating that the central concern of this Part of the Act is increasing the effectiveness of the penalties for anti-social behaviour.

10.2 The provisions were largely trailed in the Home Office White Paper, *Respect and Responsibility – Taking a Stand against Anti-Social Behaviour*,[1] and are largely technical amendments to existing provisions, but with the potential to make a considerable impact upon the practice of controlling anti-social behaviour, particularly of young people.

10.3 Table 10.1 sets out a summary of the provisions of this Part of the Act.

Table 10.1		
Summary of the provisions of Part 9 of the Anti-social Behaviour Act 2003		
Section	**Summary**	**Comment**
85–86	Amendments to the Crime and Disorder Act 1998 in connection with anti-social behaviour orders	Increases the flexibility and availability of ASBOs, for instance, by enabling county councils and housing action trusts to apply for the orders, and local authorities to prosecute for breaches Enables the youth court to lift restrictions on publication of names
87	Amends the Criminal Justice and Police Act 2001 in connection with penalty notices	Lowers the lower age limit at which penalty notices can be given from 18 to 16 and provides a power to the Secretary of State to further lower the age
88	Amends the Powers of Criminal Courts (Sentencing) Act 2000 in connection with curfew orders and supervision orders	Schedule 2 to the Act extends the potential duration of a curfew order and a supervision order and allows for supervision orders to include a period of intensive foster parenting

---

[1] Cm 5778 (March 2003).

Table 10.1		
Summary of the provisions of Part 9 of the Anti-social Behaviour Act 2003		
Section	Summary	Comment
89	Amends the Police Reform Act 2002 by extending the powers of community support officers	New powers are give to community support officers to stop cycles on the footpath and to accredited persons to issue fixed penalty notices for disorder
90	Amends the Children and Young Persons Act 1969 in connection with local authority reports	Provides for the court to be able to order the local authority to report on where a child is likely to be accommodated if the child is remanded to local authority accommodation
91	Powers of arrest and s 222 of the Local Government Act 1972	Provides a new power for the court to attach in certain circumstances a power of arrest to injunctions under s 222 of the Local Government Act 1972

Anti-social behaviour orders

Legislative background

10.4   The Crime and Disorder Act 1998 provided a range of civil court orders to law enforcement agencies and RSLs designed to tackle anti-social behaviour for the benefit of the community. The civil nature of the court orders avoids the evidential requirements of criminal prosecutions which may be particularly difficult in cases of anti-social behaviour and may also involve costs which are disproportionate to the offence. The best known and most widely applicable of those orders is the anti-social behaviour order (ASBO), the details of which are set out in s 1 of the Crime and Disorder Act 1998. The ASBO is generally obtained by way of complaint to the magistrates' court acting in its civil capacity.

10.5   The Government believes that ASBOs are extremely valuable:

> 'Home Office research published in 2002 found that the orders had delivered real improvement in the quality of life to communities around the country; its use of civil law procedures and the wide powers granted to courts to impose conditions once satisfied that an ASBO was necessary were widely welcomed. But the research also made clear that these new procedures had brought new problems with them, and these problems were part of the explanation for the fact that in some parts of the country ASBOs were being very little used by practitioners.'[1]

10.6   In order to encourage greater use of ASBOs, s 1 of the Crime and Disorder Act 1998 was substantially amended by the Police Reform Act 2002. The amendments made by the Anti-social Behaviour Act 2003 therefore are a third attempt by the Government in a very short period of time to ensure that the ASBO achieves what it is intended to achieve.

10.7   The total number of ASBOs made by the courts by the end of June 2003 was 1,372. The total number of refusals up to 30 June 2003 was 35.[2] There are a number of features of the ASBO which make it particularly useful as a tool to promote community safety.

[1]   *A Guide to Anti-social Behaviour Orders and Acceptable Behaviour Contracts* (Home Office, November 2002).

[2]   Home Office Research directorate.

10.8 First, despite the fact that the order is a civil order, there is no need for the victim to make a personal application for the order and therefore it reduces any fears of intimidation. The evidence for proving these grounds may be presented anonymously. However, it should be noted that, despite the civil nature of the order, because of its serious implications for the alleged perpetrator, the court should apply the criminal standard of proof.[1]

10.9 Secondly, any applicant for the order must consult with the police and the local authority, and if the applicant is the police or the local authority they must consult the other so the process of application emphasises the partnership approach which is a feature of the Crime and Disorder Act 1998.

10.10 Thirdly, the scope of the order is wide. A person (a child over 10 or an adult) can be made subject to an ASBO if the court is satisfied on a balance of probabilities that the person has caused the harassment, alarm or distress as defined in the Crime and Disorder Act 1998, or might have done so.[2] Once the magistrates' court accepts that an order is necessary to protect local people from further acts, the court is able to impose those prohibitions which it deems necessary to protect people from further anti-social acts.[3]

10.11 Home Office guidance indicates the range of behaviours which could be targeted by an ASBO:

> 'The most common behaviour tackled by ASBOs is general loutish and unruly conduct such as verbal abuse, harassment, assault, graffiti and excessive noise. ASBOs have also been used to combat racial harassment, drunk and disorderly behaviour, throwing missiles, vehicle crime and prostitution. Many other problems, for instance the use of air guns, would also lend themselves to this approach.'[4]

10.12 Fourthly, interim orders are available[5] to ensure that the community is protected as soon as possible from anti-social activities. A recent decision of the High Court[6] examined the operation of interim ASBOs. The judge rejected the argument that interim orders could only be made in exceptional circumstances where there was a compelling urgency to justify an application without notice. Rather:

> 'the power to make such orders was a necessary weapon in the judicial armour, enabling the court to do justice in circumstances where it was necessary to act urgently to protect the interests of a party, or where it was necessary to act without notice to a prospective defendant in order to ensure that the order of the court was effective.'

10.13 Finally, as a result of amendments made by the Police Reform Act 2002, the orders can operate to prohibit behaviour over a wide geographical area.[7] Home Office guidance explains:

---

[1] *Clingham v Royal Borough of Kensington and Chelsea; R v Crown Court at Manchester ex parte McCann and others* [2002] UKHL 39, [2003] 1 AC 787.

[2] Crime and Disorder Act 1998, s 1.

[3] Ibid, s 1(6).

[4] *A Guide to Anti-social Behaviour Orders and Acceptable Behaviour Contracts* (Home Office, November 2002).

[5] Crime and Disorder Act 1998, s 1D.

[6] *R (on the application of Kenny) v Leeds Magistrates' Court; R (on the application of M) v Secretary of State for Constitutional Affairs and the Lord Chancellor and another* [2003] All ER (D) 104 (Dec). The judge explained the test for making an interim order under s 1D is whether it is just to do so pending the determination of the main application. The court has to balance the need to protect the public against the impact that the order sought would have upon the defendant. It would need to consider the seriousness of the behaviour in issue, the urgency with which it was necessary to take steps to control such behaviour and whether it was necessary for orders to be made without notice in order for them to be effective. On the other side of the equation, it would have to consider the degree to which the order would impede the defendant's rights as a free citizen to go where he pleased and to associate with whomsoever he pleased. Where a defendant was under 18, the court had to have regard to the principle that the defendant's best interests were a primary consideration when addressing the question of whether it was just to make an order.

[7] Crime and Disorder Act 1998, s 1(1B)(b).

'The power to make an order over a wide area is for use where there is reason to believe that the person concerned may move or has already moved. It goes some way to addressing the problem of offenders moving to other areas and continuing the behaviour. An order covering a wider area could address problems such as ticket touting at different train stations, anti-social behaviour on trains and help deal with the minority of the travelling community who persistently engage in anti-social behaviour around the country. Any evidence of the itinerant nature of the defendant's lifestyle; evidence that the individual may move to another area; or wide geographical spread of offending behaviour should be submitted with the application file. The applicant does not have to prove that anti-social behaviour will occur elsewhere, just show that it is likely to. The more serious the behaviour, the more likely that the court will grant a geographically wide order.'[1]

10.14 Applications for ASBOs can be made by the local authority, the police, RSLs[2] or the British Transport Police (BTP).[3] RSLs' powers to apply for ASBOs are limited to situations where they need to take action either against their tenants or in order to protect their tenants.[4] The BTP's powers are similarly limited to those people who are on or near premises that they police.[5]

10.15 One of the effects of this Part of the Anti-social Behaviour Act 2003 is to increase the range of applicants to include county councils and housing action trusts.

10.16 ASBOs are also available to criminal courts (ie the magistrates' court, the youth court and the Crown Court), following conviction for a criminal offence.[6] In these circumstances, there is no need for an application. The ASBO can be suspended until completion of a sentence of imprisonment. ASBOs are available to a county court where the court is already dealing with proceedings relating to anti-social behaviour, such as possession proceedings. Both the recipient of the ASBO and the appropriate authority (the police, the local authority or the RSL) must be party to proceedings. However, the local authority can apply to be joined to proceedings. The standard criteria for making ASBOs apply.

10.17 Although the ASBO is obtained in civil proceedings, breach of the order is a criminal offence. Doing anything in breach of the order is a criminal offence. On summary conviction, the magistrates' court can hand down a sentence of 6 months in prison or a £1,000 fine. The breach can be dealt with in the Crown Court with a maximum sentence of 5 years and an unlimited fine. Either court can impose a community penalty.

10.18 Orders must last for not less than 2 years[7] and can last indefinitely. Although there are provisions to vary the order, the court cannot discharge an order that has not lasted for 2 years, unless all parties agree.

The provisions in detail

10.19 The provisions amend ss 1–1E of the Crime and Disorder Act 1998. These sections have already been amended extensively as a result of the Police Reform Act 2002. We have provided a copy of the amended sections in Appendix 2.

10.20 County councils and housing action trusts are added to the authorities who may apply for ASBOs under s 1 of the Crime and Disorder Act 1998. Housing action trusts are bodies, established under Part IIII of the HA 1988, which take over some of a local authority's housing stock to improve the housing stock and/or its management or to improve the general environment of an area.

---

[1]   *A Guide to Anti-social Behaviour Orders and Acceptable Behaviour Contracts* (Home Office, November 2002).
[2]   Crime and Disorder Act 1998, s 1(1A) (amended by s 61(4) of the Police Reform Act 2002).
[3]   Ibid, s 1(1A).
[4]   Ibid, s 1(1B)(d).
[5]   Ibid, s 1(1B)(c).
[6]   Ibid, s 1C.
[7]   Ibid, s 1(1B), (7).

10.21 County councils were added to the list in response to requests by the County Councils Network and to a Liberal Democrat-proposed amendment. The Government explained that it enabled it to recognise the important work carried out by county councils in combating anti-social behaviour.[1]

10.22 The same consultation requirements that are imposed upon other relevant authorities are imposed upon housing action trusts and county councils.[2]

10.23 Applications for ASBOs by housing action trusts are limited to applications for orders which are for the protection from anti-social behaviour of people who reside in or who are in the vicinity of premises provided or managed by the housing action trusts. Similarly, applications by county councils are limited to orders necessary to protect people within the county council administrative area.[3]

10.24 Local authorities and county councils are given the power to take proceedings against someone who has breached the ASBO where they obtained the order or when the person who has breached the ASBO lives or appears to live in the local government area.[4]

10.25 The Children and Young Persons Act 1933 restricts the people who have a right to attend hearings in the youth court. The provisions[5] extend the list to include a representative of the council who obtained the ASBO or in whose area the young person resides when the youth court is hearing proceedings for breach of the ASBO. The original explanatory notes to the Bill explained:

> 'This will enable the authority to monitor the proceedings and report back on the outcome to colleagues, as well as to support witnesses and victims as necessary.'

10.26 The powers of county courts to make ASBOs are limited to people who are party to the county court proceedings. Relevant authorities who are party to proceedings are enabled to apply to have someone they consider to have acted in an anti-social manner which is relevant to the proceedings to be made party to the proceedings.[6] So, for instance, where a local authority is evicting a tenant because of the anti-social behaviour of someone else, that person can be joined to the proceedings and an ASBO made to restrain his or her future conduct. This avoids the cost and inconvenience of issuing separate proceedings for an ASBO when the evidence would be predominantly the same. Where an application is unrelated the appropriate forum is the magistrates' court.

10.27 Courts have a power to make parenting orders when making ASBOs on children and young people. Parenting orders are orders under the Crime and Disorder Act 2003.[7] The Government considers that the power is too rarely used:

> 'between June 2000 and December 2001 only nine Parenting Orders were made in this way – whereas more than 200 ASBOs were granted against juveniles in the same period. That is why we will place an obligation on a court to consider a Parenting Order where a person under the age of 16 has been given an ASBO.'[8]

10.28 The Government has honoured that commitment in the Act. It provides[9] for an amendment to s 9 of the Crime and Disorder Act 1998 so that when a court makes an ASBO on a child under 16 the court must make a parenting order at the same time unless it does not consider the

[1] *Hansard*, HL Deb, 3 November 2003, col 543.
[2] Crime and Disorder Act 1998, s 1E.
[3] Ibid, s 1(1B)(aa) and (d).
[4] Ibid, s 1(10A).
[5] Section 85(4), which inserts a new subs (10A) into s 1 of the Crime and Disorder Act 1998.
[6] Crime and Disorder Act 1998, s 1B(3A)–(3C).
[7] Ibid, s 8.
[8] *Respect and Responsibility – Taking a Stand against Anti-social Behaviour* (Home Office, March 2003), Cm 5778.
[9] Section 85(8).

relevant condition is satisfied.[1] If it does not make a parenting order, it must explain why not in open court. Section 9 of the Crime and Disorder Act 1998 as amended is reproduced in Appendix 3.

10.29 The Government has used the opportunity provided by the passage of the Act to clarify certain procedures relating to the imposition of ASBOs. A court may make an ASBO following conviction for a criminal offence. It may do so either at the request of the prosecutor or when it decides it is appropriate to do so. In making its decision, the court may consider evidence from the prosecution and the defence including evidence which would not have been admissible in the criminal proceedings which preceded.[2]

10.30 Similar provisions amend the Football Spectators Act 1989. CPS prosecutors are also enabled to conduct applications for ASBOs on conviction for anti-social behaviour and football banning orders.[3]

10.31 The Act also amends the operation of proceedings for breach of ASBOs. A local authority where a person subject to an order resides or appears to reside can now prosecute for breach of the order alongside the CPS.[4]

10.32 The Act removes inconsistencies about the freedom of the press to report ASBOs made against children. Under the Crime and Disorder Act 1998, applications for ASBOs against juveniles are generally heard as civil matters in the magistrates' court where there are no automatic reporting restrictions, although the court has the power to impose restrictions to protect the identity of a person under 18. Youth courts may make ASBOs following conviction for other offences. When youth courts make ASBOs, automatic reporting restrictions apply.[5]

10.33 The Government considers that the imposition of reporting restrictions may restrict the effectiveness of the order 'if the effectiveness of the ASBO will largely depend on the wider community knowing the details'.[6]

10.34 The Act therefore removes the anomaly by removing the automatic reporting restrictions in the youth court when it makes an ASBO.[7] However, the court retains discretion to apply reporting restrictions where it considers it to be appropriate and the court will also be required to consider the welfare of the child under the Children and Young Persons Act 1933. Automatic reporting restrictions will continue to apply to the conviction which precedes the ASBO.[8]

10.35 This provision attracted a great deal of hostile parliamentary comment. For instance:

> 'One of several concerns for many is the danger or perpetuating in broader society what is begun in the family. The children are bad at home they become bad in their neighbourhoods, they develop a pariah status among their peers and adults, and finally they are named and photographed in the local newspaper, which is a certificate of their badness and failure. The adult world inadvertently colludes with what began in the dysfunctional family at the start of the child's life.'[9]

10.36 Another observation in the Lords pointed out the damaging consequences of *The Sun* newspaper's 'Stop a Yob' campaign:

---

[1] Crime and Disorder Act 1998, s 8(6). The relevant condition is that the parenting order would be desirable in the interests of preventing any repetition of the kind of behaviour which led to the child safety order, ASBO or sex offender order being made.

[2] Crime and Disorder Act 1998, s 1C(3), inserted by s 86(1).

[3] Section 86(5).

[4] Section 86(3), inserting new provisions into s 1C of the Crime and Disorder Act 1998.

[5] Children and Young Persons Act 1933, s 39.

[6] *A Guide to Anti-social Behaviour Orders and Acceptable Behaviour Contracts* (Home Office, November 2002).

[7] Section 86(3), inserting a new subs (9C) into s 1C of the Crime and Disorder Act 1998.

[8] *Hansard*, HL Deb, 3 November 2003, col 548.

[9] Ibid, col 544.

'This is the antithesis of responsible, local community involvement; it is vigilantism of the press. It is very difficult and dangerous to use publicity in this way because people interpret and react to information in an extremely unpredicatable way. When difficult, dysfunctional and often disturbed youngsters are concerned, whose behaviour is indeed unpleasant and intimidating, the risks are magnified. Such children are rarely shamed or humiliated into positive social behaviour. They are not only demonised by the process in the eyes of some, they could equally become anti-heroes in the eyes of others.'[1]

10.37 The Government's response was to note the concerns but to point out that:

'We must also however deliver for the communities that, regrettably, are sometime subjected to terrible behaviour. ... We want courts to think much more carefully about whether to grant restriction orders for children, which as noble Lords will know, are dealt with in a significantly different way from those for adults. The court must say whether it will lift or impose restrictions. For the children it is a case of whether restrictions are lifted; for adults it is whether they are imposed. We though that in the area of anti-social behaviour orders, it was appropriate to have a similar system.'

Fixed penalty notices

Legislative background

10.38 The Criminal Justice and Police Act 2001 gave the power to issue fixed penalty notices to 18-year-olds and over for anti-social behaviour. The fixed penalty provisions have been piloted in four areas as part of a Home Office project.

10.39 The Home Office reports that:

'the pilot schemes are progressing successfully in four areas (West Midlands, Essex, Croydon and North Wales). As of 5 January 2003 a total of 1835 FPNs had been issued. An overall payment rate of 60% is being achieved and only 2% are ending up in court.'[2]

The Home Secretary indicated[3] that, by the end of March 2003, 3,000 fixed penalty notices had been issued in the four pilot areas. The Government indicated that initial information from the pilots shows that most fixed penalty notices are given for alcohol-related anti-social behaviour in town centres on a Friday or Saturday night.[4]

10.40 The Police Reform Act 2002 extended the power to issue fixed penalty notices for disorder to community support officers.[5]

10.41 Certain offences attract a fine of £80. These include:

- wasting police time;
- knowingly giving a false alarm to a fire brigade; and
- using threatening words or behaviour likely to cause alarm, harassment or distress under s 5 of the Public Order Act 1986.

Other offences attract a fine of £40. These include:

- being drunk in a highway, other public place or licensed premises;
- throwing fireworks in a thoroughfare;
- trespassing on a railway, throwing stones, etc at trains or other things on railways, and
- disorderly behaviour while drunk in a public place.

---

[1]   *Hansard*, HL Deb, 3 November 2003, col 546
[2]   *Respect and Responsibility – Taking a Stand against Anti-social Behaviour*, Cm 578 (Home Office, March 2003).
[3]   In the Second Reading in the House of Commons: 8 April 2003.
[4]   *Hansard*, HC Standing Committee, 15 May 2003.
[5]   Schedule 4 to the Police Reform Act 2002.

10.42 The Government explained that:

> 'The new powers will protect the public from rowdy behaviour while saving police and court time. They will not be used to tackle racially-motivated crime, domestic incidents, football-related incidents or in any cases where people or property are hurt. The powers are discretionary and will be used by officers where appropriate. All the usual powers will be available to arrest and charge an offender to be dealt with in the courts if necessary. Payment of a penalty involves no admission of guilt or record of criminal conviction, though the alleged offender has the right to opt for trial by court and risk conviction. Failure to pay the penalty or opt for trial by court may lead to a fine equivalent to one and a half times the amount of the penalty being imposed on the defaulter.'[1]

10.43 The Government indicated that it will continue to consult with the police to see whether other offences should attract fixed penalty notices.[2] The Anti-social Behaviour Act 2003 itself provides for new fixed penalty notices for offences relating to environmental anti-social behaviour.[3]

The provisions in detail

10.44 Section 87 of the Anti-social Behaviour Act 2003 extends the fixed penalty notice scheme to 16- and 17-year-olds.[4] The section also provides the Secretary of State with the power to extend fixed penalty notices to children aged 10 and over. The power can only be exercised using the affirmative action procedure which requires a vote in Parliament.[5]

10.45 If the Secretary of State chooses, with the approval of Parliament, to extend the scheme, the section also provides a power for the relevant statutory instrument to contain a provision for the parent or guardian of a child under 16 to be notified of the imposition of the penalty notice and for the parent or guardian to be liable to pay the penalty.

10.46 The section also provides for the Secretary of State to set different levels of penalty for different age groups, although there is no indication that 16- and 17-year-olds are to pay at a different level to adults.[6] This is despite the fact only a very small number of 16- and 17-year-olds are in employment and those that are, are not protected by the minimum wage.

10.47 The explanatory notes to the Bill stated that:

> 'The extension of the scheme to 16- and 17-year-olds will be piloted and supplementary guidance will be issued to the police on the use of their discretion. The power to extend the scheme to a younger age group at this stage will be revisited in the light of the outcome of these pilots for 16- and 17-year-olds'.[7]

Baroness Scotland, in the Lords, explained that the Government wants 'to pursue only that which works effectively' and suggested that the pilots provided a useful 'suck it and see' exercise.[8]

10.48 This provision and, in particular, the power to lower the age limit still further, has attracted extensive adverse comment. For instance, Liberty suggests that 'this could lead to the unacceptable situation whereby relatively affluent parents are able to buy their children out of trouble, whereas less affluent parents may face prosecution if they are unable to afford the fines'. Children's organisations argue that lowering the age for fixed penalty notices is simply applying adult sanctions to children.

---

[1]   The crime reduction website at http://www.crimereduction.gov.uk/antisocialbehaviour.
[2]   *Respect and Responsibility – Taking a Stand against Anti-social Behaviour*, Cm 578 (Home Office, March 2003).
[3]   See discussion at **7.75–7.83**.
[4]   Section 87(2), amending s 2(1) of the Criminal Justice and Police Act 2001.
[5]   Section 87(9).
[6]   Section 87(4), amending s 3(1) of the Criminal Justice and Police Act 2001.
[7]   Bill 83 – EN.
[8]   *Hansard*, HL Deb, 3 November 2003, col 554.

10.49 The Liberal Democrats in the Lords argued that:

'a 10-year-old cannot give informed consent to the fixed penalty notice or have the capacity to understand the consequences of accepting one, as required by Code C of PACE. It is an inappropriate sanction for children so young. Of itself, it could not promote positive social behaviour. It would fall on the family to pay. It therefore fails to meet the objective of a swift and direct response to disorderly behaviour on the part of such a young person.'[1]

10.50 However, the Government remains convinced of the value of the proposals in preventing anti-social behaviour taking root:

'Extension of this scheme would give the police the power to tackle such behaviour. A notice will act as a deterrent, but it will not leave the young person with a criminal conviction, recognising this age groups' youth and vulnerability ... Further it will encourage the police to take action against anti-social behaviour in the street which is not being dealt with at present.'[2]

Curfew orders and supervision orders

Legislative background

10.51 Curfew orders[3] and supervision orders are community sentences provided for within the Powers of Criminal Courts (Sentencing) Act 2000.

10.52 Curfew orders are orders requiring an offender to remain, for periods specified in the order, at a specified place. They are available to the courts for offenders aged 10 and over. The provisions prior to the implementation of the amendments made by Sch 2 to the Anti-social Behaviour Act 2003 allow the court to impose a curfew for between 2 and 12 hours a day for up to 3 months, or, for a juvenile of 16 or 17, up to 6 months.[4] The order must not interfere with the juvenile's education or religious practices. The order can be enforced by electronic tagging if the monitoring facilities exist in the juvenile's home area.[5]

10.53 The Government has reported that:

'Curfew orders with electronic monitoring or "tagging" have proved very successful since their introduction nationally for 10–15-year-olds on 1 February 2001. More than 3,600 orders have been made. The pilots of curfew orders for 10–15 year olds between March 1998 and February 2000 demonstrated that they worked well for juveniles. The reaction of the offenders and their families was generally positive with the acknowledgement that in many cases it may have kept the young offender out of custody.

Curfew orders take into account health, safety and welfare issues. Before making a curfew order on an offender under 16, under the Powers of Criminal Courts (Sentencing) Act 2000, the court must obtain and consider information about his family circumstances and the likely effect of such an order on those circumstances. The court must also consider, under the attitude of persons likely to be affected by the enforced presence there of the offender. In the case of persons under 16 this would normally be the family.'[6]

10.54 Supervision orders are available to the courts after a finding of guilt against someone aged between 10 and 17 in any criminal proceedings other than murder. The court can designate the local authority, a probation officer, or a member of the youth offending team as supervisor. An order can be made for up to 3 years, which means that it can continue after the supervisee

---

[1] *Hansard*, HL Deb, 3 November 2003, col 552.

[2] Ibid, col 553.

[3] Not to be confused with local child curfew schemes under ss 14 and 15 of the Crime and Disorder Act 1998.

[4] Powers of Criminal Courts (Sentencing) Act 2000, ss 37–40.

[5] Ibid, s 13.

[6] Letter from Home Secretary to Joint Committee on Human Rights appended to their 13th Report, HC 766, 9 June 2003.

reaches 18. The order must be made for a minimum of 6 months. The criminal supervision order is distinct from a civil supervision order which is provided for in the Children Act 1989.[1]

10.55 A range of conditions can be attached to a supervision order, such as a requirement to reside with a named individual, requirements as to specified activities and a requirement to reside in local authority accommodation where there has been a breach of a supervision order and the court is satisfied that the offending or the non-compliance results from the circumstances in which the juvenile is living and that a residence requirement will help towards rehabilitation.[2]

10.56 'Specified activities' might include participation in an Intensive Supervision and Surveillance Programme (ISSP) or drug treatment, where young person is aged 16 or over. A supervision order can also require the offender to observe a curfew in one or more designated places for up to 10 hours, between 6.00 pm and 6.00 am.

10.57 The Youth Justice Board explains that:

> 'ISSP is the most rigorous non-custodial intervention available for young offenders. As its name suggests, it combines unprecedented levels of community-based surveillance with a comprehensive and sustained focus on tackling the factors that contribute to the young person's offending behaviour. ISSP targets the most active repeat young offenders, and those who commit the most serious crimes.'[3]

10.58 The provisions of the Powers of Criminal Courts Sentencing Act 2000 prior to the implementation of Sch 2 to the Anti-social Behaviour Act 2003 limit the total number of days during which the offender may be required to comply with the directions of the supervisor to 90.

The provisions in detail

10.59 The purpose of the provisions within the Anti-social Behaviour Act 2003 is to strengthen and extend the range of sanctions available to the criminal courts when dealing with juveniles. The Government explained:[4]

> 'the orders help to keep young offenders at home, off the streets, and away from places at times where they may be more likely to re-offend. They are often used as a last resort before custody, and thus help to keep the family together. The Government's view is that they are an appropriate and proportionate response to offending by young people.'

10.60 Section 88 of the Act provides that Sch 2 to the Act, which amends the existing provisions relating to supervision orders and curfew orders within the Powers of Criminal Courts (Sentencing) Act 2000, shall have effect.

10.61 It removes the 3-month restriction on the duration of a curfew order for children between 10 and 16 and thereby increases the maximum length of a curfew order from 3 months to 6 months.[5]

10.62 The Schedule makes it clear that a curfew order and a supervision order may be imposed at the same time. It also increases the maximum period during which the offender may be required by a supervision order to comply with specific directions of the supervising officer or specific requirements of the court as to activities etc from 90 days to 180 days.

---

[1] Children Act 1989, s 35.

[2] Powers of Criminal Courts (Sentencing) Act 2000, Sch 6.

[3] Website of Youth Justice Board.

[4] In a letter responding to queries raised by the Joint Committee on Human Rights appended to their 13th report, HC 766, 9 June 2003.

[5] Paragraph 2(2), which amends s 27 of the Powers of Criminal Courts (Sentencing) Act 2000.

10.63 The current night-time restrictions imposed on supervision orders by the Powers of Criminal Courts (Sentencing) Act 2000 are removed by the Act so that restrictions on whereabouts can be imposed at any hour of the day.[1]

10.64 These changes allow the Youth Justice Board to increase the length of its ISSP which is designed to tackle the most serious persistent young offenders. The Government announced in November 2003 that the ISSP programme would be available nationwide to provide the courts with a credible alternative to custodial sentences and secure remands. The Minister explained that ISSP:

'combines unprecedented levels of supervision, including electronic monitoring, with programmes designed to prevent re-offending by directly addressing the behaviour that led them to offend in the first place. The programme was launched in July 2001 in 22 areas and since then has been progressively introduced across the country. It will now be available as an option for all Youth Offending Teams for serious persistent offenders in their area'.[2]

10.65 The Home Office explained:

'The main reason for these changes is to strengthen the Youth Justice Board's administrative Intensive Supervision and Surveillance Programme (ISSP). ISSP is targeting serious and persistent young offenders who would otherwise receive a custodial sentence. The programme makes use of existing curfew and supervision order legislation to provide a well structured and supervised community alternative to custody. ISSP uses the curfew order to closely monitor the offender's behaviour in the community whilst the supervision order allows the young offender to be placed on a programme designed to reduce the risk of further offending.

The Government wants to make ISSP even more credible to the courts in order to divert away from custody those serious and persistent offenders who could be safely managed and rehabilitated in the community under close supervision. The changes in this Bill will allow ISSP to be available for a total maximum of 12 months (6 months intensive, 6 months less intensive).'[3]

10.66 The Government intends to issue guidance to the courts advising them to consider the use of these extended curfew orders and intensive supervision orders only for those on ISSP, or for the most persistent and serious offenders who would otherwise have received a custodial sentence.[4]

10.67 The National Youth Agency raises issues about the increased resources required to underpin the provisions. They point out that:

'All the evidence points to very intensive intervention in the early part of an order as being the form of service delivery that has the best results. There may be a few cases where lengthier interventions are necessary, but part of the skill in delivering effective interventions lies in avoiding dependency.'[5]

10.68 Paragraph 4 of Schedule 2 enables the court to include in a supervision order a requirement for 'intensive fostering' which will require the offender to live with local authority foster parents for a specified period which cannot exceed one year.[6] The requirement can only be imposed when the offence is punishable with imprisonment in the case of an offender aged 18 or over. This new requirement is available only in the case of an offender who would otherwise meet the criteria for a custodial sentence and whose offending is to a great extent due to his home circumstances. The court must decide that the imposition of a foster parent residence requirement will assist in the child's rehabilitation.[7]

---

[1] Schedule 2, para 4(3) and (4), amending Sch 6, paras 3 and 4 of the Powers of Criminal Courts (Sentencing) Act 2000.

[2] Hazel Blear's speech at the Youth Justice Board's annual convention, 11 November 2003.

[3] Letter from Home Secretary to Joint Committee on Human Rights appended to their 13th Report, HC 766, 9 June 2003.

[4] Ibid.

[5] www.nya.org.uk.

[6] Paragraph 5A(5) of Sch 6 to the Powers of Criminal Courts (Sentencing) Act 2000.

[7] Paragraph 5A of Sch 6 to the Powers of Criminal Courts (Sentencing) Act 2000.

10.69 The explanatory notes to the Bill explain that:

'Measures to allow fostering as an option for use with the supervision order will be piloted with approximately 20 places per year taking on average of 26 young people and each placement lasting an average of 9 months.'[1]

The intensive fostering will provide 24-hour support services to the foster carers, educational and family support and therapeutic intervention.

10.70 The child must be legally represented before a foster parent residence requirement is made.[2] The only exceptions to this are if the child lost his or her right to representation because of his or her conduct or, having been informed of his or her right to apply for representation, he or she refuses or fails to apply for it.[3]

10.71 The Local Government Association (LGA) expressed some caution about the value of intensive fostering. Their priority is to work with the child and their family together unless it is 'manifestly unsafe to do so'. The process of reintegration of a child back into the family must be considered an essential part of intensive fostering. They stressed 'the need for this option to be clearly seen as integral to the looked after service with local authorities assessing need and commissioning the fostering service'.

10.72 Some reassurance for the LGA's concerns is provided by the Home Office:

'The young person subject to a fostering requirement will be a "looked after" child for the purposes of the Children Act 1989. The local authority has a duty under the 1989 Act to promote contact between a "looked after" child and the natural family. It is likely that the level of contact will be far higher than if the young person had gone into custody. It is also possible that as preparations are made to return the young person home, they will be able to spend longer periods with the family, possibly including whole weekends. Furthermore, the requirement gives the local authority and Youth Offending Team the flexibility to be able to determine the level of contact between the young person and their family.'[4]

10.73 The LGA also had concerns about the resources needed to provide intensive fostering:

'There are great concerns about where the additional foster carers needed for this work will come from. There are already serious shortages for children in need. Local authorities will struggle if the foster carers in whom they have heavily invested are to be taken away from mainstream care.'

10.74 It is clear that the role of the foster parents will be very challenging:

'The fostering requirement as part of a supervision order is intended to be a child centred alternative to custody. It is available only in very tightly drawn circumstances, where a young person would otherwise have received a custodial sentence, and where their offending behaviour was due to a significant extent to the circumstances in which they were living. This could include poor parenting with insufficient supervision, a chaotic lifestyle and criminal or anti-social influences. The fostering provision provides the young person with a caring stable home life with specially trained foster parents who receive back-up support.'[5]

10.75 The court has to consult with the relevant local authority about whether the foster parent requirement is an appropriate response. The requirement can only be imposed by the court in areas where an intensive fostering scheme has been established.[6]

10.76 The Government's view is that the fostering requirement is a positive and child-centred response to serious and persistent young offenders and offers a constructive and less damaging

---

[1]   Bill 83 – EN.
[2]   Paragraph 5A(6) of Sch 6 to the Powers of Criminal Courts (Sentencing) Act 2000.
[3]   Paragraph 5A(6)(a) and (b) of Sch 6 to the Powers of Criminal Courts (Sentencing) Act 2000.
[4]   Letter to Joint Committee on Human Rights from The Rt Hon David Blunkett MP, Home Secretary.
[5]   Ibid.
[6]   Powers of Criminal Courts (Sentencing) Act 2000, Sch 6, para 5A(7).

alternative to custody. The intervention benefits the young person, the family and the wider community.

Community support officers and accredited persons

Legislative background

10.77 The Police Reform Act 2002 created the new civilian role of police community support officer. A community support officer is a uniformed police authority employee under the direction and control of a chief officer of police who can be designated by that chief officer with a specific range of police powers set out in Part 1 of Sch 4 to the Police Reform Act 2002.

10.78 The role of the police community support officer, introduced into London in September 2002, is described by the Metropolitan Police as follows:

'They perform routine duties, assist and support police officers, gather intelligence, carry out security patrols and provide public reassurance through a permanent street presence. PCSOs are not intended to replace police officers but to enable officers to better utilise their wider and specialist skills ... But where possible they will attend to matters that don't require police powers and often distract officers from more appropriate duties.'

10.79 *Respect and Responsibility*[1] explains that:

'a wide range of agencies, from the public, private and voluntary sectors are involved in vitally important community safety work in support of the police. This includes street crime wardens and members of the private security industry who work in shopping centres and sports grounds.'

The Police Reform Act 2002 enables the police to establish and maintain accreditation schemes.[2] These accredit suitably skilled and trained non-police employees involved in the provision of community safety with powers to undertake specified functions in support of the police. For example, a chief officer may accredit neighbourhood wardens employed by the local authority or a social landlord, with powers to address antisocial behaviour. Regulations will be in place to enable the Chief Constable of the British Transport Police to maintain a railway safety accreditation scheme, which will be similar to those of Home Office police forces.

10.80 *Respect and Responsibility* explains that:

'The introduction of community support officers and community safety accreditation schemes has given the police, local authorities and other agencies a range of additional options for tackling anti-social behaviour and minor disorder.'

The provisions in detail

10.81 Section 89[3] of the Act amends the Police Reform Act 2002 by adding the power to stop cyclists to the powers conferred on community support officers and accredited persons. They already have the power to issue fixed penalty notices for cycling on the pavement. The amendment is designed to make the existing power more effective.

10.82 The power only applies when the community support officer or accredited person believes that an offence of cycling on the pavement has been committed. Failing to stop a cycle when required to do so is an offence under the Road Traffic Act 1988 and is liable to a fixed penalty notice of £30.

---

[1] *Respect and Responsibility – Taking a Stand against Anti-social Behaviour* (Home Office, March 2003), Cm 5778.
[2] Police Reform Act 2002, s 40.
[3] Section 89(3), amending Part 1 of Sch 4 to the Police Reform Act 2002 and s 89(6), inserting a new para 8A into Sch 5 to the Police Reform Act 2002.

10.83 The section[1] also adds the power to issue fixed penalty notices for disorder under the Criminal Justice and Police Act 2001 to the powers that can be conferred on suitably trained persons who are accredited under either a community safety accreditation scheme or a railway safety accreditation scheme. This power is already available to community support officers. However, offences which require that the offender is drunk are excluded from the power.[2]

10.84 The explanatory notes to the Bill[3] list the relevant offences which are currently available to community safety officers which will become available to accredited persons as follows:

- use of insulting or abusive behaviour to cause harassment, alarm or distress;
- throwing fireworks in a thoroughfare;
- trespassing on a railway;
- throwing stones, etc at trains or other things on railways;
- buying or attempting to buy alcohol for consumption in a bar in licensed premises by a person under 18;
- knowingly giving a false alarm to the fire brigade;
- wasting police time or giving a false report;
- consumption of alcohol in a designated public place;
- using a public communications system for sending messages known to be false in order to cause annoyance.

10.85 This extension to the powers of accredited persons fulfils the commitment in *Respect and Responsibility*.[4]

10.86 Section 89[5] also provides the Secretary of State with the opportunity to exclude inappropriate offences of disorderly behaviour from being made available to accredited persons or community support officers. This new power was explained by the Government as follows:

'It is sensible to provide a power to restrict which new penalty offences may be used by CSOs and accredited persons, in recognition of their different roles and powers in the extended police family. The clause allows the Secretary of State to distinguish different penalty notice offences for disorder, determining which should be exclusively for the police and which may be extended to CSOs or accredited persons. This is particularly important in the case of accredited persons who do not have the powers of arrest available to police officers or the powers of detention being piloted by CSOs.'[6]

All extensions to the powers are subject to parliamentary scrutiny under the affirmative procedure.

10.87 There were two types of response in Parliament to these provisions. First, amendments were proposed to widen the scope of the provision to respond to the use of skateboards and in-line skates on footpaths. However, the Government pointed out that the result of the amendments would move the legal use of skateboards and roller skates from footways to roadways:

'these devices are not designed for use in traffic – that is for sure – and displacing them on to roads would undoubtedly be dangerous for both skaters and other road users.'[7]

They suggested that there were already sufficient powers to make by-laws to deal with the problem under s 235 of the Local Government Act 1972.

10.88 In contrast, the second type of response was opposed in principle to the extension of policing powers to civilians:

---

[1] Section 89(5), amending para 1(2) of Sch 5 to the Police Reform Act 2002.
[2] These are offences within s 12 of the Licensing Act 1872 and s 91 of the Criminal Justice Act 1967.
[3] Bill 83 – EN.
[4] *Respect and responsibility – taking a stand against anti-social behaviour*, Cm 5778 (Home Office, March 2003).
[5] Section 89(4), inserting a new para 15A into Part 1 of Sch 4 to the Police Reform Act 2002, and s 89(7) inserting a new para 9A into Sch 5 to the Police Reform Act 2002.
[6] *Hansard*, HC Standing Committee G, col 305.
[7] *Hansard*, HL Deb, 17 September 2003, col 1039.

'There is concern about public transparency, accountability and professional capability and about the piecemeal extension of police powers to civilian bodies not under the direct supervision of the police. ... We see the creation of second and third tier policing with increasingly obscure boundaries of accountability and professionalism as very disturbing.'[1]

10.89 The Government pointed out that:

'there are a number of safeguards already in place to ensure that the powers are given only in appropriate circumstances. Chief Officers will be responsible for ensuring that anybody given these powers is suitable and more importantly, properly trained. As an additional safeguard the clause allows the Secretary of State to determine which penalty notices for disorder should be exclusively for police and which are appropriate to be extended to community support officers and accredited persons.'

The purpose of the powers is to enable communities to deal with 'lower level incidents of disorder, "quickly and effectively".'[2]

Local authority reports on bail

Legislative background

10.90 Young people can currently be fostered on remand, under the Children and Young Persons Act 1969 provided they are remanded to local authority accommodation. As *Respect and Responsibility* explains:

'It is not often taken up as courts do not have the confidence that fostering will be an option. We will introduce a power that allows the court to require local authorities to undertake an initial investigation of the young person's circumstances and advise on how it would exercise its responsibilities should the young person be remanded to local authority accommodation. This will facilitate dialogue between courts and local authorities, and we will encourage, through guidance, fostering to be taken up as a remand option where this is deemed appropriate.'[3]

10.91 Section 23A of the Children and Young Persons Act 1969 provides that, where a court does not grant bail, remands and committals of a child or young person charged with or convicted of an offence must be to local authority accommodation.

10.92 Section 23(4) of the Children and Young Persons Act 1969 gives the court the power to impose a security requirement when remanding a child to local authority accommodation. However, by s 23(5) of the Children and Young Persons Act 1969, the court may not impose a security requirement in respect of a child who has not reached the age of 12. There is, therefore, a gap in the law for serious or persistent offenders aged under 12.

Provisions in detail

10.93 Section 90 introduces a new s 23B into the Children and Young Persons Act 1969. The section applies to children of 10- and 11-years-old who have been charged with serious offences or who are persistent offenders.

10.94 The section enables the court to order a local authority to make a report specifying where the child would be placed if the court decided to remand the child to local authority accommodation. The court will then be able to make an informed decision on the options available to them.

---

[1] *Hansard*, HL Deb, 17 September 2003, col 1040.

[2] Ibid, col 1040.

[3] *Respect and Responsibility – Taking a Stand against Anti-social Behaviour*, Cm 5778 (Home Office, March 2003).

10.95 The Act[1] allows the Secretary of State to extend the court power to 12–16-year-olds who met the criteria for a secure remand, and whose behaviour was due, to a significant extent, to their home circumstances.

Section 222 of the Local Government Act 1972

Legislative background

10.96 Section 222 of the Local Government Act 1972 provides a power for a local authority to prosecute or defend legal proceedings where it considers it to be expedient to do so for the promotion or protection of the interests of the inhabitants of its area.

10.97 This power includes instituting proceedings for public nuisance, provided that an authority considers it expedient for the promotion and protection of the interests of the inhabitants of its area. As public nuisance is also a crime, this indicates that local authorities are not restrained from commencing proceedings where the activity it seeks to restrain is a crime. Local authority use of s 222 of the Local Government Act 1972 is constrained by judicial review.

10.98 This understanding of the law was confirmed by the Court of Appeal in *Nottingham City Council v Z (A Child)*.[2] In this case, a local authority successfully sought an injunction restraining the defendant from entering a housing estate in its area. The authority claimed that a lot of dealing in drugs was going on publicly on the estate and that the defendant was associating there with well-known drug dealers and had himself been in possession of drugs and had been arrested on suspicion of dealing in drugs.

10.99 Section 222 therefore has the potential to be used to prevent a range of anti-social behaviour. It was recently used to prevent five defendants from entering into any part of an identified area of the Royal Borough of Kensington and Chelsea for any purpose, from entering any residential property within any part of the Royal Borough where controlled drugs were being sold or consumed, or from entering any block of flats or residential premises within the area of which the local authority was the owner, freehold or leasehold.[3]

10.100 The local authority said that the injunction was necessary in order to prevent the continuation of a public nuisance that was created – and had been created – over a number of years by the five defendants through the way in which they started up, operated and managed crack houses.

10.101 The local authority gave evidence that the crack houses were set up in premises where there was a vulnerable local authority tenant on a number of estates and as the authority closed one crack house, another one was opened and the resultant misery repeated. The High Court judge stated that:

> 'The evidence as to the degree of nuisance which is caused by the activities of the setting up of crack houses is shown graphically and powerfully by the whole range of the evidence which has been produced, whether from the police or from local authority managers or from – occasionally – tenants. It is quite clear that there is a public nuisance which is created by the large numbers of people who attend at the crack house; by the shouting, screaming, associated prostitution, the leaving of drug paraphernalia, urine, faeces and so on the common parts, the endless noise through the night, the intimidation and so on.'

10.102 The judge continued:

> 'It is also quite clear that those are activities which are seriously damaging to the well-being of the tenants

---

[1]   Section 90, inserting s 23B(6) into the Children and Young Persons Act 1969.
[2]   [2001] EWCA Civ 1248.
[3]   *Royal Borough of Kensington & Chelsea v Williams and Others* [2003] EWHC 1933, [2002] 1 WLR 607.

and in particular to the well-being of the vulnerable tenants who are targeted by those who seek to set up crack houses. They are targeted because they are the most vulnerable to pressure, or favours, or favours, or other intimidation to enable their consent to be gained to the use of their premises for dealing in, or taking crack cocaine.'

10.103   The judge found that the authority was entitled to the injunction not only on the basis of public nuisance but also to protect its legitimate property interest.

10.104   It is quite possible to see that use of s 222 of the Local Government Act 1972 could be used in conjunction with the powers of Part 1 of the Anti-social Behaviour Act 2003 to provide an effective remedy for crack houses. Individual properties used for dealing in crack could be closed and the organisers of the crack house forbidden from entering the estate or a wider local authority area.

10.105   However, as with all injunctions other than those restraining domestic violence and injunctions under ss 152 and 153 of the Housing Act 1996, there is no ability for a court to attach a power of arrest prior to breach of the order. A penal notice can be attached, but that requires enforcement via contempt proceedings. The Anti-social Behaviour Act 2003 addresses this problem.

The provisions in detail

10.106   Section 91 of the Act amends s 222 of the Local Government Act 1972. It enables a court which grants an injunction which prohibits conduct capable of causing nuisance or annoyance to a person to attach a power of arrest to any provision of the injunction if the conditions set out in the section apply.

10.107   The conditions[1] are that the conduct consists of or includes the use or threatened use of violence, or there is a significant risk of harm to the person that the injunction was designed to protect.

10.108   This considerably extends the scope of local authorities to obtain powers of arrest when seeking to restrain anti-social conduct or conduct capable of being anti-social.

10.109   The Government explained that:

'the purpose of the amendments is to ensure that injunctions that prohibit anti-social behaviour obtained by local authorities in any proceedings can be properly enforced. Where the conduct prohibited includes violence, threatened violence or a risk of significant harm, we want to give the courts the right to attach a power of arrest to the injunction. The changes that the amendments make is modest, but the practical effect may be significant.'[2]

Conclusion

10.110   This Part of the Act is largely concerned with increasing the effectiveness of measures that the government has already put in place elsewhere and fulfilling the commitments made in the White Paper, *Respect and Responsibility*.

10.111   *Respect and Responsibility* is clear:

'We must be much tougher about forcing people not to behave anti-socially. When people break the rules, there must be consequences for them: consequences that are swift, proportionate and that change the pattern of their behaviour. And where those who are responsible for tackling anti-social behaviour fail to do so, we must intervene. Unless laws are enforced the signal is clear – if those in a position to act do not

---

[1]   Set out in s 91(3).

[2]   *Hansard*, HL Deb, 23 October 2003, col 1797.

do so, then others will not join inn. Those who have both the power and the responsibility to act must do so.'

10.112 This Part of the Act ensures the relevant powers are in place, now it depends on enforcement and resources.

APPENDIX 1

ANTI-SOCIAL BEHAVIOUR ACT 2003

2003 Chapter 38

CONTENTS

PART 1
PREMISES WHERE DRUGS USED UNLAWFULLY

1   **Closure notice**

(1)   This section applies to premises if a police officer not below the rank of superintendent (the authorising officer) has reasonable grounds for believing—

    (a)   that at any time during the relevant period the premises have been used in connection with the unlawful use, production or supply of a Class A controlled drug, and

    (b)   that the use of the premises is associated with the occurrence of disorder or serious nuisance to members of the public

(2)   The authorising officer may authorise the issue of a closure notice in respect of premises to which this section applies if he is satisfied—

    (a)   that the local authority for the area in which the premises are situated has been consulted;

    (b)   that reasonable steps have been taken to establish the identity of any person who lives on the premises or who has control of or responsibility for or an interest in the premises.

(3)   An authorisation under subsection (2) may be given orally or in writing, but if it is given orally the authorising officer must confirm it in writing as soon as it is practicable.

(4)   A closure notice must—

    (a)   give notice that an application will be made under section 2 for the closure of the premises;

    (b)   state that access to the premises by any person other than a person who habitually resides in the premises or the owner of the premises is prohibited;

    (c)   specify the date and time when and the place at which the application will be heard;

    (d)   explain the effects of an order made in pursuance of section 2;

    (e)   state that failure to comply with the notice amounts to an offence;

    (f)   give information about relevant advice providers.

(5)   The closure notice must be served by a constable.

(6)   Service is effected by—

    (a)   fixing a copy of the notice to at least one prominent place on the premises,

    (b)   fixing a copy of the notice to each normal means of access to the premises,

(c)   fixing a copy of the notice to any outbuildings which appear to the constable to be used with or as part of the premises,

(d)   giving a copy of the notice to at least one person who appears to the constable to have control of or responsibility for the premises, and

(e)   giving a copy of the notice to the persons identified in pursuance of subsection (2)(b) and to any other person appearing to the constable to be a person of a description mentioned in that subsection.

(7)   The closure notice must also be served on any person who occupies any other part of the building or other structure in which the premises are situated if the constable reasonably believes at the time of serving the notice under subsection (6) that the person's access to the other part of the building or structure will be impeded if a closure order is made under section 2.

(8)   It is immaterial whether any person has been convicted of an offence relating to the use, production or supply of a controlled drug.

(9)   The Secretary of State may by regulations specify premises or descriptions of premises to which this section does not apply.

(10)   The relevant period is the period of three months ending with the day on which the authorising officer considers whether to authorise the issue of a closure notice in respect of the premises.

(11)   Information about relevant advice providers is information about the names of and means of contacting persons and organisations in the area that provide advice about housing and legal matters.

2   Closure order

(1)   If a closure notice has been issued under section 1 a constable must apply under this section to a magistrates' court for the making of a closure order.

(2)   The application must be heard by the magistrates' court not later than 48 hours after the notice was served in pursuance of section 1(6)(a).

(3)   The magistrates' court may make a closure order if and only if it is satisfied that each of the following paragraphs applies—

(a)   the premises in respect of which the closure notice was issued have been used in connection with the unlawful use, production or supply of a Class A controlled drug;

(b)   the use of the premises is associated with the occurrence of disorder or serious nuisance to members of the public;

(c)   the making of the order is necessary to prevent the occurrence of such disorder or serious nuisance for the period specified in the order.

(4)   A closure order is an order that the premises in respect of which the order is made are closed to all persons for such period (not exceeding three months) as the court decides.

(5)   But the order may include such provision as the court thinks appropriate relating to access to any part of the building or structure of which the premises form part.

(6)   The magistrates' court may adjourn the hearing on the application for a period of not more than 14 days to enable—

(a)   the occupier of the premises,

(b)   the person who has control of or responsibility for the premises, or

(c)   any other person with an interest in the premises,

to show why a closure order should not be made.

(7)   If the magistrates' court adjourns the hearing under subsection (6) it may order that the closure notice continues in effect until the end of the period of the adjournment.

(8) A closure order may be made in respect of all or any part of the premises in respect of which the closure notice was issued.

(9) It is immaterial whether any person has been convicted of an offence relating to the use, production or supply of a controlled drug.

3 Closure order: enforcement

(1) This section applies if a magistrates' court makes an order under section 2.

(2) A constable or an authorised person may—

(a) enter the premises in respect of which the order is made;

(b) do anything reasonably necessary to secure the premises against entry by any person.

(3) A person acting under subsection (2) may use reasonable force.

(4) But a constable or authorised person seeking to enter the premises for the purposes of subsection (2) must, if required to do so by or on behalf of the owner, occupier or other person in charge of the premises, produce evidence of his identity and authority before entering the premises.

(5) A constable or authorised person may also enter the premises at any time while te order has effect for the purpose of carrying out essential maintenance of or repairs to the premises.

(6) In this section and in section 4 an authorised person is a person authorised by the chief officer of police for the area in which the premises are situated.

4 Closure of premises: offences

(1) A person commits an offence if he remains on or enters premises in contravention of a closure notice.

(2) A person commits an offence if—

(a) he obstructs a constable or an authorised person acting under section 1(6) or 3(2),

(b) he remains on premises in respect of which a closure order has been made, or

(c) he enters the premises.

(3) A person guilty of an offence under this section is liable on summary conviction—

(a) to imprisonment for a period not exceeding six months, or

(b) to a fine not exceeding level 5 on the standard scale,

or to both such imprisonment and fine.

(4) But a person does not commit an offence under subsection (1) or subsection (2)(b) or (c) if he has a reasonable excuse for entering or being on the premises (as the case may be).

(5) A constable in uniform may arrest a person he reasonably suspects of committing or having committed an offence under this section.

5 Extension and discharge of closure order

(1) At any time before the end of the period for which a closure order is made or extended a constable may make a complaint to an appropriate justice of the peace for an extension or further extension of the period for which it has effect.

(2) But a complaint must not be made unless it is authorised by a police officer not below the rank of superintendent—

(a)   who has reasonable grounds for believing that it is necessary to extend the period for which the closure order has effect for the purpose of preventing the occurrence of disorder or serious nuisance to members of the public, and

(b)   who is satisfied that the local authority has been consulted about the intention to make the complaint.

(3)   If a complaint is made to a justice of the peace under subsection (1) the justice may issue a summons directed to—

(a)   the persons on whom the closure notice relating to the closed premises was served under subsection (6)(d) or (e) or (7) of section 1;

(b)   any other person who appears to the justice to have an interest in the closed premises but on whom the closure notice was not served,

requiring such person to appear before the magistrates' court to answer to the complaint.

(4)   If the court is satisfied that the order is necessary to prevent the occurrence of disorder or serious nuisance for a further period it may extend the period for which the order has effect by a period not exceeding three months.

(5)   But a closure order must not have effect for more than six months.

(6)   Any of the following persons may make a complaint to an appropriate justice of the peace for an order that a closure order is discharged—

(a)   a constable;

(b)   the local authority;

(c)   a person on whom the closure notice relating to the closed premises was served under subsection (6)(d) or (e) or (7) of section 1;

(d)   a person who has an interest in the closed premises but on whom the closure notice was not served.

(7)   If a complaint is made under subsection (6) by a person other than a constable the justice may issue a summons directed to such constable as he thinks appropriate requiring the constable to appear before the magistrates' court to answer to the complaint.

(8)   The court must not make an order discharging a closure order unless it is satisfied that the closure order is no longer necessary to prevent the occurrence of disorder or serious nuisance to members of the public

(9)   If a summons is issued in accordance with subsection (3) or (7), a notice stating the date, time and place at which the complaint will be heard must be served on—

(a)   the persons to whom the summons is directed if it is issued under subsection (3);

(b)   the persons mentioned in subsection (6)(c) and (d) (except the complainant) if the summons is issued under subsection (7);

(c)   such constable as the justice thinks appropriate (unless he is the complainant);

(d)   the local authority (unless they are the complainant).

(10)   An appropriate justice of the peace is a justice of the peace acting for the petty sessions area in which the premises in respect of which a closure order is made are situated.

6   Appeals

(1)   This section applies to—

(a)   an order under section 2 or 5;

(b)   a decision by a court not to make an order under either of those sections.

(2)   An appeal against an order or decision to which this section applies must be brought to the Crown Court before the end of the period of 21 days beginning with the day on which the order or decision is made.

(3)   An appeal against an order under section 2 or 5(4) may be brought by—

    (a)   a person on whom the closure notice relating to the closed premises was served under section 1(6)(d) or (e);

    (b)   a person who has an interest in the closed premises but on whom the closure notice was not served.

(4)   An appeal against the decision of a court not to make such an order may be brought by—

    (a)   a constable;

    (b)   the local authority.

(5)   On an appeal under this section the Crown Court may make such order as it thinks appropriate.

7   Access to other premises

(1)   This section applies to any person who occupies or owns any part of a building or structure—

    (a)   in which closed premises are situated, and

    (b)   in respect of which the closure order does not have effect.

(2)   A person to whom this section applies may at any time while a closure order has effect apply to—

    (a)   the magistrates' court in respect of an order made under section 2 or 5;

    (b)   the Crown Court in respect of an order made under section 6.

(3)   If an application is made under this section notice of the date, time and place of the hearing to consider the application must be given to every person mentioned in section 5(6).

(4)   On an application under this section the court may make such order as it thinks appropriate in relation to access to any part of a building or structure in which closed premises are situated.

(5)   It is immaterial whether any provision has been made as mentioned in section 2(5).

8   Reimbursement of costs

(1)   A police authority or a local authority which incurs expenditure for the purpose of clearing, securing or maintaining the premises in respect of which a closure order has effect may apply to the court which made the order for an order under this section.

(2)   On an application under this section the court may make such order as it thinks appropriate in the circumstances for the reimbursement (in full or in part) by the owner of the premises of the expenditure mentioned in subsection (1).

(3)   But an application for an order under this section must not be entertained unless it is made not later than the end of the period of three months starting with the day the closure order ceases to have effect.

(4)   An application under this section must be served on—

    (a)   the police authority for the area in which the premises are situated if the application is made by the local authority;

    (b)   the local authority if the application is made by a police authority;

    (c)   the owner of the premises.

9   Exemption from liability for certain damages

(1)   A constable is not liable for relevant damages in respect of anything done or omitted to be done by him in the performance or purported performance of his functions under this Part.

(2)   A chief officer of police is not liable for relevant damages in respect of anything done or omitted to be done by a constable under his direction or control in the performance or purported performance of the constable's functions under this Part.

(3)   Subsections (1) and (2) do not apply—

    (a)   if the act or omission is shown to have been in bad faith;

    (b)   so as to prevent an award of damages made in respect of an act or omission on the ground that the act or omission was unlawful by virtue of section 6(1) of the Human Rights Act 1998 (c 42).

(4)   This section does not affect any other exemption from liability for damages (whether at common law or otherwise).

(5)   Relevant damages are damages in proceedings for judicial review or for the tort of negligence or misfeasance in public duty.

10   Compensation

(1)   This section applies to any person who incurs financial loss in consequence of—

    (a)   the issue of a closure notice, or

    (b)   a closure order having effect.

(2)   A person to whom this section applies may apply to—

    (a)   the magistrates' court which considered the application for a closure order;

    (b)   the Crown Court if the closure order was made or extended by an order made by that Court on an appeal under section 6.

(3)   An application under this section must not be entertained unless it is made not later than the end of the period of three months starting with whichever is the later of—

    (a)   the day the court decides not to make a closure order;

    (b)   the day the Crown Court dismisses an appeal against a decision not to make a closure order;

    (c)   the day a closure order ceases to have effect.

(4)   On an application under this section the court may order the payment of compensation out of central funds if it is satisfied—

    (a)   that the person had no connection with the use of the premises as mentioned in section 1(1),

    (b)   if the person is the owner or occupier of the premises, that he took reasonable steps to prevent the use,

    (c)   that the person has incurred financial loss as mentioned in subsection (1), and

    (d)   having regard to all the circumstances it is appropriate to order payment of compensation in respect of that loss.

(5)   Central funds has the same meaning as in enactments providing for the payment of costs.

11   Interpretation

(1)   References to a controlled drug and (however expressed) to the production or supply of a controlled drug must be construed in accordance with the Misuse of Drugs Act 1971 (c 38).

(2)   A Class A controlled drug is a controlled drug which is a Class A drug within the meaning of section 2 of that Act.

(3)   Premises includes—

(a)   any land or other place (whether enclosed or not);

(b)   any outbuildings which are or are used as part of the premises.

(4)   A closure notice is a notice issued under section 1.

(5)   A closure order is—

(a)   an order made under section 2;

(b)   an order extended under section 5;

(c)   an order made or extended under section 6 which has the like effect as an order made or extended under section 2 or 5 (as the case may be).

(6)   Each of the following is a local authority in relation to England—

(a)   a district council;

(b)   a London borough council;

(c)   a county council for an area for which there is no district council;

(d)   the Common Council of the City of London in its capacity as a local authority;

(e)   the Council of the Isles of Scilly.

(7)   Each of the following is a local authority in relation to Wales—

(a)   a county council;

(b)   a county borough council.

(8)   References to a local authority are to the local authority for the area in which premises—

(a)   to which a closure notice applies are situated;

(b)   in respect of which a closure order has effect are situated.

(9)   Closed premises are premises in respect of which a closure order has effect.

(10)   A person is the owner of premises if either of the following paragraphs applies to him—

(a)   he is a person (other than a mortgagee not in possession) who is for the time being entitled to dispose of the fee simple in the premises, whether in possession or in reversion;

(b)   he is a person who holds or is entitled to the rents and profits of the premises under a lease which (when granted) was for a term of not less than three years.

(11)   This section applies for the purposes of this Part.

PART 2
HOUSING

12   Anti-social behaviour: landlords' policies and procedures

(1)   In Part 8 of the Housing Act 1996 (c 52) before section 219 (power of Secretary of State to give directions as to certain charges by social landlords) there is inserted the following section—

'218A   Anti-social behaviour: landlords' policies and procedures

(1)   This section applies to the following landlords—

(a)   a local housing authority;

(b)   a housing action trust;

(c)   a registered social landlord.

(2)   The landlord must prepare—

(a)   a policy in relation to anti-social behaviour;

(b)   procedures for dealing with occurrences of anti-social behaviour.

(3)   The landlord must not later than 6 months after the commencement of section 12 of the Anti-social Behaviour Act 2003 publish a statement of the policy and procedures prepared under subsection (2).

(4)   The landlord must from time to time keep the policy and procedures under review and, when it thinks appropriate, publish a revised statement.

(5)   A copy of a statement published under subsection (3) or (4)—

(a)   must be available for inspection at all reasonable hours at the landlord's principal office;

(b)   must be provided on payment of a reasonable fee to any person who requests it.

(6)   The landlord must also—

(a)   prepare a summary of its current policy and procedures;

(b)   provide without charge a copy of the summary to any person who requests it.

(7)   In preparing and reviewing the policy and procedures the landlord must have regard to guidance issued—

(a)   by the Secretary of State in the case of a local housing authority or a housing action trust;

(b)   by the Relevant Authority under section 36 in the case of a registered social landlord.

(8)   Anti-social behaviour is any conduct to which section 153A or 153B applies.

(9)   Relevant Authority has the same meaning as in Part 1.'

(2)   In section 36(2) of that Act (functions of the Housing Corporation relating to guidance and corresponding functions relating to Wales) after paragraph (h) there is inserted the following paragraph—

'(i)   the policy and procedures a landlord is required under section 218A to prepare and from time to time revise in connection with anti-social behaviour.'

13   Injunctions against anti-social behaviour on application of certain social landlords

(1)   The Housing Act 1996 (c 52) is amended as follows.

(2)   Sections 152 (power to grant injunctions against anti-social behaviour) and 153 (power of arrest for breach of certain injunctions against anti-social behaviour) are omitted.

(3)   Before section 154 (power of arrest in ex parte applications) there are inserted the following sections—

'153A Anti-social behaviour injunction

(1)   This section applies to conduct—

(a)   which is capable of causing nuisance or annoyance to any person, and

(b)   which directly or indirectly relates to or affects the housing management functions of a relevant landlord.

(2)   The court on the application of a relevant landlord may grant an injunction (an anti-social behaviour injunction) if each of the following two conditions is satisfied.

(3)   The first condition is that the person against whom the injunction is sought is engaging, has engaged or threatens to engage in conduct to which this section applies.

(4)   The second condition is that the conduct is capable of causing nuisance or annoyance to any of the following—

(a)   a person with a right (of whatever description) to reside in or occupy housing accommodation owned or managed by the relevant landlord;

(b) a person with a right (of whatever description) to reside in or occupy other housing accommodation in the neighbourhood of housing accommodation mentioned in paragraph (a);

(c) a person engaged in lawful activity in or in the neighbourhood of housing accommodation mentioned in paragraph (a);

(d) a person employed (whether or not by the relevant landlord) in connection with the exercise of the relevant landlord's housing management functions.

(5) It is immaterial where conduct to which this section applies occurs.

(6) An anti-social behaviour injunction prohibits the person in respect of whom it is granted from engaging in conduct to which this section applies.

153B Injunction against unlawful use of premises

(1) This section applies to conduct which consists of or involves using or threatening to use housing accommodation owned or managed by a relevant landlord for an unlawful purpose.

(2) The court on the application of the relevant landlord may grant an injunction prohibiting the person in respect of whom the injunction is granted from engaging in conduct to which this section applies.

153C Injunctions: exclusion order and power of arrest

(1) This section applies if the court grants an injunction under subsection (2) of section 153A or 153B and it thinks that either of the following paragraphs applies—

(a) the conduct consists of or includes the use or threatened use of violence;

(b) there is a significant risk of harm to a person mentioned in section 153A(4).

(2) The court may include in the injunction a provision prohibiting the person in respect of whom it is granted from entering or being in—

(a) any premises specified in the injunction;

(b) any area specified in the injunction.

(3) The court may attach a power of arrest to any provision of the injunction.

153D Injunction against breach of tenancy agreement

(1) This section applies if a relevant landlord applies for an injunction against a tenant in respect of the breach or anticipated breach of a tenancy agreement on the grounds that the tenant—

(a) is engaging or threatening to engage in conduct that is capable of causing nuisance or annoyance to any person, or

(b) is allowing, inciting or encouraging any other person to engage or threaten to engage in such conduct.

(2) The court may proceed under subsection (3) or (4) if it is satisfied—

(a) that the conduct includes the use or threatened use of violence, or

(b) that there is a significant risk of harm to any person.

(3) The court may include in the injunction a provision prohibiting the person in respect of whom it is granted from entering or being in—

(a) any premises specified in the injunction;

(b) any area specified in the injunction.

(4) The court may attach a power of arrest to any provision of the injunction.

(5) Tenancy agreement includes any agreement for the occupation of residential accommodation owned or managed by a relevant landlord.

153E Injunctions: supplementary

(1) This section applies for the purposes of sections 153A to 153D.

(2)   An injunction may—

   (a)   be made for a specified period or until varied or discharged;

   (b)   have the effect of excluding a person from his normal place of residence.

(3)   An injunction may be varied or discharged by the court on an application by—

   (a)   the person in respect of whom it is made;

   (b)   the relevant landlord.

(4)   If the court thinks it just and convenient it may grant or vary an injunction without the respondent having been given such notice as is otherwise required by rules of court.

(5)   If the court acts under subsection (4) it must give the person against whom the injunction is made an opportunity to make representations in relation to the injunction as soon as it is practicable for him to do so.

(6)   The court is the High Court or a county court.

(7)   Each of the following is a relevant landlord—

   (a)   a housing action trust;

   (b)   a local authority (within the meaning of the Housing Act 1985);

   (c)   a registered social landlord.

(8)   A charitable housing trust which is not a registered social landlord is also a relevant landlord for the purposes of section 153D.

(9)   Housing accommodation includes—

   (a)   flats, lodging-houses and hostels;

   (b)   any yard, garden, outhouses and appurtenances belonging to the accommodation or usually enjoyed with it;

   (c)   in relation to a neighbourhood, the whole of the housing accommodation owned or managed by a relevant landlord in the neighbourhood and any common areas used in connection with the accommodation.

(10)   A landlord owns housing accommodation if either of the following paragraphs applies to him—

   (a)   he is a person (other than a mortgagee not in possession) who is for the time being entitled to dispose of the fee simple in the premises, whether in possession or in reversion;

   (b)   he is a person who holds or is entitled to the rents and profits of the premises under a lease which (when granted) was for a term of not less than three years.

(11)   The housing management functions of a relevant landlord include—

   (a)   functions conferred by or under any enactment;

   (b)   the powers and duties of the landlord as the holder of an estate or interest in housing accommodation.

(12)   Harm includes serious ill-treatment or abuse (whether physical or not).'

(4)   In section 154—

   (a)   in subsection (1) for 'section 152(6) or section 153' there is substituted 'section 153C(3) or 153D(4)';

   (b)   in subsection (1)(b) for '152(1)(a) or section 153(5)(a)' there is substituted 'section 153A(4)'.

(5)   In section 155—

   (a)   in subsection (1) for 'section 152(6) or section 153' there is substituted 'section 153C(3) or 153D(4)';

   (b)   in subsection (3) for 'section 152(6) or section 153' there is substituted 'section 153C(3) or 153D(4)'.

(6)   In section 157—

   (a)   in subsection (1) for 'section 152(6) or section 153' there is substituted 'section 153C(3) or 153D(4)';

(b)   in subsection (3) for 'section 152(6) or section 153' there is substituted 'section 153C(3) or 153D(4)'.

(7)   In section 158—

(a)   in subsection (1) the entries relating to 'child', 'harm', 'health' and 'ill-treatment' are omitted;

(b)   subsection (2) is omitted.

14   Security of tenure: anti-social behaviour

(1)   In the Housing Act 1985 (c 68) section 82 (which makes provision in relation to security of tenure) is amended as follows—

(a)   in subsection (1) for the words from 'of the court' to the end of the subsection there is substituted 'mentioned in subsection (1A)';

(b)   after subsection (1) there is inserted the following subsection—

'(1A)   These are the orders—

(a)   an order of the court for the possession of the dwelling-house;

(b)   an order under subsection (3);

(c)   a demotion order under section 82A.'

(2)   After section 82 of that Act there is inserted the following section—

'82A   Demotion because of anti-social behaviour

(1)   This section applies to a secure tenancy if the landlord is—

(a)   a local housing authority;

(b)   a housing action trust;

(c)   a registered social landlord.

(2)   The landlord may apply to a county court for a demotion order.

(3)   A demotion order has the following effect—

(a)   the secure tenancy is terminated with effect from the date specified in the order;

(b)   if the tenant remains in occupation of the dwelling-house after that date a demoted tenancy is created with effect from that date;

(c)   it is a term of the demoted tenancy that any arrears of rent payable at the termination of the secure tenancy become payable under the demoted tenancy;

(d)   it is also a term of the demoted tenancy that any rent paid in advance or overpaid at the termination of the secure tenancy is credited to the tenant's liability to pay rent under the demoted tenancy.

(4)   The court must not make a demotion order unless it is satisfied—

(a)   that the tenant or a person residing in or visiting the dwelling-house has engaged or has threatened to engage in conduct to which section 153A or 153B of the Housing Act 1996 (anti-social behaviour or use of premises for unlawful purposes) applies, and

(b)   that it is reasonable to make the order.

(5)   Each of the following has effect in respect of a demoted tenancy at the time it is created by virtue of an order under this section as it has effect in relation to the secure tenancy at the time it is terminated by virtue of the order—

(a)   the parties to the tenancy;

(b)   the period of the tenancy;

(c)   the amount of the rent;

(d)   the dates on which the rent is payable.

(6)   Subsection (5)(b) does not apply if the secure tenancy was for a fixed term and in such a case the demoted tenancy is a weekly periodic tenancy.

(7)   If the landlord of the demoted tenancy serves on the tenant a statement of any other express terms of the secure tenancy which are to apply to the demoted tenancy such terms are also terms of the demoted tenancy.

(8)   For the purposes of this section a demoted tenancy is—

     (a)   a tenancy to which section 143A of the Housing Act 1996 applies if the landlord of the secure tenancy is a local housing authority or a housing action trust;

     (b)   a tenancy to which section 20B of the Housing Act 1988 applies if the landlord of the secure tenancy is a registered social landlord.'

(3)   Section 83 of that Act is amended as follows—

     (a)   in subsection (1) for the words from 'the possession' to the second 'tenancy' substitute 'an order mentioned in section 82(1A)';

     (b)   in subsection (2)(b) for the words from 'an order' to 'tenancy' substitute 'the order';

     (c)   after subsection (4) insert-

        '(4A)   If the proceedings are for a demotion order under section 82A the notice—

           (a)   must specify the date after which the proceedings may be begun;

           (b)   ceases to be in force twelve months after the date so specified.';

     (d)   in subsection (5) for 'or (4)' substitute '(4) or (4A)'.

(4)   In the Housing Act 1988 (c 50) after section 6 (which makes provision about fixing the terms of a statutory periodic tenancy) there is inserted the following section—

'6A   Demotion because of anti-social behaviour

(1)   This section applies to an assured tenancy if the landlord is a registered social landlord.

(2)   The landlord may apply to a county court for a demotion order.

(3)   A demotion order has the following effect—

     (a)   the assured tenancy is terminated with effect from the date specified in the order;

     (b)   if the tenant remains in occupation of the dwelling-house after that date a demoted tenancy is created with effect from that date;

     (c)   it is a term of the demoted tenancy that any arrears of rent payable at the termination of the assured tenancy become payable under the demoted tenancy;

     (d)   it is also a term of the demoted tenancy that any rent paid in advance or overpaid at the termination of the assured tenancy is credited to the tenant's liability to pay rent under the demoted tenancy.

(4)   The court must not make a demotion order unless it is satisfied—

     (a)   that the tenant or a person residing in or visiting the dwelling-house has engaged or has threatened to engage in conduct to which section 153A or 153B of the Housing Act 1996 (anti-social behaviour or use of premises for unlawful purposes) applies, and

     (b)   that it is reasonable to make the order.

(5)   The court must not entertain proceedings for a demotion order unless—

     (a)   the landlord has served on the tenant a notice under subsection (6), or

     (b)   the court thinks it is just and equitable to dispense with the requirement of the notice.

(6)   The notice must—

     (a)   give particulars of the conduct in respect of which the order is sought;

     (b)   state that the proceedings will not begin before the date specified in the notice;

(c) state that the proceedings will not begin after the end of the period of twelve months beginning with the date of service of the notice.

(7) The date specified for the purposes of subsection (6)(b) must not be before the end of the period of two weeks beginning with the date of service of the notice.

(8) Each of the following has effect in respect of a demoted tenancy at the time it is created by virtue of an order under this section as it has effect in relation to the assured tenancy at the time it is terminated by virtue of the order—

(a) the parties to the tenancy;

(b) the period of the tenancy;

(c) the amount of the rent;

(d) the dates on which the rent is payable.

(9) Subsection (8)(b) does not apply if the assured tenancy was for a fixed term and in such a case the demoted tenancy is a weekly periodic tenancy.

(10) If the landlord of the demoted tenancy serves on the tenant a statement of any other express terms of the assured tenancy which are to apply to the demoted tenancy such terms are also terms of the demoted tenancy.

(11) For the purposes of this section a demoted tenancy is a tenancy to which section 20B of the Housing Act 1988 applies.'

(5) Schedule 1 amends the Housing Act 1996 (c 52) and the Housing Act 1985 (c 68).

15 Demoted assured shorthold tenancies

(1) In the Housing Act 1988 (c 50) after section 20A (duty of landlord to provide statement of terms for certain tenancies) there is inserted the following section—

'20B Demoted assured shorthold tenancies

(1) An assured tenancy is an assured shorthold tenancy to which this section applies (a demoted assured shorthold tenancy) if—

(a) the tenancy is created by virtue of an order of the court under section 82A of the Housing Act 1985 or section 6A of this Act (a demotion order), and

(b) the landlord is a registered social landlord.

(2) At the end of the period of one year starting with the day when the demotion order takes effect a demoted assured shorthold tenancy ceases to be an assured shorthold tenancy unless subsection (3) applies.

(3) This subsection applies if before the end of the period mentioned in subsection (2) the landlord gives notice of proceedings for possession of the dwelling house.

(4) If subsection (3) applies the tenancy continues to be a demoted assured shorthold tenancy until the end of the period mentioned in subsection (2) or (if later) until one of the following occurs—

(a) the notice of proceedings for possession is withdrawn;

(b) the proceedings are determined in favour of the tenant;

(c) the period of six months beginning with the date on which the notice is given ends and no proceedings for possession have been brought.

(5) Registered social landlord has the same meaning as in Part 1 of the Housing Act 1996.'

(2) In section 21 of that Act (recovery of possession on expiry or termination of assured shorthold tenancy) after subsection (5) there is inserted the following subsection—

'(5A) Subsection (5) above does not apply to an assured shorthold tenancy to which section 20B (demoted assured shorthold tenancies) applies.'

(3) In Schedule 2A to that Act (assured tenancies which are not shorthold tenancies) after paragraph 5 (former secure tenancies) there is inserted the following paragraph—

'5A.   Former demoted tenancies

An assured tenancy which ceases to be an assured shorthold tenancy by virtue of section 20B(2) or (4).'

16   Proceedings for possession: anti-social behaviour

(1)   In the Housing Act 1985 (c 68) after section 85 (which extends the court's discretion in certain proceedings for possession) there is inserted the following section—

'85A   Proceedings for possession: anti-social behaviour

(1)   This section applies if the court is considering under section 84(2)(a) whether it is reasonable to make an order for possession on ground 2 set out in Part 1 of Schedule 2 (conduct of tenant or other person).

(2)   The court must consider, in particular—

(a)   the effect that the nuisance or annoyance has had on persons other than the person against whom the order is sought;

(b)   any continuing effect the nuisance or annoyance is likely to have on such persons;

(c)   the effect that the nuisance or annoyance would be likely to have on such persons if the conduct is repeated.'

(2)   In the Housing Act 1988 (c 50) after section 9 (which extends the court's discretion in certain proceedings for possession) there is inserted the following section—

'9A   Proceedings for possession: anti-social behaviour

(1)   This section applies if the court is considering under section 7(4) whether it is reasonable to make an order for possession on ground 14 set out in Part 2 of Schedule 2 (conduct of tenant or other person).

(2)   The court must consider, in particular—

(a)   the effect that the nuisance or annoyance has had on persons other than the person against whom the order is sought;

(b)   any continuing effect the nuisance or annoyance is likely to have on such persons;

(c)   the effect that the nuisance or annoyance would be likely to have on such persons if the conduct is repeated.'

17   Devolution: Wales

In Schedule 1 to the National Assembly for Wales (Transfer of Functions) Order 1999 (S.I. 1999/672) references to the following Acts are to be treated as references to those Acts as amended by virtue of this Part—

(a)   the Housing Act 1985;

(b)   the Housing Act 1988;

(c)   the Housing Act 1996 (c 52).

PART 3
PARENTAL RESPONSIBILITIES

Parenting orders under the 1998 Act

18   Parenting orders under the 1998 Act

(1)   Section 8 of the Crime and Disorder Act 1998 (c 37) is amended as follows.

(2)   For subsections (4) and (5) substitute—

'(4)   A parenting order is an order which requires the parent—

(a)   to comply, for a period not exceeding twelve months, with such requirements as are specified in the order, and

(b)   subject to subsection (5) below, to attend, for a concurrent period not exceeding three months, such counselling or guidance programme as may be specified in directions given by the responsible officer.

(5)   A parenting order may, but need not, include such a requirement as is mentioned in subsection (4)(b) above in any case where a parenting order under this section or any other enactment has been made in respect of the parent on a previous occasion.'

(3)   After subsection (7) insert—

'(7A)   A counselling or guidance programme which a parent is required to attend by virtue of subsection (4)(b) above may be or include a residential course but only if the court is satisfied—

(a)   that the attendance of the parent at a residential course is likely to be more effective than his attendance at a non-residential course in preventing any such repetition or, as the case may be, the commission of any such further offence, and

(b)   that any interference with family life which is likely to result from the attendance of the parent at a residential course is proportionate in all the circumstances.'

Truancy and exclusion from school

19   Parenting contracts in cases of exclusion from school or truancy

(1)   This section applies where a pupil has been excluded on disciplinary grounds from a relevant school for a fixed period or permanently.

(2)   This section also applies where a child of compulsory school age has failed to attend regularly at a relevant school at which he is a registered pupil.

(3)   A local education authority or the governing body of a relevant school may enter into a parenting contract with a parent of the pupil or child.

(4)   A parenting contract is a document which contains—

(a)   a statement by the parent that he agrees to comply with such requirements as may be specified in the document for such period as may be so specified, and

(b)   a statement by the local education authority or governing body that it agrees to provide support to the parent for the purpose of complying with those requirements.

(5)   The requirements mentioned in subsection (4) may include (in particular) a requirement to attend a counselling or guidance programme.

(6)   The purpose of the requirements mentioned in subsection (4)—

(a)   in a case falling within subsection (1), is to improve the behaviour of the pupil,

(b)   in a case falling within subsection (2), is to ensure that the child attends regularly at the relevant school at which he is a registered pupil.

(7)   A parenting contract must be signed by the parent and signed on behalf of the local education authority or governing body.

(8)   A parenting contract does not create any obligations in respect of whose breach any liability arises in contract or in tort.

(9)   Local education authorities and governing bodies of relevant schools must, in carrying out their functions in relation to parenting contracts, have regard to any guidance which is issued by the appropriate person from time to time for that purpose.

20   Parenting orders in cases of exclusion from school

(1)   This section applies where—

(a)   a pupil has been excluded on disciplinary grounds from a relevant school for a fixed period or permanently, and

(b)   such conditions as may be prescribed in regulations made by the appropriate person are satisfied.

(2)   A local education authority may apply to a magistrates' court for a parenting order in respect of a parent of the pupil.

(3)   If such an application is made, the court may make a parenting order in respect of a parent of the pupil if it is satisfied that making the order would be desirable in the interests of improving the behaviour of the pupil.

(4)   A parenting order is an order which requires the parent—

(a)   to comply, for a period not exceeding twelve months, with such requirements as are specified in the order, and

(b)   subject to subsection (5), to attend, for a concurrent period not exceeding three months, such counselling or guidance programme as may be specified in directions given by the responsible officer.

(5)   A parenting order under this section may, but need not, include a requirement mentioned in subsection (4)(b) in any case where a parenting order under this section or any other enactment has been made in respect of the parent on a previous occasion.

(6)   A counselling or guidance programme which a parent is required to attend by virtue of subsection (4)(b) may be or include a residential course but only if the court is satisfied that the following two conditions are fulfilled.

(7)   The first condition is that the attendance of the parent at a residential course is likely to be more effective than his attendance at a non-residential course in improving the behaviour of the pupil.

(8)   The second condition is that any interference with family life which is likely to result from the attendance of the parent at a residential course is proportionate in all the circumstances.

21   Parenting orders: supplemental

(1)   In deciding whether to make a parenting order under section 20, a court must take into account (amongst other things)—

(a)   any refusal by the parent to enter into a parenting contract under section 19 in respect of the pupil in a case falling within subsection (1) of that section, or

(b)   if the parent has entered into such a parenting contract, any failure by the parent to comply with the requirements specified in the contract.

(2) Before making a parenting order under section 20 in the case of a pupil under the age of 16, a court must obtain and consider information about the pupil's family circumstances and the likely effect of the order on those circumstances.

(3) Subsections (3) to (7) of section 9 of the Crime and Disorder Act 1998 (c 37) (supplemental provisions about parenting orders) are to apply in relation to a parenting order under section 20 as they apply in relation to a parenting order under section 8 of that Act.

(4) The appropriate person may by regulations make provision as to how the costs associated with the requirements of parenting orders under section 20 (including the costs of providing counselling or guidance programmes) are to be borne.

(5) Local education authorities, head teachers and responsible officers must, in carrying out their functions in relation to parenting orders, have regard to any guidance which is issued by the appropriate person from time to time for that purpose.

22 Parenting orders: appeals

(1) An appeal lies to the Crown Court against the making of a parenting order under section 20.

(2) Subsections (2) and (3) of section 10 of the Crime and Disorder Act 1998 (appeals against parenting orders) are to apply in relation to an appeal under this section as they apply in relation to an appeal under subsection (1)(b) of that section.

23 Penalty notices for parents in cases of truancy

(1) After section 444 of the Education Act 1996 (c 56) (failure to secure regular attendance at school of registered pupil) insert—

'444A Penalty notice in respect of failure to secure regular attendance at school of registered pupil

(1) Where an authorised officer has reason to believe—

(a) that a person has committed an offence under section 444(1), and

(b) that the school to which the offence relates is a relevant school in England,

he may give the person a penalty notice in respect of the offence.

(2) A penalty notice is a notice offering a person the opportunity of discharging any liability to conviction for the offence under section 444(1) to which the notice relates by payment of a penalty in accordance with the notice.

(3) Where a person is given a penalty notice, proceedings for the offence to which the notice relates (or an offence under section 444(1A) arising out of the same circumstances) may not be instituted before the end of such period as may be prescribed.

(4) Where a person is given a penalty notice, he cannot be convicted of the offence to which the notice relates (or an offence under section 444(1A) arising out of the same circumstances) if he pays a penalty in accordance with the notice.

(5) Penalties under this section shall be payable to local education authorities in England.

(6) Sums received by a local education authority under this section may be used by the authority for the purposes of any of its functions which may be specified in regulations.

444B Penalty notices: supplemental

(1) Regulations may make—

(a) provision as to the form and content of penalty notices,

(b) provision as to the monetary amount of any penalty and the time by which it is to be paid,

(c) provision for determining the local education authority to which a penalty is payable,

(d)   provision as to the methods by which penalties may be paid,

(e)   provision as to the records which are to be kept in relation to penalty notices,

(f)   provision as to the persons who may be authorised by a local education authority or a head teacher to give penalty notices,

(g)   provision limiting the circumstances in which authorised officers of a prescribed description may give penalty notices,

(h)   provision for or in connection with the withdrawal, in prescribed circumstances, of a penalty notice, including—

    (i)   repayment of any amount paid by way of penalty under a penalty notice which is withdrawn, and

    (ii)   prohibition of the institution or continuation of proceedings for the offence to which the withdrawn notice relates (and any offence under section 444(1A) arising out of the same circumstances),

(i)   provision for a certificate—

    (i)   purporting to be signed by or on behalf of a prescribed person, and

    (ii)   stating that payment of any amount paid by way of penalty was or, as the case may be, was not received on or before a date specified in the certificate,

to be received in evidence of the matters so stated,

(j)   provision as to the action to be taken if a penalty is not paid in accordance with a penalty notice,

(k)   provision for or in connection with the preparation of codes of conduct in relation to the giving of penalty notices,

(l)   such other provision in relation to penalties or penalty notices as the Secretary of State thinks necessary or expedient.

(2)   Without prejudice to the generality of subsection (1) or section 569(4), regulations under subsection (1)(b) may make provision for penalties of different amounts to be payable in different cases or circumstances (including provision for the penalty payable under a penalty notice to differ according to the time by which it is paid).

(3)   Local education authorities, head teachers and authorised officers shall, in carrying out their functions in relation to penalty notices, have regard to any guidance which is published by the Secretary of State from time to time in relation to penalty notices.

(4)   In this section and section 444A—

'authorised officer' means—

    (a)   a constable,

    (b)   an officer of a local education authority in England who is authorised by the authority to give penalty notices, or

    (c)   an authorised staff member,

'authorised staff member' means—

    (a)   a head teacher of a relevant school in England, or

    (b)   a member of the staff of a relevant school in England who is authorised by the head teacher of the school to give penalty notices,

'penalty' means a penalty under a penalty notice,

'penalty notice' has the meaning given by section 444A(2),

'relevant school' means—

    (a)   a maintained school,

    (b)   a pupil referral unit,

    (c)   an Academy,

        (d)   a city technology college, or

        (e)   a city college for the technology of the arts.'

(2)   In section 572 of that Act (service of notices and other documents) for 'served on any person may be served' substitute 'served on, or given to, any person may be served or given'.

(3)   In paragraph 1(2) of Schedule 4 to the Police Reform Act 2002 (c 30) (powers of community support officers to issue fixed penalty notices) after paragraph (a) insert—

        '(aa)   the power of a constable to give a penalty notice under section 444A of the Education Act 1996 (penalty notice in respect of failure to secure regular attendance at school of registered pupil);'.

(4)   After paragraph 1(3) of that Schedule insert—

        '(4)   In its application to an offence which is an offence by reference to which a notice may be given to a person in exercise of the power mentioned in sub-paragraph (2)(aa), sub-paragraph (1) shall have effect as if for the words from 'who he has reason to believe' to the end there were substituted 'in the relevant police area who he has reason to believe has committed a relevant fixed penalty offence'.'

(5)   In paragraph 2 of that Schedule (power to detain etc) after sub-paragraph (6) insert—

        '(7)   In its application to an offence which is an offence by reference to which a notice may be given to a person in exercise of the power mentioned in paragraph 1(2)(aa), sub-paragraph (2) of this paragraph shall have effect as if for the words 'has committed a relevant offence in the relevant police area' there were substituted 'in the relevant police area has committed a relevant offence'.'

(6)   In paragraph 1(2) of Schedule 5 to that Act (powers of accredited persons to issue fixed penalty notices) before paragraph (b) insert—

        '(ab)   the power of a constable to give a penalty notice under section 444A of the Education Act 1996 (penalty notice in respect of failure to secure regular attendance at school of registered pupil);'.

(7)   After paragraph 1(3) of that Schedule insert—

        '(4)   In its application to an offence which is an offence by reference to which a notice may be given to a person in exercise of the power mentioned in sub-paragraph (2)(ab), sub-paragraph (1) shall have effect as if for the words from 'who he has reason to believe' to the end there were substituted 'in the relevant police area who he has reason to believe has committed or is committing a relevant fixed penalty offence'.'

(8)   In paragraph 2 of that Schedule (power to require giving of name and address) after sub-paragraph (3) insert—

        '(4)   In its application to an offence which is an offence by reference to which a notice may be given to a person in exercise of the power mentioned in paragraph 1(2)(ab), sub-paragraph (1) of this paragraph shall have effect as if for the words 'has committed a relevant offence in the relevant police area' there were substituted 'in the relevant police area has committed a relevant offence'.'

(9)   The National Assembly for Wales may by order amend sections 444A and 444B of the Education Act 1996 (c 56) by removing the words 'in England' in each place where they occur.

(10)   Where an order is made under subsection (9), any functions of the Secretary of State under sections 444A and 444B of the Education Act 1996 which by virtue of the order become exercisable in relation to Wales are to be treated as if they had been transferred to the National Assembly for Wales by an Order in Council under section 22 of the Government of Wales Act 1998 (c 38).

24   Interpretation

In this section and sections 19 to 21—

'the appropriate person' means—

        (a)   in relation to England, the Secretary of State, and

(b)   in relation to Wales, the National Assembly for Wales,

'child of compulsory school age' has the same meaning as in the 1996 Act, and 'child' is to be construed accordingly,

'head teacher' includes acting head teacher, teacher in charge and acting teacher in charge,

'local education authority' has the same meaning as in the 1996 Act,

'parent', in relation to a pupil or child, is to be construed in accordance with section 576 of the 1996 Act, but does not include a person who is not an individual,

'pupil' is to be construed in accordance with section 3(1) and (1A) of the 1996 Act,

'registered pupil' has the meaning given by section 434(5) of the 1996 Act,

'relevant school' means—

(a)   a qualifying school as defined in section 1(3) of the Education Act 2002 (c 32), or

(b)   a pupil referral unit as defined in section 19(2) of the 1996 Act,

'responsible officer', in relation to a parenting order, means one of the following who is specified in the order, namely—

(a)   an officer of a local education authority, and

(b)   a head teacher or a person nominated by a head teacher,

but a person falling within paragraph (b) may not be specified in the order without his consent,

'the 1996 Act' means the Education Act 1996 (c 56).

Criminal conduct and anti-social behaviour

25   Parenting contracts in respect of criminal conduct and anti-social behaviour

(1)   This section applies where a child or young person has been referred to a youth offending team.

(2)   The youth offending team may enter into a parenting contract with a parent of the child or young person if a member of that team has reason to believe that the child or young person has engaged, or is likely to engage, in criminal conduct or anti-social behaviour.

(3)   A parenting contract is a document which contains—

(a)   a statement by the parent that he agrees to comply with such requirements as may be specified in the document for such period as may be so specified, and

(b)   a statement by the youth offending team that it agrees to provide support to the parent for the purpose of complying with those requirements.

(4)   The requirements mentioned in subsection (3)(a) may include (in particular) a requirement to attend a counselling or guidance programme.

(5)   The purpose of the requirements mentioned in subsection (3)(a) is to prevent the child or young person from engaging in criminal conduct or anti-social behaviour or further criminal conduct or further anti-social behaviour.

(6)   A parenting contract must be signed by the parent and signed on behalf of the youth offending team.

(7)   A parenting contract does not create any obligations in respect of whose breach any liability arises in contract or in tort.

(8)   Youth offending teams must, in carrying out their functions in relation to parenting contracts, have regard to any guidance which is issued by the Secretary of State from time to time for that purpose.

26   Parenting orders in respect of criminal conduct and anti-social behaviour

(1)   This section applies where a child or young person has been referred to a youth offending team.

(2)   A member of the youth offending team may apply to a magistrates' court for a parenting order in respect of a parent of the child or young person.

(3)   If such an application is made, the court may make a parenting order in respect of a parent of the child or young person if it is satisfied—

    (a)   that the child or young person has engaged in criminal conduct or anti-social behaviour, and

    (b)   that making the order would be desirable in the interests of preventing the child or young person from engaging in further criminal conduct or further anti-social behaviour.

(4)   A parenting order is an order which requires the parent—

    (a)   to comply, for a period not exceeding twelve months, with such requirements as are specified in the order, and

    (b)   subject to subsection (5), to attend, for a concurrent period not exceeding three months, such counselling or guidance programme as may be specified in directions given by the responsible officer.

(5)   A parenting order under this section may, but need not, include a requirement mentioned in subsection (4)(b) in any case where a parenting order under this section or any other enactment has been made in respect of the parent on a previous occasion.

(6)   A counselling or guidance programme which a parent is required to attend by virtue of subsection (4)(b) may be or include a residential course but only if the court is satisfied that the following two conditions are fulfilled.

(7)   The first condition is that the attendance of the parent at a residential course is likely to be more effective than his attendance at a non-residential course in preventing the child or young person from engaging in further criminal conduct or further anti-social behaviour.

(8)   The second condition is that any interference with family life which is likely to result from the attendance of the parent at a residential course is proportionate in all the circumstances.

27   Parenting orders: supplemental

(1)   In deciding whether to make a parenting order under section 26, a court must take into account (amongst other things)—

    (a)   any refusal by the parent to enter into a parenting contract under section 25 in respect of the child or young person, or

    (b)   if the parent has entered into such a parenting contract, any failure by the parent to comply with the requirements specified in the contract.

(2)   Before making a parenting order under section 26 in the case of a child or a young person under the age of 16, a court must obtain and consider information about the child or young person's family circumstances and the likely effect of the order on those circumstances.

(3)   Subsections (3) to (7) of section 9 of the 1998 Act (supplemental provisions about parenting orders) are to apply in relation to a parenting order under section 26 as they apply in relation to a parenting order under section 8 of that Act.

(4)   Members of youth offending teams and responsible officers must, in carrying out their functions in relation to parenting orders, have regard to any guidance which is issued by the Secretary of State from time to time for that purpose.

28 Parenting orders: appeals

(1) An appeal lies to the Crown Court against the making of a parenting order under section 26.

(2) Subsections (2) and (3) of section 10 of the 1998 Act (appeals against parenting orders) are to apply in relation to an appeal under this section as they apply in relation to an appeal under subsection (1)(b) of that section.

29 Interpretation and consequential amendment

(1) In this section and sections 25 to 28—

'anti-social behaviour' means behaviour by a person which causes or is likely to cause harassment, alarm or distress to one or more other persons not of the same household as the person,

'child' has the same meaning as in the 1998 Act,

'criminal conduct' means conduct which—

      (a)   constitutes a criminal offence, or

      (b)   in the case of conduct by a person under the age of 10, would constitute a criminal offence if that person were not under that age,

'guardian' has the same meaning as in the Children and Young Persons Act 1933 (c 12),

'parent' includes guardian,

'responsible officer', in relation to a parenting order, means a member of a youth offending team who is specified in the order,

'the 1998 Act' means the Crime and Disorder Act 1998 (c 37),

'young person' has the same meaning as in the 1998 Act,

'youth offending team' means a team established under section 39 of the 1998 Act.

(2) In section 38(4) of the 1998 Act (meaning of 'youth justice services') after paragraph (e) insert—

    '(ee)   the performance by youth offending teams and members of youth offending teams of functions under sections 25 to 27 of the Anti-social Behaviour Act 2003;'.

PART 4
DISPERSAL OF GROUPS ETC

30 Dispersal of groups and removal of persons under 16 to their place of residence

(1) This section applies where a relevant officer has reasonable grounds for believing—

      (a)   that any members of the public have been intimidated, harassed, alarmed or distressed as a result of the presence or behaviour of groups of two or more persons in public places in any locality in his police area (the 'relevant locality'), and

      (b)   that anti-social behaviour is a significant and persistent problem in the relevant locality.

(2) The relevant officer may give an authorisation that the powers conferred on a constable in uniform by subsections (3) to (6) are to be exercisable for a period specified in the authorisation which does not exceed 6 months.

(3) Subsection (4) applies if a constable in uniform has reasonable grounds for believing that the presence or behaviour of a group of two or more persons in any public place in the relevant locality has resulted, or is likely to result, in any members of the public being intimidated, harassed, alarmed or distressed.

(4) The constable may give one or more of the following directions, namely—

(a)   a direction requiring the persons in the group to disperse (either immediately or by such time as he may specify and in such way as he may specify),

(b)   a direction requiring any of those persons whose place of residence is not within the relevant locality to leave the relevant locality or any part of the relevant locality (either immediately or by such time as he may specify and in such way as he may specify), and

(c)   a direction prohibiting any of those persons whose place of residence is not within the relevant locality from returning to the relevant locality or any part of the relevant locality for such period (not exceeding 24 hours) from the giving of the direction as he may specify;

but this subsection is subject to subsection (5).

(5)   A direction under subsection (4) may not be given in respect of a group of persons—

(a)   who are engaged in conduct which is lawful under section 220 of the Trade Union and Labour Relations (Consolidation) Act 1992 (c 52), or

(b)   who are taking part in a public procession of the kind mentioned in section 11(1) of the Public Order Act 1986 (c 64) in respect of which—

    (i)   written notice has been given in accordance with section 11 of that Act, or

    (ii)   such notice is not required to be given as provided by subsections (1) and (2) of that section.

(6)   If, between the hours of 9pm and 6am, a constable in uniform finds a person in any public place in the relevant locality who he has reasonable grounds for believing—

(a)   is under the age of 16, and

(b)   is not under the effective control of a parent or a responsible person aged 18 or over,

he may remove the person to the person's place of residence unless he has reasonable grounds for believing that the person would, if removed to that place, be likely to suffer significant harm.

(7)   In this section any reference to the presence or behaviour of a group of persons is to be read as including a reference to the presence or behaviour of any one or more of the persons in the group.

31   Authorisations: supplemental

(1)   An authorisation—

(a)   must be in writing,

(b)   must be signed by the relevant officer giving it, and

(c)   must specify-(i) the relevant locality,

    (ii)   the grounds on which the authorisation is given, and

    (iii)   the period during which the powers conferred by section 30(3) to (6) are exercisable.

(2)   An authorisation may not be given without the consent of the local authority or each local authority whose area includes the whole or part of the relevant locality.

(3)   Publicity must be given to an authorisation by either or both of the following methods—

(a)   publishing an authorisation notice in a newspaper circulating in the relevant locality,

(b)   posting an authorisation notice in some conspicuous place or places within the relevant locality.

(4)   An 'authorisation notice' is a notice which—

(a)   states the authorisation has been given,

(b)   specifies the relevant locality, and

(c)   specifies the period during which the powers conferred by section 30(3) to (6) are exercisable.

(5)   Subsection (3) must be complied with before the beginning of the period mentioned in subsection (4)(c).

(6)   An authorisation may be withdrawn by—

    (a)   the relevant officer who gave it, or

    (b)   any other relevant officer whose police area includes the relevant locality and whose rank is the same as or higher than that of the relevant officer mentioned in paragraph (a).

(7)   Before the withdrawal of an authorisation, consultation must take place with any local authority whose area includes the whole or part of the relevant locality.

(8)   The withdrawal of an authorisation does not affect the exercise of any power pursuant to that authorisation which occurred prior to its withdrawal.

(9)   The giving or withdrawal of an authorisation does not prevent the giving of a further authorisation in respect of a locality which includes the whole or any part of the relevant locality to which the earlier authorisation relates.

(10)   In this section 'authorisation' means an authorisation under section 30.

32   Powers under section 30: supplemental

(1)   A direction under section 30(4)—

    (a)   may be given orally,

    (b)   may be given to any person individually or to two or more persons together, and

    (c)   may be withdrawn or varied by the person who gave it.

(2)   A person who knowingly contravenes a direction given to him under section 30(4) commits an offence and is liable on summary conviction to—

    (a)   a fine not exceeding level 4 on the standard scale, or

    (b)   imprisonment for a term not exceeding 3 months,

or to both.

(3)   A constable in uniform may arrest without warrant any person he reasonably suspects has committed an offence under subsection (2).

(4)   Where the power under section 30(6) is exercised, any local authority whose area includes the whole or part of the relevant locality must be notified of that fact.

33   Powers of community support officers

(1)   Part 1 of Schedule 4 to the Police Reform Act 2002 (c 30) (powers of community support officers) is amended as follows.

(2)   In paragraph 2 (power to detain etc) after sub-paragraph (6)(a) insert—

    '(aa)   an offence under section 32(2) of the Anti-social Behaviour Act 2003; or'.

(3)   After paragraph 4 insert—

    '4A   *Power to disperse groups and remove young persons to their place of residence*

        Where a designation applies this paragraph to any person, that person shall, within the relevant police area, have the powers which, by virtue of an authorisation under section 30 of the Anti-social Behaviour Act 2003, are conferred on a constable in uniform by section 30(3) to (6) of that Act (power to disperse groups and remove persons under 16 to their place of residence).

    4B(1)   Where a designation applies this paragraph to any person, that person shall, within the relevant police area, have the power of a constable under section 15(3) of the Crime and Disorder Act 1998 (power to remove child to their place of residence).

(2)   Section 15(1) of that Act shall have effect in relation to the exercise of that power by that person as if the reference to a constable in that section were a reference to that person.

(3)   Where that person exercises that power, the duty in section 15(2) of that Act (duty to inform local authority of contravention of curfew notice) is to apply to him as it applies to a constable.'

34   Code of practice

(1)   The Secretary of State may issue a code of practice about—

(a)   the giving or withdrawal of authorisations under section 30, and

(b)   the exercise of the powers conferred by section 30(3) to (6).

(2)   The Secretary of State may from time to time revise the whole or any part of a code of practice issued under this section.

(3)   The Secretary of State must lay any code of practice issued by him under this section, and any revisions of such a code, before Parliament.

(4)   In giving or withdrawing an authorisation under section 30, a relevant officer must have regard to any code of practice for the time being in force under this section.

(5)   In exercising the powers conferred by section 30(3) to (6), a constable in uniform or community support officer must have regard to any code of practice for the time being in force under this section.

(6)   A code of practice under this section may make different provision for different cases.

35   Authorisations by British Transport Police

(1)   For the purposes of the giving of an authorisation under section 30 by a relevant officer who is an officer of the British Transport Police Force, section 30(1) is to have effect as if for 'in his police area' there were substituted 'which forms part of property in relation to which he has all the powers and privileges of a constable by virtue of section 31(1)(a) to (f) of the Railways and Transport Safety Act 2003'.

(2)   Where such an authorisation is given by such an officer, section 31(6)(b) is to have effect as if for 'whose police area includes the relevant locality' there were substituted 'who is an officer of the British Transport Police Force'.

36   Interpretation

In this Part—

'anti-social behaviour' means behaviour by a person which causes or is likely to cause harassment, alarm or distress to one or more other persons not of the same household as the person,

'local authority' means—

(a)   in relation to England, a district council, a county council that is the council for a county in which there are no district councils, a London borough council, the Common Council of the City of London or the Council of the Isles of Scilly,

(b)   in relation to Wales, a county council or a county borough council,

'public place' means-(a) any highway, and

(b)   any place to which at the material time the public or any section of the public has access, on payment or otherwise, as of right or by virtue of express or implied permission,

'relevant locality' has the same meaning as in section 30,

'relevant officer' means a police officer of or above the rank of superintendent.

PART 5
FIREARMS

37   Possession of air weapon or imitation firearm in public place

(1)   In section 19 of the Firearms Act 1968 (c 27) (offence to carry firearm in public place) for the words from 'a loaded shot gun' to the end of the section substitute—

'(a)   a loaded shot gun,

(b)   an air weapon (whether loaded or not),

(c)   any other firearm (whether loaded or not) together with ammunition suitable for use in that firearm, or

(d)   an imitation firearm.'

(2)   In Part I of Schedule 6 to that Act (punishment) in the entry relating to section 19—

(a)   in the second column (general nature of offence) for 'loaded firearm' substitute 'firearm or imitation firearm', and

(b)   in the third column (mode of prosecution) after 'not' insert 'in the case of an imitation firearm or'.

(3)   The following shall be inserted after paragraph 5 of Schedule 1A to the Police and Criminal Evidence Act 1984 (c 60) (arrestable offences)—

'5A   Firearms Act 1968

An offence under section 19 of the Firearms Act 1968 (carrying firearm or imitation firearm in public place) in respect of an air weapon or imitation firearm.'

38   Air weapons: age limits

(1)   The Firearms Act 1968 shall be amended as follows.

(2)   In section 22 (acquisition and possession of firearms by minors)—

(a)   in subsection (4) for 'fourteen' substitute 'seventeen', and

(b)   omit subsection (5).

(3)   In section 23 (the heading to which becomes 'Exceptions from s 22(4)')—

(a)   in subsection (2) omit 'or (5)', and

(b)   after subsection (2) insert-

'(3)   It is not an offence under section 22(4) of this Act for a person of or over the age of fourteen to have with him an air weapon or ammunition on private premises with the consent of the occupier.

(4)   But where a person has with him an air weapon on premises in circumstances where he would be prohibited from having it with him but for subsection (3), it is an offence for him to use it for firing any missile beyond those premises.'

(4)   In section 24(4) (offence to give air weapon or ammunition to person under fourteen)—

(a)   in paragraph (a) for 'fourteen' substitute 'seventeen', and

(b)   in paragraph (b) for 'that age' substitute 'the age of seventeen'.

(5)   In Part I of Schedule 6 (punishment)—

(a)   in the entry relating to section 22(4) in the second column (general nature of offence) for '14' substitute '17',

(b)   omit the entry relating to section 22(5),

(c)   in the entry relating to section 23(1) in the second column for '14' substitute '17',

(d)   after that entry insert—

'Section 23(4)	Person under 17 making improper use of air weapon on private premises	Summary	A fine of level 3 on the standard scale	Paragraphs 7 and 8 of Part II of this Schedule apply.'

and

(e)   in the entry relating to section 24(4) in the second column for '14' substitute '17'.

(6)   In Part II of that Schedule (supplementary)—

(a)   in paragraph 7 for '22(4) or (5), 23(1)' substitute '22(4), 23(1) or (4)', and

(b)   in paragraph 8 for '22(3), (4) or (5), 23(1)' substitute '22(3) or (4), 23(1) or (4)'.

39   Prohibition of certain air weapons

(1)   The Firearms Act 1968 (c 27) shall be amended as follows.

(2)   In section 1(3)(b) after 'air pistol' insert 'which does not fall within section 5(1) and which is'.

(3)   In section 5 (weapons subject to general prohibition) after subsection (1)(ae) insert—

'(af) any air rifle, air gun or air pistol which uses, or is designed or adapted for use with, a self-contained gas cartridge system;'.

(4)   If at the time when subsection (3) comes into force a person has in his possession an air rifle, air gun or air pistol of the kind described in section 5(1)(af) of the Firearms Act 1968 (inserted by subsection (3) above)—

(a)   section 5(1) of that Act shall not prevent the person's continued possession of the air rifle, air gun or air pistol,

(b)   section 1 of that Act shall apply, and

(c)   a chief officer of police may not refuse to grant or renew, and may not revoke or partially revoke, a firearm certificate under Part II of that Act on the ground that the person does not have a good reason for having the air rifle, air gun or air pistol in his possession.

(5)   But subsection (4)(a) to (c) shall not apply to possession in the circumstances described in section 8 of that Act (authorised dealing).

(6)   In section 1 of the Firearms (Amendment) Act 1988 (c 45)—

(a)   in subsection (4), omit the word 'or' at the end of paragraph (a) and after paragraph (b) insert—'; or

(c)   any air rifle, air gun or air pistol which is not for the time being specified in that subsection but appears to him to be specially dangerous,', and

(b)   after subsection (4) insert-

'(4A)   An order under subsection (4)—

(a)   may provide for a provision of the principal Act to apply with or without modification or exception in relation to anything added to subsection (1) of section 5 by the order,

(b)   may impose conditions in respect of any application, modification or exception provided for by the order (which may, in particular, include provision requiring a person to obtain a certificate in accordance with an enactment referred to or applied by the order),

(c)   may make provision generally or by reference to a particular purpose or circumstance,

(d)   may confer a function on the Secretary of State or another specified person, and

(e)   may make transitional, consequential or incidental provision.'

PART 6
THE ENVIRONMENT

Noise

40   Closure of noisy premises

(1)   The chief executive officer of the relevant local authority may make a closure order in relation to premises to which this section applies if he reasonably believes that—

(a)   a public nuisance is being caused by noise coming from the premises, and

(b)   the closure of the premises is necessary to prevent that nuisance.

(2)   This section applies to premises if—

(a)   a premises licence has effect in respect of them, or

(b)   a temporary event notice has effect in respect of them.

(3)   In this section 'closure order' means an order which requires specified premises to be kept closed during a specified period which—

(a)   does not exceed 24 hours, and

(b)   begins when a manager of the premises receives written notice of the order.

(4)   A person commits an offence if without reasonable excuse he permits premises to be open in contravention of a closure order.

(5)   A person guilty of an offence under this section shall be liable on summary conviction to—

(a)   imprisonment for a term not exceeding three months,

(b)   a fine not exceeding £20,000, or

(c)   both.

41   Closure of noisy premises: supplemental

(1)   Where a closure order is made in relation to premises, the chief executive officer of the relevant local authority—

(a)   may cancel the closure order by notice in writing to a manager of the premises,

(b)   shall cancel the order as soon as is reasonably practicable if he believes that it is no longer necessary in order to prevent a public nuisance being caused by noise coming from the premises, and

(c)   shall give notice of the order as soon as is reasonably practicable to the licensing authority for the area in which the premises are situated.

(2)   The chief executive officer of a local authority may authorise an environmental health officer of the authority to exercise a power or duty of the chief executive officer under section 40(1) or under subsection (1) above; and—

(a)   authority under this subsection may be general or specific, and

(b)   a reference in section 40(1) or subsection (1) above to a belief of the chief executive officer includes a reference to a belief of a person authorised under this subsection.

(3)   In section 40 and this section—

'chief executive officer' of an authority means the head of the paid service of the authority designated under section 4 of the Local Government and Housing Act 1989 (c 42),

'environmental health officer' of an authority means an officer authorised by the authority for the purpose of exercising a statutory function in relation to pollution of the environment or harm to human health,

'licensing authority' has the same meaning as in the Licensing Act 2003 (c 17),

'manager' in relation to premises means—

    (a)   a person who holds a premises licence in respect of the premises,

    (b)   a designated premises supervisor under a premises licence in respect of the premises,

    (c)   the premises user in relation to a temporary event notice which has effect in respect of the premises, and

    (d)   any other person who works at the premises in a capacity (paid or unpaid) which enables him to close them,

'premises licence' has the same meaning as in the Licensing Act 2003,

'relevant local authority' in relation to premises means an authority which has statutory functions, for the area in which the premises are situated, in relation to minimising or preventing the risk of pollution of the environment or of harm to human health, and

'temporary event notice' has the same meaning as in the Licensing Act 2003 (and is to be treated as having effect in accordance with section 170(6) of that Act).

42   Dealing with noise at night

(1)   The Noise Act 1996 (c 37) is amended as follows.

(2)   For section 1 (sections 2 to 9 only apply to area of local authority if authority have so resolved or an order by Secretary of State so provides) substitute—

'1   Application of sections 2 to 9

Sections 2 to 9 apply to the area of every local authority in England and Wales.'

(3)   For section 2(1) (local authority under duty to investigate complaint of noise from dwelling at night) substitute—

    '(1)   A local authority in England and Wales may, if they receive a complaint of the kind mentioned in subsection (2), arrange for an officer of the authority to take reasonable steps to investigate the complaint.'

(4)   In section 2(7) (power of local authority to act in relation to dwelling within area of other authority) omit the words from 'and accordingly' to the end.

(5)   In section 9 (section 8: supplementary), for subsection (4) substitute—

    '(4)   A local authority may use any sums it receives under section 8 (its 'penalty receipts') only for the purposes of functions of its that are qualifying functions.

        (4A)   The following are qualifying functions for the purposes of this section—

        (a)   functions under this Act, and

        (b)   functions of a description specified in regulations made by the Secretary of State.

        (4B)   Regulations under subsection (4A)(b) may (in particular) have the effect that a local authority may use its penalty receipts for the purposes of any of its functions.

(4C)   A local authority must supply the Secretary of State with such information relating to the use of its penalty receipts as the Secretary of State may require.

(4D)   The Secretary of State may by regulations—

    (a)   make provision for what a local authority is to do with its penalty receipts—

        (i)   pending their being used for the purposes of qualifying functions of the authority;

        (ii)   if they are not so used before such time after their receipt as may be specified by the regulations;

    (b)   make provision for accounting arrangements in respect of a local authority's penalty receipts.

(4E)   The provision that may be made under subsection (4D)(a)(ii) includes (in particular) provision for the payment of sums to a person (including the Secretary of State) other than the local authority.

(4F)   Before making regulations under this section, the Secretary of State must consult—

    (a)   the local authorities to which the regulations are to apply, and

    (b)   such other persons as the Secretary of State considers appropriate.'

(6)   In section 11 (interpretation and subordinate legislation), in subsection (3) after 'order', in the first place where it occurs, insert 'or regulations'.

(7)   The reference to the Noise Act 1996 (c 37) in Schedule 1 to the National Assembly for Wales (Transfer of Functions) Order 1999 (S.I. 1999/672) is to be treated as referring to that Act as amended by this section.

Penalty notices for graffiti and fly-posting

43   Penalty notices for graffiti and fly-posting

(1)   Where an authorised officer of a local authority has reason to believe that a person has committed a relevant offence in the area of that authority, he may give that person a notice offering him the opportunity of discharging any liability to conviction for that offence by payment of a penalty in accordance with the notice.

(2)   But an authorised officer may not give a notice under subsection (1) if he considers that the commission of the offence—

    (a)   in the case of a relevant offence falling within section 44(1)(c), also involves the commission of an offence under section 30 of the Crime and Disorder Act 1998 (c 37), or

    (b)   in the case of any other relevant offence, was motivated (wholly or partly) by hostility—

        (i)   towards a person based upon his membership (or presumed membership) of a racial or religious group, or

        (ii)   towards members of a racial or religious group based on their membership of that group.

(3)   In the case of a relevant offence falling within section 44(1)(f), an authorised officer may not give a notice to a person under subsection (1) in relation to the display of an advertisement unless he has reason to believe that that person personally affixed or placed the advertisement to, against or upon the land or object on which the advertisement is or was displayed.

(4)   Where a person is given a notice under subsection (1) in respect of an offence—

    (a)   no proceedings may be instituted for that offence (or any other relevant offence arising out of the same circumstances) before the expiration of the period of fourteen days following the date of the notice, and

    (b)   he may not be convicted of that offence (or any other relevant offence arising out of the same circumstances) if before the expiration of that period he pays the penalty in accordance with the notice.

(5)   A notice under subsection (1) must give such particulars of the circumstances alleged to constitute the offence as are necessary for giving reasonable information of the offence.

(6)   A notice under subsection (1) must also state—

         (a)   the period during which, by virtue of subsection (4), proceedings will not be instituted for the offence,

         (b)   the amount of the penalty, and

         (c)   the person to whom and the address at which the penalty may be paid.

(7)   Without prejudice to payment by any other method, payment of a penalty in pursuance of a notice under subsection (1) may be made by pre-paying and posting a letter containing the amount of the penalty (in cash or otherwise) to the person mentioned in subsection (6)(c) at the address so mentioned.

(8)   Where a letter is sent in accordance with subsection (7) payment is to be regarded as having been made at the time at which that letter would be delivered in the ordinary course of post.

(9)   A notice under subsection (1) must be in such form as the appropriate person may by order prescribe.

(10)   Subject to subsection (11), the penalty payable in pursuance of a notice under subsection (1) is £50.

(11)   The appropriate person may by order substitute a different amount for the amount for the time being specified in subsection (10).

44   Meaning of relevant offence

(1)   'Relevant offence' means—

         (a)   an offence under paragraph 10 of section 54 of the Metropolitan Police Act 1839 (c 47) (affixing posters etc),

         (b)   an offence under section 20(1) of the London County Council (General Powers) Act 1954 (defacement of streets with slogans etc),

         (c)   an offence under section 1(1) of the Criminal Damage Act 1971 (c 48) (damaging property etc) which involves only the painting or writing on, or the soiling, marking or other defacing of, any property by whatever means,

         (d)   an offence under section 131(2) of the Highways Act 1980 (c 66) (including that provision as applied by section 27(6) of the Countryside Act 1968 (c 41)) which involves only an act of obliteration,

         (e)   an offence under section 132(1) of the Highways Act 1980 (painting or affixing things on structures on the highway etc),

         (f)   an offence under section 224(3) of the Town and Country Planning Act 1990 (c 8) (displaying advertisement in contravention of regulations).

(2)   This section has effect for the purposes of the interpretation of section 43.

45   Penalty receipts

(1)   Penalties which are payable in pursuance of notices under section 43(1) are payable to local authorities.

(2)   In any proceedings a certificate which—

         (a)   purports to be signed by or on behalf of the person responsible for the financial affairs of a local authority, and

         (b)   states that payment of a penalty payable in pursuance of a notice under section 43(1) was or was not received by a date specified in the certificate,

     is evidence of the facts stated.

(3)   A local authority may use any sums it receives in respect of penalties payable to it in pursuance of notices under section 43(1) (its 'penalty receipts') only for the purposes of functions of its that are qualifying functions.

(4)   The following are qualifying functions for the purposes of this section—

(a)   functions under section 43, and

(b)   functions of a description specified in regulations made by the appropriate person.

(5)   Regulations under subsection (4)(b) may (in particular) have the effect that a local authority may use its penalty receipts for the purposes of any of its functions.

(6)   A local authority must supply the appropriate person with such information relating to its use of its penalty receipts as the appropriate person may require.

(7)   The appropriate person may by regulations—

(a)   make provision for what a local authority is to do with its penalty receipts—

(i)   pending their being used for the purposes of qualifying functions of the authority;

(ii)   if they are not so used before such time after their receipt as may be specified by the regulations;

(b)   make provision for accounting arrangements in respect of a local authority's penalty receipts.

(8)   The provision that may be made under subsection (7)(a)(ii) includes (in particular) provision for the payment of sums to a person (including the appropriate person) other than the local authority.

(9)   Before making regulations under this section, the appropriate person must consult—

(a)   the local authorities to which the regulations are to apply, and

(b)   such other persons as the appropriate person considers appropriate.

46   Powers of police civilians

(1)   In paragraph 1 of Schedule 4 to the Police Reform Act 2002 (c 30) (powers of community support officers to issue fixed penalty notices)—

(a)   at the end of sub-paragraph (2)(c) omit 'and', and

(b)   after sub-paragraph (2)(c) insert-

'(ca)   the power of an authorised officer of a local authority to give a notice under section 43(1) of the Anti-social Behaviour Act 2003 (penalty notices in respect of graffiti or fly-posting); and'.

(2)   In paragraph 1 of Schedule 5 to that Act (powers of accredited persons to issue fixed penalty notices)—

(a)   at the end of sub-paragraph (2)(b) omit 'and', and

(b)   after sub-paragraph (2)(b) insert-

'(ba)   the power of an authorised officer of a local authority to give a notice under section 43(1) of the Anti-social Behaviour Act 2003 (penalty notices in respect of graffiti or fly-posting); and'.

47   Interpretation etc

(1)   In this section and sections 43 and 45—

'advertisement' and 'land' have the meanings given by section 336(1) of the Town and Country Planning Act 1990 (c 8),

'appropriate person' means—

(a)   in relation to England, the Secretary of State, and

(b)   in relation to Wales, the National Assembly for Wales, 'authorised officer' means an officer of a local authority who is authorised in writing by the authority for the purpose of giving notices under section 43(1),

'local authority' means an authority in England and Wales which is a litter authority for the purposes of section 88 of the Environmental Protection Act 1990 (c 43),

'racial group' and 'religious group' have the meanings given by section 28(4) and (5) of the Crime and Disorder Act 1998 (c 37).

(2) Section 28(2) of the Crime and Disorder Act 1998 is to apply for the purposes of section 43(2)(b)(i) as it applies for the purposes of section 28(1)(a) of that Act.

(3) The appropriate person may issue guidance—

(a) about the exercise of the discretion to give notices under section 43(1), and

(b) about the giving of such notices.

Removal of graffiti

48 Graffiti removal notices

(1) This section applies where a local authority is satisfied—

(a) that a relevant surface in an area has been defaced by graffiti, and

(b) that the defacement is detrimental to the amenity of the area or is offensive.

(2) The authority may serve a notice (a 'graffiti removal notice') upon any person who is responsible for the surface imposing the requirement mentioned in subsection (3).

(3) That requirement is a requirement that the defacement be removed, cleared or otherwise remedied within a period specified in the notice being not less than 28 days beginning with the day on which the notice is served.

(4) If the requirement mentioned in subsection (3) is not complied with, the authority or any person authorised by the authority may remove, clear or otherwise remedy the defacement.

(5) In exercising the power under subsection (4) the authority or any person authorised by the authority may enter any land to the extent reasonably necessary for that purpose.

(6) A graffiti removal notice must explain the effect of subsections (4) and (5) and sections 49 and 51.

(7) Subject to subsection (8), section 160 of the Environmental Protection Act 1990 (c 43) has effect in relation to graffiti removal notices as if they were notices within subsection (2) of that section.

(8) Where after reasonable enquiry a local authority is unable to ascertain the name or proper address of any person who is responsible for a relevant surface, the authority may—

(a) affix a graffiti removal notice to the surface, and

(b) enter any land to the extent reasonably necessary for that purpose;

and that notice shall be treated as having been served upon a person responsible for the surface.

(9) In this section a 'relevant surface' is any of the following surfaces, whether internal or external or open to the air or not—

(a) the surface of any street or of any building, structure, apparatus, plant or other object in or on any street;

(b) the surface of any land owned, occupied or controlled by a statutory undertaker or of any building, structure, apparatus, plant or other object in or on any such land;

(c) the surface of any land owned, occupied or controlled by an educational institution (including its governing body) or of any building, structure, apparatus, plant or other object in or on any such land.

(10) But a surface is not a relevant surface unless—

(a)   in the case of a surface within subsection (9)(a), the street is public land;

(b)   in the case of a surface within subsection (9)(b) or (c)-(i) the land is public land,

   (ii)   the surface is visible from public land, or

   (iii)   the surface is otherwise visible to members of the public using the services or facilities of the statutory undertaker or educational institution in question or any other statutory undertaker or educational institution.

(11)   A person is responsible for a relevant surface if—

(a)   where it is the surface of any land (including a street), he owns, leases, occupies, controls, operates or maintains the land, and

(b)   where it is the surface of any other thing mentioned in subsection (9), he owns, leases, occupies, controls, operates or maintains the thing.

(12)   In this section and in sections 49 to 52—

'educational institution' has the meaning given by section 98(2) of the Environmental Protection Act 1990,

'graffiti' includes painting, writing, soiling, marking or other defacing by whatever means,

'graffiti removal notice' has the meaning given by subsection (2),

'local authority' means an authority in England and Wales which is a litter authority for the purposes of section 88 of the Environmental Protection Act 1990 (c 43),

'proper address' is to be read in accordance with section 160(4) and (5) of the Environmental Protection Act 1990,

'public land' means land to which the public are entitled or permitted to have access with or without payment (including any street to which the public are so entitled or permitted),

'statutory undertaker' has the meaning given by section 98(6) of the Environmental Protection Act 1990,

'street' has the meaning given by section 48(1) of the New Roads and Street Works Act 1991 (c 22).

49   Recovery of expenditure

(1)   A local authority may recover from the person on whom a graffiti removal notice was served expenditure reasonably incurred in exercise of the power under section 48(4).

(2)   A local authority may not recover expenditure from a person under subsection (1) unless it has served on that person a notice which sets out the amount of, and details of, the expenditure which it proposes to recover.

(3)   Section 160 of the Environmental Protection Act 1990 has effect in relation to notices under subsection (2) as if they were notices within subsection (2) of that section.

50   Guidance

(1)   The Secretary of State must issue guidance to local authorities in England for the purposes of sections 48 and 49.

(2)   The National Assembly for Wales must issue guidance to local authorities in Wales for the purposes of sections 48 and 49.

(3)   A local authority must have regard to any guidance issued to it under this section.

51   Appeals

(1)   A person on whom a graffiti removal notice is served may, within the period of 21 days beginning with the day on which it is served, appeal against the notice to a magistrates' court on any of the following grounds.

(2)   They are—

(a)   that the defacement is neither detrimental to the amenity of the area nor offensive,

(b)   that there is a material defect or error in, or in connection with, the notice,

(c)   that the notice should be served on another person.

(3)   Where an appeal under subsection (1) is brought, the graffiti removal notice shall be of no effect pending the final determination or withdrawal of the appeal.

(4)   On the determination of such an appeal, the magistrates' court must do one of the following—

(a)   quash the notice,

(b)   modify the notice,

(c)   dismiss the appeal.

(5)   Where the court modifies the notice or dismisses the appeal, it may extend the period specified in the notice.

(6)   A person on whom a notice under section 49(2) is served may, within the period of 21 days beginning with the day on which it is served, appeal to a magistrates' court on the grounds that the expenditure which the authority is proposing to recover is excessive.

(7)   On the determination of an appeal under subsection (6), the magistrates' court must do either of the following—

(a)   confirm that the amount which the authority is proposing to recover is reasonable, or

(b)   substitute a lower amount as the amount which the authority is entitled to recover.

52   Exemption from liability in relation to graffiti removal notices

(1)   None of the persons mentioned in subsection (2) is to have any liability to any person responsible for the relevant surface for damages or otherwise (whether at common law or otherwise) arising out of anything done or omitted to be done in the exercise or purported exercise of—

(a)   the power under subsection (4) of section 48 (including as provided for in subsection (5) of that section), or

(b)   the power under subsection (8) of that section.

(2)   Those persons are—

(a)   in the case of the power mentioned in subsection (1)(a)—

(i)   the local authority and any employee of the authority, and

(ii)   any person authorised by the authority under section 48(4) and the employer or any employee of that person, and

(b)   in the case of the power mentioned in subsection (1)(b), the local authority and any employee of the authority.

(3)   Subsection (1) does not apply—

(a)   if the act or omission is shown to have been in bad faith;

(b)   to liability arising out of a failure to exercise due care and attention;

(c)   so as to prevent an award of damages made in respect of an act or omission on the ground that the act or omission was unlawful by virtue of section 6(1) of the Human Rights Act 1998 (c 42).

(4)   This section does not affect any other exemption from liability (whether at common law or otherwise).

(5)   Section 48(11) is to apply for the purposes of this section as it applies for the purposes of that section.

Advertisements

53   Display of advertisements in contravention of regulations

In section 224(3) of the Town and Country Planning Act 1990 (c 8) (offence of displaying advertisement in contravention of regulations) for 'level 3', in both places where it occurs, substitute 'level 4'.

Aerosol paints

54   Sale of aerosol paint to children

(1)   A person commits an offence if he sells an aerosol paint container to a person under the age of sixteen.

(2)   In subsection (1) 'aerosol paint container' means a device which—

(a)   contains paint stored under pressure, and

(b)   is designed to permit the release of the paint as a spray.

(3)   A person guilty of an offence under this section shall be liable on summary conviction to a fine not exceeding level 4 on the standard scale.

(4)   It is a defence for a person charged with an offence under this section in respect of a sale to prove that—

(a)   he took all reasonable steps to determine the purchaser's age, and

(b)   he reasonably believed that the purchaser was not under the age of sixteen.

(5)   It is a defence for a person charged with an offence under this section in respect of a sale effected by another person to prove that he (the defendant) took all reasonable steps to avoid the commission of an offence under this section.

Waste and litter

55   Unlawfully deposited waste etc

(1)   The Control of Pollution (Amendment) Act 1989 (c 14) is amended in accordance with subsections (2) and (3).

(2)   In subsection (1) of section 7 (further enforcement provisions) for 'relevant authority' substitute 'waste regulation authority'.

(3)   After subsection (1) of section 9 (interpretation) insert—

'(1A)   In sections 5 to 7 above 'regulation authority' also means a waste collection authority falling within section 30(3)(a), (b) or (bb) of the Environmental Protection Act 1990.'

(4)   After section 59 of the Environmental Protection Act 1990 (c 43) insert—

'59A   Directions in relation to exercise of powers under section 59

(1)   The Secretary of State may issue directions setting out categories of waste to which a waste regulation authority or waste collection authority in England and Wales should give priority for the purposes of exercising its powers under section 59 above.

(2)   Priorities set out in directions under subsection (1) above may be different for different authorities or areas.

(3)   But nothing in this section or in any directions issued under it affects any power of an authority under section 59 above.'

(5)   In section 71 of the Environmental Protection Act 1990 (c 43) (obtaining information from persons and authorities), after subsection (3) insert—

    '(4)   The Secretary of State may, by notice in writing, require a waste regulation authority or waste collection authority in England and Wales to supply to him, or to such other person as may be specified in the notice, such information as may be so specified in respect of—

        (a)   cases where the authority has exercised any powers under section 59 above, and

        (b)   cases where the authority has taken action under any other enactment in respect of any deposit or other disposal of controlled waste in contravention of section 33(1) above.'

(6)   Subsection (15) of section 108 of the Environment Act 1995 (c 25) (powers of enforcing authorities and persons authorised by them) is amended in accordance with subsections (7) to (9).

(7)   In the definition of 'enforcing authority' after paragraph (b) insert—

    '(ba)   a waste collection authority;'.

(8)   After the definition of 'pollution control functions' in relation to the Agency or SEPA insert—

    '"pollution control functions", in relation to a waste collection authority, means the functions conferred on it by section 59 of the Environmental Protection Act 1990;'.

(9)   After the definition of 'premises' insert—

    '"waste collection authority" shall be construed in accordance with section 30(3)(a), (b) and (bb) of the Environmental Protection Act 1990.'

(10)   The reference to the Environmental Protection Act 1990 in Schedule 1 to the National Assembly for Wales (Transfer of Functions) Order 1999 (SI 1999/672) is to be treated as referring to that Act as amended by this section.

56   Extension of litter authority powers to take remedial action

(1)   For section 92(10) of the Environmental Protection Act 1990 (restriction on remedial action by litter authorities) substitute—

    '(10)   Subsection (9) above does not apply in relation to any land to which subsection (11) or (12) below applies.

    (11)   This subsection applies to any relevant Crown land which is occupied for naval, military or air force purposes.

    (12)   This subsection applies to any relevant land of a statutory undertaker in relation to which the Secretary of State has specified, by order, that it is requisite or expedient that, in the national interest, subsection (9) above should not apply.'

(2)   The reference to the Environmental Protection Act 1990 (c 43) in Schedule 1 to the National Assembly for Wales (Transfer of Functions) Order 1999 (SI 1999/672) is to be treated as referring to that Act as amended by this section.

PART 7
PUBLIC ORDER AND TRESPASS

57   Public assemblies

In section 16 of the Public Order Act 1986 (c 64) (which defines 'public assembly' for the purposes of the power in section 14 of that Act to impose conditions on public assemblies), in the definition of 'public assembly' for '20' substitute '2'.

58   Raves

(1)   Section 63 of the Criminal Justice and Public Order Act 1994 (c 33) (powers in relation to raves) is amended as follows.

(2)   In subsection (1) for '100' substitute '20'.

(3)   After subsection (1) insert—

    '(1A)   This section also applies to a gathering if—

        (a)   it is a gathering on land of 20 or more persons who are trespassing on the land; and

        (b)   it would be a gathering of a kind mentioned in subsection (1) above if it took place on land in the open air.'

(4)   In subsection (2) omit 'in the open air'.

(5)   In subsection (7) for 'this section' substitute 'subsection (6) above'.

(6)   After subsection (7) insert—

    '(7A)   A person commits an offence if—

        (a)   he knows that a direction under subsection (2) above has been given which applies to him, and

        (b)   he makes preparations for or attends a gathering to which this section applies within the period of 24 hours starting when the direction was given.

    (7B)   A person guilty of an offence under subsection (7A) above is liable on summary conviction to imprisonment for a term not exceeding three months or a fine not exceeding level 4 on the standard scale, or both.'

59   Aggravated trespass

(1)   The Criminal Justice and Public Order Act 1994 is amended as follows.

(2)   In section 68 (offence of aggravated trespass), in subsection (1) (which defines the offence by reference to trespass on land in the open air and lawful activity on land in the open air) omit 'in the open air' in both places where those words appear.

(3)   In section 69 (powers to remove persons committing or participating in aggravated trespass), in subsection (1) (which confers the power by reference to trespass on land in the open air) omit 'in the open air' in both places where those words appear.

60   Power to remove trespassers: alternative site available

After section 62 of the Criminal Justice and Public Order Act 1994 (c 33) insert—

'62A   Power to remove trespassers: alternative site available

    (1)   If the senior police officer present at a scene reasonably believes that the conditions in subsection (2) are satisfied in relation to a person and land, he may direct the person—

(a)   to leave the land;

(b)   to remove any vehicle and other property he has with him on the land.

(2)   The conditions are—

(a)   that the person and one or more others ('the trespassers') are trespassing on the land;

(b)   that the trespassers have between them at least one vehicle on the land;

(c)   that the trespassers are present on the land with the common purpose of residing there for any period;

(d)   if it appears to the officer that the person has one or more caravans in his possession or under his control on the land, that there is a suitable pitch on a relevant caravan site for that caravan or each of those caravans;

(e)   that the occupier of the land or a person acting on his behalf has asked the police to remove the trespassers from the land.

(3)   A direction under subsection (1) may be communicated to the person to whom it applies by any constable at the scene.

(4)   Subsection (5) applies if—

(a)   a police officer proposes to give a direction under subsection (1) in relation to a person and land, and

(b)   it appears to him that the person has one or more caravans in his possession or under his control on the land.

(5)   The officer must consult every local authority within whose area the land is situated as to whether there is a suitable pitch for the caravan or each of the caravans on a relevant caravan site which is situated in the local authority's area.

(6)   In this section—

"caravan" and "caravan site" have the same meanings as in Part 1 of the Caravan Sites and Control of Development Act 1960;

"relevant caravan site" means a caravan site which is—

(a)   situated in the area of a local authority within whose area the land is situated, and

(b)   managed by a relevant site manager;

"relevant site manager" means—

(a)   a local authority within whose area the land is situated;

(b)   a registered social landlord;

"registered social landlord" means a body registered as a social landlord under Chapter 1 of Part 1 of the Housing Act 1996.

(7)   The Secretary of State may by order amend the definition of 'relevant site manager' in subsection (6) by adding a person or description of person.

(8)   An order under subsection (7) must be made by statutory instrument and is subject to annulment in pursuance of a resolution of either House of Parliament.'

61   Failure to comply with direction: offences

After section 62A of the Criminal Justice and Public Order Act 1994 (c 33) (inserted by section 60) insert—

'62B   Failure to comply with direction under section 62A: offences

(1)   A person commits an offence if he knows that a direction under section 62A(1) has been given which applies to him and—

(a)   he fails to leave the relevant land as soon as reasonably practicable,or

(b)   he enters any land in the area of the relevant local authority as a trespasser before the end of the relevant period with the intention of residing there.

(2)   The relevant period is the period of 3 months starting with the day on which the direction is given.

(3)   A person guilty of an offence under this section is liable on summary conviction to imprisonment for a term not exceeding 3 months or a fine not exceeding level 4 on the standard scale or both.

(4)   A constable in uniform who reasonably suspects that a person is committing an offence under this section may arrest him without a warrant.

(5)   In proceedings for an offence under this section it is a defence for the accused to show—

    (a)   that he was not trespassing on the land in respect of which he is alleged to have committed the offence, or

    (b)   that he had a reasonable excuse—

        (i)   for failing to leave the relevant land as soon as reasonably practicable, or

        (ii)   for entering land in the area of the relevant local authority as a trespasser with the intention of residing there, or

    (c)   that, at the time the direction was given, he was under the age of 18 years and was residing with his parent or guardian.'

62   Failure to comply with direction: seizure

(1)   After section 62B of the Criminal Justice and Public Order Act 1994 (inserted by section 61) insert—

'62C   Failure to comply with direction under section 62A: seizure

(1)   This section applies if a direction has been given under section 62A(1) and a constable reasonably suspects that a person to whom the direction applies has, without reasonable excuse—

    (a)   failed to remove any vehicle on the relevant land which appears to the constable to belong to him or to be in his possession or under his control; or

    (b)   entered any land in the area of the relevant local authority as a trespasser with a vehicle before the end of the relevant period with the intention of residing there.

(2)   The relevant period is the period of 3 months starting with the day on which the direction is given.

(3)   The constable may seize and remove the vehicle.'

(2)   In section 67(1) (retention and charges for seized vehicles) after 'section 62(1)' insert , '62C(3)'.

63   Common land: modifications

After section 62C of the Criminal Justice and Public Order Act 1994 (c 33) (inserted by section 62) insert—

'62D   Common land: modifications

(1)   In their application to common land sections 62A to 62C have effect with these modifications.

(2)   References to trespassing and trespassers have effect as if they were references to acts, and persons doing acts, which constitute—

    (a)   a trespass as against the occupier, or

    (b)   an infringement of the commoners' rights.

(3)   References to the occupier—

    (a)   in the case of land to which the public has access, include the local authority and any commoner;

    (b)   in any other case, include the commoners or any of them.

(4)   Subsection (1) does not—

    (a)   require action by more than one occupier, or

(b)   constitute persons trespassers as against any commoner or the local authority if they are permitted to be there by the other occupier.

(5)   In this section 'common land', 'commoner' and 'the local authority' have the meanings given by section 61.'

64   Interpretation

After section 62D of the Criminal Justice and Public Order Act 1994 (inserted by section 63) insert—

'62E   Sections 62A to 62D: interpretation

(1)   Subsections (2) to (8) apply for the interpretation of sections 62A to 62D and this section.

(2)   "Land" does not include buildings other than—

(a)   agricultural buildings within the meaning of paragraphs 3 to 8 of Schedule 5 to the Local Government Finance Act 1988, or

(b)   scheduled monuments within the meaning of the Ancient Monuments and Archaeological Areas Act 1979.

(3)   "Local authority2 means—

(a)   in Greater London, a London borough or the Common Council of the City of London;

(b)   in England outside Greater London, a county council, a district council or the Council of the Isles of Scilly;

(c)   in Wales, a county council or a county borough council.

(4)   "Occupier", "trespass", "trespassing" and "trespasser" have the meanings given by section 61 in relation to England and Wales.

(5)   "The relevant land" means the land in respect of which a direction under section 62A(1) is given.

(6)   "The relevant local authority" means—

(a)   if the relevant land is situated in the area of more than one local authority (but is not in the Isles of Scilly), the district council or county borough council within whose area the relevant land is situated;

(b)   if the relevant land is situated in the Isles of Scilly, the Council of the Isles of Scilly;

(c)   in any other case, the local authority within whose area the relevant land is situated.

(7)   "Vehicle" has the meaning given by section 61.

(8)   A person may be regarded as having a purpose of residing in a place even if he has a home elsewhere.'

PART 8
HIGH HEDGES

Introductory

65   Complaints to which this Part applies

(1)   This Part applies to a complaint which—

(a)   is made for the purposes of this Part by an owner or occupier of a domestic property; and

(b)   alleges that his reasonable enjoyment of that property is being adversely affected by the height of a high hedge situated on land owned or occupied by another person.

(2)   This Part also applies to a complaint which—

(a)   is made for the purposes of this Part by an owner of a domestic property that is for the time being unoccupied, and

(b)   alleges that the reasonable enjoyment of that property by a prospective occupier of that property would be adversely affected by the height of a high hedge situated on land owned or occupied by another person,

as it applies to a complaint falling within subsection (1).

(3)   In relation to a complaint falling within subsection (2), references in sections 68 and 69 to the effect of the height of a high hedge on the complainant's reasonable enjoyment of a domestic property shall be read as references to the effect that it would have on the reasonable enjoyment of that property by a prospective occupier of the property.

(4)   This Part does not apply to complaints about the effect of the roots of a high hedge.

(5)   In this Part, in relation to a complaint —

'complainant' means—

(a)   a person by whom the complaint is made; or

(b)   if every person who made the complaint ceases to be an owner or occupier of the domestic property specified in the complaint, any other person who is for the time being an owner or occupier of that property;

and references to the complainant include references to one or more of the complainants;

'the neighbouring land' means the land on which the high hedge is situated; and

'the relevant authority' means the local authority in whose area that land is situated.

66   High hedges

(1)   In this Part 'high hedge' means so much of a barrier to light or access as—

(a)   is formed wholly or predominantly by a line of two or more evergreens; and

(b)   rises to a height of more than two metres above ground level.

(2)   For the purposes of subsection (1) a line of evergreens is not to be regarded as forming a barrier to light or access if the existence of gaps significantly affects its overall effect as such a barrier at heights of more than two metres above ground level.

(3)   In this section 'evergreen' means an evergreen tree or shrub or a semi-evergreen tree or shrub.

67   Domestic property

(1)   In this Part 'domestic property' means—

(a)   a dwelling; or

(b)   a garden or yard which is used and enjoyed wholly or mainly in connection with a dwelling.

(2)   In subsection (1) 'dwelling' means any building or part of a building occupied, or intended to be occupied, as a separate dwelling.

(3)   A reference in this Part to a person's reasonable enjoyment of domestic property includes a reference to his reasonable enjoyment of a part of the property.

Complaints procedure

68   Procedure for dealing with complaints

(1)   This section has effect where a complaint to which this Part applies—

    (a)   is made to the relevant authority; and

    (b)   is accompanied by such fee (if any) as the authority may determine.

(2)   If the authority consider—

    (a)   that the complainant has not taken all reasonable steps to resolve the matters complained of without proceeding by way of such a complaint to the authority, or

    (b)   that the complaint is frivolous or vexatious,

the authority may decide that the complaint should not be proceeded with.

(3)   If the authority do not so decide, they must decide—

    (a)   whether the height of the high hedge specified in the complaint is adversely affecting the complainant's reasonable enjoyment of the domestic property so specified; and

    (b)   if so, what action (if any) should be taken in relation to that hedge, in pursuance of a remedial notice under section 69, with a view to remedying the adverse effect or preventing its recurrence.

(4)   If the authority decide under subsection (3) that action should be taken as mentioned in paragraph (b) of that subsection, they must as soon as is reasonably practicable—

    (a)   issue a remedial notice under section 69 implementing their decision;

    (b)   send a copy of that notice to the following persons, namely—

        (i)   every complainant; and

        (ii)   every owner and every occupier of the neighbouring land; and

    (c)   notify each of those persons of the reasons for their decision.

(5)   If the authority—

    (a)   decide that the complaint should not be proceeded with, or

    (b)   decide either or both of the issues specified in subsection (3) otherwise than in the complainant's favour,

they must as soon as is reasonably practicable notify the appropriate person or persons of any such decision and of their reasons for it.

(6)   For the purposes of subsection (5)—

    (a)   every complainant is an appropriate person in relation to a decision falling within paragraph (a) or (b) of that subsection; and

    (b)   every owner and every occupier of the neighbouring land is an appropriate person in relation to a decision falling within paragraph (b) of that subsection.

(7)   A fee determined under subsection (1)(b) must not exceed the amount prescribed in regulations made—

    (a)   in relation to complaints relating to hedges situated in England, by the Secretary of State; and

    (b)   in relation to complaints relating to hedges situated in Wales, by the National Assembly for Wales.

(8)   A fee received by a local authority by virtue of subsection (1)(b) may be refunded by them in such circumstances and to such extent as they may determine.

69   Remedial notices

(1)   For the purposes of this Part a remedial notice is a notice—

    (a)   issued by the relevant authority in respect of a complaint to which this Part applies; and

    (b)   stating the matters mentioned in subsection (2).

(2)   Those matters are—

    (a)   that a complaint has been made to the authority under this Part about a high hedge specified in the notice which is situated on land so specified;

    (b)   that the authority have decided that the height of that hedge is adversely affecting the complainant's reasonable enjoyment of the domestic property specified in the notice;

    (c)   the initial action that must be taken in relation to that hedge before the end of the compliance period;

    (d)   any preventative action that they consider must be taken in relation to that hedge at times following the end of that period while the hedge remains on the land; and

    (e)   the consequences under sections 75 and 77 of a failure to comply with the notice.

(3)   The action specified in a remedial notice is not to require or involve—

    (a)   a reduction in the height of the hedge to less than two metres above ground level; or

    (b)   the removal of the hedge.

(4)   A remedial notice shall take effect on its operative date.

(5)   'The operative date' of a remedial notice is such date (falling at least 28 days after that on which the notice is issued) as is specified in the notice as the date on which it is to take effect.

(6)   'The compliance period' in the case of a remedial notice is such reasonable period as is specified in the notice for the purposes of subsection (2)(c) as the period within which the action so specified is to be taken; and that period shall begin with the operative date of the notice.

(7)   Subsections (4) to (6) have effect in relation to a remedial notice subject to—

    (a)   the exercise of any power of the relevant authority under section 70; and

    (b)   the operation of sections 71 to 73 in relation to the notice.

(8)   While a remedial notice has effect, the notice—

    (a)   shall be a local land charge; and

    (b)   shall be binding on every person who is for the time being an owner or occupier of the land specified in the notice as the land where the hedge in question is situated.

(9)   In this Part—

'initial action' means remedial action or preventative action, or both;

'remedial action' means action to remedy the adverse effect of the height of the hedge on the complainant's reasonable enjoyment of the domestic property in respect of which the complaint was made; and

'preventative action' means action to prevent the recurrence of the adverse effect.

70   Withdrawal or relaxation of requirements of remedial notices

(1)   The relevant authority may—

    (a)   withdraw a remedial notice issued by them; or

    (b)   waive or relax a requirement of a remedial notice so issued.

(2)   The powers conferred by this section are exercisable both before and after a remedial notice has taken effect.

(3)   Where the relevant authority exercise the powers conferred by this section, they must give notice of what they have done to—

(a)   every complainant; and

(b)   every owner and every occupier of the neighbouring land.

(4)   The withdrawal of a remedial notice does not affect the power of the relevant authority to issue a further remedial notice in respect of the same hedge.

Appeals

71   Appeals against remedial notices and other decisions of relevant authorities

(1)   Where the relevant authority—

(a)   issue a remedial notice,

(b)   withdraw such a notice, or

(c)   waive or relax the requirements of such a notice,

each of the persons falling within subsection (2) may appeal to the appeal authority against the issue or withdrawal of the notice or (as the case may be) the waiver or relaxation of its requirements.

(2)   Those persons are—

(a)   every person who is a complainant in relation to the complaint by reference to which the notice was given; and

(b)   every person who is an owner or occupier of the neighbouring land.

(3)   Where the relevant authority decide either or both of the issues specified in section 68(3) otherwise than in the complainant's favour, the complainant may appeal to the appeal authority against the decision.

(4)   An appeal under this section must be made before—

(a)   the end of the period of 28 days beginning with the relevant date; or

(b)   such later time as the appeal authority may allow.

(5)   In subsection (4) 'the relevant date'—

(a)   in the case of an appeal against the issue of a remedial notice, means the date on which the notice was issued; and

(b)   in the case of any other appeal under this section, means the date of the notification given by the relevant authority under section 68 or 70 of the decision in question.

(6)   Where an appeal is duly made under subsection (1), the notice or (as the case may be) withdrawal, waiver or relaxation in question shall not have effect pending the final determination or withdrawal of the appeal.

(7)   In this Part 'the appeal authority' means—

(a)   in relation to appeals relating to hedges situated in England, the Secretary of State; and

(b)   in relation to appeals relating to hedges situated in Wales, the National Assembly for Wales.

72   Appeals procedure

(1)   The appeal authority may by regulations make provision with respect to—

(a)   the procedure which is to be followed in connection with appeals to that authority under section 71; and

(b)   other matters consequential on or connected with such appeals.

(2)   Regulations under this section may, in particular, make provision—

(a)   specifying the grounds on which appeals may be made;

(b)   prescribing the manner in which appeals are to be made;

(c)   requiring persons making appeals to send copies of such documents as may be prescribed to such persons as may be prescribed;

(d)   requiring local authorities against whose decisions appeals are made to send to the appeal authority such documents as may be prescribed;

(e)   specifying, where a local authority are required by virtue of paragraph (d) to send the appeal authority a statement indicating the submissions which they propose to put forward on the appeal, the matters to be included in such a statement;

(f)   prescribing the period within which a requirement imposed by the regulations is to be complied with;

(g)   enabling such a period to be extended by the appeal authority;

(h)   for a decision on an appeal to be binding on persons falling within section 71(2) in addition to the person by whom the appeal was made;

(i)   for incidental or ancillary matters, including the awarding of costs.

(3)   Where an appeal is made to the appeal authority under section 71 the appeal authority may appoint a person to hear and determine the appeal on its behalf.

(4)   The appeal authority may require such a person to exercise on its behalf any functions which—

(a)   are conferred on the appeal authority in connection with such an appeal by section 71 or 73 or by regulations under this section; and

(b)   are specified in that person's appointment;

and references to the appeal authority in section 71 or 73 or in any regulations under this section shall be construed accordingly.

(5)   The appeal authority may pay a person appointed under subsection (3) such remuneration as it may determine.

(6)   Regulations under this section may provide for any provision of Schedule 20 to the Environment Act 1995 (c 25) (delegation of appellate functions) to apply in relation to a person appointed under subsection (3) with such modifications (if any) as may be prescribed.

(7)   In this section, 'prescribed' means prescribed by regulations made by the appeal authority.

73   Determination or withdrawal of appeals

(1)   On an appeal under section 71 the appeal authority may allow or dismiss the appeal, either in whole or in part.

(2)   Where the appeal authority decides to allow such an appeal to any extent, it may do such of the following as it considers appropriate—

(a)   quash a remedial notice or decision to which the appeal relates;

(b)   vary the requirements of such a notice; or

(c)   in a case where no remedial notice has been issued, issue on behalf of the relevant authority a remedial notice that could have been issued by the relevant authority on the complaint in question.

(3)   On an appeal under section 71 relating to a remedial notice, the appeal authority may also correct any defect, error or misdescription in the notice if it is satisfied that the correction will not cause injustice to any person falling within section 71(2).

(4)   Once the appeal authority has made its decision on an appeal under section 71, it must, as soon as is reasonably practicable—

(a)   give a notification of the decision, and

(b) if the decision is to issue a remedial notice or to vary or correct the requirements of such a notice, send copies of the notice as issued, varied or corrected,

to every person falling within section 71(2) and to the relevant authority.

(5) Where, in consequence of the appeal authority's decision on an appeal, a remedial notice is upheld or varied or corrected, the operative date of the notice shall be—

(a) the date of the appeal authority's decision; or

(b) such later date as may be specified in its decision.

(6) Where the person making an appeal under section 71 against a remedial notice withdraws his appeal, the operative date of the notice shall be the date on which the appeal is withdrawn.

(7) In any case falling within subsection (5) or (6), the compliance period for the notice shall accordingly run from the date which is its operative date by virtue of that subsection (and any period which may have started to run from a date preceding that on which the appeal was made shall accordingly be disregarded).

Powers of entry

74 Powers of entry for the purposes of complaints and appeals

(1) Where, under this Part, a complaint has been made or a remedial notice has been issued, a person authorised by the relevant authority may enter the neighbouring land in order to obtain information required by the relevant authority for the purpose of determining—

(a) whether this Part applies to the complaint;

(b) whether to issue or withdraw a remedial notice;

(c) whether to waive or relax a requirement of a remedial notice;

(d) whether a requirement of a remedial notice has been complied with.

(2) Where an appeal has been made under section 71, a person authorised—

(a) by the appeal authority, or

(b) by a person appointed to determine appeals on its behalf,

may enter the neighbouring land in order to obtain information required by the appeal authority, or by the person so appointed, for the purpose of determining an appeal under this Part.

(3) A person shall not enter land in the exercise of a power conferred by this section unless at least 24 hours' notice of the intended entry has been given to every occupier of the land.

(4) A person authorised under this section to enter land—

(a) shall, if so required, produce evidence of his authority before entering; and

(b) shall produce such evidence if required to do so at any time while he remains on the land.

(5) A person who enters land in the exercise of a power conferred by this section may—

(a) take with him such other persons as may be necessary;

(b) take with him equipment and materials needed in order to obtain the information required;

(c) take samples of any trees or shrubs that appear to him to form part of a high hedge.

(6) If, in the exercise of a power conferred by this section, a person enters land which is unoccupied or from which all of the persons occupying the land are temporarily absent, he must on his departure leave it as effectively secured against unauthorised entry as he found it.

(7) A person who intentionally obstructs a person acting in the exercise of the powers under this section is guilty of an offence and shall be liable, on summary conviction, to a fine not exceeding level 3 on the standard scale.

Enforcement powers etc

75   Offences

(1)   Where—

    (a)   a remedial notice requires the taking of any action, and

    (b)   that action is not taken in accordance with that notice within the compliance period or (as the case may be) by the subsequent time by which it is required to be taken,

every person who, at a relevant time, is an owner or occupier of the neighbouring land is guilty of an offence and shall be liable, on summary conviction, to a fine not exceeding level 3 on the standard scale.

(2)   In subsection (1) 'relevant time'—

    (a)   in relation to action required to be taken before the end of the compliance period, means a time after the end of that period and before the action is taken; and

    (b)   in relation to any preventative action which is required to be taken after the end of that period, means a time after that at which the action is required to be taken but before it is taken.

(3)   In proceedings against a person for an offence under subsection (1) it shall be a defence for him to show that he did everything he could be expected to do to secure compliance with the notice.

(4)   In any such proceedings against a person, it shall also be a defence for him to show, in a case in which he—

    (a)   is not a person to whom a copy of the remedial notice was sent in accordance with a provision of this Part, and

    (b)   is not assumed under subsection (5) to have had knowledge of the notice at the time of the alleged offence,

that he was not aware of the existence of the notice at that time.

(5)   A person shall be assumed to have had knowledge of a remedial notice at any time if at that time—

    (a)   he was an owner of the neighbouring land; and

    (b)   the notice was at that time registered as a local land charge.

(6)   Section 198 of the Law of Property Act 1925 (c 20) (constructive notice) shall be disregarded for the purposes of this section.

(7)   Where a person is convicted of an offence under subsection (1) and it appears to the court—

    (a)   that a failure to comply with the remedial notice is continuing, and

    (b)   that it is within that person's power to secure compliance with the notice,

the court may, in addition to or instead of imposing a punishment, order him to take the steps specified in the order for securing compliance with the notice.

(8)   An order under subsection (7) must require those steps to be taken within such reasonable period as may be fixed by the order.

(9)   Where a person fails without reasonable excuse to comply with an order under subsection (7) he is guilty of an offence and shall be liable, on summary conviction, to a fine not exceeding level 3 on the standard scale.

(10)   Where a person continues after conviction of an offence under subsection (9) (or of an offence under this subsection) to fail, without reasonable excuse, to take steps which he has been ordered to take under subsection (7), he is guilty of a further offence and shall be liable, on summary conviction, to a fine not exceeding one-twentieth of that level for each day on which the failure has so continued.

76   Power to require occupier to permit action to be taken by owner

Section 289 of the Public Health Act 1936 (c 49) (power of court to require occupier to permit work to be done by owner) shall apply with any necessary modifications for the purpose of giving an owner of land to which a remedial notice relates the right, as against all other persons interested in the land, to comply with the notice.

77   Action by relevant authority

(1)   This section applies where—

(a)   a remedial notice requires the taking of any action; and

(b)   that action is not taken in accordance with that notice within the compliance period or (as the case may be) after the end of that period when it is required to be taken by the notice.

(2)   Where this section applies—

(a)   a person authorised by the relevant authority may enter the neighbouring land and take the required action; and

(b)   the relevant authority may recover any expenses reasonably incurred by that person in doing so from any person who is an owner or occupier of the land.

(3)   Expenses recoverable under this section shall be a local land charge and binding on successive owners of the land and on successive occupiers of it.

(4)   Where expenses are recoverable under this section from two or more persons, those persons shall be jointly and severally liable for the expenses.

(5)   A person shall not enter land in the exercise of a power conferred by this section unless at least 7 days' notice of the intended entry has been given to every occupier of the land.

(6)   A person authorised under this section to enter land—

(a)   shall, if so required, produce evidence of his authority before entering; and

(b)   shall produce such evidence if required to do so at any time while he remains on the land.

(7)   A person who enters land in the exercise of a power conferred by this section may—

(a)   use a vehicle to enter the land;

(b)   take with him such other persons as may be necessary;

(c)   take with him equipment and materials needed for the purpose of taking the required action.

(8)   If, in the exercise of a power conferred by this section, a person enters land which is unoccupied or from which all of the persons occupying the land are temporarily absent, he must on his departure leave it as effectively secured against unauthorised entry as he found it.

(9)   A person who wilfully obstructs a person acting in the exercise of powers under this section to enter land and take action on that land is guilty of an offence and shall be liable, on summary conviction, to a fine not exceeding level 3 on the standard scale.

78   Offences committed by bodies corporate

(1)   Where an offence under this Part committed by a body corporate is proved to have been committed with the consent or connivance of, or to be attributable to any neglect on the part of—

(a)   a director, manager, secretary or other similar officer of the body corporate, or

(b)   any person who was purporting to act in any such capacity,

he, as well as the body corporate, shall be guilty of that offence and be liable to be proceeded against and punished accordingly.

(2)   Where the affairs of a body corporate are managed by its members, subsection (1) applies in relation to the acts and defaults of a member in connection with his functions of management as if he were a director of the body corporate.

Supplementary

79   Service of documents

(1)   A notification or other document required to be given or sent to a person by virtue of this Part shall be taken to be duly given or sent to him if served in accordance with the following provisions of this section.

(2)   Such a document may be served—

    (a)   by delivering it to the person in question;

    (b)   by leaving it at his proper address; or

    (c)   by sending it by post to him at that address.

(3)   Such a document may—

    (a)   in the case of a body corporate, be served on the secretary or clerk of that body;

    (b)   in the case of a partnership, be served on a partner or a person having the control or management of the partnership business.

(4)   For the purposes of this section and of section 7 of the Interpretation Act 1978 (c 30) (service of documents by post) in its application to this section, a person's proper address shall be his last known address, except that—

    (a)   in the case of a body corporate or their secretary or clerk, it shall be the address of the registered or principal office of that body; and

    (b)   in the case of a partnership or person having the control or the management of the partnership business, it shall be the principal office of the partnership.

(5)   For the purposes of subsection (4) the principal office of—

    (a)   a company registered outside the United Kingdom, or

    (b)   a partnership carrying on business outside the United Kingdom,

shall be their principal office within the United Kingdom.

(6)   If a person has specified an address in the United Kingdom other than his proper address within the meaning of subsection (4) as the one at which he or someone on his behalf will accept documents of a particular description, that address shall also be treated for the purposes of this section and section 7 of the Interpretation Act 1978 as his proper address in connection with the service on him of a document of that description.

(7)   Where—

    (a)   by virtue of this Part a document is required to be given or sent to a person who is an owner or occupier of any land, and

    (b)   the name or address of that person cannot be ascertained after reasonable inquiry,

the document may be served either by leaving it in the hands of a person who is or appears to be resident or employed on the land or by leaving it conspicuously affixed to some building or object on the land.

80   Documents in electronic form

(1)   A requirement of this Part—

    (a)   to send a copy of a remedial notice to a person, or

    (b)   to notify a person under section 68(4) of the reasons for the issue of a remedial notice, is not capable of being satisfied by transmitting the copy or notification electronically or by making it available on a web-site.

(2)   The delivery of any other document to a person (the 'recipient') may be effected for the purposes of section 79(2)(a)—

   (a)   by transmitting it electronically, or

   (b)   by making it available on a web-site,

   but only if it is transmitted or made available in accordance with subsection (3) or (5).

(3)   A document is transmitted electronically in accordance with this subsection if—

   (a)   the recipient has agreed that documents may be delivered to him by being transmitted to an electronic address and in an electronic form specified by him for that purpose; and

   (b)   the document is a document to which that agreement applies and is transmitted to that address in that form.

(4)   A document which is transmitted in accordance with subsection (3) by means of an electronic communications network shall, unless the contrary is proved, be treated as having been delivered at 9 a.m. on the working day immediately following the day on which it is transmitted.

(5)   A document is made available on a web-site in accordance with this subsection if—

   (a)   the recipient has agreed that documents may be delivered to him by being made available on a web-site;

   (b)   the document is a document to which that agreement applies and is made available on a web-site;

   (c)   the recipient is notified, in a manner agreed by him, of—

      (i)   the presence of the document on the web-site;

      (ii)   the address of the web-site; and

      (iii)   the place on the web-site where the document may be accessed.

(6)   A document made available on a web-site in accordance with subsection (5) shall, unless the contrary is proved, be treated as having been delivered at 9a.m. on the working day immediately following the day on which the recipient is notified in accordance with subsection (5)(c).

(7)   In this section—

   'electronic address' includes any number or address used for the purposes of receiving electronic communications;

   'electronic communication' means an electronic communication within the meaning of the Electronic Communications Act 2000 (c 7) the processing of which on receipt is intended to produce writing;

   'electronic communications network' means an electronic communications network within the meaning of the Communications Act 2003 (c 21);

   'electronically' means in the form of an electronic communication;

   'working day' means a day which is not a Saturday or a Sunday, Christmas Day, Good Friday or a bank holiday in England and Wales under the Banking and Financial Dealings Act 1971 (c 80).

81   Power to make further provision about documents in electronic form

(1)   Regulations may amend section 80 by modifying the circumstances in which, and the conditions subject to which, the delivery of a document for the purposes of section 79(2)(a) may be effected by—

   (a)   transmitting the document electronically; or

   (b)   making the document available on a web-site.

(2)   Regulations may also amend section 80 by modifying the day on which and the time at which documents which are transmitted electronically or made available on a web-site in accordance with that section are to be treated as having been delivered.

(3)   Regulations under this section may make such consequential amendments of this Part as the person making the regulations considers appropriate.

(4)   The power to make such regulations shall be exercisable—

(a)   in relation to documents relating to complaints about hedges situated in England, by the Secretary of State; and

(b)   in relation to documents relating to complaints about hedges situated in Wales, by the National Assembly for Wales.

(5)   In this section 'electronically' has the meaning given in section 80.

82   Interpretation

In this Part—

'the appeal authority' has the meaning given by section 71(7);

'complaint' shall be construed in accordance with section 65;

'complainant' has the meaning given by section 65(5);

'the compliance period' has the meaning given by section 69(6);

'domestic property' has the meaning given by section 67;

'high hedge' has the meaning given by section 66;

'local authority', in relation to England, means—

(a)   a district council;

(b)   a county council for a county in which there are no districts;

(c)   a London borough council; or

(d)   the Common Council of the City of London;

and, in relation to Wales, means a county council or a county borough council;

'the neighbouring land' has the meaning given by section 65(5);

'occupier', in relation to any land, means a person entitled to possession of the land by virtue of an estate or interest in it;

'the operative date' shall be construed in accordance with sections 69(5) and 73(5) and (6);

'owner', in relation to any land, means a person (other than a mortgagee not in possession) who, whether in his own right or as trustee for any person—

(a)   is entitled to receive the rack rent of the land, or

(b)   where the land is not let at a rack rent, would be so entitled if it were so let;

'preventative action' has the meaning given by section 69(9);

'the relevant authority' has the meaning given by section 65(5);

'remedial notice' shall be construed in accordance with section 69(1);

'remedial action' has the meaning given by section 69(9).

(2)   The Secretary of State shall not make an order containing (with or without any other provision) any provision authorised by this paragraph unless a draft of that order has been laid before Parliament and approved by a resolution of each House.'

90   Report by local authority in certain cases where person remanded on bail

After section 23A of the Children and Young Persons Act 1969 (c 54) there is inserted—

'23B   Report by local authority in certain cases where person remanded on bail

(1)   Subsection (2) below applies where a court remands a person aged 10 or 11 on bail and either—

    (a)   the person is charged with or has been convicted of a serious offence, or

    (b)   in the opinion of the court the person is a persistent offender.

(2)   The court may order a local authority to make an oral or written report specifying where the person is likely to be placed or maintained if he is further remanded to local authority accommodation.

(3)   An order under subsection (2) above must designate the local authority which is to make the report; and that authority must be the local authority which the court would have designated under section 23(2) of this Act if the person had been remanded to local authority accommodation.

(4)   An order under subsection (2) above must specify the period within which the local authority must comply with the order.

(5)   The maximum period that may be so specified is seven working days.

(6)   If the Secretary of State by order so provides, subsection (2) above also applies where—

    (a)   a court remands on bail any person who has attained the age of 12 and is under the age of 17,

    (b)   the requirement in section 23AA(3) of this Act is fulfilled, and

    (c)   in a case where he is remanded after conviction, the court is satisfied that the behaviour which constituted the offence was due, to a significant extent, to the circumstances in which the offender was living.

(7)   In this section—

'serious offence' means an offence punishable in the case of an adult with imprisonment for a term of two years or more.

'working day' means any day other than—

    (a)   a Saturday or a Sunday,

    (b)   Christmas day or Good Friday, or

    (c)   a bank holiday in England and Wales under the Banking and Financial Dealings Act 1971.'.

91   Proceedings under section 222 of the Local Government Act 1972: power of arrest attached to injunction

(1)   This section applies to proceedings in which a local authority is a party by virtue of section 222 of the Local Government Act 1972 (c 70) (power of local authority to bring, defend or appear in proceedings for the promotion or protection of the interests of inhabitants of their area).

(2)   If the court grants an injunction which prohibits conduct which is capable of causing nuisance or annoyance to a person it may, if subsection (3) below applies, attach a power of arrest to any provision of the injunction.

(3)   This subsection applies if the local authority applies to the court to attach the power of arrest and the court thinks that either—

(a)   the conduct mentioned in subsection (2) consists of or includes the use or threatened use of violence, or

(b)   there is a significant risk of harm to the person mentioned in that subsection.

(4)   Harm includes serious ill-treatment or abuse (whether physical or not).

(5)   Local authority has the same meaning as in section 222 of the Local Government Act 1972.

PART 10
GENERAL

92   Repeals

Schedule 3 contains repeals.

93   Commencement

(1)   Except as provided in subsections (2) and (3), the preceding provisions of this Act (other than subsections (9) to (11) of section 85) come into force in accordance with provision made by the Secretary of State by order.

(2)   Part 2 and sections 19 to 22, 24, 40 to 45, 47 to 52, 55, 56 and 91—

   (a)   so far as relating to England, come into force in accordance with provision made by the Secretary of State by order;

   (b)   so far as relating to Wales, come into force in accordance with provision made by the National Assembly for Wales by order.

(3)   Part 8 comes into force—

   (a)   in relation to complaints about hedges situated in England, in accordance with provision made by the Secretary of State by order;

   (b)   in relation to complaints about hedges situated in Wales, in accordance with provision made by the National Assembly for Wales by order.

94   Orders and regulations

(1)   References in this section to subordinate legislation are to—

   (a)   an order of the Secretary of State or the National Assembly for Wales under this Act;

   (b)   regulations under this Act.

(2)   Subordinate legislation—

   (a)   may make different provision for different purposes, different cases and different areas;

   (b)   may include incidental, supplemental, consequential, saving or transitional provisions (including provisions applying, with or without modification, provision contained in an enactment).

(3)   A power to make subordinate legislation is exercisable by statutory instrument.

(4)   A statutory instrument is subject to annulment in pursuance of a resolution of either House of Parliament if it contains subordinate legislation made by the Secretary of State other than—

   (a)   regulations under section 81 or 83; or

   (b)   an order under section 93.

(5)   No regulations shall be made by the Secretary of State under section 81 or 83 (whether alone or with other provisions) unless a draft of the statutory instrument containing the regulations has been laid before, and approved by a resolution of, each House of Parliament.

95   Money

There shall be paid out of money provided by Parliament any increase attributable to this Act in the sums payable out of money so provided under any other enactment.

96 Extent

(1) Parts 1 to 4 and 6 to 9 extend to England and Wales only.

(2) Part 5 and this Part do not extend to Northern Ireland.

97 Short title

This Act may be cited as the Anti-social Behaviour Act 2003.

SCHEDULES

SCHEDULE 1

Section 14

DEMOTED TENANCIES

1   In the Housing Act 1996 (c 52) after section 143 the following sections are inserted as Chapter 1A of Part 5—

'CHAPTER 1A
DEMOTED TENANCIES

General provisions

143A   Demoted tenancies

(1) This section applies to a periodic tenancy of a dwelling-house if each of the following conditions is satisfied.

(2) The first condition is that the landlord is either a local housing authority or a housing action trust.

(3) The second condition is that the tenant condition in section 81 of the Housing Act 1985 is satisfied.

(4) The third condition is that the tenancy is created by virtue of a demotion order under section 82A of that Act.

(5) In this Chapter—

(a) a tenancy to which this section applies is referred to as a demoted tenancy;

(b) references to demoted tenants must be construed accordingly.

143B   Duration of demoted tenancy

(1) A demoted tenancy becomes a secure tenancy at the end of the period of one year (the demotion period) starting with the day the demotion order takes effect; but this is subject to subsections (2) to (5).

(2) A tenancy ceases to be a demoted tenancy if any of the following paragraphs applies—

(a) either of the first or second conditions in section 143A ceases to be satisfied;

(b) the demotion order is quashed;

(c) the tenant dies and no one is entitled to succeed to the tenancy.

(3) If at any time before the end of the demotion period the landlord serves a notice of proceedings for possession of the dwelling-house subsection (4) applies.

(4) The tenancy continues as a demoted tenancy until the end of the demotion period or (if later) until any of the following occurs—

(a)   the notice of proceedings is withdrawn by the landlord;

(b)   the proceedings are determined in favour of the tenant;

(c)   the period of 6 months beginning with the date on which the notice is served ends and no proceedings for possession have been brought.

(5)   A tenancy does not come to an end merely because it ceases to be a demoted tenancy.

143C   Change of landlord

(1)   A tenancy continues to be a demoted tenancy for the duration of the demotion period if—

(a)   at the time the demoted tenancy is created the interest of the landlord belongs to a local housing authority or a housing action trust, and

(b)   during the demotion period the interest of the landlord transfers to another person who is a local housing authority or a housing action trust.

(2)   Subsections (3) and (4) apply if—

(a)   at the time the demoted tenancy is created the interest of the landlord belongs to a local housing authority or a housing action trust, and

(b)   during the demotion period the interest of the landlord transfers to a person who is not such a body.

(3)   If the new landlord is a registered social landlord or a person who does not satisfy the landlord condition the tenancy becomes an assured shorthold tenancy.

(4)   If the new landlord is not a registered social landlord and does satisfy the landlord condition the tenancy becomes a secure tenancy.

(5)   The landlord condition must be construed in accordance with section 80 of the Housing Act 1985.

Proceedings for possession

143D   Proceedings for possession

(1)   The landlord may only bring a demoted tenancy to an end by obtaining an order of the court for possession of the dwelling-house.

(2)   The court must make an order for possession unless it thinks that the procedure under sections 143E and 143F has not been followed.

(3)   If the court makes such an order the tenancy comes to an end on the date on which the tenant is to give up possession in pursuance of the order.

143E   Notice of proceedings for possession

(1)   Proceedings for possession of a dwelling-house let under a demoted tenancy must not be brought unless the landlord has served on the tenant a notice of proceedings under this section.

(2)   The notice must—

(a)   state that the court will be asked to make an order for the possession of the dwelling-house;

(b)   set out the reasons for the landlord's decision to apply for the order;

(c)   specify the date after which proceedings for the possession of the dwelling-house may be begun;

(d)   inform the tenant of his right to request a review of the landlord's decision and of the time within which the request must be made.

(3)   The date specified under subsection (2)(c) must not be earlier than the date on which the tenancy could (apart from this Chapter) be brought to an end by notice to quit given by the landlord on the same date as the notice of proceedings.

(4)   The court must not entertain proceedings begun on or before the date specified under subsection (2)(c).

(5)   The notice must also inform the tenant that if he needs help or advice—

(a) about the notice, or

(b) about what to do about the notice,

he must take the notice immediately to a Citizen's Advice Bureau, a housing aid centre, a law centre or a solicitor.

143F   Review of decision to seek possession

(1)   Before the end of the period of 14 days beginning with the date of service of a notice for possession of a dwelling-house let under a demoted tenancy the tenant may request the landlord to review its decision to seek an order for possession.

(2)   If a request is made in accordance with subsection (1) the landlord must review the decision.

(3)   The Secretary of State may by regulations make provision as to the procedure to be followed in connection with a review under this section.

(4)   The regulations may include provision—

(a)   requiring the decision on review to be made by a person of appropriate seniority who was not involved in the original decision;

(b)   as to the circumstances in which the tenant is entitled to an oral hearing, and whether and by whom he may be represented at the hearing.

(5)   The landlord must notify the tenant—

(a) of the decision on the review;

(b) of the reasons for the decision.

(6)   The review must be carried out and notice given under subsection (5) before the date specified in the notice of proceedings as the date after which proceedings for possession of the dwelling-house may be begun.

143G   Effect of proceedings for possession

(1)   This section applies if the landlord has begun proceedings for the possession of a dwelling-house let under a demoted tenancy and—

(a)   the demotion period ends, or

(b)   any of paragraphs (a) to (c) of section 143B(2) applies (circumstances in which a tenancy ceases to be a demoted tenancy).

(2)   If any of paragraphs (a) to (c) of section 143B(2) applies the tenancy ceases to be a demoted tenancy but the landlord (or the new landlord as the case may be) may continue the proceedings.

(3)   Subsection (4) applies if in accordance with subsection (2) a tenancy ceases to be a demoted tenancy and becomes a secure tenancy.

(4)   The tenant is not entitled to exercise the right to buy unless—

(a)   the proceedings are finally determined, and

(b)   he is not required to give up possession of the dwelling-house.

(5)   The proceedings must be treated as finally determined if—

(a)   they are withdrawn;

(b)   any appeal is abandoned;

(c)   the time for appealing expires without an appeal being brought.

Succession

143H   Succession to demoted tenancy

(1)   This section applies if the tenant under a demoted tenancy dies.

(2)   If the tenant was a successor, the tenancy—

(a)   ceases to be a demoted tenancy, but

(b)   does not become a secure tenancy.

(3)   In any other case a person is qualified to succeed the tenant if—

(a)   he occupies the dwelling-house as his only or principal home at the time of the tenant's death,

(b)   he is a member of the tenant's family, and

(c)   he has resided with the tenant throughout the period of 12 months ending with the tenant's death.

(4)   If only one person is qualified to succeed under subsection (3) the tenancy vests in him by virtue of this section.

(5)   If there is more than one such person the tenancy vests by virtue of this section in the person preferred in accordance with the following rules—

(a)   the tenant's spouse or (if the tenant has no spouse) the person mentioned in section 143P(1)(b) is to be preferred to another member of the tenant's family;

(b)   if there are two or more other members of the tenant's family the person preferred may be agreed between them or (if there is no such agreement) selected by the landlord.

143I   No successor tenant: termination

(1)   This section applies if the demoted tenant dies and no person is qualified to succeed to the tenancy as mentioned in section 143H(3).

(2)   The tenancy ceases to be a demoted tenancy if either subsection (3) or (4) applies.

(3)   This subsection applies if the tenancy is vested or otherwise disposed of in the course of the administration of the tenant's estate unless the vesting or other disposal is in pursuance of an order under—

(a)   section 23A or 24 of the Matrimonial Causes Act 1973 (property adjustment orders in connection with matrimonial proceedings);

(b)   section 17(1) of the Matrimonial and Family Proceedings Act 1984 (property adjustment orders after overseas divorce, etc);

(c)   paragraph 1 of Schedule 1 to the Children Act 1989 (orders for financial relief against parents).

(4)   This subsection applies if it is known that when the tenancy is vested or otherwise disposed of in the course of the administration of the tenant's estate it will not be in pursuance of an order mentioned in subsection (3).

(5)   A tenancy which ceases to be a demoted tenancy by virtue of this section cannot subsequently become a secure tenancy.

143J   Successor tenants

(1)   This section applies for the purpose of sections 143H and 143I.

(2)   A person is a successor to a secure tenancy which is terminated by a demotion order if any of subsections (3) to (6) applies to him.

(3)   The tenancy vested in him—

(a)   by virtue of section 89 of the Housing Act 1985 or section 133 of this Act;

(b)   under the will or intestacy of the preceding tenant.

(4)   The tenancy arose by virtue of section 86 of the Housing Act 1985 and the original fixed term was granted—

(a)   to another person, or

(b)   to him jointly with another person.

(5)   He became the tenant on the tenancy being assigned to him unless—

(a)   the tenancy was assigned in proceedings under section 23A or 24 of the Matrimonial Causes Act 1973 (property adjustment orders in connection with matrimonial proceedings) or section 17(1) of the Matrimonial and Family Proceedings Act 1984 (property adjustment orders after overseas divorce, etc), and

(b)   neither he nor the other party to the marriage was a successor.

(6)   He became the tenant on assignment under section 92 of the Housing Act 1985 if he himself was a successor to the tenancy which he assigned in exchange.

(7)   A person is the successor to a demoted tenancy if the tenancy vested in him by virtue of section 143H(4) or (5).

(8)   A person is the successor to a joint tenancy if he has become the sole tenant.

Assignment

143K   Restriction on assignment

(1)   A demoted tenancy is not capable of being assigned except as mentioned in subsection (2).

(2)   The exceptions are assignment in pursuance of an order made under—

(a)   section 24 of the Matrimonial Causes Act 1973 (property adjustment orders in connection with matrimonial proceedings);

(b)   section 17(1) of the Matrimonial and Family Proceedings Act 1984 (property adjustment orders after overseas divorce, etc);

(c)   paragraph 1 of Schedule 1 to the Children Act 1989 (orders for financial relief against parents).

Repairs

143L   Right to carry out repairs

The Secretary of State may by regulations under section 96 of the Housing Act 1985 (secure tenants: right to carry out repairs) apply to demoted tenants any provision made under that section in relation to secure tenants.

Provision of information

143M   Provision of information

(1)   This section applies to a local housing authority or a housing action trust if it is the landlord of a demoted tenancy.

(2)   The landlord must from time to time publish information about the demoted tenancy in such form as it thinks best suited to explain in simple terms and so far as it considers appropriate the effect of—

(a)   the express terms of the demoted tenancy;

(b)   the provisions of this Chapter;

(c)   the provisions of sections 11 to 16 of the Landlord and Tenant Act 1985 (landlord's repairing obligations).

(3)   The landlord must ensure that information published under subsection (2) is, so far as is reasonably practicable, kept up to date.

(4)   The landlord must supply the tenant with—

(a)   a copy of the information published under subsection (2);

(b)   a written statement of the terms of the tenancy, so far as they are neither expressed in the lease or written tenancy agreement (if any) nor implied by law.

(5)   The statement required by subsection (4)(b) must be supplied on the grant of the tenancy or as soon as practicable afterwards.

Supplementary

143N Jurisdiction of county court

(1) A county court has jurisdiction—

    (a) to determine questions arising under this Chapter;

    (b) to entertain proceedings brought under this Chapter;

    (c) to determine claims (for whatever amount) in connection with a demoted tenancy.

(2) The jurisdiction includes jurisdiction to entertain proceedings as to whether a statement supplied in pursuance of section 143M(4)(b) (written statement of certain terms of tenancy) is accurate.

(3) For the purposes of subsection (2) it is immaterial that no relief other than a declaration is sought.

(4) If a person takes proceedings in the High Court which, by virtue of this section, he could have taken in the county court he is not entitled to recover any costs.

(5) The Lord Chancellor may make such rules and give such directions as he thinks fit for the purposes of giving effect to this section.

(6) The rules and directions may provide—

    (a) for the exercise by a district judge of a county court of any jurisdiction exercisable under this section;

    (b) for the conduct of proceedings in private.

(7) The power to make rules must be exercised by statutory instrument subject to annulment in pursuance of a resolution of either House of Parliament.

143O Meaning of dwelling house

(1) For the purposes of this Chapter a dwelling-house may be a house or a part of a house.

(2) Land let together with a dwelling-house must be treated for the purposes of this Chapter as part of the dwelling-house unless the land is agricultural land which would not be treated as part of a dwelling-house for the purposes of Part 4 of the Housing Act 1985.

143P Members of a person's family

(1) For the purposes of this Chapter a person is a member of another's family if—

    (a) he is the spouse of that person;

    (b) he and that person live together as a couple in an enduring family relationship, but he does not fall within paragraph (c);

    (c) he is that person's parent, grandparent, child, grandchild, brother, sister, uncle, aunt, nephew or niece.

(2) For the purposes of subsection (1)(b) it is immaterial that two persons living together in an enduring family relationship are of the same sex.

(3) For the purposes of subsection (1)(c)—

    (a) a relationship by marriage must be treated as a relationship by blood;

    (b) a relationship of the half-blood must be treated as a relationship of the whole blood;

    (c) a stepchild of a person must be treated as his child.'

2(1) The Housing Act 1985 (c 68) is amended as follows.

(2) In section 105 (requirement to consult secure tenants on certain housing management matters) after subsection (6) there is inserted the following subsection—

    '(7) For the purposes of this section—

        (a) secure tenants include demoted tenants within the meaning of section 143A of the Housing Act 1996;

(b)   secure tenancies include demoted tenancies within the meaning of that section.'

(3)   In section 171B (extent of preserved right to buy) after subsection (1) there is inserted the following subsection—

'(1A)   A person to whom this section applies ceases to have the preserved right to buy if the tenancy of a relevant dwelling-house becomes a demoted tenancy by virtue of a demotion order under section 6A of the Housing Act 1988.'

(4)   In Schedule 1 (tenancies which are not secure tenancies) after paragraph 1A (introductory tenancies) there is inserted the following paragraph—

'1B   A tenancy is not a secure tenancy if it is a demoted tenancy within the meaning of section 143A of the Housing Act 1996.'

(5)   In Schedule 4 (qualifying period for right to buy and discount) after paragraph 9 (the tenant condition) there is inserted the following paragraph—

'9A   The tenant condition is not met during any period when a tenancy is a demoted tenancy by virtue of section 20B of the Housing Act 1988 or section 143A of the Housing Act 1996.'

SCHEDULE 2

Section 88

CURFEW ORDERS AND SUPERVISION ORDERS

Interpretation

1   In this Schedule 'the 2000 Act' means the Powers of Criminal Courts (Sentencing) Act 2000 (c 6).

Curfew orders

2(1)   Section 37 of the 2000 Act (curfew orders) is amended as follows.

(2)   Subsection (4) (which limits to three months the duration of a curfew order made in respect of a person aged under 16 on conviction) is omitted.

(3)   For subsection (12) there is substituted—

'(12)   In this Act, "responsible officer", in relation to an offender subject to a curfew order, means—

(a)   where the offender is also subject to a supervision order, the person who is the supervisor in relation to the supervision order, and

(b)   in any other case, the person who is responsible for monitoring the offender's whereabouts during the curfew periods specified in the order.'

Supervision orders

3   After section 64 of the 2000 Act there is inserted—

'64A   Supervision orders and curfew orders

Nothing in this Chapter prevents a court which makes a supervision order in respect of an offender from also making a curfew order in respect of him.'

4(1)   Schedule 6 to the 2000 Act (requirements which may be included in supervision orders) is amended as follows.

(2)   In paragraph 2(5) (total number of days during which offender may be required to comply with directions of supervisor not to exceed 90), for '90' there is substituted '180'.

(3)   In paragraph 3 (requirements as to activities, reparation, night restrictions etc)—

(a)   sub-paragraph (2)(e) (night restriction) is omitted, and

      (b)   in sub-paragraph (3) (total number of days in respect of which an offender may be subject to requirements imposed by virtue of any of sub-paragraph (2)(a) to (e) not to exceed 90)—

            (i)   for the words ', (d) or (e)' there is substituted 'or (d)', and

            (ii)   for '90' there is substituted '180'.

(4)   Paragraph 4 (night restrictions) is omitted.

(5)   After paragraph 5 there is inserted—

Requirement to live for specified period with local authority foster parent

5A(1)   Where the conditions mentioned in sub-paragraph (2) below are satisfied, a supervision order may impose a requirement ('a foster parent residence requirement') that the offender shall live for a specified period with a local authority foster parent.

(2)   The conditions are that—

      (a)   the offence is punishable with imprisonment in the case of an offender aged 18 or over;

      (b)   the offence, or the combination of the offence and one or more offences associated with it, was so serious that a custodial sentence would normally be appropriate (or, where the offender is aged 10 or 11, would normally be appropriate if the offender were aged 12 or over); and

      (c)   the court is satisfied that—

            (i)   the behaviour which constituted the offence was due to a significant extent to the circumstances in which the offender was living, and

            (ii)   the imposition of a foster parent residence requirement will assist in his rehabilitation.

(3)   A foster parent residence requirement shall designate the local authority who are to place the offender with a local authority foster parent under section 23(2)(a) of the Children Act 1989, and that authority shall be the authority in whose area the offender resides.

(4)   A court shall not impose a foster parent residence requirement unless—

      (a)   the court has been notified by the Secretary of State that arrangements for implementing such a requirement are available in the area of the designated authority;

      (b)   the notice has not been withdrawn; and

      (c)   the court has consulted the designated authority.

(5)   Subject to paragraph 5(2A) of Schedule 7 to this Act, the maximum period which may be specified in a foster parent residence requirement is twelve months.

(6)   A court shall not impose a foster parent residence requirement in respect of an offender who is not legally represented at the relevant time in that court unless—

      (a)   he was granted a right to representation funded by the Legal Services Commission as part of the Criminal Defence Service for the purposes of the proceedings but the right was withdrawn because of his conduct; or

      (b)   he has been informed of his right to apply for such representation for the purposes of the proceedings and has had opportunity to do so, but nevertheless refused or failed to apply.

(7)   In sub-paragraph (6) above—

      (a)   'the relevant time' means the time when the court is considering whether or not to impose the requirement, and

      (b)   'the proceedings' means—

            (i)   the whole proceedings, or

            (ii)   the part of the proceedings relating to the imposition of the requirement.

(8)   A supervision order imposing a foster parent residence requirement may also impose any of the requirements mentioned in paragraphs 2, 3, 6 and 7 of this Schedule.

(9)   If at any time while a supervision order imposing a foster parent residence requirement is in force, the supervisor notifies the offender—

       (a)   that no suitable local authority foster parent is available, and

       (b)   that the supervisor has applied or proposes to apply under paragraph 5 of Schedule 7 for the variation or revocation of the order,

the foster parent residence requirement shall, until the determination of the application, be taken to require the offender to live in local authority accommodation (as defined by section 163 of this Act).

(10)   This paragraph does not affect the power of a local authority to place with a local authority foster parent an offender to whom a local authority residence requirement under paragraph 5 above relates.

(11)   In this paragraph 'local authority foster parent' has the same meaning as in the Children Act 1989.'

Consequential amendments

5   In section 21 of the Children Act 1989 (c 41) (provision of accommodation for children in police protection or detention or on remand, etc.) in subsection (2)(c)(ii) after '2000' there is inserted 'or a foster parent residence requirement under paragraph 5A of that Schedule'.

6(1)   Schedule 7 to the 2000 Act (breach, revocation and amendment of supervision orders) is amended as follows.

(2)   In paragraph 2 (breach of requirement of supervision order)—

       (a)   in sub-paragraph (1), after '5' there is inserted ', 5A',

       (b)   in sub-paragraph (2)(a)(ii) after 'subject to' there is inserted 'sub-paragraph (2A) below and', and

       (c)   after sub-paragraph (2) there is inserted—

        '(2A)   The court may not make a curfew order under sub-paragraph (2)(a)(ii) above in respect of an offender who is already subject to a curfew order.'

(3)   In paragraph 5 (revocation and amendment of supervision order)—

       (a)   after sub-paragraph (2) there is inserted—

        '(2A)   In relation to a supervision order imposing a foster parent residence requirement under paragraph 5A of Schedule 6 to this Act, the power conferred by sub-paragraph (1)(b)(ii) above includes power to extend the period specified in the requirement to a period of not more than 18 months beginning with the day on which the requirement first had effect.', and

       (b)   sub-paragraph (3)(b) and the word 'or' immediately preceding it are omitted.

SCHEDULE 3

Section 92

REPEALS

Short title and chapter	Extent of repeal
Firearms Act 1968 (c 27)	Section 22(5). In section 23(2) the words 'or (5)'. In Part 1 of Schedule 6, the entry relating to section 22(5).
Prosecution of Offences Act 1985 (c 23)	In section 3(2), the word 'and' after paragraph (f).
Firearms (Amendment) Act 1988 (c 45)	In section 1(4), the word 'or' at the end of paragraph (a).
Criminal Justice and Public Order Act 1994 (c 33)	In section 63(2), 'in the open air'. In section 68(1), 'in the open air' in both places. In section 69(1), 'in the open air' in both places.
Noise Act 1996 (c 37)	In section 2(7) the words from 'and accordingly' to the end.

Housing Act 1996 (c 52)	Sections 152 and 153. In section 158— (a) in subsection (1), the entries relating to 'child', 'harm', 'health' and 'ill-treatment'; (b) subsection (2).
Crime and Disorder Act 1998 (c 37)	In section 1(1A), the word 'or' after paragraph (c).
Powers of Criminal Courts (Sentencing) Act 2000 (c 6)	Section 37(4). In Schedule 6— (a) in paragraph 3(2), the words 'and paragraph 4 below' and paragraph (e), and (b) paragraph 4. In Schedule 7, paragraph 5(3)(b) and the word 'or' immediately preceding it.
Police Reform Act 2002 (c 30)	In Schedule 4, the word 'and' at the end of paragraph 1(2)(c). In Schedule 5, the word 'and' at the end of paragraph 1(2)(b).

'local government area' means—

    (a)   in relation to England, a district or London borough, the City of London, the Isle of Wight and the Isles of Scilly;

    (b)   in relation to Wales, a county or county borough.

'policed premises' has the meaning given by section 53(3) of the British Transport Commission Act 1949.

1A   Power of Secretary of State to add to relevant authorities

The Secretary of State may by order provide that the chief officer of a body of constables maintained otherwise than by a police authority is, in such cases and circumstances as may be prescribed by the order, to be a relevant authority for the purposes of section 1 above.

1B   Orders in county court proceedings

(1)   This section applies to any proceedings in a county court ('the principal proceedings').

(2)   If a relevant authority—

    (a)   is a party to the principal proceedings, and

    (b)   considers that a party to those proceedings is a person in relation to whom it would be reasonable for it to make an application under section 1,

it may make an application in those proceedings for an order under subsection (4).

(3)   If a relevant authority—

    (a)   is not a party to the principal proceedings, and

    (b)   considers that a party to those proceedings is a person in relation to whom it would be reasonable for it to make an application under section 1,

it may make an application to be joined to those proceedings to enable it to apply for an order under subsection (4) and, if it is so joined, may apply for such an order.

(3A)   *Subsection (3B) applies if a relevant authority is a party to the principal proceedings and considers—*

    (a)   that a person who is not a party to the proceedings has acted in an anti-social manner, and

    (b)   that the person's anti-social acts are material in relation to the principal proceedings.

(3B)   *The relevant authority may—*

    (a)   make an application for the person mentioned in subsection (3A) (a) to be joined to the principal proceedings to enable an order under subsection (4) to be made in relation to that person;

    (b)   if that person is so joined, apply for an order under subsection (4).

(3C)   *But a person must not be joined to proceedings in pursuance of subsection (3B) unless his anti-social acts are material in relation to the principal proceedings.*

(4)   If, on an application for an order under this subsection, it is proved that the conditions mentioned in section 1(1) are fulfilled as respects that other party, the court may make an order which prohibits him from doing anything described in the order.

(5)   Subject to subsection (6), the *person* against whom an order under this section has been made and the relevant authority on whose application that order was made may apply to the county court which made an order under this section for it to be varied or discharged by a further order.

(6)   Except with the consent of the relevant authority and the person subject to the order, no order under this section shall be discharged before the end of the period of two years beginning with the date of service of the order.

(7)   Subsections (5) to (7) and (10) to (12) of section 1 apply for the purposes of the making and effect of orders made under this section as they apply for the purposes of the making and effect of anti-social behaviour orders.

1C   Orders on conviction in criminal proceedings

(1)   This section applies where a person (the 'offender') is convicted of a relevant offence.

(2)   If the court considers—

   (a)   that the offender has acted, at any time since the commencement date, in an anti-social manner, that is to say in a manner that caused or was likely to cause harassment, alarm or distress to one or more persons not of the same household as himself, and

   (b)   that an order under this section is necessary to protect persons in any place in England and Wales from further anti-social acts by him,

it may make an order which prohibits the offender from doing anything described in the order.

(3)   The court may make an order under this section

   (a)   *if the prosecutor asks it to do so, or*

   (b)   *if the court thinks it is appropriate to do so.*

(3A)   *For the purpose of deciding whether to make an order under this section the court may consider evidence led by the prosecution and the defence.*

(3B)   *It is immaterial whether evidence led in pursuance of subsection (3A) would have been admissible in the proceedings in which the offender was convicted.*

(4)   An order under this section shall not be made except—

   (a)   in addition to a sentence imposed in respect of the relevant offence; or

   (b)   in addition to an order discharging him conditionally.

(5)   An order under this section takes effect on the day on which it is made, but the court may provide in any such order that such requirements of the order as it may specify shall, during any period when the offender is detained in legal custody, be suspended until his release from that custody.

(6)   An offender subject to an order under this section may apply to the court which made it for it to be varied or discharged.

(7)   In the case of an order under this section made by a magistrates' court, the reference in subsection (6) to the court by which the order was made includes a reference to any magistrates' court acting for the same petty sessions area as that court.

(8)   No application may be made under subsection (6) for the discharge of an order before the end of the period of two years beginning with the day on which the order takes effect.

(9)   Subsections (7), (10) and (11) of section 1 apply for the purposes of the making and effect of orders made by virtue of this section as they apply for the purposes of the making and effect of anti-social behaviour orders.

(9A)   *The council for the local government area in which a person in respect of whom an anti-social behaviour order has been made resides or appears to reside may bring proceedings under section 1(10) (as applied by subsection (9) above) for breach of an order under subsection (2) above.*

(9B)   *Subsection (9C) applies in relation to proceedings in which an order under subsection (2) is made against a child or young person who is convicted of an offence.*

(9C)   *In so far as the proceedings relate to the making of the order –*

   (a)   *section 49 of the Children and Young Persons Act 1933 (c 12) (restrictions on reports of proceedings in which children and young persons are concerned) does not apply in respect of the child or young person against whom the order is made;*

   (b)   *section 39 of that Act (power to prohibit publication of certain matter) does so apply.*

(10) In this section—

'child' and 'young person' have the same meaning as in the *Children and Young Persons Act 1933 (c 12);*

'the commencement date' has the same meaning as in section 1 above;

'the court' in relation to an offender means—

    (a)   the court by or before which he is convicted of the relevant offence; or

    (b)   if he is committed to the Crown Court to be dealt with for that offence, the Crown Court; and

'relevant offence' means an offence committed after the coming into force of section 64 of the Police Reform Act 2002 (c 30).

1D   Interim orders

(1) The applications to which this section applies are—

    (a)   an application for an anti-social behaviour order; and

    (b)   an application for an order under section 1B.

(2) If, before determining an application to which this section applies, the court considers that it is just to make an order under this section pending the determination of that application ('the main application'), it may make such an order.

(3) An order under this section is an order which prohibits the defendant from doing anything described in the order.

(4) An order under this section—

    (a)   shall be for a fixed period;

    (b)   may be varied, renewed or discharged;

    (c)   shall, if it has not previously ceased to have effect, cease to have effect on the determination of the main application.

(5) Subsections (6), (8) and (10) to (12) of section 1 apply for the purposes of the making and effect of orders under this section as they apply for the purposes of the making and effect of anti-social behaviour orders.

1E   Consultation requirements

(1) This section applies to—

    (a)   applications for an anti-social behaviour order; and

    (b)   applications for an order under section 1B.

(2) Before making an application to which this section applies, the council for a local government area shall consult the chief officer of police of the police force maintained for the police area within which that local government area lies.

(3) Before making an application to which this section applies, a chief officer of police shall consult the council for the local government area in which the person in relation to whom the application is to be made resides or appears to reside.

(4) Before making an application to which this section applies, a relevant authority other than a council for a local government area or a chief officer of police shall consult—

    (a)   the council for the local government area in which the person in relation to whom the application is to be made resides or appears to reside; and

    (b)   the chief officer of police of the police force maintained for the police area within which that local government area lies.

(5) *Subsection (4)(a) does not apply if the relevant authority is a county council for a county in which there are no districts.*

APPENDIX 3

CRIME AND DISORDER ACT 1998, s 9
(as amended by the Police Reform Act 2002)

Amendments made by the Anti-social Behaviour Act 2003 are shown in italics.

1998 c 37

9   Parenting orders: supplemental

(1)   Where a person under the age of 16 is convicted of an offence, the court by or before which he is so convicted—

    (a)   if it is satisfied that the relevant condition is fulfilled, shall make a parenting order; and

    (b)   if it is not so satisfied, shall state in open court that it is not and why it is not.

(1A)   Subsection (1) above has effect subject to section 19(5) of, and paragraph 13(5) of Schedule 1 to, the Powers of Criminal Courts (Sentencing) Act 2000.

(1B)   If an anti-social behaviour order is made in respect of a person under the age of 16 the court which makes the order —

    (a)   must make a parenting order if it is satisfied that the relevant condition is fulfilled;

    (b)   if it is not so satisfied, must say in open court that it is not and why it is not.

(2)   Before making a parenting order—

    (a)   in a case falling within paragraph (a) of subsection (1) of section 8 above;

    (b)   in a case falling within paragraph (b) or (c) of that subsection, where the person concerned is under the age of 16; or

    (c)   in a case falling within paragraph (d) of that subsection, where the person to whom the offence related is under that age,

a court shall obtain and consider information about the person's family circumstances and the likely effect of the order on those circumstances.

(3)   Before making a parenting order, a court shall explain to the parent in ordinary language—

    (a)   the effect of the order and of the requirements proposed to be included in it;

    (b)   the consequences which may follow (under subsection (7) below) if he fails to comply with any of those requirements; and

    (c)   that the court has power (under subsection (5) below) to review the order on the application either of the parent or of the responsible officer.

(4)   Requirements specified in, and directions given under, a parenting order shall, as far as practicable, be such as to avoid—

    (a)   any conflict with the parent's religious beliefs; and

    (b)   any interference with the times, if any, at which he normally works or attends an educational establishment.

(5)   If while a parenting order is in force it appears to the court which made it, on the application of the responsible officer or the parent, that it is appropriate to make an order under this subsection, the court may make an order discharging the parenting order or varying it—

    (a)   by cancelling any provision included in it; or

    (b)   by inserting in it (either in addition to or in substitution for any of its provisions) any provision that could have been included in the order if the court had then had power to make it and were exercising the power.

(6)   Where an application under subsection (5) above for the discharge of a parenting order is dismissed, no further application for its discharge shall be made under that subsection by any person except with the consent of the court which made the order.

(7)   If while a parenting order is in force the parent without reasonable excuse fails to comply with any requirement included in the order, or specified in directions given by the responsible officer, he shall be liable on summary conviction to a fine not exceeding level 3 on the standard scale.